MORNING & EVENING
DEVOTIONAL

Beauty

&

Grace

BroadStreet
PUBLISHING

BroadStreet Publishing Group LLC
Savage, MN, USA
Broadstreetpublishing.com

Beauty & Grace: A Morning & Evening Devotional

ISBN 978-1-4245-5745-5 (faux)
ISBN 978-1-4245-5746-2 (e-book)

Devotional entries composed by Stephanie Sample.

Design by Chris Garborg | garborgdesign.com
Editing services by Michelle Winger | literallyprecise.com

Printed in China.

18 19 20 21 22 23 24   7 6 5 4 3 2 1

Your beauty should

come from within you—

the beauty of a gentle

and quiet spirit that will

never be destroyed and

is very precious to God.

1 PETER 3:4 NCV

Introduction

We know from Scripture that the unfading beauty of a gentle and quiet spirit is of great worth in God's sight. But how do we find quiet in a busy world, and embrace this definition of beauty that is not at all popular?

This morning & evening devotional will encourage you to spend time with God at the beginning and end of each day, experiencing his peace and joy, and being refreshed in his presence. Let anxiety melt away and be filled with the assurance that your Creator cherishes you because he made you.

Walk confidently in the beauty and grace that God has purposed for you.

The Crown

You shall be a crown of beauty in the hand of the Lord,
and a royal diadem in the hand of your God.

ISAIAH 62:3 ESV

Beginnings are wonderful, aren't they? So much possibility, potential, and promise accompany the first part of a journey, a story, a year. Let's enjoy it, this feeling of newness. Let's take this verse and declare a season of beauty and grace in our actions, our speech, and our thoughts.

Whether silently in your heart or boldly aloud, speak it out. *I will be a crown of beauty in the hand of the Lord.* Today, this traditional day of new beginnings, offer him everything: the parts you're proud of, the parts that need polishing, and the ones that feel broken. Hand it all over and behold the beautiful crown he renders.

Father God, I give you my day, my year, my life. I know before the day is over I'll need to hand it over again, so I ask you to strengthen me through your Holy Spirit to keep surrendering— again and again—so you can continue making a thing of beauty of it all.

The LORD will hold you in his hand for all to see—
a splendid crown in the hand of God.

Your Father already sees you this way: radiant, glowing, a
symbol of great value in his kingdom. How does that make
you feel? Are there parts of your life you would like to beautify
before him?

Refusing shame, guilt, or obligation, acting purely on your
love for him, spend some time prayerfully considering
the parts of your crown you'd like to polish. As you do this,
remain open to seeing the areas you shine in as well.

God, to know you hold me in your hand, that you show me off as
a treasure, is simply overwhelming. Gratefully, I ask you to reveal
your favorite things about me, and to help me embrace them. I also
welcome your loving invitation to grow—to shine brighter—and I
pray for the courage to do so.

Spend time with this prayer and notice what he brings to mind.

Affordable Extravagance

From his fullness we have all received, grace upon grace.

JOHN 1:16 NRSV

There's an old saying that you can never have too much of a good thing. One can quickly poke holes in this aphorism by considering midday sun, rain, or even cheesecake, but when it comes to grace, it holds true. Can he forgive us too many times? Show us too much tenderness, or display too much compassion?

We draw on the well of his unconditional love again and again, as we find ourselves perpetually in need of forgiveness—in need of a little grace. And how would he have us respond to this gratuitous love? By giving it away. In light of the generous, unmerited love our Father extends to us, it's an affordable extravagance. His supply—our supply—is endless, so why not pass it on?

God, as I meditate on the bottomless well of your grace, gratitude wells up in me. Let grace spill over, nourishing relationships and situations everywhere I turn. May I never lose sight of your unconditional love, and may that truth inspire me to pass it on: grace upon grace, thanks upon thanks, love upon love.

Out of his fullness we have all received grace in place of grace already given.

JOHN 1:16 NIV

Like a field of wildflowers, or a patch of daisies in your own garden, what starts as a few blooms on a few plants multiplies. So it is with grace.

The grace we receive when we first fall in love with Jesus doesn't leave us; like a flower going to seed, grace is replanted every time we ask for forgiveness, acknowledge a weakness, or extend grace to another.

Father, as I end this day, I thank you for scattering seeds of grace throughout my life. Send me to sleep with a picture of the blooms you've brought forward. Thank you for multiplying love, forgiveness, and truth in me, and help me to re-seed those blessings in others.

Where can you scatter more seeds of grace?

Swept into Him

Let that abide in you which you heard from the beginning. If what you heard from the beginning abides in you, you also will abide in the Son and in the Father.

1 John 2:24, NKJV

Most homes, even those of the most organized among us, end up with junk drawer. Maybe a junk closet, junk room, or a garage you can no longer park in is more your situation. No matter how large your clutter-catcher is, the problem is the same: space. Everything that enters your home needs a spot, and the more that comes in, the fewer the open spaces. Eventually, be it a yard sale, donation, or a storage unit, something's got to go.

Our hearts and minds are basically the same. Everything allowed inside takes up room. One of the most wonderful gifts of a relationship with Jesus is the space his Spirit claims in our lives. The more we invite him in, the more junk gets cleared away. His peace pushes out anxiety. His patience banishes our short temperedness. His joy leaves no room for contention.

God, abide in me! Take all the space you need; nothing I've collected compares to the beauty of your Spirit. Let my heart make way for all you want to bring.

Let that abide in you which you heard from the beginning. If what you heard from the beginning abides in you, you also will abide in the Son and in the Father.

1 JOHN 2:24 NASB

The reality of God in us, and we in him is a beautiful one. Because he is everywhere, when he comes to us we are swept into him.

Like a sponge in the ocean, at once saturated and contained by his vastness, our lives are forever connected. We are influenced and changed by God in us. We are protected through residing in him.

God, tonight I thank you for mysteries too big for me to fully comprehend. Beyond even the depth of the oceans, my life in you is limitless. Your life in me is a gift.

What does considering your oneness with God do in your heart?

He Is With You

> "Fear not, for I am with you;
> be not dismayed, for I am your God;
> I will strengthen you, I will help you,
> I will uphold you with my righteous right hand."

ISAIAH 41:10 ESV

"I am with you." Sometimes, that's all we need to hear, isn't it? It's why we have those special few on speed dial: the friend, the sister, the mentor who says, "I'm here" and instantly the crisis grows smaller. The presence of another—minus even words or touch—is enough to quiet an anxious spirit. And when that "other" is God? What can this, or any day throw at us that we, with his strengthening help, can't handle?

Even weak, we are strong. Even trembling, we remain upright. Our God is just that strong, just that for us, just that good. Even on a day that's hard, his arms are waiting. He is with you.

God, how strengthening it is to know you are always with me! What a beautiful hope it gives me to sense your presence. I have nothing to fear, ever, because I have you.

> *"Fear not, for I am with you;*
> *be not dismayed, for I am your God.*
> *I will strengthen you, yes, I will help you,*
> *I will uphold you with My righteous right hand."*

ISAIAH 41:10 NKJV

Think back to your childhood, and a time you were frightened, then calmed. Perhaps Dad shone a flashlight under a bed you were certain housed a monster, revealing instead an old suitcase and a stuffed bear. That mysterious noise turned out to be a tree branch against the eaves, or a squirrel in the rain gutter. Once you understood how safe you were, your fears were even funny.

Take that joyous laughter to any grown-up fears you may be facing. Upheld by God, who never leaves you, you are strong enough to shine the light at anything.

Lord God, I'm so grateful for your presence! As I drift into sleep tonight, may I dream of walking beside you. May I sense your nearness as I face my fears, and together, may we laugh at them.

Where do you need to ask God to reveal his presence and quiet a fear?

Every Good Thing

Whatever is good and perfect is a gift coming down to us from God our Father, who created all the lights in the heavens. He never changes or casts a shifting shadow.

JAMES 1:17 NLT

Who in your life always seems to come up with the perfect gift? From a scarf that perfectly matches your eyes, to a care-package of herbal teas, an empty journal and a beautiful pen, this person just gets you, and so what they give you is always just right. Good gift-givers are themselves a gift.

Consider our Lord, and the intimate way he attends to us. What if we could start seeing not just the obvious gifts, but *every good thing* as a gift from above? Pay special attention today to all the good you see, hear and experience, and consider the Father as the author of it all.

God, you are the ultimate giver. From the smell of brewing coffee to a perfectly timed green light, you love to make me smile. Thank you! May I spend this and every day in grateful awe of all you do.

Every gift God freely gives us is good and perfect, streaming down from the Father of lights, who shines from the heavens with no hidden shadow or darkness and is never subject to change.

JAMES 1:17 TPT

Along with all the good and perfect things about our Father lies this incredible treasure: he never changes! Even the most loving relationships, the most stable job, the most well-behaved child is bound to change.

Only one thing is certain, and it's the goodness of our Lord. He simply can't be any other way.

God, what a good Father you are! I never have to wonder with you; you are always for me, always in the light, always good. Thank you for all the ways you love me, and all the perfect gifts you bestow.

What is the best gift God gave you today?

Beauty Beneath

The LORD said to Samuel, "Don't look at how handsome Eliab is or how tall he is, because I have not chosen him. God does not see the same way people see. People look at the outside of a person, but the LORD looks at the heart."

1 SAMUEL 16:7 NCV

Were you ever blinded by a beautiful smile or arresting eyes, only to discover you didn't connect emotionally? Or perhaps you've experienced the opposite, and someone who didn't strike you as attractive initially became one of the most beautiful people you know as the relationship grew.

Because true beauty comes from the heart, a first impression can be quite different from how we eventually see people. This is the Holy Spirit at work in our world, revealing hearts, even changing what our eyes see as character shines through.

God, I love how you see us, and I love when you allow me glimpses through your eyes! As I move through my day today, open my eyes to true beauty, Lord. Let me see into hearts in love with you, and hearts in need of you, and let me respond from mine.

The LORD said to Samuel, "Do not look on his appearance or on the height of his stature, because I have rejected him. For the LORD sees not as man sees: man looks on the outward appearance, but the LORD looks on the heart."

1 SAMUEL 16:7 ESV

Most of us have a nighttime beauty routine. At minimum, we wash off the day. On the other end are more complicated regimens employing all sorts of creams, lotions, serums, and potions designed to make us appear more beautiful.

As you stand before your mirror tonight, together with God, examine the beauty beneath your skin. Ask him to show you today's moments of true beauty and also the less attractive ones. Rather than beat yourself up for thoughts, words, or behaviors that were less than lovely, let him help you see them as opportunities to grow more like him.

Father, I confess I sometimes spend more time wanting to be outwardly beautiful that I do pursuing a heart like yours. Make me beautiful, Lord! Give me a heart inclined toward yours, and let that radiance be my best feature.

What's your favorite physical attribute? What is the loveliest thing about your heart?

Even Though

"Whenever you stand praying, if you have anything against anyone, forgive him that your Father in heaven may also forgive you your trespasses."

MARK 11:25 NKJV

Forgiveness is one of those topics it's tempting to attach a "Yeah, but…" or an "Even though…?" to. We know forgiveness is important, and we know we're commanded to give it, but it's often easier said than done. "Yeah, but he did *this*," we think. "I'm expected to forgive her even though she did *that?*" we ask.

In a word, yes. Jesus was crystal clear. After all, forgiveness is why he came, why he suffered and died, and why he rose. And just as his forgiveness frees us from our sins, our forgiveness frees us from anger, resentment, and broken relationships. Did you catch that? Forgiving frees *us!* Oh, how he loves us. Even the hardest commands are for our good.

Jesus, you're simply amazing. Not only do you forgive me—daily— for all my failings, you do it for everyone who loves you. And still you keep giving, by helping us banish unforgiveness from our own hearts. Thank you, God, for your redemptive, gracious love.

"Whenever you stand praying, if you find that you carry something in your heart against another person, release him and forgive him so that your Father in heaven will also release you and forgive you of your faults."

MARK 11:25 TPT

Which sounds more like you?

"I have struggled to forgive, despite a heartfelt apology and deep remorse?"

or

"I have forgiven someone who wasn't sorry, who didn't even ask me to."

What feelings come up as you consider these two scenarios? Where is Jesus in each?

God, thank you for showing me it is I who am set free when I drop the chains I've wrapped around people who have wronged me. Make me gracious, offering release where it isn't deserved or even wanted. I invite you to take over my heart in the area of forgiveness, and I ask you to forgive me for the times it's hard.

As you close your day, meditate on the healing nature of forgiveness given and received.

A Whisper Away

Not that I was ever in need, for I have learned how to be content with whatever I have.

PHILIPPIANS 4:11 NLT

It's easy to be content when the laundry's done, the bills are paid, the cupboards are full, and the to do list is empty. Even someone who has never known God's comfort can sit back and smile on an evening like that. But what about those other days, when none of the above is true? Picture yourself in the midst of chaos…utterly at peace. Can you see it?

How we answer that question depends a great deal on where Christ is in the picture. Can you see him? What if he's right there, sitting on top of the dryer, keeping you company as you sort and fold? Sense his compassion as you transfer today's undone tasks to tomorrow's list. Notice the change in your breathing, the smile upon your face, as you remember Jesus is right there with you.

Lord Jesus, I simply cannot hold on to my stress and to you at the same time. Thank you! Thank you for making even the most mundane tasks lovely, and even the most stressful situations peaceful. Help me remember as I go through this day that you are right here with me, seeing to my every need.

Not that I speak from want, for I have learned to be content in whatever circumstances I am.

PHILIPPIANS 4:11 NASB

How long did your contentment last today? About as long as your attentiveness to Jesus' presence? On a good day, we recognize the drift and race back toward the warm glow of his contentment. On a more "normal" day, we are swept up in life's current and carried along—sometimes for hours—before we realize what's happened.

It's okay. We're here now, and so is he. Contentment is just a whisper away: *Jesus.*

God, you are an anchor of contentment. Some days I stay close and all is peace. Other times I need to ask you to shorten my rope, or to calm the waves. Thank you for not moving or cutting me loose. Thank you for teaching me that you, and not my circumstances, are the answer to a contented life.

Where do you need more peace? Invite Jesus' presence in the circumstance, and watch it transform you.

That Dream

> *"I know that you can do all things;*
> *no purpose of yours can be thwarted."*
>
> JOB 42:2 NIV

We all know someone who seems unstoppable, don't we? That person who, when she's on the job, we know it will get done. When he gets in the game, the other team might as well go home. As amazing as those people are, their will, tenacity, and capacity pale in comparison our Lord's.

That dream you get when you are praying and asking for direction, that desire in your heart to make a difference, the one that just won't go away? If God has planted this purpose in you, it's going to happen. Fear, resistance, and procrastination might as well go home.

Father God, I have dreams only you know about, and only you could have given me. I know this because there is no way I can realize them on my own. I know this because there are days I am not even sure I want to try, and yet my heart won't let go of them. Thank you, God, for God-sized dreams and the ability you plant and replant in me to bring them to fruition.

> *"I know that you can do anything,*
> *and no one can stop you."*
>
> JOB 42:2 NLT

Imagine for a moment this prayer of Job's is actually God speaking to you. "I know that you can do anything, and that no one can stop you."

When your will is joined with his, he *does* speak this over you. He believes in you; he is proud of you! God knows exactly why he made you, and he knows exactly what you need to fulfill your purpose. Listen to him, and believe.

God, I want to believe I can do anything you ask of me. Let your Holy Spirit fill me with the passion, confidence, and will to make you proud.

What is your God-given dream? How are you pursuing it?

All Wise

Who is wise and understanding among you? Show by your good life that your works are done with gentleness born of wisdom.

JAMES 3:13 NRSV

What does wisdom mean to you? Do you picture a white-haired grandma, spouting out pearls of advice? The dictionary combines experience, knowledge, and good judgment to define it. With these terms, it's fairly safe to say we are all wise in some regard.

Rather than wait for the rocking chair days, let's pay attention to where our experience, knowledge, and good judgment could be a blessing today. As wonderful as it feels to be over, past, or through something, might we benefit someone by revisiting those days? Gently, lovingly, with an eye ever on the Father, is there someone you can bless with your wisdom?

God, give me eyes to see where my experience can ease the road of another. Show me where my knowledge can edify, and where my good judgement, gained through trial and error, can spare someone an error or two. Give me gentleness and humility, born of love, as I move to be of help. Remind me always that everything I've gained is from and for you.

If you consider yourself to be wise and one who understands the ways of God, advertise it with a beautiful, fruitful life guided by wisdom's gentleness. Never brag or boast about what you've done and you'll prove that you're truly wise.

JAMES 3:13 TPT

Just as there are areas of life in which we are wise, there are those where we are in need of wisdom.

Spend some time in prayer over an area of your life in which you feel stuck. Is there a mistake you repeat or a cycle you can't seem to break? Ask God to bring someone wise into your situation.

God, sometimes I marvel at how I can be so together in some ways and such a mess in others! Thank you for making me so complex. Thank you for opportunities to share the wisdom you've given me, and for bringing wise people into my life for the areas in which I have much growing left to do. Let both my wisdom and my lack be a blessing.

How are you wise? Where do you need the wisdom of another?

Ripples to Waves

Remember to welcome strangers, because some who have done this have welcomed angels without knowing it.

HEBREWS 13:2 NCV

Who is the best hostess you know—that dear soul whose door is always open and whose table is always full? It's not hard to think of someone, is it? The gift of hospitality is easy to recognize and wonderful to benefit from. Perhaps that warm hostess is you. Opening your home, filling it with friends, and filling their bellies is food for your soul.

While hospitality is a gift of the Spirit, coming to some as naturally as breath, others among us are more inclined to attend than to host. Just the thought of entertaining makes us uncomfortable. The cleaning, the shopping, the cooking, the cleaning again? "I'll bring the bread," we say tentatively. But what might we be missing out on? Who knows who God has sent to help us open our hearts along with our homes?

God, you know me so well. Whether you made me a born entertainer or whether I'm more of a bread-bringer, I want to experience every blessing you have for me! I want to know every angel you set in my path, and give my heart every opportunity to bless another. Give me a heart of hospitality, Father.

Do not neglect to show hospitality to strangers, for thereby some have entertained angels unawares.

HEBREWS 13:2 ESV

Won't it be fun to get to heaven and have it all make sense? To see all the interconnected threads, all the ripple effects of every tiny act of kindness?

As you end your day today, imagine a world where hospitality comes as naturally as breath. See ripples turn to waves as strangers are revealed as angels.

Precious God, remind me! Remind me every single person I meet is a child of yours or an angel in disguise. Make me generous with my words, my time, and my table. Send me an angel to bless, that I may know a heart that's truly open.

Where in your life can you show greater hospitality? Does God bring anyone specific to mind?

Passionate and Powerful

> *I love You, O LORD, my strength.*
>
> PSALM 18:1 NASB

"Don't you just love these?" There are words of great weight we have come to toss around as lightly as snowflakes. Words like love, the most powerful of all actions or emotions, get attached to things like cookies, colors, or athletes and celebrities we'll never actually know. *Awesome* can as easily describe a brownie as the power of God to lift an affliction or transform a heart.

Today, let's meditate on what it means to love God, then purpose to notice our casual use of heavy terms. Let the "I love you," we offer our Father carry a singular weight. Let the brownies be yummy, and God alone be awesome.

God, I want to honor you with the reverence you deserve. I know you know I don't consider you equal with a delicious dessert, but Holy Spirit, I invite you to show me how liberally I speak as though I do. Let my love be true love and my awe be genuine awe. I love you, Lord.

Lord, I passionately love you and I'm bonded to you!
I want to embrace you, for now you've become my power!

PSALM 18:1 TPT

The expanded version of this verse gives us further insight into how David was feeling when he wrote this Psalm. Feelings have degrees; we obviously don't love God and brownies, our children and the color green, or our parents and our favorite football player in the same way.

The love David had for God—the love the Lord wants us all to have—is passionate, binding, and powerful. It's also the way he loves us. How much strength can we gather from a love like that? How much hope?

Father God, I want to love you with all the passion I have. I want to need you, as David did, every moment. Increase my desire for you, God, and strengthen me through the bond of our shared affection.

Imagine yourself in a deep, loving embrace with your Creator. How does it feel?

Truth Matters

I have no greater joy than this, to hear that my children are walking in the truth.

3 JOHN 1:4 NRSV

How is your relationship with the truth? The deeper we dig into this question, the more likely it is we're realizing it's a relationship that could do some growing. While few followers of Christ are outright liars, once we consider embellishment, exaggeration, omission, and the like, it's easy to see we all have room for improvement.

And why does this matter? Notice how often Jesus refers to the truth in the Gospels. Whether starting a sentence with "I tell you the truth," declaring himself to be the truth, or indicating truth as the gateway to freedom, it's clear truth matters to our Lord.

Dear Jesus, I want to walk in the truth, because I know that's where you are. I consider myself an honest person, and I know how much I value honesty in my relationships, so I ask you to show me any areas of my life where truth is lacking. Whether I am prone to exaggerate, embellish, or even behave differently alone that I do around others, show me the truth and give me the courage to join you there!

Nothing gives me greater joy than to hear that my children are following the way of truth.

3 JOHN 1:4 NCV

Whether or not you have ever raised a child, chances are you've been lied to by one. It's almost charming, isn't it, the way they so boldly insist on something so clearly false? Gently, we explain the importance of being honest. "You need to be honest so people will trust you," we say. In later years, these stories become family legends, often the source of great laughter.

The older people get, the more that innocent charm wears off. There's nothing funny about being lied to by a teenager, a roommate, a co-worker, a spouse. Lies hurt, but honesty brings joy, and no wonder: Jesus himself is truth. A relationship based on truth is one where Jesus can live.

God, because you are the truth, I want more truth! Bring honesty and openness to my relationships, so you can dwell among us. Infuse my life with the joy that comes from following your way, and help me be a safe place for others to share their truth with me.

How might you infuse more honesty into your walk?

There Is Joy

Those who sow with tears will reap with songs of joy.
PSALM 126:5 NIV

How do you define joy? Is it just intense happiness, or is it more complex, more unexplainable than that? Reading Bible verses that contain the word, a theme emerges. Biblically speaking, joy is often connected to its opposites: sorrow, pain, and tears. Frequently, joy springs from places we wouldn't expect it.

When we're able to celebrate a life while mourning a death, there is joy. When we have hope for the future despite a present disappointment or disaster, there again is joy. With God as our shepherd, our supply and our strength, intense happiness—joy—is possible, even in the saddest of circumstances. Could it be that the contrast between where we are and how the Lord is holding our hearts is the reason for the intensity? Could it be that God is not only the source of joy, but joy itself? What a joy it is even to wonder such things!

God, you are my joy! Because I've been able to smile on even my darkest day, I know you will redeem every circumstance of my life. You bring joy from every tear, laughter from every sorrow, and pleasure from every pain. May I remember this every day, and may I be a guiding light for others in their own search for joy.

Those who sow in tears shall reap with joyful shouting.
PSALM 126:5 NASB

It's a common experiment, the first many of us ever conducted: place a dried bean inside a wet paper towel, then place the paper towel in a plastic bag. Within days, sprouts emerge. Factors like the amount of moisture and the amount of light have an effect on how quickly your bean will grow, but almost without fail, your bean will grow.

In a time of sorrow or transition, God's Word teaches us that as we plant tiny seeds of hope, eventually we'll reap in joy. It probably won't grow as quickly as those beans, but it will grow.

God, you are so faithful! I can't see what you're doing underground, but because of your promises, I know roots are forming, hope is sprouting, and one day joy will burst forth from this place. Thank you for hope, for your faithfulness, and for joy.

When has God shown himself faithful by bringing joy to your heart?

Selflessness

*"Greater love has no one than this:
to lay down one's life for one's friends."*

JOHN 15:13 NIV

In a society that seems to grow more self-oriented every day, the New Testament notion of selflessness is certainly counter-cultural. Particularly as young women are finding a voice in the very important conversation about equality, the idea that we would willingly place our own wants below those of our friends, neighbors, and even people half way around the world can be controversial.

What then do we make of this call to selflessness? Are we to skip over it, or, can we look past our first, bristly reaction and find the imbedded gift? The moment we stop thinking about ourselves—start giving ourselves away—is the moment we realize that letting go of "me" is what makes way for "us." Standing up for "my rights" becomes standing up for "our rights." Laying down "my life" means joining with yours and together being swept up into Christ's.

God, I can't lie to you. This one is hard! Lay down my life? What if no one picks it up, or someone tramples it? Inspire me to forget "me"—even for a day—and become absorbed in loving and serving someone else. Show me that less of me makes room for more of you and that as I become more like you, choosing others becomes automatic.

"The greatest love a person can show is to die for his friends."

What would you die for? Fortunately for most people, this is a
question we'll never need to prove our answer to. It's the stuff
of journal writing, or perhaps Bible study conversation, but
not a serious decision.

And yet, for Jesus, it was. John didn't share these words of
Jesus in his Gospel so we'd all rush into burning buildings
and otherwise throw ourselves into harm's way to save
one another; he shared it so we could try and comprehend
the incredible depth of Jesus' love for us. Willingly,
premeditatedly, and through indescribable pain, Jesus
proved his answer. He was willing to die for you.

Jesus, as I lay down to rest, help me lay down my life. Your selfless
love is more than I can fathom. Facing fear and unbearable pain,
you literally gave your life. For me. For us. The next time I don't feel
like participating in a meal train, or taking a turn in the toddler
room at church, please, God, flood me with awareness of what you
gave up for me. I am so very grateful.

How selfless or selfish do you believe you are? Ask the Lord to
reveal the truth to you.

Sleep in Peace

I will both lie down in peace, and sleep;
for You alone, O LORD, make me dwell in safety.

PSALM 4:8 NKJV

Ah, peace. Just to speak the word starts to bring the feeling on. Long before his birth, Isaiah called Jesus the Prince of Peace, and Jesus himself mentions peace over 100 times in the Bible, so it seems reasonable to believe it's important to him.

Most of us would say it's important to us too, but do our lives reflect this? Do we lie down in peace, or do we bring unfinished business, worries, and our smart phones to bed with us? As we sleep, does Jesus inhabit our dreams or does the chatter of our busyness continue to occupy us even then? Awake now and ready for a new day, let us pray for the peace of Christ to rule our thoughts and actions.

Lord God, I do want peace! I want to bring you, your calm and loving Spirit, into all my interactions. As stressors arise, let your peace remind me it's just a moment, just a decision. Help me to choose well, and again flood me with peace as I move forward. All day long, bring me to peace.

I go to bed and sleep in peace,
because, LORD, only you keep me safe.

Regardless of the day, how done the to-do list is, how
resolved the issues, we can go to bed and sleep in peace. We
may need to lay our concerns out one by one, giving them
over to the Lord and his infinitely more capable plans. We
may need to shift our minds entirely off ourselves by praying
for others or reading the Word. We may simply need to pray,
"Lord, bring your peace."

The method is not nearly so important as the intention. Let
the Prince of Peace rock you to sleep tonight. May you drift
off easily and quietly, and may you wake restored.

Jesus, Prince of peace, help me shed the day. Turn my thoughts to
the comfort and safety you alone provide and let the certainty of
your love for me bring my mind and body to peace. May I rest and
be refreshed and dream of you.

How might you tweak (or establish) your nighttime routine to
invite peaceful sleep?

When I Worship

Oh come, let us worship and bow down;
let us kneel before the LORD, our Maker!

PSALM 95:6 ESV

How do you worship God? At first, the answer might seem obvious. We go to church, we sing the songs, we read our Bibles. But are we worshipping? Are we sure? Somewhere along the line, Sunday worship became, for many of us, for us. We go to church to learn, to be inspired, to see our friends. We sing along because we love the song. We read our Bibles because again, we want to learn—or be inspired—or even out of habit.

While being inspired by the teaching and moved by the music and enjoying the fellowship of our brothers and sisters are all wonderful things, let us take an inventory of those things we do for God. Not to beat ourselves up, but to rightfully raise *him* up, let us be mindful of our worship.

Father God, I have allowed my worship of you to become about me. Forgive me. The next time I sing a song to you without even thinking of you, invade my heart with love for you. As I read my Bible to keep up with my plan, overwhelm me with gratitude for the one who breathed every word to life. God, let my worship be worthy!

Come and kneel before this Creator-God;
come and bow before the mighty God, our majestic maker!

PSALM 95:6 TPT

No matter how and where you worship, you've probably
encountered someone more demonstrative than yourself.
Hands a little higher, voice a little louder, maybe even
dancing up front or face down in the aisle, they seem a little
freer, a little more surrendered, a little less self-conscious.

How do you feel around these free spirits? Are you
comfortable asking God to show you how surrendered he
wants you to be when you worship him? If you're an aisle
dancer, are you comfortable asking God if your focus is truly
all on him?

Dear God, you and I both know how self-conscious or free I am when
I worship. This is a little scary for me, but I want to ask you, Father,
to help me forget everything but you during my worship. Whether
alone in my room or in a church of thousands, help me turn all my
attention to you, and let me give you all the glory you deserve.

What addition can you make to the ways and times you
worship God?

Confident in Hope

Such confidence we have through Christ before God.

2 CORINTHIANS 3:4 NIV

Side by side are two runners. Thirteen miles ahead is a finish line. Runner number one has been training for weeks, following a schedule of runs, stretching, and rest all geared toward getting her to the finish line. Because she's prepared, she feels ready and excited for the run. Runner number two hasn't run more than a few blocks in five years, but she ran track in high school—and she knows a lot of people who have run half-marathons. She figures if they can do it, she can do it. Both are confident, but one with more reason.

Where does your confidence come from? While ambition and a healthy sense of our capability are helpful, even admirable qualities, the confidence we gain from a disciplined life surrendered to Christ is something we can take straight to the altar of God.

Father God, as a child, I approach your throne with the needs, the dreams, and the desires of my heart. Because I am in Christ, I know you are for me. I am confident in my hope, as I am confident in your goodness. Because I believe in Jesus, I believe I can do these things you've placed in my heart. Thank you, God, for confidence born of faith.

We are confident of all this because of our great trust in God through Christ.

2 CORINTHIANS 3:4 NLT

How would you rate your overall confidence? Do you find yourself feeling stronger and more assured in some aspects of life than others? Maybe you feel invincible at work, but you constantly question yourself at home, or vice versa.

Turning specifically to your faith, how strong, truly, is your confidence in God? Do you believe he hears your prayers, and that he is always for you? Finish your day by reflecting on the times God has worked good in your life, and let your confidence soar.

God, what confidence I have is from abilities, blessings, or provisions you have given me. What confidence I lack is in areas I am trying too hard to control on my own. The more I consider who you are and what you've done, the more I realize I can trust you with everything. Your goodness is all the confidence I need.

Consider an area where you feel vulnerable in the light of God's promises.

It Will Be Done

Heal me, O Lord, and I shall be healed;
save me, and I shall be saved,
for You are my praise.

JEREMIAH 17:14 NKJV

By the time we reach adulthood, most of us carry a few scars.
Tracing their lines, we might even get a twinge—if only from
memory—of the pain we felt when the wound was fresh.
Formerly broken bones may still ache on rainy days. Long-
ago sprains, though healed, may never feel as strong.

This is why we need God's healing! When he repairs a broken
life there is no scar. All is new. All is well. Our memories
may invite us to return to the pain, but our Lord never will.
He invites us to wholeness, safety, and peace. His healing is
complete, and it is ours for the asking.

God, thank you for your healing love! Thank you for making me
new, for restoring what was broken and bruised. On the days I'm
tempted to re-open those wounds, remind me of the work you've
already done—the healing that is already mine. You have saved
me, so I am saved.

Heal me, O Lord, and I will be healed;
save me and I will be saved,
for You are my praise.

Jeremiah 17:14 NASB

"If you want to make sure it gets done, ask …." Some people are just known for their reliability. Within an office, a family, a circle of friends, it doesn't take long to figure out who we can count on to make the deadline, host the party, or take out the recycling.

This prayer of Jeremiah's speaks volumes of faith. "Lord, if you do it, it will be done." With the confidence of God's love we don't need to wonder. If he takes away the sickness, it's gone. If he mends the wound, it is healed.

God, what can I add to this prayer? Heal me, and I will be healed.
Save me and I am saved. I praise you, God, and I trust you. Your
healing is complete and your salvation is forever. Thank you for
your unfailing love.

Is there a wound in you only God can heal? What will it take for you to let him?

As They Are

Accept one another, then, just as Christ accepted you, in order to bring praise to God.

ROMANS 15:7 NIV

It's easy to come up with ways other people could change for the better, isn't it? If she could keep a secret. If he would stop bragging about his possessions. We know Christ calls us to live in harmony with one another, but sometimes others can make this challenging. We start to notice sins and flaws, and the next thing we know, it's all we can see.

Romans 15:7 reminds us to accept one another... as Christ accepted us. Broken, imperfect, and sinful, Jesus loves us just as we are. If this is how our Savior feels about us, then truly, who are we to place conditions on our acceptance of one another? Yes, everyone in our lives could improve. But we bring glory to God by loving them as they are.

God, thank you for accepting me in all my brokenness. You see past my sins and shortcomings and you love me for me. Help me to see others as you see them, and to glorify you by accepting them for them.

Welcome one another, therefore, just as Christ has welcomed you,
for the glory of God.

ROMANS 15:7 NRSV

It's one thing to be more accepting of the people in our lives, and quite another to be more welcoming and accepting in general. As much as we might struggle to be more gracious toward a gossipy friend or a neighbor with a bit too much braggadocio, how much more challenging is it to extend that grace to the addict on the corner, or the shockingly rude customer on the phone? How about that politician that gets under your skin?

And yet, this is exactly what we are called to do. Jesus loves that dirty, shivering addict exactly as much as he loves us. His heart beats for yours and the politician's with the same abiding love. How much glory, then, do we bring him when we extend grace, acceptance, and love despite agreement or understanding?

Dear God, let it be so! When treated rudely, let me respond with your kindness. When my initial reaction is disgust, replace it with your compassion. Grant me empathy, god that defies reason and instinct. Open my heart so others will see you there.

Invite the Holy Spirit to bring you an opportunity to practice true acceptance.

The Real Prize

"Be strong, and let us be courageous for our people and for the cities of our God; and may the Lord *do what seems good to him."*

1 Chronicles 19:13 nrsv

Pause for a moment and read the verse aloud. For many of us, the first part of this verse is easy to rally around. Be strong! Have courage! Let's do this! But how about that second half? Can you easily say, "Whatever seems good to you, God" or do you typically struggle for control, ask for certain outcomes, want things to go your way? Is surrender to his plan easy for you, or a constant challenge?

In the words of Joab to his army, we find a perfect model of surrender: be strong for those we serve; be courageous for the Kingdom of God, and may the Lord's will be done. Nothing for us, all for God and those he has given us to serve. Oh, that we could achieve such devotion!

God, I want to use my strength for others, my courage to carry out your will. I want to want only what seems good to you. Grant me the faithfulness of Joab, God, that I may willingly surrender to your perfect will.

> *"Be courageous! Let us fight bravely for our people and the cities of our God. May the Lord's will be done."*

1 Chronicles 19:13 NLT

"Your Kingdom come, your will be done, unless it interferes with my happiness." If we were fully honest before God, our version of the Lord's Prayer might sound more like this. What if what he wills for my team to lose? What if he wills the other candidate to get the job? What if God's plan is to grow my character through a season of loss and struggle?

This is where courage comes in. As we trust him, we see that it's in the brave fighting we best glorify him. It's how we fight: bravely. It's why we fight: for our people and the cities of our God. Winning is a bonus; the real prize is surrendering to his will.

Perfect Father, grant me this courage! As I sleep this night, loosen my grip on my plans. Draw me toward your will, and show me where I can fight bravely to see it done.

What cause, issue, or people come to mind again and again when you think of fighting bravely? How can you step in?

Whatever He Whispers

> *"I, the LORD your God, hold your right hand;*
> *it is I who say to you, 'Fear not, I am the one who helps you.'"*
>
> ISAIAH 41:13 NIV

Looking back on the most frightening and difficult things we've ever done, we often wonder where we found the courage. It seems impossible now that we actually passed that test; we felt so unprepared! How did we face that diagnosis, and the months of uncertainty that followed? Where did the words come from, and where did our tears go, when we stood up and gave that eulogy?

Scripture tells us again and again our help comes from God himself. He is the inner voice saying, "You can do this. You are strong enough. I've got you." That sudden burst of inspiration, endurance, or eloquence? That was the Lord squeezing your hand.

God, what a thrill it is to know you hold my hand! You stay close enough, always, to sense when I need a whisper of encouragement. The courage, the strength, the power that seems to come from nowhere—it all comes from you. You are my constant help, and the only help I need.

> *"I am the LORD your God, who holds your right hand,*
> *and I tell you, 'Don't be afraid. I will help you.'"*
>
> ISAIAH 41:13 NCV

Look down at your right hand. Open and close it. Turn it over. In a moment, close your eyes and try to sense the presence of God beside you, holding your hand. Don't give up too quickly; give your thoughts time to settle on him. What is he giving your courage for? What is he promising you will not face alone?

Rest with him awhile, allowing his presence to wash over you. Whatever he whispers, believe it.

Father God, I confess I don't come to this sweet space with you nearly enough. How incredible it is to know you are right here, always, no matter how long it takes me to return. Speak to me, Father. Tell me I can do it, face it, make you proud, and then—help me believe it.

How often do you sense God's presence?

49

Ready to See

Open my eyes that I may see wonderful things in your law.
PSALM 119:18 NIV

Have you ever been the last to get a joke? As everyone else wiped tears of laughter from their eyes, you smiled and thought, "Huh?" But then, suddenly, the extra layer of meaning was illuminated and your laughter became as genuine as everyone else's. Or maybe, seeing an old movie through adult eyes, you understand why your parents didn't want you watching it as a child.

We call these "Aha" moments, and Bible reading provides an endless series of them. As we go deeper into the Word, God opens our eyes to fresh revelations, allowing stories we thought we knew to become fresh and exciting. Passages we've taken for granted take on sudden weight and significance when the Lord opens our eyes.

Father, in the words of the psalmist, open my eyes. Illuminate layer upon layer of meaning. Show me the beauty hidden within your Word. Surprise me with wisdom; delight me with depth. I'm ready to see.

Open my eyes, that I may behold wondrous things out of your law.

PSALM 119:18 ESV

As a little girl, it may not have made sense to you that you couldn't have cake for breakfast, lunch, and dinner. By the time you reached a certain age, though, you understood the wisdom of this rule. Speed limits can feel like a nuisance, especially to a young driver, but as we gain experience, we appreciate the safety of slower-moving cars in neighborhoods and around blind curves.

So it is with God's law. The more he illuminates our understanding, the more we understand every command is handed down in love. Every rule is designed with our best life in mind.

God, I confess I don't always enjoy obeying your laws. They sometimes conflict with my comfort, and cut down on my fun. And yet, each time I do, I gain something. Open my eyes further, God! Show me all the good that awaits when I follow your ways.

Is there a rule or law in Scripture you struggle to embrace? Let the Holy Spirit help you by opening your eyes to its loving intent.

Showing Kindness

God is working in you, giving you the desire and the power to do what pleases him.

PHILIPPIANS 2:13 NLT

When did you last act with spontaneous kindness? Whether you were moved to buy a homeless man a meal, to support someone running a charity race, or simply to smile at the cashier scanning your groceries, these impulsive acts of goodness are evidence of the Spirit at work in you.

The more we tune into God, the more his heart works into us. As we consider his perfect love, he provides us with opportunities—big and small—to express this love to others. When we look to him for inspiration, he responds by inspiring us to be kind. When our desire is to reflect his heart with our actions, he empowers us to do so.

God, you make me so much better than I am on my own! Thank you for allowing me to see the people I encounter, and inspiring me to do what I can to show them your kindness. Today and every day, God, help me to see and to seize each opportunity to please you by sharing your love.

It is God who is at work in you, both to will and to work for His good pleasure.

PHILIPPIANS 2:13 NASB

When we please others, by meeting a need or fulfilling a desire, we please the Lord. It's one of the reasons he inspires us to be kind; our kindness gives him pleasure. He loves it when one of his children is the beneficiary of a generous act or thoughtful gesture. All the more wonderful when another he calls "child" made it happen.

In these moments, both hearts grow more like his; both are invited to know him more. Oh, how we delight him by delighting one another!

God, like a little girl eager to please her papa, so I long to please you. How creative you are, giving me a desire to do good things. I make you proud by making someone's day, bringing joy to us all. Thank you for your work in me, Father. May I grow in kindness and generosity, that I may be more and more pleasing to you.

How important is it to you to delight your Father?

Perfectly Loved

"If a man has a hundred sheep but one of the sheep gets lost, he will leave the other ninety-nine on the hill and go to look for the lost sheep. I tell you the truth, if he finds it he is happier about that one sheep than about the ninety-nine that were never lost."

MATTHEW 18:12-13 NCV

Regardless of how beautifully or how imperfectly you were loved by your earthly father, your heavenly Father's love knows no limit. Rest in that thought a moment. There is nothing you can do to change how he feels about you, and there is no point at which you have gone too far for him to come after you. Astonishing, isn't it?

We spend so much time trying to make ourselves more lovable—from beauty routines to creating the perfect home to saying yes to every request—it's easy to forget we are already perfectly loved. More than we can imagine, our Father loves us.

Father, I try to comprehend your love and I just can't. How can it be that no matter where I wander, no matter how many times, you come after me? Thank you for loving me perfectly, no matter how imperfectly I return it. I know you don't require it, but of love and gratitude, I want to be the child you deserve.

"What do you think? If a man has a hundred sheep, and one of them goes astray, does he not leave the ninety-nine and go to the mountains to seek the one that is straying? And if he should find it, assuredly, I say to you, he rejoices more over that sheep than over the ninety-nine that did not go astray."

MATTHEW 18:12-13 NKJV

Think of the person you love most fiercely, most protectively, most desperately here on earth. Imagine them hurting. Imagine them lost. What would you do to help save them, bring them back? The passion you feel, and the lengths you would go to are but a tiny fraction of what God feels for you, of what he would do for you.

And once you'd succeeded, saved your loved one, how much joy can you imagine feeling? Again, it cannot compare. He adores you. He adores you.

Oh, Lord! I am in awe. Tonight, I take a break from considering my flaws, counting my sins. Tonight, I simply rest in your love. Washing over me, wave after wave, let me see what you see when you look at me.

Are you comfortable with the thought of being perfectly loved? Take your feelings, whatever they are, to your Father.

Find Peace Here

Those of steadfast mind you keep in peace because they trust in you.
ISAIAH 26:3 NRSV

If you were to form a mental picture of chaos, what would you see? Impossible deadlines, commitments on top of commitments, long lists and short hours? How about peace? What picture comes to mind?

Most of us picture getting *away*. Whether our minds took us to a hot bath or a tropical island, we're definitely not *here*. The trouble with this image, though it's wonderful, is that it's fleeting. Whether bathtub or Bali, we can't stay. Rather than going to a peaceful place, let's start over, inviting peace right into our chaos. Let the Holy Spirit quiet your movements. Let Jesus slow your thoughts. Say his name. Find peace here.

Lord Jesus, I love how you come into my chaos with your peace. As I slow my breath and think of you, you envelop me in quiet joy. As I trust you with this load, you lighten it. As I commit my weakness to you, you help me see the ways I'm being strengthened. Thank you, God, for bringing peace here.

You will keep in perfect peace all who trust in you,
all whose thoughts are fixed on you!

Earlier today, in order to picture peace, we shifted our
thoughts. Imagining a place where cares were few and all was
quiet, chaos diminished. God promises this peace can be
ours any time, any place, anywhere. How? By thinking of him.

Fixing our thoughts on the Lord and all his goodness, we see
it is simply impossible to remain unsettled. The more we
train our minds to stay with him, the more perfect peace is
ours—no matter the circumstances. The more we place our
trust in him, the less we have to steal our peace.

God, as I end this day, will you help me shift my thoughts? Each
worry, as it comes to mind, I turn over to you. I marvel at the
creative ways you've cared for me in the past, and I imagine the
glories you have in store for the future. Because I know you are
faithful, because I know you are good, I will sleep in peace.

As you close your eyes tonight, speak the name of Jesus.
Imagine his presence. Let him bring you peace.

57

With Love

Let all that you do be done in love.

1 CORINTHIANS 16:14 NRSV

Imagine a day where you determined to live out this extraordinary command. What would that look like? Take a lingering whiff of your coffee. Smile at yourself in the mirror as you get ready for your day, and mean it. Drive with love. Work with love. Run errands and open mail and cook and clean and engage…with love. How long did you last, even in your imagination?

Let's try it. We'll probably stumble. We'll rebel, certainly. Yes, we'll forget. But once we remember, we can begin again.

Jesus, I want to live this day in love. Please stay close to me, because I know I will stumble without you. Overwhelm me with your love, so I won't rebel. Remind me, so I can't forget.

Do everything in love.

1 CORINTHIANS 16:14, NIV

If we consider this command carefully, we see we're to act in love. This is not necessarily the same thing as acting with love. There may not be a way to lovingly scrub a pan or navigate rush hour, but there is a way to be in love as we do it.

Recall a time you were newly in love. Remember how you floated through the days? To feel that again, we need simply turn our thoughts to Jesus, the lover of our souls.

God, I want to be in love with you! Beyond my first crush, beyond the earthly love of my life, I want to carry that feeling: joy, bliss, anticipation, everywhere I go. Sing me to sleep with the song of your love for me, and let it be mine for you.

How did it go today? Even now, as you consider the day, do it in love. Rather than dwell on the times you failed, give yourself grace. Love yourself. Love the memory of the day you tried to bring love everywhere you went.

Wrapped in Love

Blessed be the God and Father of our Lord Jesus Christ, the Father of mercies and God of all comfort, who comforts us in all our affliction, so that we may be able to comfort those who are in any affliction, with the comfort with which we ourselves are comforted by God.

2 CORINTHIANS 1:3-4, ESV

To be held by the Father is a comfort like no other. As we climb like children into that space that feels like it was made just for us, he holds us sweetly, but also with sureness. He's here to soothe and also to protect. No matter what we are going through, our Abba knows how to make it better. And once we're better, he invites us to pass it on.

Part of his beautiful design is that we would give away what's been so generously given to us. Once we've known his comfort in the face of disappointment, we can be there for a friend facing bad news. Once he's loved us through loss, we're uniquely equipped to walk alongside someone else through theirs. And through it all, we—and they—are drawn ever closer to him.

God, on the days I need your comfort, wrap me up and hold me close. On the days I need to be a comforter, open my arms toward the one who needs me. Give me words, wisdom, and compassion. Let me be a warm, soft blanket—a conduit of your comfort.

Praise be to the God and Father of our Lord Jesus Christ. God is the Father who is full of mercy and all comfort. He comforts us every time we have trouble, so when others have trouble, we can comfort them with the same comfort God gives us.

2 CORINTHIANS 1:3-4 NCV

After a long day, sometimes all we want to do is crawl under the comforter and rest. The warmth, the weight, the softness and even the smell wrap us up and invite us to relax.

This is how our Father God wants us to think of him. The God of all comfort wants us to crawl under his weight, feel his warmth, experience the softness of his compassion.

Notice how many times the word comfort is repeated in the verse. This isn't an accident; it's so we don't miss the message. We are comforted so that we will comfort. Our Father wants us to experience the incomparable warmth of being the comforted and the comforter. He wants to wrap us in love, and he wants us to become love.

God, as I settle into bed tonight and sink into sleep, make me aware of your presence! Allow me to feel the warmth and reassurance that only you can provide. And when I wake, equip me to give it away. I can always come back for more, and you will always give it.

Are you more a seeker or a giver of comfort? How might God be inviting you to move toward the other?

Defeating the Mighty

We have this treasure in jars of clay to show that this all-surpassing power is from God and not from us.

2 CORINTHIANS 4:7 NIV

In the age of social media, every day brings another inspiring story. Here's a theme we're probably all familiar with: someone displays miraculous strength, saving someone else. A mother saves her toddler by lifting a car. A man saves a buddy by moving a 500-pound boulder. A vacationing couple swims out into a riptide, saving a drowning stranger. It's such a lovely image, the tiny defeating the mighty.

This is God at his most transparent. When our frail, fragile bodies do things they can't, it's because he can. And it doesn't have to be lifting a car: for some of us, not lifting that glass to our lips is a feat of equally miraculous strength. Either way, it's a chance to bring him glory.

God, I may not save anyone's life today, but I can still bring glory to you with my life. Every time I am more kind, more patient, more restrained, it's because of you. Let me never forget this, and let me give you all the credit.

We have this treasure in earthen vessels that the excellence
of the power may be of God and not of us.

2 Corinthians 4:7 NKJV

When God calls us out of our comfort zone, our first instinct is often to think of all the reasons we can't. Or shouldn't. Or just plain won't. We dwell on our capacity, forgetting the One who calls us is the same one who will equip us.

We are like Esther, wondering, "What if I fail?" We are like Moses, saying, "But I'm not even a good speaker!" But that's the point, isn't it? That's always been the point. The weaker we are, the stronger he is. The more unlikely the hero, the more the signs point upward.

God, forgive me for the times I've felt you urging me toward
something bigger, something possibly great, and stayed put. I
don't want to fail, and I know I'm not great, so I pretend I didn't
hear you. I hear you. And the next time you ask me, I'll remember
where my strength comes from—and say yes.

Do you have a crazy, impossible dream that just won't go away? Maybe you've been ignoring an invitation to move toward something that feels beyond you. Could God be inviting you to display his glory?

You're Beautiful

You are altogether beautiful, my love;
there is no flaw in you.
SONG OF SOLOMON 4:7 NRSV

Have you ever had a friend refer to herself as ugly? You didn't agree with her, did you? "No!" we say, "You're beautiful! You're so beautiful. I wish you could see yourself the way I see you." And we mean it. We mean it because we love her and we mean it because it's true. There is beauty in every face because we all reflect the face of God.

Imagine how the Bridegroom feels when we call ourselves ugly, poking at the parts we don't like and complaining about everything that makes us unique. "No, my darling. You are beautiful. So beautiful. Let me show you what I see when I look at you. Those aren't flaws; those are jewels. And you, my beautiful one, are a crown." Believe him.

Oh, Jesus, can it be true that you see only beauty in me? Will you give me your eyes? Help me believe I'm flawless. Let me radiate your beauty, with eyes that see, a mouth that encourages, ears that listen. Shine from inside me, God, and I will see it.

Every part of you is so beautiful, my darling.
Perfect is your beauty, without flaw within.

SONG OF SOLOMON 4:7 TPT

Let's be honest. This is a hard one. Every woman has a list of things she'd like to change; some spend thousands of dollars and hours pursuing an idealized beauty. Consider this: do you think Solomon's bride was truly perfect, inside and out? Of course not! Because he adored her, she was perfect to him.

The invitation to see ourselves as beautiful is an invitation to see ourselves as adored. It's a beckoning to forget the freckles, look past the lines, and see the radiance of a woman chosen by the King himself.

God, only you are flawless. When you speak these words over me, you are reminding me where beauty comes from. Thank you, Jesus for choosing, for loving, for cherishing me. What a beautiful thing!

How hard would it be for you to make a conscious choice to focus on seeing your beauty? Ask Jesus to lend you his eyes, and begin.

Destiny

This vision is for a future time.
It describes the end, and it will be fulfilled.
If it seems slow in coming, wait patiently,
for it will surely take place.
It will not be delayed.

HABAKKUK 2:3 NLT

Watching a gifted athlete, or listening to a brilliant singer, words like "destiny" come to mind. Some talents are so extraordinary; they simply have to be used and shared. *She was born for this*, we think. *What am I born for?* we might think next.

We may not all sing like angels or swing a golf club like we were born holding it, but we do all have a destiny. Some of us know what it is; we're just not ready. The timing isn't right. Others among us aren't even sure we have one. Take heart. God knows exactly why he made you. He knows what he gave you to do, and who he gave you to love, and exactly how long it's going to be before you fulfill his plans. It might not feel like it today, but you're right on schedule.

God, I love believing I have a purpose. It doesn't need to be grand, but if it is, I'm willing to step up when you call me. And if it isn't, remind me it's big to you. Help me prepare by paying attention to the people, places, and assignments you put in front of me. I trust your timing, God, and I ask you to help me wait—with patience and with faith.

The vision is yet for an appointed time;
but at the end it will speak, and it will not lie.
Though it tarries, wait for it;
because it will surely come, it will not tarry.

HABAKKUK 2:3 NKJV

Not only do you have a destiny, but all of humanity does. Daily, we are moving toward a promised end, where heaven and earth are renewed and we will live together with God forever. Whether you long for this day, or whether eternity seldom crosses your mind, allow this promise to assure you: what God promises, God delivers.

If something feels late, or even forgotten, know that it is not. His timing is perfect and his love is boundless.

Father God, thank you for your Word! Promises in Scripture, though made to people living thousands of years before me, speak to me and remind me you are faithful. You are truthful. You are good. Whatever you have for me, I eagerly await. Whatever you want from me, I will eagerly do.

Does God's timing feel slow in an area of your life? What reason might he have for waiting?

Love, Not Perfection

Those who wait for perfect weather will never plant seeds;
those who look at every cloud will never harvest crops.

ECCLESIASTES 11:4 NCV

I already blew my eating plan with that bagel, so I might as well have this cupcake. I'm tired. The kitchen can wait until morning. Ugh, I'm going to be late. I'll just skip the party. Sound familiar? It's so easy to talk ourselves into procrastination, especially when the circumstances are less than ideal. But really, how often *are* they ideal? If we waited to be in the mood, perfectly rested, on time and batting 1000 on the day, we would never accomplish anything. The world would simply stop.

But it doesn't, does it? It hasn't, has it? With his help and through our faith in him, God inspires and empowers us to do it now, arrive late anyway, skip the cupcake. He reminds us, through mercies renewed every morning, that each day, each decision, each moment is an opportunity. A beautiful afternoon can come from the ugliest morning. Go ahead. Plant the seed.

Precious God, thank you for inspiration! Thank you for hope.
I've seen it before, how one bad decision can derail my whole day
when I forget that each hour is its own. And I've seen it the other
way, when you step in and whisper, "Go ahead. Just begin."
And so, I will.

He who observes the wind will not sow,
and he who regards the clouds will not reap.

ECCLESIASTES 11:4 ESV

Taken too literally, this verse can seem foolish. Who goes sailing on a windless day? Who goes ahead with an outdoor wedding on a day the forecast calls for hail and high winds? Preparedness is important; it's responsible to plan. Of course this is true.

Rather than suggest we disregard obvious warning signs, Solomon is reminding us where to focus. It's the wedding, not the weather. It's making food choices that honor our bodies, not an all-or-nothing battle. It's time with our friends, not being on time. It's love, not perfection.

Dear God, I thank you for having people to love, projects to do, and things to celebrate. All I need to do is to look for the love, and I know where to focus; I know what to do.

Have you been watching the sky, waiting for perfection? Where can you turn your focus toward love?

As You Would

Bear one another's burdens, and thereby fulfill the law of Christ.

GALATIANS 6:2 NASB

The day we accepted Christ, he became one with us. Through his Spirit, we now share a heart. In particular, Jesus wants to show us what breaks his heart. He wants it to break ours, so that we will act.

The stories of Jesus at work in the world are stories of compassion. The feeding, the healing, the teaching, the command—again and again—to love one another. This is what he wants from us. This is how we honor him.

Precious Jesus, in your life you modeled compassion and in your death you made sure all would have an opportunity to express and receive it. Show me someone who needs a friend, a child who needs a meal. Show me a stranger who has never met you. Empower me to love them as you would, to take on their need, their pain and hunger. Break my heart, God, for the things that cause you pain.

Love empowers us to fulfill the law of the Anointed One as we carry each other's troubles.

GALATIANS 6:2 TPT

From the beginning, God made us for relationships. With the creation of Eve, he expressed his intent that we do life together. He wants to be connected to us, and he wants us connected to one another. This includes sharing our burdens. When you are struggling, is it easy for you to receive help? Does anyone even know you need it, or are you too busy being strong for everyone else?

Just as we fulfill the law by helping others, we also do so when we allow others to help us.

Father God, just as you help me to extend compassion, please help me to receive it! Remind me I am honoring you when I let someone in. Remind me I am seeing more of you—the part that lives in them—when I allow them to meet me in my struggle, to carry some of the weight. What a beautiful design, each helping another. Creative, compassionate God, you are so very good.

Which is easier for you, to give or receive help? Invite the Holy Spirit to help you with both.

For the Run

> *Not that I have already obtained this or am already perfect,*
> *but I press on to make it my own,*
> *because Christ Jesus has made me his own.*
>
> PHILIPPIANS 3:12 ESV

You likely don't remember the day, but do you recall the general time you realized you had stopped growing? Your pants stopped getting too short; your shoes stopped getting too tight. For women, the shoe thing is kind of a thrill. These will still fit next summer? Let the collection commence!

Shortly after we stopped growing physically, we realized how very far we still had to grow. True friendships deepened, while others faded away. The more complicated our choices became, the easier it was to see who believed as we did, valued what we valued. Whether eighteen or eighty, if we are growing in Christ, the process continues to this day. It never really ends.

God, I'm so far from perfect, but because of you, I'm closer than I was yesterday. I strive for this not because I need to earn your love or out of competition, but because becoming better means becoming more like you. Because I belong to you, I want to represent you well.

Not that I have already obtained this or have already reached the goal; but I press on to make it my own, because Christ Jesus has made me his own.

The treadmill has passionate spokespeople on both sides. For lovers, it's a space-efficient, joint-friendly, non-weather-dependent means of running as far as one wants. Detractors would argue you're actually not running anywhere. Let's assume Paul would have been in the former group.

We don't press on toward the goal of being Christ-like with any expectation of getting there. We keep running because it makes us stronger, faster, healthier, better. We keep running for the run itself. We keep running because every step brings us closer to Jesus.

Jesus, I know I'll never "get there," but that's okay. I like it here. In fact, I love it. I love getting closer to you, knowing more of you, becoming better. Thank you for a goal I'll never reach; it means I get to keep running, right up to my last breath, toward you. And really, what else is there?

Christ made you his own so you could spend your life pursuing him, becoming stronger and better every day. What does this inspire you to attempt next?

Better Together

"Have I not commanded you? Be strong and courageous! Do not tremble or be dismayed, for the Lord your God is with you wherever you go."

JOSHUA 1:9 NASB

Women love to travel with other women. Not all men understand this, and some will joke endlessly about it, but trips to the restroom, concession stand, track meet, or pretty much anywhere just feel better together. It's not that we're fearful, it's just that companionship is a delight. When our friends ask us to accompany them, we don't roll our eyes, we go. We go because we want to.

And so it is with God. Isn't that amazing? Through the Spirit of God, we have a constant companion. On those days no one can join you in the bleachers, tune in to the presence of the Lord. He's right there, cheering for the team. He's there because he wants to be, and that goes for all the moments. The silly, the scary and the sublime, every moment of your life is important enough to the Spirit to accompany you.

Lord Jesus, what a friend you are! You're never too busy. You always have time for me. When I'm afraid, you're here. When I'm overjoyed, you're here. Bored, lonely, excited, busy, stressed, and at peace, you are here. Alone or with friends, you are here. Thank you God, for your constant presence.

"Have I not commanded you? Be strong and courageous. Do not be frightened, and do not be dismayed, for the LORD your God is with you wherever you go."

JOSHUA 1:9 ESV

Test results. Rough neighborhood. Job interview. Raging storm. Some moments test our courage, require all our strength. What a comfort it is to know our Lord is always with us!

How impossible is it for fear to remain when we remember the powerful presence of the God who split the sea! Take courage from his promise to never leave you. Draw strength from the assurance he is here, now and on the day of your doubt.

God, you are my courage. You are my strength. The days I doubt are the days I forget you are with me. Thank you for the constant reminders in your Word, and through your actions in my life. The words of comfort you speak, the waves of peace you send, the incredible way you have of calming me in the storm, they sustain me.

What fear could God wipe away as you recall his presence and sovereignty?

Proud Papa

Whether you turn to the right or to the left, your ears will hear a voice behind you, saying, "This is the way; walk in it."

ISAIAH 30:21 NIV

So many choices! It seems we are always in the middle of considering, making, or living with the results of a decision. Factor in the mundane ones, like smoothie or scrambled eggs, and we see our life is one choice after another. Our breakfast is clearly less impactful than a career change or whether to put a child in a traveling sports program, but each decision forms a step on our path, becomes a brick in the wall of our past. If only we could be sure we were making the right ones.

Well, we can! As children of our God, with the earnest desire to follow him in our hearts, he promises to guide our steps. We need only be still enough to hear his voice, and then willing enough to follow his direction.

God, thank you for leading me from behind. I confess there are times I wish you'd run ahead, wave your arms and shout, "Over here!" but I see your way is best. Gently, you encourage me step by step. A wrong turn is not a disaster when I have you whispering, "this way." A dark path is not so intimidating when your light points toward the best next step. Help me to hear you, God, and then help me to go.

Your ears shall hear a word behind you, saying, "This is the way, walk in it, whenever you turn to the right hand or whenever you turn to the left."

ISAIAH 30:21 NKJV

Because of free will, God will never force us onto the right road. Notice the verse doesn't say he's ahead of us, pulling us along. It doesn't even say he's beside us, moving as we do. He's behind us.

This means the only way to get our next whisper is to take a step. And we needn't fear it being the wrong one; that's why he's there. Even if we do step wrong—and we will—his voice guides us back to right.

Father, once again I am captivated by your creativity. You show me where to go by allowing me to move. Like a father teaching his child to ride a bike, you steady me, encourage me, and give me directions from behind, but it is I who turn the pedals, I who steer the handlebars. Thank you for running behind me, proud Papa, and cheering me on.

What way is God encouraging you to go? How willingly are you walking in it?

A Little Wobbly

Direct my footsteps according to your word;
let no sin rule over me.

PSALM 119:133 NIV

Is there an old family photo of you in your mama's high heels, tiny feet barely making it past the arch, stubby legs only slightly longer than the shoes? What is it about those shoes that, even as the littlest girls, make us feel beautiful? They're certainly not comfortable or easy to move in, but we all want to feel elegant and those narrow, pointy pumps have a way of bringing out our inner princess. Whether you wear them daily or save them for special occasions, chances are, your steps get a little wobbly at times.

Stepping out in faith is similar. Getting used to walking in these shoes, we're a little shaky and uncertain. People in taller, prettier shoes seem to be everywhere, and they're making it look so much more graceful than we feel. Guess what: the beautifully coiffed woman in the stilettos? She's teetering too. This is one of many reasons we need the Holy Spirit. The Helper is a strong, steady arm, directing our steps, keeping us steady in the Word, and steering us away from sin.

Holy Spirit, thank you for how you direct my steps. Thank you for the strong arm that steadies me. This walk is beautiful, and I wouldn't trade it for all the shoes in a designer store, but I'd be lying if I said it was easy and without pain. I'm so grateful I have you to hold me up.

Prepare before me a path filled with your promises,
and don't allow even one sin to have dominion over me.

PSALM 119:133 TPT

From a steadying arm, directing each step and keeping us upright, to a path maker paving our way with promises, God's Word and his character are full of fresh surprises.

A path filled with promises sounds heavenly, doesn't it? Like a trail of flower petals leading to a candlelit proposal, the Lord makes a wonderful way for us to walk. And paving over every obstacle, he makes it safe.

God, I love the thought of stepping into promise after promise.
Thank you for preparing my path, holding my arm, and keeping
me safe. I do feel like a princess when I walk with you, my King.

Take a moment to appreciate the beautiful nuances in Scripture. How wonderful it is that the original language can lead to such layered, lovely translations! Which translation speaks to your heart more powerfully tonight?

You Are Loved

I am convinced that neither death, nor life, nor angels, nor principalities, nor things present, nor things to come, nor powers, nor height, nor depth, nor any other created thing, will be able to separate us from the love of God, which is in Christ Jesus our Lord.

ROMANS 8:38-39 NASB

Who doesn't love an epic, romantic gesture? Moments in film featuring desperate airport dashes or overcoat-wearing, boombox-wielding heroes become etched on our hearts. Even if no one has ever moved a mountain to get to us, we easily imagine the lengths we would go to prove, save, or declare our love. Whether bestie or baby, spouse or sister, loving deeply transcends reason, obstacles, and even death.

Why? Because this is how Christ loves us. Thanks to his limitless power, there is nothing that can keep him from the ones he loves. You are cherished beyond comprehension. You are adored beyond reason. You are pursued beyond the boundaries of time and space.

Oh, Jesus, how can you love me so? When I picture you, robe flowing, racing through time itself to pull me to you, it takes my breath away. I want to be that desperate to get to you too, Lord. Remove the distractions and clear the obstacles keeping me from pursuing you with all my heart. It's what I desire, it's what you deserve.

I am sure that neither death, nor life, nor angels, nor ruling spirits, nothing now, nothing in the future, no powers, nothing above us, nothing below us, nor anything else in the whole world will ever be able to separate us from the love of God that is in Christ Jesus our Lord.

ROMANS 8:38-39 NCV

Have you ever totally blown it? Maybe you failed at an important opportunity or ruined a relationship and now forgiveness feels impossible. Please know, there is no way—no possible way—to blow it with God.

Once you have his heart, it's yours forever. Before you even sin, you are forgiven. Before you even love, you are loved. Forever, wherever, however. You are loved.

God, thank you for your incomprehensible love. Thank you for the mountains you move, the spirits you overrule, and the sins, slights, and oversights you forgive to keep me in your love. You amaze me, God. I cannot blow it with you, and that just blows me away.

Have you consistently believed this beautiful truth about God since you've began your walk with him? How does the depth of his love make you feel?

Gift of Peace

*"I am leaving you with a gift—peace of mind and heart.
And the peace I give is a gift the world cannot give.
So don't be troubled or afraid."*

JOHN 14:27 NLT

Have you ever wondered why it's so hard to find peace in this world? Jesus' words to his disciples here give us the answer. We are looking in the wrong place. Peace is not of this world, it's of heaven. Peace doesn't come from a blooming meadow or a tranquil pool. It comes from Jesus.

We can certainly find peaceful moments this side of heaven, but, because we are here in the temporary world, the feelings those lovely places and quiet moments provide will be temporary, as well. True peace from above is eternal and always available to those who seek it. True peace paves the way for joy to shine through in even our darkest times.

God, I confess to looking for peace where it cannot be found. I seek out solace, space, and beauty and expect my heart to be at rest. Only you can give me what I am searching for. You long to give peace even more than I long to receive it. Thank you, God, for your gift of peace.

"I leave the gift of peace with you—my peace. Not the kind of fragile peace given by the world, but my perfect peace. Don't yield to fear or be troubled in your hearts—instead, be courageous!"

JOHN 14:27 TPT

This morning we focused on the Lord's peace, which is ours for as long as we will remain in it. This evening let's turn our attention to the second half of this verse. After promising his disciples peace, Jesus tells them not to yield to fear or to be troubled. This implies they had a choice.

We also have a choice. Fear will come; that's inevitable. It is up to us whether we invite fear to stay and push our peace out the door, or we push fear away and choose to have our peace remain.

God, how empowering this is! Knowing peace is a gift and fear is a choice, I have more control over my emotional state than I realized. As opposites, fear and peace cannot live together. As the gatekeeper, I get to decide who stays. What an easy choice! Peace, make yourself at home in my heart.

What burdens or fears threaten your peace? Share them with Jesus and ask that he give you the courage to choose peace instead.

Home

*Your faithfulness continues throughout all generations;
you established the earth, and it stands.*

PSALM 119:90 NASB

Most families have someone fascinated with the family tree: a precious old uncle or a curious cousin. This relative has spent hours poring over old records and tracing generations. They may have even visited the ruins of an ancient castle or family farmstead. They are fascinated because there is something profound about a family's legacy, and something beautiful about its stories of struggle, change, triumph, and love.

This is especially true in the story of God's family—our family—and the enduring legacy of his abiding love and faithfulness. No war, no plague, no wave from the sea, or meteor from the sky has erased us from this earth. Nothing has changed his love for us, and nothing ever will.

God, thank you for making me a part of your family. Thank you for giving me your Word and the stories of your love throughout the generations. You love all of us as your chosen people, and your faithfulness so great! I am in awe. I am so grateful to be yours.

Your faithfulness endures to all generations;
you have established the earth, and it stands fast.

PSALM 119:90 ESV

What is the oldest thing you own? Whether a centuries-old family heirloom or a tattered baby blanket, the things we own with a history hold special meaning. Who have you loved the longest, and who has loved you? Even if they are not in our day-to-day lives, shared history creates an unbreakable bond. Reunited after months, years, or even decades, we fall easily into familiar patterns when we see them again. It's as if no time has passed at all.

Now consider this earth, the place we call home. The best scientific estimates place its age at around 4.5 billion years. Just as those waves, wars and meteors didn't destroy us, they didn't destroy the home our Father built us. Through it all, every blaze, and every bomb, and throughout the passing of time, our earth stands fast.

God, when I consider all your hands have made, and the enduring beauty, strength and resilience of this gorgeous planet, awe is the only appropriate response. Great is your faithfulness, great are your gifts to us, and great you are, oh God.

What creation of God's do you find most amazing?
Talk to him about it.

Wear Love

Let not steadfast love and faithfulness forsake you;
bind them around your neck;
write them on the tablet of your heart.

PROVERBS 3:3 ESV

It doesn't take long when studying God's Word to realize the value he places on love and loyalty. Scarcely a page goes by without a mention of how the Father loves his children, and how he wants us to love one another.

In this verse the instructions are graphic. Wear love around your neck. Write faithfulness on your heart. It's that important. What do you suppose following those instructions would look like in your day-to-day life? With faithfulness imprinted on our hearts, would it be harder to betray a confidence? Would the weight of love around our necks help us to slow down and notice someone who could use our help?

God, the love you have for me and the faithfulness you have shown me are the model I wish to imitate to others. I want to carry love and faithfulness everywhere I go. Bind me to them so I can't wander off and leave them behind, or trade them for a quick, careless thrill.

> *Hold on to loyal love and don't let go,*
> *and be faithful to all that you've been taught.*
> *Let your life be shaped by integrity,*
> *with truth written upon your heart.*

PROVERBS 3:3 TPT

The verses above urge us to remember who we are called to be. Our experiences have taught us valuable lessons, so let us not stray from what we have learned.

Love matters, so we must wear it always. Integrity counts, and it's a wonderful foundation to build a life upon. Truth is so important, it deserves to be written on our hearts.

God, thank you for your wonderful Word. The Bible is so rich with instruction on how to be my best, so filled with encouragement, admonishment, and wisdom I can't get enough of it. Thank you for teaching me how to live, for telling me who I am, and for calling me yours. I love you so.

If you were to write a truth on your heart, what would it be?

She Is Radiant

All of us who have had that veil removed can see and reflect the
glory of the Lord. And the Lord—who is the Spirit—makes us more
and more like him as we are changed into his glorious image.

2 CORINTHIANS 3:18 NLT

Picture a traditional bride, veiled and dressed in white, as she comes down the aisle toward her groom. Wedding guests see a hint of her beauty, but most of her radiance is hidden behind the veil. Until the moment the bridegroom raises it, the veil obscures much of her wedding-day glory. As the first to see her, he is dazzled by her beauty. The glow of love and anticipation have made her lovelier than ever before. She turns to face the guests and they are also dazzled. She is radiant.

Paul uses this same picture to describe what happens to us when we become one with Christ. Veil removed, we can fully see and be seen by our glorious Bridegroom. The longer we look at him, the more we reflect him. The more we reflect him, the more dazzling we become.

God, let me gaze at you forever, and make me a mirror! I want to
reflect your beauty and light always. No matter what I face, let me
shine with the radiance of one who is chosen by you. When others
are drawn to me, let me direct them to you. You are the Beautiful
One. by loving you I am made beautiful too.

We can all draw close to him with the veil removed from our faces.
And with no veil we all become like mirrors who brightly reflect
the glory of the Lord Jesus. We are being transfigured into his very
image as we move from one brighter level of glory to another. And
this glorious transfiguration comes from the Lord, who is the Spirit.

2 CORINTHIANS 3:18 TPT

Another purpose of a veil is separation. Like a mosquito
net or a curtain that filters the sun, the veil forms a barrier
between two sides. With the veil removed, there is nothing
keeping us from getting right next to the Lord. He will be
close enough to touch, and his glory unobscured.

Imagine what it will be like once the veil is removed forever.
Imagine when Jesus is right before your eyes: his presence
so powerful and his light so strong. We will become more
and more like him, blooming like a flower moved from the
greenhouse to the garden.

Jesus, I want to be so near to you it's impossible to tell where I end,
and you begin. I want to be planted in your garden and nourished
by your light, ever growing, blooming, and radiant. Thank you for
your Spirit, living in me, who makes this possible, and who makes
me glorious.

How much of Jesus' radiance are you reflecting? How much is
still hidden?

89

Peace, Life, and Freedom

Letting your sinful nature control your mind leads to death. But letting the Spirit control your mind leads to life and peace.

ROMANS 8:6 NLT

If you've ever conquered a long-term habit, you know how difficult it is. Whether nail biting, smoking, eating—too much or too little—lying, or even drugs, the habits we don't control eventually control us. No wonder, then, we struggle so mightily against surrender. Holding on is a hard pattern to break. And why should we surrender? Control is good, right?

Oh, if ever there were a case for letting go and surrendering our control, it is here in Romans 6. When we, as sinful beings, insist on controlling things ourselves, the result is death. Yet when we turn our lives over to the Spirit, peace, life, and freedom await. Peace. Life. Freedom. We can surrender to those promises.

Holy Spirit, I surrender. My way is hard and seems to be leading me nowhere. Even my best intentions can't compare with your perfect peace and sweet surrender. The life I want is the one you offer when I uncross my arms, raise them up, and allow you to carry me.

If people's thinking is controlled by the sinful self, there is death. But if their thinking is controlled by the Spirit, there is life and peace.

ROMANS 8:6 NCV

Sometimes, seemingly out of nowhere, a preposterous thought comes to mind. Something we would never do or say just pops into our heads. *Where on earth did that thought come from?* we ask ourselves. Immediately, we reject it; it's so clearly not us.

What if we applied that same outright rejection to every thought that would take us from peace, life and freedom? What if instead we returned again and again to the Spirit? And to every flash of anger, or anxiety, or impatience we respond, "Where did that come from? That's not who I am." There is truth in this response. You were not created to be angry, anxious or impatient. The beautiful, perfect peace of Christ is always available; we need only choose to let it rule.

Prince of peace, help control my thoughts. Take every stray, negative thought and cast it out. Remind me that I have everything I need, I am exactly as I should be, and you and your perfect peace are my sustenance. Thank you, God, that an anxious mind can be quieted simply by speaking your name. Jesus, Jesus, Jesus.

What is the easiest way for the enemy to disrupt your peace? Be aware of this scheme and refuse to allow it. Give the Holy Spirit control.

God of Hope

May the God of hope fill you with all joy and peace in believing,
so that you may abound in hope by the power of the Holy Spirit.

ROMANS 15:13 NRSV

Think of the last time you used the words "I hope" in a sentence. Often, when we say we hope what we actually mean is we want, and somewhat against the odds. "I hope I'm not late!" is more likely to mean, "I'm probably going to be late, but I'd love to be wrong about that."

When we hope, we don't just want. True hope carries with it an expectancy beyond mere desire because what we want can be had. When the Holy Spirit fills us with hope, this wonderful anticipation ushers in joy and peace too. All will be well; there is nothing to fear. Whatever we hope for, we can turn to our Lord. He is the God of hope.

God of hope, I hope for more hope! As I trust you, and as you prove yourself faithful time and again, may my expectancy grow. May I believe that every good thing I hope for in our name is already mine.

May God, the inspiration and fountain of hope, fill you to overflowing with uncontainable joy and perfect peace as you trust in him. And may the power of the Holy Spirit continually surround your life with his super-abundance until you radiate with hope!

ROMANS 15:13 TPT

Picture a vase filled with ping pong balls with a pitcher of water next to it. Imagine slowly pouring the water into the vase. At first, the water fills the crevices between the balls but, eventually, the balls begin to float and spill out of the vase.

Hope works the same way. Every worry, doubt, distraction and fear in our hearts is just a ball of air. The more hope pours in through our faith in the Lord, the more those empty balls float up and out. Gone. Only hope remains. Hope, and the Spirit who brings it.

Holy Spirit, thank you! I invite you to please pour hope, peace and joy into me until the lesser things are crowded out and I am left overflowing with your goodness.

What "empty balls of air" is the Spirit ready to remove from your heart?

Love not Sacrifice

*"I want you to show love, not offer sacrifices.
I want you to know me more than I want burnt offerings."*

HOSEA 6:6 NLT

If someone said they loved you— even brought you flowers every day—but never made time for you, never really talked to you, would you truly feel loved by them? How connected can you feel to someone you're never actually connecting with?

Since God is the author of love, why would we expect him to feel any differently? He loves it when we profess our love for him. He loves it when we sacrifice our time and money for the things he cares about. But he feels most loved by us when we reach out to connect with him. Pray, journal, sing, or get into his creation or quietly meditate. How we connect isn't nearly so important as that we connect. He wants to know us, and he wants us to know him.

God, I want you to know how much I love you. I don't just want to impress you with my generosity or my Bible knowledge; I want to move you with the depth of my affection for you. I want to share my dreams with you, and I want to know your dreams. I want to share my heart with you, and I want to know yours.

> *"I desire steadfast love and not sacrifice,*
> *the knowledge of God rather than burnt offerings."*
>
> HOSEA 6:6 ESV

It's amazing, isn't it, that the God of the Universe, love himself, wants more of you?

What matters most to him is that you love him. He wants to be seen and known and felt and heard by you. More than he wants your service, your gifts, your attendance, and your obedience, he wants your love.

God, I love you so! Thank you for this beautiful invitation to slow down, seek your face, and just be with you. I will still sacrifice. I'll give, I'll go, and I'll serve, but never in place of simply being with you. Let me constantly discover more of who you are, and make sure you know how much I love you.

What happens in your heart when you realize that what the Lord most wants from you is you?

Beauty in the Ordinary

> *This is the day the LORD has made;*
> *we will rejoice and be glad in it.*
>
> PSALM 118:24 NKJV

As you look outside this morning, the joyful part of today may not be immediately obvious. Even in warmer climates, winter is winter. Nature seems a little less alive. The air is not quite as warm. In colder places, the novelty of those boots, scarves, and hats we couldn't wait to wear back in October has worn off.

Looking at your schedule may not make a reason for gladness any more apparent. Keep looking. A patch of blue sky, a warm hug, a thoughtful text, the furry belly of your sweet pet, all are reminders we have a loving Father who makes certain each and every day contains a reason to rejoice and be glad.

God, no matter the weather, no matter the circumstances, that you made this day is reason for rejoicing. When there's beauty outside, I am glad of it. When my day brings delights, I am overjoyed. Yet even in the cold and gray, even in the doldrums of a day like so many others, there is you, Creator God, and the unending joy that lives inside every heart that knows you.

> *This is the day which the LORD has made;*
> *Let us rejoice and be glad in it.*
>
> PSALM 118:24 NASB

What was the best meal you ever made? Whether it was a gourmet creation from the blog of a celebrity chef, or the most sublime burger ever to grace your grill, that meal stands out. If you cooked at that level daily, nothing would stand out or be special.

Perhaps God creates ordinary days for the same reason we eat the same sandwich nearly every day for lunch: so sushi with your girlfriends, or Mexican with your favorite man, will stand out. Maybe he made this day just this way so that we would have the chance, right now, to recognize the beauty in the ordinary.

God, thank you for making this day! Thank you for its highs and lows, no matter how indistinguishable they were. Thank you that there is joy in the simple, ordinary act of eating a meal, stroking a pet, or hearing from a friend. I am so very, very glad of it.

What are you glad for today? In what can you rejoice? If no event comes to mind, ponder the creativity of our Lord.

Boasting in Weakness

If I must boast, I will boast of the things that show my weakness.
2 CORINTHIANS 11:30 NRSV

You are amazing! How did you feel when you read that?
Did you feel affirmed, or a bit uncomfortable? Pleased, or
patronized? When someone gives you a sincere compliment,
are you able to receive it with the same level of sincerity? This
is tricky for many of us, as we tread that fine line we've walked
since little girls, the one between graciousness and fear of
appearing vain.

One of the many wonderful things about life in Christ is that
we can cast this worry aside. Once we grasp that every good
thing about us is a gift from him, we are free to appreciate
being appreciated. Not only that, we also get to call attention
to the awesome work he does through our weak places.
Consider responding like this: "Thank you! Let me tell you,
that was all God. My human side wanted to run for the hills.
I can't believe the courage he gave me to hang in there."
Doesn't that feel good?

*Father, I thank you for my gifts and my flaws. Each time I am
generous despite my inner tendency toward holding back, or I am
brave despite inner fear, I know for certain it is you at work in me.
What a gift this is! Holy Spirit, make me bold to share the ways
you work to make me better. let my testimony inspire others to
invite you to move in them.*

If I must brag, I will brag about the things that show I am weak.

2 CORINTHIANS 11:30 NCV

"If I must brag…" What do you suppose Paul meant by this? When would we ever be called to brag? If we are meant to do everything for the glory of God, surely there will be times when calling attention to the beautiful transformation the Lord has worked in us is important.

A sister stuck believing she can never overcome her selfishness will be blessed to know it is only by the power of the Holy Spirit you are able to behave selflessly. An addict caught in hopelessness will find hope in your story of overcoming. So, brag you must. Someone's hope may depend on it.

God, I come before you tonight humbled by the way you have already transformed me. I am so excited to see what is yet to come. Embolden me to share your great work, Father! Show me someone who needs to know just how lost I'd be without you, so I may boast about your glory over my weaknesses.

Spend some time honestly reflecting on the ways God has changed you. What innate weakness has he overridden in order to do something wonderful through you?

Truest Friendship

*A dear friend will love you no matter what,
and a family sticks together through all kinds of trouble.*

PROVERBS 17:17 TPT

By the time we reach adulthood, or sometimes even earlier, we realize not all friendships are forever. Once friendship is about more than liking the same princess movie and living on the same block, and once secrets and boys and envy enter the picture, only the truest of friendships survive. Oh, what a gift those friendships are!

A friend who has seen the ugliest part of you and chooses to keep looking, or a girlfriend who has been hurt by you and chosen to forgive, is a treasure. Who are your treasures? Whether you have a tight-knit tribe who have loved one another since primary school, or just one special girlfriend who totally gets you, thank God for friendship today.

God, thank you for friends! Thank you that no matter how much of me they see, or how much of me they know, their love remains. How amazing it is to know that you—who know everything there is to know about me—love me even more. Jesus, what a friend you are.

A friend loves at all times,
and a brother is born for adversity.

PROVERBS 17:17 NKJV

Tonight, turn your focus to the second half of the verse above. Whether biologically related to you or not, who are the family, the brothers and sisters, you know will be there in a crisis?

Sometimes the answer surprises us. Crisis comes and those who show up and refuse to leave us are not always those we may have expected. Months may have passed since you last saw them, but your need is the only invitation they need to come back into your life. What a gift they are, these sisters, brothers, and mothers. Let us receive them gladly.

Father, I love how many different ways there are to love, and how many different people you've chosen for me. From lifelong friends to brand new ones, and from running buddies to siblings, you cover every area of my life with love and friendship. I especially thank you, God, for those who will never let me struggle alone.

Spend some time prayerfully considering your friendships. Thank God for each person, and the unique way they love you.

Both Necessary

After sending them home, he went up into the hills by himself to pray. Night fell while he was there alone.

MATTHEW 14:23 NLT

It's the classic introvert/extrovert test question: Everyone in the house will be gone for the entire weekend. Do you plan a party, a girls' night out, or a quiet weekend alone with the remote, a book, and your coziest blanket? Perhaps you choose a little we time *and* a little me time.

Jesus is a perfect model of balance. He clearly adored his closest friends; they were constant companions for three years. His comfort with the crowd is obvious as well: multitudes followed him everywhere, eager for the next healing or teaching event, and he repeatedly gave them all he had. Yet, tucked into these stories, we see another Jesus as well, a Jesus who guarded and cherished time alone. Both were necessary. Both made him who he was. Whichever we gravitate toward, may we seek and receive balance.

God, you know my heart. You know where I am filled and where I am drained. Thank you for caring for me so intimately, for making sure I have opportunities to grow and nurture the public and the private me. Thank you for showing me how much I need them both.

After He had sent the crowds away, He went up on the mountain by Himself to pray; and when it was evening, He was there alone.

MATTHEW 14:23 NASB

It would be easy to stop our consideration of Jesus' alone time here, recognizing the example of balance he set by healing then restoring, teaching then retreating. It's a wonderful lesson, but also an incomplete one. Jesus didn't retreat to find a hot spring and get in touch with himself. As nice as that sounds, and as pleasant as a good soak can be, Jesus went off by himself to pray.

He knew—as we do through his teaching—that alone is never really alone. The Holy Spirit is always with us, connecting, rejuvenating, and replenishing our stores of patience and peace. Let us not waste our alone time being alone! Rather, let us draw on the intimacy with our Lord that is only possible when we are alone with him. Share your heart. Listen to his.

Dearest Jesus, I cherish my alone time because of the incredible opportunity to be alone with you. As I retreat to the quiet, may I be filled with a sense of your presence and a desire to bare my soul before you. As I do, may I be restored and refilled with your incomparable goodness.

How often do you carve out time to be alone with Jesus? No matter how much it is, know he wants even more. What steps can you take to "go up on the mountain" and meet him more regularly?

Silent Before God

For God alone, O my soul, wait in silence,
for my hope is from him.

PSALM 62:5 ESV

Take a moment right now and just listen. Is there music, a television playing, or a conversation near enough for you to hear? Perhaps you hear the hum of electricity, or the whirring of the furnace. Regardless, in this century, total silence is a rarity. For the hearing, there is always sound to be heard.

How, then, do we wait in silence? Where do we find the Lord if we can't escape sound? We listen for him. Before you focused on the sounds around you, could you hear the furnace? Though a song was playing, were you tuned in? The key to finding and hearing from God is to create silence in our minds, to tune our hearts to his, and to listen. No matter where we are, we can wait in silence for the hope of his message to us.

Oh, Lord. So much noise competes for my attention, yet all I want to hear is your voice. Even as I pray, thoughts race through my mind. Help me a stillness, God, where I can hear you and nothing else. Here in the silence, meet me as I wait.

I am standing in absolute stillness, silent before the one I love,
waiting as long as it takes for him to rescue me.
Only God is my Savior, and he will not fail me.

PSALM 62:5 TPT

Reread the verse slowly, imagining yourself living this out. How long could you stand silent before God? How long could you wait for your moment or turn with him What a beautiful picture of patience and faith!

Can we trust him enough, and we love him enough, to be content to simply gaze upon him and wait? No pleading, desperate prayers, no passionate singing or dancing, just stillness. Stillness, silence, and waiting.

Precious Jesus, I come into your presence, quiet and still, and eagerly wait to hear from you.

Tonight, practice stillness. Be kind to yourself when it's difficult. Tomorrow, and the next day, and the day after that, try again.

Ever Want

> *Delight yourself in the LORD;*
> *and he will give you the desires of your heart.*
>
> PSALM 37:4 NASB

As a little girl, what did you dream of? A steady diet of princess movies often results in dreams of marrying a prince. A visit to a farm has us longing for a horse of our own. At the time, we can't fathom anything more wonderful. As we grow, we learn our odds of becoming royal, and the realities of caring for an equine pet, and our heart's desire changes. Still, we continue to long for things that require hope.

As we follow Christ, we learn he longs to fulfill these hopes, to answer these prayers. Whatever my heart desires? Perhaps. It depends on the source of the desire. If our dreams are for things of the world—riches, fame, or a flawless face, Jesus may not agree this is what we need. But when our hearts are beating for him, and knowing and pleasing him is our highest aim, we can be assured our dreams are aligned with his will.

Jesus, you delight me! the more I want you, the more you promise to give me. It's amazing. You're amazing. The more of you I have, the less anything else—even those things that seemed so important before—can compare. You are my heart's desire.

Enjoy serving the Lord,
and he will give you what you want.

There's a wonderful simplicity to this message. If what you
want is to make the Lord happy, he'll provide a way to make it
happen. If what you want is to make yourself happy, his help
is not guaranteed. Wanting to make him happy will invariably
make us happier in the long run.

When we long for the things of this world, Jesus knows that
even if he gives us all we crave, we will still be filled with
longing. Until we fall in love with our Savior, our hearts will
always have an empty space. There is simply nothing in this
world that can satisfy us. Only when we long for Jesus alone
will we finally get all we could ever want.

God, I confess that while I do love serving you, it is not always
my top priority. I do love to worship you, but many other things
compete for my attention. Yet, in your perfect way, you fill me with
a longing only you can fill. Draw me to you until I'm close enough
to see you're all I've ever wanted.

What is your heart's true desire? Ask the Spirit to show you
the root of this longing. If it is not from him, what will it take
for you to let it go and join your dream to his instead?

Everlasting Love

The LORD has appeared of old to me, saying:
"Yes, I have loved you with an everlasting love;
therefore with lovingkindness I have drawn you."

JEREMIAH 31:3 NKJV

How did God draw you to him? Whether you cannot remember a time you did not know and love him, or whether you first felt him in the wake of a devastating loss, know that your path to him was carefully laid. He knew just what it would take to get you here, and, with lovingkindness, he brought you along.

Perhaps you found the Lord in the wake of a devastating loss, or a painful situation. If your road to him was hard, the above verse may seem confusing. You may wonder how losing a loved one, or suffering through abuse or neglect, counts as lovingkindess. Believe in his everlasting love for you. He loved you enough to watch you suffer—though it broke his heart—through whatever it took to bring you home.

Dear God, I see now how everything that happened had to happen. If not for the pain, how would I know joy? Though it hurt sometimes, and I couldn't always feel your love, I recognize now hard it must have been for you to wait for me and witness my pain. Thank you for your everlasting love. It's so good to be home!

The LORD appeared to him from far away. "I have loved you with an everlasting love; therefore I have continued my faithfulness to you."

JEREMIAH 31:3 ESV

Is there someone you have loved their entire life: a child you carried, a niece or nephew, or a younger sibling? There's an extra depth to the love we have for those we've known "forever." To think that God loves all of us even more deeply than this, because he has truly known us for all time.

Since before time began, he has loved everyone. Whether they returned that love from their first awareness of him, or whether they died refusing his every overture, he never stops loving any of his children. And he never will.

God, your love is forever. Everlasting. Whether I succeed or fail, and regardless of how imperfectly I reciprocate, you love me. Thank you for your faithfulness, God. With your help, may I one day deserve it.

Spend a little time thinking of all the ways God has stuck by you, thanking him for everyone.

Free to Love

You, my brothers and sisters, were called to be free. But do not use your freedom to indulge the flesh; rather, serve one another humbly in love.

GALATIANS 5:13 NIV

Picture total freedom. What's gone from your life? Perhaps the first things that come to mind are obligations: job, bills, kids, commitments. But, as we continue to imagine being completely free, we may think of other burdens, like pain, guilt, grief, and regret. Imagine all that melting away. It's not difficult to see which kind of freedom Jesus calls us to, is it?

Christ doesn't come into our lives to untether us from responsibility. He comes to break the chains of emotional and spiritual bondage. He sets us free from the baggage that hinders us from fully embracing the people he's given us to love or the mission he's called us to serve. In him, we are free to love, free to give, and free to serve with all our hearts.

Precious God, I don't always ask for true freedom, do I? I think I need less to do, or fewer people depending on me, but you show me the truth. By setting me free from the pain in my heart, you free me to give others all I have.

Beloved ones, God has called us to live a life of freedom in the Holy
Spirit. But don't view this wonderful freedom as an opportunity to
set up a base of operations in the natural realm. Freedom means
that we become so completely free of self-indulgence that we
become servants of one another, expressing love in all we do.

GALATIANS 5:13 TPT

What would you have done with an entire weekend of
freedom when you were a teenager? Some of us are blushing
just thinking of it. Those of us with teenager children are
probably praying. Just because you can, doesn't mean you
should.

Paul wanted to make sure the Galatians understood that
forgiveness from sin and freedom from the old law is not an
invitation to party like it's 1999. Just because we'll be forgiven
for our worst choices doesn't mean there won't be other
painful consequences. By focusing our freedom on how to best
love one another, we remain free from the trappings of sin.

Jesus, is there no end to the freedom you provide? Not only do you
forgive me for every poor or selfish choice, you also set me free from
the desire repeat those mistakes. The closer I am to you, the freer
I am from the sins that could weigh me down and hurt me. Come
close, Lord!

What old wound has Jesus released you from? What former
desire to sin has he delivered you from? What has he replaced
those old feelings with? Spend some time enjoying the
beautiful gift of true freedom.

Made Perfect

With one sacrifice he made perfect forever those who are being made holy.

HEBREWS 10:14 NCV

You are perfect. You, right now, as you are, are perfect. This concept of perfection isn't referring to your reflection in the mirror, the thoughts in your head, or the condition of your heat. It's about Jesus. The day you accepted the free gift of his sacrifice, you were made perfect.

In order to better understand what this means, we need only consider one of the synonyms of perfection: complete. It is finished. When he died on the cross for our sins, he removed all our transgressions from the Book of Life and completed the impossible task of making us holy.

Father, what do you see when you look at me? I want to see past the surface, past the things I'd like to fix, and see what you see. I want to see myself finished, complete, and holy. Will you show me?

By one offering He has perfected forever
those who are being sanctified.

HEBREWS 10:14, NKJV

What would you be willing to endure for a million dollars? A whole television empire has grown around exploring this question. People's tolerance for physical pain, betrayal, emotional fatigue, and worse, are put to the test in the hopes of winning big money. How much pain is worth it for the money?

What if instead of winning money, you were helping your loved ones? What would you go through in order to guarantee their permanent safety, comfort and happiness? Now, think of what Jesus endured—for you. Imagine how perfectly worth it it feels to him each time someone accepts his sacrifice.

Oh Jesus, I couldn't do what you did. Somewhere between the garden and the cross, I would have crumbled under the weight. You're awesome, Lord. Thank you for your strength and love. Only through you am I made worthy of your perfect sacrifice.

For now, and for as long as you can, believe you are perfect. Cast aside any other view of yourself and see what the Lord sees. See who he believed was worth dying for.

Invite His Will

I appeal to you therefore, brothers and sisters, by the mercies
of God, to present your bodies as a living sacrifice, holy and
acceptable to God, which is your spiritual worship.

ROMANS 12:1 NRSV

Surrender can be scary. We hear the word and we picture a
desperate fugitive, coming outside with arms raised to face
a multitude of snipers, police, and S.W.A.T. forces with
all guns pointed towards him. Or, perhaps, we picture the
ravaged shell of a person who has surrendered to addiction,
or a nation admitting defeat after a bloody war.

Yes, surrender can be scary, especially when it means
surrendering to an enemy. But because God is for us and
not against us, surrender to him is entirely different. Giving
our heart to God means abandoning our resistance. Instead,
we accept his plans. We invite his will. And, surprisingly,
beautifully, we find freedom.

God, I know there are areas of my heart I am struggling to let go of.
I know your plans are perfect, and your will for me is peace. I want
to surrender my whole heart to you, God, and end the struggle. I
want your peace.

Beloved friends, what should be our proper response to God's
marvelous mercies? I encourage you to surrender yourselves to God
to be his sacred, living sacrifices. And live in holiness, experiencing
all that delights his heart. For this becomes your genuine
expression of worship.

ROMANS 12:1 TPT

If you surrendered your life to Christ more than a day ago,
you've already learned that while conversion is a one-
time thing, surrender most certainly is not. We offer him
everything, and we mean it. Sincerely, we pledge to trust
him with all we have. Then, ever so slowly, bit by bit, we start
taking things back. We begin to think we could manage things
better. Our eyes wander from following his path, and we
begin to follow our own.

He knows. He's always right there watching, waiting for us to
hand it all back to him, and remember the delight of letting
him hold the reins.

God, I surrender to you. You're not too busy for my relationships.
My ideas for work and finances are not superior to yours. Even my
physical well-being is better off in your hands. Take it all, God, the
major and the mundane. Take my heart and take my plans. I'm so
eager to see where you lead.

What one area of your life could most benefit from letting
God lead? What is stopping you from handing it over? Let
him heal the piece of your heart that is resisting him, then
trust him—again—with the whole thing.

Pain Shared

Jesus wept.

JOHN 11:35 NKJV

When someone we love is hurting, we hurt with them. We cry alongside our newly jobless neighbors, bereaved girlfriends, and disappointed daughters. Compassion is as natural as breath when we are one with the Spirit, because the tears we cry are his. It breaks his heart to see us broken.

The verse above, the shortest in most translations, is also one of the most beautiful. Jesus was grieved by the pain his dear friends were experiencing. Even though he was going to dry their tears and raise Lazarus from the dead, in that moment, their pain was his pain—and it moved him to tears.

Jesus, the image of you weeping with your friends is at once so beautiful and so sad. As I better understand the depth of your compassion, I am filled with even more love for you. I am overwhelmed at how much pain you feel when I am in pain. Oh, how you love me.

Then tears streamed down Jesus' face.

JOHN 11:35 TPT

Sit for a moment with the picture of Jesus' tearstained face in your mind. Imagine the river of compassion in those tears, not just for the moment, but for the heartbreaking moments to follow. These dear friends, who loved him so, would soon watch Jesus himself suffer and die.

Knowing his heart, so filled with love and grace, can you imagine the sorrow contained in those tears?

God, how much grief we must cause you? How enormous, giving, and gracious your heart is to contain it all! You are so very beautiful, my God. Thank you for the tears you've cried for me.

Most translations of John 11:35 contain just two words: Jesus wept. Why do you think this powerful little sentence was given its own verse?

The First Thing

I rise before dawn and cry for help;
I put my hope in your words.

PSALM 119:147 NRSV

For a morning person, this verse seems quite reasonable. Whether the sun is up or not, they're awake early and eager to greet the day. For the night owls, rising before the dawn sounds, well, like something they would rather not do. They like their sleep. They're comfortable right here between our sheets. Must we all rise before dawn to cry out to God and find our hope?

While Scripture does frequently encourage early rising, it's not so much the hour of the day that matters as the eagerness of the heart. The Psalmist simply cannot wait to get with God. Regardless of the height of the sun, is time with the Father the first thing on your mind?

God, before anyone or anything can distract me, before I've even fully awakened, I want to meet with you. Hear me, God, as I call out to you. Teach me as I turn to your Word. Fill me with your hope, so it can spill over into my day.

I wake up early in the morning and cry out.
I hope in your word.

PSALM 119:147 NCV

How we end our day is just as important as how we begin it.

If we fall asleep to late-night television, how likely are we to wake with thoughts of the Savior? If we drift off with our smartphones still in hand, might they be the first thing we reach for as we wake? Instead, let us find sleep while seeking the Father.

Here in the quiet of evening, I call to you again. Father, help me to end this day in a way that sets me up for a hopeful tomorrow. Invite me to finish as I began, with you. Reviewing the day, I thank you for all the ways you met me. I ask you to wake me tomorrow, so we can do it all again.

What is your nighttime routine? Are there changes you could make to how you end that would improve how you begin?

The Way Is Clear

> "I am about to do a new thing;
> now it springs forth, do you not perceive it?
> I will make a way in the wilderness and rivers in the desert."
>
> ISAIAH 43:19 NRSV

Hiking a time-worn trail, our thoughts don't often focus on the tremendous amount of thought and labor that went into its creation. A well-laid path seems like it belongs and has always been there. A slight detour quickly illustrates the effort it took as roots, bushes and branches trip our feet and obstruct our progress. To continue this way would eventually render us lost, stranded, or injured.

Similarly, when we follow God's path, things just make sense. Sure, we may stumble a little, but for the most part, the way is clear and the destination reachable. Only when we stop to consider it, or when we wander from it, do we fully appreciate the intricacies of his involvement.

Father, you plan my path with such thought and creativity! You see a way through the densest wilderness and you go ahead of me, pulling up the brambles. Help me to notice and appreciate the way you remove that which would entangle me, making the route so clear.

> *"Behold, I will do something new,*
> *now it will spring forth; will you not be aware of it?*
> *I will even make a roadway in the wilderness, rivers in the desert."*

ISAIAH 43:19 NASB

We may only see a desert, but the Lord always knows where the springs are. As we face a seemingly impenetrable forest, the Father knows the best way through. He is inviting us to watch, listen, and notice how he works.

Nothing is too difficult for God. Nothing out of reach. The path is coming, and it leads to a spring. All we need to do is follow. Adventure and refreshment await if only we will take notice.

God, where there is no way, you make a way. Where the earth is dry you spring up a well and invite me to join you! Thank you, God, for all you make possible. I lay my challenges before you and invite you to carve the way through.

What dense forest lies in your way? What desert? Turn your attention to the Lord and let him show you something new.

Sustained

"When you pass through the waters, I will be with you;
and when you pass through the rivers, they will not sweep over you.
When you walk through the fire, you will not be burned;
the flames will not set you ablaze."

ISAIAH 43:2 NIV

Which part of this verse captured your attention—the danger
or God's presence with you in it? Your answer tells you
something about how close to that rushing water or raging
fire you are right now. Are you chest-deep in cold, rushing
water? Are you close enough to the fire to feel its heat on your
skin? Or, are you safe now, grateful for the way he kept you
afloat or prevented the flames from reaching you?

Regardless of how we relate to it, this promise contains two
important truths. First, this life will try you. Second, God
will sustain you. Expect the trial, but don't sit and wait for it.
Expect his presence when it comes, but don't spend your time
frantically scanning the horizon for potential danger. The
reason God will be with you then is that he is with you now.
He never leaves you. No matter how close or how far you are
from those icy waters or searing flames, settle into the safety
of the Father who is always there.

God, you are so faithful! When the water rises, I'm not carried
away. Though the flames come close, I'm never consumed. You
stay with me. You carry me to safety. You sustain me, God, through
every trial.

"When you go through deep waters, I will be with you.
When you go through rivers of difficulty, you will not drown.
When you walk through the fire of oppression,
you will not be burned up;
the flames will not consume you."

Isaiah 43:2 NLT

Most of us are a little broken—it's a rare person who gets through life completely unscathed. A misunderstanding of verses like this can leave us wondering who God was talking to, because based on what we've lived, it sure wasn't us. We may feel like he let us drown or get burned but, dear friends, we have never been abandoned.

We must remember this world is not our home. God protects our eternal souls, and they cannot be consumed, overwhelmed, or taken away by anything on this earth. We are his. First, last, and always, we are his. Even if the river drowns us, we live on. Even if the smoke and flames overpower us, they can never overpower him.

Eternal God, thank you for love that transcends this earthly
life. Thank you for the promise of protection even in the midst of
unimaginable pain. What a comfort it is to know that within your
embrace no harm can come to me. I rest in that promise.

Come before God with your true feelings about the fires and floods you've experienced or may experience in the future. Do you need the Holy Spirit's help to believe they won't overtake you?

We're Already In

When you live a life of abandoned love,
surrendered before the awe of God,
here's what you'll experience:
Abundant life. Continual protection.
And complete satisfaction!

PROVERBS 19:23 TPT

As advertisements go, Proverbs 19:23 puts forth a rather persuasive pitch for joining your life to God's. Abundant life? Yes, please! Continual protection? Let us in! Complete satisfaction? Where do we sign?

Here's the best part of all: we already signed. We're already in. The day we fell in love with Jesus and asked him into our hearts, all this and more was ours. To claim it, we need only remain in his love. To experience it, we need only give the Father our awe.

God, thank you for letting me in on the best deal ever. An overflowing life, completely safe and satisfying, is more than I could hope for before I met you. now it's mine to live and to share. What an awesome, generous God you are!

> *The fear of the L*ORD *is life indeed;*
> *filled with it one rests secure and suffers no harm.*

PROVERBS 19:23 NRSV

When we are reclined on the beach, hearing gentle waves rhythmically hit the shore, the ocean doesn't seem particularly fearsome. Jumping from a ship into twelve-foot swells and with no land in sight? It's hard to imagine anything more terrifying. It's a matter of perspective. From land, it's easy to forget the ocean's vastness and power. From the center, it's impossible to think of anything else.

This is what it means to fear God. To fear him is to respect him—to remember his vastness, to stand in awe of his power. Let us remain at the center of our faith, constantly aware of all he can, has, and will do, and find our secure rest there.

Father God, I am awed by you. What little I know is more than enough for me to realize your greatness is beyond measure, and your power without limit. This knowledge gives me life. how easy it is to rest secure knowing I am protected by a limitless God.

Does your fear of the Lord bring you a feeling of safety? Work through this with the Spirit and allow your awe of him to fill you with peace.

Heart Directions

May the Lord direct your hearts to the love of God and to the steadfastness of Christ.

2 Thessalonians 3:5 ESV

Popular culture says the key to happiness is to follow your heart. The idea is that by pursuing our passions we're most likely to end up in a good place. It seems like lovely advice, but only as long as we're sure our hearts know the way. Could your heart use directions from time to time?

A young woman choosing partying with friends over hard work or study, or a middle-aged, married woman acting on a flirtation that makes her heart flutter—both women could be following their hearts. Yet the heart can be deceptive. The heart's wants can be based on selfish, unhealthy, or irresponsible desires. God's heart, though, is steady and true. He knows exactly where we need to go. His unwavering love for us will make certain we get there.

God, direct my heart. Speak into my heart and fill it with your love for me. Lead me toward purpose and stability. Direct me to Jesus, my ultimate home.

May the Lord lead your hearts into God's love and Christ's patience.

2 THESSALONIANS 3:5 NCV

Visit any public venue and you're likely to see a child sprinting away from their parents. Their excitement can't be contained in their little bodies. They bolt because they are so certain they know where to go. We hear their harried parents call out to their child. "Slow down!" Whether by allowing her to temporarily believe she is lost, or by explaining the potential dangers of running off, the parents will try and teach her to stay close.

As a little girl, how often did you charge ahead, running headlong without looking back? How often do you do it still today? We know the Lord has plans for us, so each time we think we see a glimpse of what's next, we bolt. No looking left and right, no checking the rearview mirror, we just go. "Slow down," our Savior calls. May we listen and learn to stay close.

I confess it, Father. I try to rush you sometimes. Like a little girl in pursuit of the ice cream truck, I run ahead. I'm eager to arrive where you're leading me, so sometimes I forget to wait and follow. Thank you for your loving patience. Thank you for making sure I'm never lost.

Still your mind and ask the Father where he's leading your heart.

Pain Has Purpose

Jesus answered, "It was neither that this man sinned,
nor his parents; but it was so that the works of God
might be displayed in him."

JOHN 9:3 NASB

In Jesus' time, it was common to believe people with afflictions were being punished for either their own sins or those of a family member. Among the many incredible lessons about the heart of God that Jesus taught, he also set the record straight on this account. The man referred to in the verse, blind since birth, was sightless so that everyone witnessing—and everyone who would ever read this story— would see the awesome power of God.

Pain has purpose, dear friend. It draws us to the Father and gives us a chance to experience his compassion and healing. It may feel like punishment but believe Jesus' words, it's not.

Father, I know you don't punish me. Things beyond my control and messes I get into all on my own are opportunities for me to witness all you are able to do. Don't let me be blinded by pain. Heal me, Lord. Show me your glory and restore my sight.

*Jesus answered, "Neither this man nor his parents sinned,
but that the works of God should be revealed in him."*

JOHN 9:3 NKJV

Stories like the one in the verse above may seem unfair.
Especially if we have been in our own season of affliction,
we may even think God is being cruel. This poor man had
to spend his entire life blind just so Jesus could perform a
miracle? Ask yourself, though, what the man would say.

Always in darkness, he met Jesus who brought him into the
light. The first face he ever saw was that of the Son of God.
The hands who healed him were the hands of the Christ. Do
you suppose he'd tell you it was worth it?

*Oh, Jesus, I hope to one day proclaim your glory has triumphed
over every affliction in my life! Already I see where I was and
where I am, and I can say with certainty it was worth it. I didn't
love the pain, but oh, how I love the healer.*

What opportunities has the Lord taken in your life to display
his glory? Where would you like him to reveal it next?

Light in Darkness

*In him was life, and that life was the light of all mankind. The
light shines in the darkness, and the darkness has not overcome it.*

JOHN 1:4-5 NIV

Unless you are trying to sleep, what is the first thing you
look for in the dark? Light. We require illumination to find
our way. When light and dark are used figuratively, the same
truth applies. There is a reason a tough season is referred to
as a dark time. It's hard to see the way through. Obstacles are
everywhere.

In our own darkness, Jesus is a constant source of life-giving,
soul-nurturing light. He is likewise constant for all those who
love him. For those who have yet to know him, let us *be* light.
Let us bring his words, his presence, and his grace and peace
everywhere we go.

*Because you never leave me, God, I am never lost in darkness. I
need only turn to face you. As you are ever with me, I can also light
someone's way. Thank you, precious Jesus, for your constant glow.*

The Word gave life to everything that was created,
and his life brought light to everyone.
The light shines in the darkness,
and the darkness can never extinguish it.

JOHN 1:4-5 NLT

In God's creation total darkness is rare. Halfway around the world, the sun still finds a way—on all but the cloudiest of nights—to reflect off the moon. The lights of a billion stars, unfathomably far away, still make their way to earth. There is always a little light because light is stronger than the dark.

In the darkest room, a single candle will change everything. It doesn't matter how dark that room is meant to be, that tiny flame will always succeed. As long as it's there, the room cannot be shrouded in darkness.

God, on the days my hope is as big as the sun, you are that light. You are life. On the days darkness tries to overtake me, you send a star. You light a flame. You bring hope on the light, God, and light always wins.

Go to the darkest place you can. Is there yet a beam of light beneath the door? The glow of an appliance? Total darkness is rare. If you do find it, you can always light a candle or flashlight. Thank Jesus for being light in the darkness.

Our Worries

Cast all your anxiety on him, because he cares for you.

1 PETER 5:7 NRSV

"Can you talk? I really need to vent." What would we do without our friends who always have an ear when we need to release a little bit of steam? Yet, as compassionate as they are, their empathy can only go so far. Your bestie will gladly listen as you lament the bills, the baby who won't sleep, or the hard-to-please boss, but she can't take away the anxiety they create in your heart.

Jesus can. He loves you so deeply. He doesn't want you to continue struggling under the weight of your worries. *Give them to me,* he offers. And what an offer it is. Anything keeping you awake, robbing your joy, or filling you with worry, you can cast on him.

God, your offer to take all my worries is so beautiful yet I struggle with it. I don't know why, but I seem to want to carry my anxiety on my own. Will you strengthen me, Mighty God? Help me not to carry more, but to courageously accept your offer to stand up tall and hand my burdens to you.

Give all your worries to him, because he cares about you.

1 PETER 5:7 NCV

Just as we wouldn't be disappointed in our dear friend for not paying an unexpected bill or offering to potty-train a stubborn toddler, we must be careful not to misunderstand Jesus' offer. He wants our worries, not our responsibilities. He'll take the anxiety, not its source.

It's still an awesome offer. How much more gracefully can we approach our obligations when we are not weighed down with worry, consumed with concern?

I trust you, God. Knowing you will carry me, and knowing worry is not your plan for me, I can meet every challenge with confidence and patience. All will be well. Because of your great care for me, all will be well.

How much lighter will you be once you cast aside your worries and trust God with the outcome of your difficulties?

Loving Intercession

We constantly pray for you, that our God may make you worthy of his calling, and that by his power he may bring to fruition your every desire for goodness and your every deed prompted by faith.

2 THESSALONIANS 1:11 NIV

Do you have someone in life who often tells you they are praying for you? Maybe a parent, a sibling or a close friend? What a gift they are! Since they have a heart to see you thrive, why not help them by sharing your God-given dreams with them?

We know the Lord answers the prayers of the faithful, so, as we invite others to pray for us, we can be confident he will hear them. Our desire to find and fulfill our purpose, our longing to be worthy of the great love of Christ, and the acts we perform in obedience to his calling: all will be blessed by their loving intercession.

God, thank you for the pray-ers in my life. I don't want to take them for granted. Knowing they want to see me reach my every dream is a gift. Having their sincere prayers for my growth and success is a blessing. Hear their prayers.

We always pray for you, that our God may make you worthy of his calling and may fulfill every resolve for good and every work of faith by his power,

2 THESSALONIANS 1:11 ESV

It is with good reason that most churches encourage small groups. We are wired for connection. We are called to intercede for one another. We are made for love. Do you believe this?

To study God's Word with others and encourage each other to grow in faith is a beautiful, life-giving experience. Having people who constantly pray for you—and having people to constantly pray for—is a wonderful gift. As we take our eyes of our own concerns to lift up those of our friends, the Lord sees and rewards our compassion. As we share the load together, our own burden grows lighter.

Father, thank you for the gift of Spiritual friendship. A friend in Christ is a priceless blessing. May I treasure mine, and may I be a treasure to them.

Friend, do you have a group of women to pray with? If you do, thank the Father for them. If you do not, ask the Lord to lead you to the ladies he's chosen for you. Pay attention: this is a prayer he longs to answer.

Flung Wide Open

Though you have not seen Him, you love Him, and though you do not see Him now, but believe in Him, you greatly rejoice with joy inexpressible and full of glory,

1 PETER 1:8 NASB

What are your thoughts on love at first sight? Does a soul recognize its other half instantly, or are we stitched together with our mates slowly over time? How about love in the absence of sight? Could you fall for someone based solely on the words he wrote to you and the things he did for you, even if you never saw his face?

Of course, you can, and you have. The day you fell in love with Jesus, the eyes of your heart were flung wide open. Though you won't lay eyes on him until you meet in heaven, your soul has already seen his beauty and found its missing half.

Oh, Jesus, how I love you! The most beautiful thing I'll ever see is something I've never seen at all, and yet I know it will be amazing. My heart knows. Oh, what joy, what inexpressible joy, I will feel the day I see you face to face.

Whom having not seen you love. Though now you do not see Him, yet believing, you rejoice with joy inexpressible and full of glory.

1 PETER 1:8 NKJV

This beautiful picture of love is also a picture of faith. It is through faith we can rejoice in a promise. Trust allows us to revel in that we have yet to witness. We believe he is who he says he is and, believing, we love. Oh, how we love.

And how he loves us for it! We didn't ask for proof, we just opened our hearts and let truth in. We didn't demand evidence, our souls simply accepted what he offered, and we loved. How can this be? How can we, doubting and fickle, have such great capacity for love and faith? Only through him. In this truth, we find yet another reason to love.

God, thank you for this joyful love! It's as if you are rewarding me for my faith, or thanking me for believing you, by granting me glory. It's almost more than I can handle, and It's definitely more than I can describe. Thank you, Jesus. I love you.

How did you first fall in love with Jesus? Was it slow, like a friendship that grew into more, or all at once, like a bolt of lightning?

Unshakeable

I know how to live on almost nothing or with everything. I have learned the secret of living in every situation, whether it is with a full stomach or empty, with plenty or little. For I can do everything through Christ, who gives me strength.

PHILIPPIANS 4:12-13 NLT

Can you imagine feeling at peace no matter what circumstances you're in? Whether laid off, promoted, proposed to, dumped, selected, or rejected, you remain faithful and content? That kind of unshakeable peace seems extraordinary, perhaps even impossible, yet it's ours to take hold of.

Paul, after learning about this incredible gift, decided it was too wonderful to remain hidden. In the middle of his letter to the Philippians, he passed it along to them. Jesus is our supply. Whether we need help staying hopeful, or staying humble, the Lord gives us the strength.

God, I confess I find this easier to believe on the good days than the tough ones. When all seems right with the world, "God is good!" rolls effortlessly off my tongue. Give me the strength of Paul, Lord. Whether from a prison cell, from a hospital bed, or from feeling alone and forgotten, let me boast of your sustaining peace.

I know what it is to have little, and I know what it is to have plenty. In any and all circumstances I have learned the secret of being well-fed and of going hungry, of having plenty and of being in need. I can do all things through him who strengthens me.

PHILIPPIANS 4:12-13 NRSV

Want to be unshakeable? Get your strength from Christ. When your source of power comes from him, instead of your wallet, abilities, or the mirror, the supply is constant. There are no blackouts and no surges, just a steady stream.

With our faith resting securely in him, discontentment cannot gain a foothold. When our identity comes from his greatness, ego can't take any ground. The Lord is constant, and so is his peace. He is consistent, and so is his supply.

Jesus, your steadiness appeals to me. I want to remain grounded in your on my best days and to trust the center still holds on my worst. Like so many things about you, your consistency is awesome, Lord. Thank you for this offer of contentment and peace. May I be wise enough to claim it.

Can you imagine being truly unshakeable? How different would life be if you got off the roller coaster ride of circumstance?

Power and Grace

He said to me, "My grace is sufficient for you, for my power is made perfect in weakness." Therefore I will boast all the more gladly about my weaknesses, so that Christ's power may rest on me.

2 CORINTHIANS 12:9 NIV

Picture a tug-of-war contest. One side, all burly athletes, is dominating the other, a group of children. Which side would you be most inclined to jump in and help? Who would be more appreciative? God loves to come alongside us in all our endeavors, but he especially enjoys helping us when we are overpowered.

When we are feeling perfectly capable on our own, we are far less likely to appreciate—or even notice—the Lord's assistance. When we are outmanned, unqualified, and unprepared, his help is obvious and welcome. Be on the lookout for moments that were "all him" and give him the glory he deserves.

Father, thank you for all the ways you help me. I'm sure I'm not aware of all you do but I certainly notice when you intervene and make me kinder, stronger, more patient, or more capable than usual. Your grace is sufficient, Lord. It is more than enough, and I am more than grateful.

He has said to me, "My grace is sufficient for you, for power is perfected in weakness." Most gladly, therefore, I will rather boast about my weaknesses, so that the power of Christ may dwell in me.

2 CORINTHIANS 12:9 NASB

Hidden in the final words of this verse is a remarkable concept. Why would we boast about our weaknesses? So that the power of Christ may dwell in us. Yes, please!

If admitting we sometimes struggle to be patient, occasionally fail to hold our tongue, and often feel incapable of loving the way we should will invite Jesus to send his power, let the confessions begin. As he helps us conquer these challenges, let our lives be a billboard for his power and grace.

God, send your grace. You know my weaknesses. Rather than pretend I've got it all together, encourage me to be open about where I fall short. Then, when you help me rise above my shortcomings, others see will your power and be drawn in to your grace for themselves.

What weakness are you working hard to hide? How might a "boast" about it be a blessing to someone else, or an opportunity to let God display his awesome power?

Many Parts

If the whole body were an eye, it would not be able to hear. If the whole body were an ear, it would not be able to smell. If each part of the body were the same part, there would be no body. But truly God put all the parts, each one of them, in the body as he wanted them.

1 CORINTHIANS 12:17-18 NCV

It's nearly impossible to experience a spectacular display of talent—whether painting, song, novel or even a touchdown run—and not feel a longing to be able to perform at that same level. A captivating speaker is bound to make us yearn for the podium. A beautiful dance may stir us to dig out the old pink slippers. These feelings are both natural and a lovely tribute to the way God gifted the artists.

The important thing is not to become fixated on someone else's gifts, lest we miss out on discovering our own. If I, a mediocre singer at best, am obsessed with becoming a vocalist, I may never realize my potential as a chef, nurse, or accountant. The world needs us to use the gifts we do have far more than to work on acquiring the ones we wish we had.

Father God, thank you for the way you made me. Thank you for the way you made everyone else and the amazing gifts you've given them. By making us all unique, you ensure a world of endless delights, provision, and beauty.

If the whole body were an eye, where would be the hearing? If the whole were hearing, where would be the smelling? But now God has set the members, each one of them, in the body just as He pleased.

1 CORINTHIANS 12:17-18 NKJV

Imagine a country with nothing but athletes, a state with only doctors, or a city with only singers. It's unthinkable, almost laughable. No great athlete can become so without coaches, teachers, groundskeepers, equipment designers, assembly line workers, farmers, and so on.

We need each other. Even right now, someone else's greatness depends on yours.

God, I love your creativity! Your endless capacity for weaving things together amazes me. Let this inspire me to do my part with excellence, gratitude, and pride. Remind how significant my purpose is, and how vital my role is.

How important do you consider your "work?" Ask God to help you grasp the big picture and realize just how many people are affected by what you do.

How Eager

"*What no eye has seen, nor ear heard, nor the heart of man imagined, what God has prepared for those who love him.*"

1 CORINTHIANS 2:9 ESV

Recall the most stunning sunset you've ever seen. Mentally replay the most gorgeous piece of music you've ever heard. Sit with these sensations for a moment. Now, consider this, what you saw and what you heard are paltry compared to what the Lord has waiting for us in heaven. He can't wait to reveal it to us.

Every sense will be completely dazzled by the glory of heaven. Our minds can't comprehend it; we can't even dream it. The most delicious feasts, the most luxurious textures, and the most divine fragrances we've experienced so far will seem bland, scratchy, and faint next to the glories of God's kingdom.

God, the beauty I've experienced here on earth is so sublime that I can't imagine how much better things could be. What sounds more beautiful than a symphony? What scent is sweeter than a field of flowers? yet you promise the best is yet to come. I can't wait to see what you've prepared, God.

"Things never discovered or heard of before, things beyond our ability to imagine these are the many things God has in store for all his lovers."

1 Corinthians 2:9 TPT

When expecting a special guest, we take extra care in our preparations, fresh sheets, soft towels, and a fridge filled with their favorites. We plan meaningful activities, fluff the pillows, and light a fire. God is infinitely more excited and immeasurably more prepared for our homecoming than we could be for any guest.

He knows exactly what moves us, what stirs us, what overwhelms our hearts with joy and, having collected all those things together, he's going to multiply them and then multiply them again. That's how much God longs for our return. That's how eager he is for us to come home.

Father God, I am so excited to see my room! I truly can't imagine the beauty that awaits me in heaven, but I love trying. It blows my mind to realize how carefully you've prepared a place for me. Thank you for loving me so well.

Knowing how glorious heaven promises to be, what do you imagine you will find?

What Compassion

> *While they were stoning Stephen, he prayed, "Lord Jesus, receive my spirit." Then he knelt down and cried out in a loud voice, "Lord, do not hold this sin against them." When he had said this, he died.*

ACTS 7:59-60 NRSV

Staring into the eyes of your murderer, how likely is it your final words would be spent begging God to forgive them? In the case of Stephen's death, this unbelievable act of grace is exactly what transpired. The effect the love of Christ can have on a human heart is extraordinary.

What compassion it takes to see past the crime into the brokenness of the criminal and pray for their soul! Only Jesus can make us so forgiving, gracious, and selfless. On his own power, Stephen would have undoubtedly had something very different to say, as would we. When empowered by Christ, though, we can share his love with anyone.

Jesus, how great your love is in bridging the gap between killer and victim and producing selfless grace. Fill me with the love of Stephen, God, that I may set an example, even with my dying breath, of how to live in perfect love.

As they stoned him, Stephen prayed, "Lord Jesus, receive my
spirit." He fell to his knees, shouting, "Lord, don't charge them
with this sin!" And with that, he died.

ACTS 7:59-60 NLT

Stephen's last act is nearly impossible to imagine. How could
he be so filled with Jesus' lovingkindness that he wanted his
murderers to be forgiven?

Perhaps the first verse holds the answer. Just before he asked
for their forgiveness, he asked for Jesus to receive his spirit.
Perhaps, in so doing, there was an exchange and it was not
Stephen, but the Holy Spirit within him, offering such a
compassionate gesture.

God, if this is true, I need to ask you to receive my spirit every
day. Replace my selfish thoughts with selflessness. In place of my
impatience, fill me with peace. Make me extraordinary, Jesus, by
filling me with you.

If you were to exchange your spirit with his Holy Spirit, what
are some of the compassionate gestures Jesus would do
through you? To whom would he reach out in reconciliation?

Founded on Faith

> *"The rain descended, the floods came, and the winds blew and beat on that house; and it did not fall, for it was founded on the rock."*
>
> MATTHEW 7:25 NKJV

Life's most difficult situations are often compared to storms. Considering the passage above, it's easy to see why. Issues pour upon us, calamities rise around us, and problems beat against us, sometimes all at once. These tough times are often when our faith is tested. When we face disaster, we learn how solid our foundation is. Relying on our own strength—or counting on others to be our source of stability—we may find ourselves flattened once the clouds recede.

A life founded on faith in God, built according to his Word, and assembled with his truth is solid and able to withstand even the strongest of storms. We may find ourselves battered, but we will be standing. With Christ as our foundation, strong and certain, we remain upright.

Lord Jesus, I will build my life on you. Your Word will be my cornerstone and your sacrifice and grace my pillars. Because I'm founded in you, I can't be toppled. Whatever the storm, whatever the test, I'll remain—because you remain.

> *"The rain came down, the streams rose, and the winds blew and beat against that house; yet it did not fall, because it had its foundation on the rock."*
>
> MATTHEW 7:25 NIV

The last time you went through a storm, how did you respond? Were you fearful, or faithful; panicked, or patient; desperate, or devout? Don't think of this as a time to be self-critical, but instead as an invitation to become more self-aware.

If illness sends us into a spiral of fear, or bad news produces a storm of short-temperedness, this may be the Lord's way of telling us it's time to restructure. The more our lives are built on believing God, learning his Word, and following his ways, the steadier we remain in a trial.

Father God, I invite you to show me the areas in my life that I have built on unsteady ground. You know which rooms in my house need remodeling. With your help, I'll replace fear and desperation with a devout faith in your goodness. The next time a storm comes, I'll be stronger than ever.

Tonight, pray for someone you know who is going through a storm. Ask God to shore up their foundation and reinforce it with his faithfulness.

Get Wisdom

Wisdom is the most important thing; so get wisdom.
If it costs everything you have, get understanding.

PROVERBS 4:7 NASB

Can you imagine needing to understand or explain traffic
if all the lights were shades of green? If it's grass-green, go
ahead. If it's tulip-green, you'd better hurry because once it
gets to pine-green, you have to stop. We'd all be hopelessly
confused.

Green means go. Red means stop. This basic pattern is one
that is easily taught and learned, even for young children. Our
safety depends on understanding and following this system,
so it was designed to be simple. While a lot of the Bible is
poetic and symbolic, certain instructions, like this one, are
as straightforward as a stoplight. Why? Because they're that
important. Wisdom? It's a really big deal.

God, thank you for making sure I can't miss the really big lessons.
Because you want me safe and wise, you make your most
important instructions the easiest to follow. Help me get wisdom,
God, and thank you for reminding me how much it matters.

*"The beginning of wisdom is: acquire wisdom;
and with all your acquiring, get understanding."*

PROVERBS 4:7 NCV

Solomon, the author of Proverbs widely attributed to be the wisest man who ever lived, goes out of his way to emphasize the value of wisdom. Nothing matters more. Start here. His urging reflects the importance of constantly seeking greater understanding.

If we want to have something, we need to go get it. Want to be strong? Get strong by exercising or working hard. Want to be fast? Get fast by running a little harder and faster every time. Want to be wise? Get wise by learning from every experience.

God, I want wisdom! Help me to ask and understand why so I can grow wiser with every success, and every mistake. I see how much it matters to you, which makes it important to me. As I would run fast in order to get faster, let me think wisely in order to get wiser.

How much effort have you placed on acquiring wisdom?

Source of Peace

Great peace have those who love Your law,
and nothing causes them to stumble.

PSALM 119:165 NKJV

If you could be guaranteed a lifetime of peace with only one small requirement, would you be interested? According to this Scripture, you can. If we love the Lord's law, we will have great peace. Nothing can trip us up. Can this be possible? Rule-following sounds anything but peaceful; it sounds tedious and exhausting.

Rule-following is exhausting but, mercifully, that is not what it means to love the law. Loving God's law means trusting his will for our lives. It means we desire to please him above everything else. When our hearts are focused on making his happy, we needn't follow a list of rules. He will keep our hearts in line with his, and this will be the source of our peace.

God, as I desire more and more to walk in step with you, I am learning to trust your will. Help me to see your law as a path to peace, God. keep me from stumbling as I go.

*Those who love your instructions have great peace
and do not stumble.*

PSALM 119:165 NLT

Which sounds more peaceful: attending an elaborate
wedding or planning every detail of it? Even those of us who
dearly love to be in charge would have to admit it is more
relaxing to be a guest at a carefully planned event than it is to
be responsible for it.

How lovely of the Lord to have taken care of our lives, down
to the smallest detail! It's up to us to accept all his careful
planning. We can be "that guest" who smuggles her own food
in and tries to persuade the DJ to play her party mix, or we
can eat the beautiful meal prepared for us and then dance for
joy no matter the song.

*Oh, Father, how I love the life you've planned for me. Your
instructions are clear and true. Every choice you have made is for
my good. What steadiness and peace I find on your sure-footed
path.*

Does the idea of following God's plans and instructions create
a peaceful or unsettled feeling in you? Discuss this with him.

A Good Struggle

My suffering was good for me,
for it taught me to pay attention to your decrees.

PSALM 119:71 NLT

When we're struggling or suffering, it's hard to imagine embracing a verse like this. How could I ever see this situation as good for me? We may even be tempted to think we'd rather just stay the way we were, to know less of God's decrees, but we would be mistaken. There is a gift hidden in every struggle.

Take encouragement from the author of this verse. King David experienced repeated mortal danger, extreme discipline due to terrible choices, and a thorough humbling of his heart. Let us believe that if he could grow to appreciate the hardest times in his life, then we—with the Lord's help—will be able to do the same.

Father, I read these words and I am filled with hope. To know that no matter what I face, you can use it to teach me, shape me, and make me better gives me courage. I won't pretend I enjoy suffering, but I do love knowing I can one day look back and see the gift you hid in the struggle.

It is good for me that I was humbled,
so that I might learn your statutes.

PSALM 119:71 NRSV

In this morning's translation, David said his suffering had been good for him. This evening's Bible version interpreted the passage another way, with David grateful for being humbled. Just as it's hard to imagine being thankful for pain, it is also a challenge to fathom being glad for humiliation, demotion, or discipline.

Yet, again, there is always blessing in the Lord's lessons! Facing our flaws invites us to acknowledge how much we need the Holy Spirit's help. Recognizing a weakness allows us to rely on the power of God. Realizing our sin opens the door to greater intimacy with our Father.

God, just as it's hard to suffer, it's tough to look at the parts of myself that need polishing. I want to embrace the gift of your humbling. I want to see it as a means of getting closer to you and experiencing more of you. Thank you, God, that even when I falter, you work it for good.

Spend some time thinking of an incident where the Father humbled you. Focus on the good that came from it.

Only Pray

Then he will pray to God, and He will accept him,
that he may see His face with joy,
And He may restore His righteousness to man.

JOB 33:26 NASB

We all long to be accepted. Some people are willing to go much farther than others to gain acceptance, but we are all united in our desire to have it. Which material possessions or physical attributes will ensure we fit in? By worldly standards, the answer changes daily.

By God's standards, though, the system is always the same: we pray to him and he accepts us. No makeover or freshly-renovated house is required. Just as we are, we are accepted. To the King of kings, we fit in.

God, when I think of the effort I've expended trying to be accepted here, I can only shake my head in bemusement. How beautiful it is to realize I need only speak your name to be welcomed by you. I pray, and you usher me in. Thank you, God, for accepting me just as I am.

He shall pray to God, and He will delight in him,
He shall see His face with joy,
For He restores to man His righteousness.

JOB 33:26 NKJV

Can you imagine if everyone you encountered found you utterly delightful? For most of us, such a favored time in our lives ended around the age of two. Yet, no baby is preoccupied with how to make people like them. These days, we tend to wonder if we're doing it right from the way we look, the actions we take, and the very words we speak. Who is it we're trying to impress? What makes their acceptance so important?

The only one worthy of such effort is the Lord, and, amazingly, he is the only one who doesn't place conditions on us becoming part of his "in crowd." He restores, he welcomes, and he loves, while we need only pray.

Oh, Lord. Heal me of my desire to attain approval by obtaining the things of this world. With joy, I accept your acceptance of me. You alone are worthy of my striving, yet you don't ask me to do so. You delight in me. You restore my joy.

In your relationships, where do you feel the most authentic? Call to mind the precious people who love you as you are. Recognize them as little glimpses of Jesus' perfect love.

Show Me

The LORD said to Moses, "I will do the very thing you have asked, because I am pleased with you and I know you by name." Then Moses said, "Now show me your glory."

EXODUS 33:17-18 NIV

If a person you'd never exchanged more than a few words with asked to borrow your car, you'd most likely hesitate. If your best friend asked, though, you'd hand the keys over in an instant. Intimacy welcomes openness. We love to do things for those we are closest to.

How intimate are you with the Lord? Has it "been awhile?" Would he be a little surprised to get a request from you, or do you talk so regularly that he already knows exactly what you need? How delighted will he be to show you his glory, to answer your prayer?

God, I want to delight you! Not simply to have my requests answered, but because I want you to know me by name. I want to be your friend, God. Will you show me your glory?

The LORD said to Moses, "This very thing that you have spoken I will do, for you have found favor in my sight, and I know you by name." Moses said, "Please show me your glory."

EXODUS 33:17-18 ESV

"Anything you want, anything at all, it's yours." Who hasn't fantasized about hearing something like that? What would we ask for? Depending on the day, our minds might jump to something simple, like a good night's sleep, something practical, like a fully paid mortgage, or something altruistic, like an end to hunger.

Having pleased God, Moses chose to *see* God. Specifically, to see his glory. What an awesome request. Would you have thought of it? Yet, what could be better? What could possibly compare?

God, am I thinking too small? I'm so fixed on things in and of this world, I forget you hold us all in your palm with room to spare. Show me your glory, Lord! Give me a glimpse of what is possible with you.

What would you ask for? Invite the Holy Spirit to show you just how big you can dream.

Uncountable Blessings

The LORD will command the blessing upon you in your barns and in all that you put your hand to, and He will bless you in the land which the LORD your God gives you.

DEUTERONOMY 28:8 NASB

"Count your blessings" has become cliché. It's one of those things we say without really even thinking about, but have you ever tried to actually do it? It only takes a few minutes to consider the people, experiences, opportunities, beauty, and second chances we've been given to realize it can't be easily done. We have been given too many blessings to count.

What kind of day might you have if you make a conscious effort to notice every good thing, thank God for giving it, and collect the blessings like tiny lights? How brightly would you glow by day's end?

God, every good thing is from you. I usually thank you for the obvious ones, but I know I often miss the little ones. No more. Holy Spirit, help me recognize every element of goodness in this day. Overwhelm me with how blessed I am to be showered with good and perfect gifts.

*The LORD your God will bless you with full barns, and he will bless
everything you do. He will bless the land he is giving you.*

DEUTERONOMY 28:8 NCV

How was your day? Were you overwhelmed by the
immeasurable lightness of God's goodness, or were you
overwhelmed by routine and responsibility, forgetting your
"blessing watch" before lunch. Either way, what ordinary
blessing did you see for the first time? Did anything
extraordinary happen?

End today as you began it by trying to count what cannot be
counted: the innumerable ways he has blessed you.

*Father, you're overwhelming. The way you rain heaven down,
whether I am paying attention or not, in order to bathe me in your
love is so very beautiful. Thank you, God, for your constant goodness.
Thank you for the gifts, good and perfect, you so freely give.*

What blessings did you notice today that you had been taking
for granted? Ask the Spirit to open your eyes even wider as you
dream tonight that you may see all the blessings in your life.

Let God Decide

This is the boldness we have in God's presence: that if we ask God for anything that agrees with what he wants, he hears us. If we know he hears us every time we ask him, we know we have what we ask from him.

1 JOHN 5:14-15 NCV

Think of a time you had to ask for something you really wanted. Maybe you wanted your parents to approve your first unsupervised trip, or perhaps you believed you were ready for more responsibility or more compensation at work. Your first goal was to get your parents—or your boss—to agree with you. However, this only works when what you ask for is what is in line with what they think is best.

It is just this way with God. When we want what's in line with his purpose, we can ask boldly, assured of his yes. Because of his great love for us, we needn't be afraid to surrender our will to his. He wants what is best for us, always!

Lord God, you know my motives, my needs, and my capabilities so much better than I. I trust you to decide what's best. Align me with your perfect will, God, so all I ever want is what you want for me.

This is the boldness we have in him, that if we ask anything according to his will, he hears us. And if we know that he hears us in whatever we ask, we know that we have obtained the requests made of him.

1 JOHN 5:14-15 NRSV

A sixteen-year-old asking to go to Fort Lauderdale with a group of college students isn't likely to get an enthusiastic yes from her parents. Mom and Dad see a bigger picture due to their combined wisdom and experience. Though she may threaten never to speak to them again, they love her enough to say no. When she grows up, she'll likely be amused she even asked—and grateful they said no.

Let us remember we are like immature teenagers compared to God. No matter how many years we live on earth, our understanding will never come close to his omniscience. Let us continually allow him to be like a good parent to us, and to trust and obey when he says no.

Father, thank you for loving me enough to tell me no. Some of the things I've begged you for over the years were not part of your plan for me. Though those disappointments hurt at the time, now I can easily see all you were saving me from and keeping me for.

What "no" from God hurt at the time and was later revealed to be a blessing?

Papa's Here

"As a mother comforts her child, so will I comfort you;
and you will be comforted over Jerusalem.
When you see this, your heart will rejoice
and you will flourish like grass."

ISAIAH 66:13-14 NIV

Few images are more precious than a mother soothing her child. She holds them close, gently swaying and whispering comforting words. "It's okay. Mama's here. I've got you." Through the prophet Isaiah, the Father promises his children that same loving comfort.

You will be comforted. You will rejoice and flourish. Papa's here. He's got you. All will be well. Believe it, friend. No matter how things look today, settle into the sway. Listen to his words and be comforted.

Abba Father, I love that I will never outgrow your arms. Your lap will always have a spot that fits me perfectly. Thank you for your loving comfort, God, and for promises of a joyful.

"I will comfort you there in Jerusalem as a mother comforts her child. When you see these things, your heart will rejoice. You will flourish like the grass!"

ISAIAH 66:13-14 NLT

Even if not today, a day will come when you are fighting tears. Guess what? There is no need to fight! Store this truth up for the day you need it, and the next time you find yourself holding back, holding it in, and barely hanging on…don't.

On that day, go ahead and cry. Cry like a baby and let your Abba's comfort wrap around you and hear his whispered words of comfort.

I may just do it, Lord. I may just open the floodgates and let all my tears come rushing out the next time they try. Who knows what comforts I've been missing by not inviting you to see and dry my tears!

What does it take for you to let your pain out? Why do you think it's easy or difficult for you?

A Wise Counselor

You will show me the path of life;
in Your presence is fullness of joy;
at Your right hand are pleasures forevermore.

PSALM 16:11 NKJV

As young people, we wonder what to do with our lives. Which
college should we attend? Is college our best path? What career
path should we embark on? Which relationships are building
us up, and which are holding us back? Whether they be
guidance counselor, pastor, parent or other trusted adult, wise
advice from someone who cares for us helps find our way.

As we get older, the world seems to expect us to figure things
out for ourselves. What a blessing that as Christ-followers,
we need never go it alone. The wisest, most wonderful
counselor of all is living inside us, and is always ready to put
us on the right path.

God, I know you want me to find the path to joy. Thank you for
sending your Spirit to make sure I do! Thank you for not expecting
me to have it all figured it out, instead sending me a wise,
wonderful counselor to show me the way.

You bring me a continual revelation of resurrection life,
the path to the bliss that brings me face-to-face with you.

PSALM 16:11 TPT

One of the most precious gifts of life in the Spirit is the "continual revelation of resurrection life," mentioned in Psalm 16. Daily, in his Word and through constant nudges, impulses and instincts we are guided. Go right instead of left; wait instead of run; call and check on that friend you can't stop thinking about.

Whether we are aware at the time or not, we are constantly being rescued, blessed, and saved, each step bringing us ever-closer to the Savior.

God, the more I notice, the more I notice you! Your Spirit, a constant source of salvation and blessing, is everywhere, guiding every step I take. Each time I listen, I feel myself draw nearer to your glory. Thank you for the intimate attention you pay to my every step. I love knowing they're each bring me nearer to you.

Think back over some of the "fortunate coincidences" or "close calls" you've experienced recently. Thank the Lord for his close attentiveness in your life — especially those times when you overlooked his involvement.

Sorrow into Dancing

> *You changed my sorrow into dancing.*
> *You took away my clothes of sadness,*
> *and clothed me in happiness.*
> *I will sing to you and not be silent.*
> *LORD, my God, I will praise you forever.*
>
> PSALM 30:11-12 NCV

There's a beautiful moment during most funerals when, if you look around, you see everyone is smiling. The stories have begun to flow, and the laughter along with them. The quirks, habits, and renowned stories that made our loved one who they were are able to bring us joy through the sadness. Happy memories ease the pain of loss.

Love endures and changes sorrow into dancing. God designed it this way. He designed *us* this way. Whatever pain we feel, through his compassion, he turns to strength. The sadness we bear, through his love, can turn to joy.

Father, your love is amazing. As I spiral into sadness, you take my hand and twirl me into joy. You transform grief to gladness, as I remember the joy of what was. My tears become songs of praise to you, as you turn my crying into laughter.

You have turned for me my mourning into dancing;
you have loosed my sackcloth and clothed me with gladness,
that my glory may sing your praise and not be silent.
O Lord my God, I will give thanks to you forever!

PSALM 30:11-12 ESV

Dear friend, perhaps you have not yet reached the place where the joy of reminiscing outweighs the sadness of loss. If you have lost someone close to you or have suffered other trials, be sure to trust God with your heart and memories. In time, he will guide you through your mourning.

Know that it's okay to dance, to laugh, and to feel glad. Picture the one you loved waiting for you in heaven. Imagine them dancing for joy and clothed in gladness. Jesus wants you to feel that same happiness, even now as you live on earth. Give him your grief and sing his praises in exchange.

God, thank you for offering me joy instead of sorrow. You are light, love, and joy. For me to remain in despair would keep me from you. You bring memories to make me laugh, people to touch my heart, and a new song that causes me to sing. How lovely you are!

Is there an old garment of grief you need to allow your Father to loosen? What gladness does he want to wrap you in?

What Is Right

Pursue peace with everyone, and the holiness without which no one will see the Lord.

HEBREWS 12:14 NRSV

Is there a peacemaker in your life? Perhaps you have a friend or relative who can't rest while others are at odds? It's likely that they are always butting heads with those who can't let go of a grudge or agree to reconciliation. What is it that makes both the peacemakers and grudge-holders so passionate?

Both have a strong conviction of what is right. Sometimes when we feel we have been wronged, all we can focus on is assigning blame and standing our ground— that's what feels like the right thing to do. For peacemaker, what's right is peace, regardless of fault or blame. According to Hebrews, we are likewise called to pursue peace this way. We are to love each other unconditionally, continually forgiving any wrongs. It is by becoming the peacemaker ourselves that we grow in holiness and see the Lord.

God, knowing I can only have you if I have peace, all my squabbles now seem silly. Holy Spirit, bring to my heart any relationships in need of healing. Inspire me to pursue the peace that leads to where you are. I don't need to be right; I need to be with you.

Make every effort to live in peace with everyone and to be holy;
without holiness no one will see the Lord.

HEBREWS 12:14 NIV

"Make every effort to live in peace…and to be holy." Lest we
be tempted think these are two separate instructions, let's
notice they are contained in the same sentence. They are not
mutually exclusive concepts, rather one fosters the other; it's
a process. Lie down and rest. Stand up and walk. One leads
naturally to the other and so we conclude: the path to holiness
is peace.

Why does this matter? Because the path to Jesus is holiness.
The author of Hebrews spells it out for us simply, so we can
understand this important truth. If you want to run, you need
to stand. If you want to see the Lord, you need to live in peace.

Jesus, I see. I understand. You are holy, and holiness does
not allow for strife. You want us—all of us—with you. For this
harmony to become reality, you urge us to reconcile. When we find
this peace, we will find you waiting.

Pray about your relationships. Are you making every effort
to live at peace with everyone and be holy? Do you feel the
Lord nudging you to take a step towards reconciliation with
anyone?

Our Sustenance

> *You are the fountain of life,*
> *the light by which we see.*
>
> PSALM 36:9 NLT

When lost in the desert, do we long for water or sand? Fumbling in the dark, do we search for light or squeeze our eyes shut? When thirsty, we crave water. In darkness, we seek light. Our bodies know what we need.

Spiritually, God is both our sustenance and the light that leads us to it. His truth is what nourishes us while his Spirit is what draws us into it. His grace is our salvation while his Son leads the way. He is author and perfecter, beginning and end, and supplier and supply. He is Lord.

God, you set me up so I cannot fail to find you! You designed me to thirst and because you love me, you became living water. You created me to seek light, and then made yourself the brightest star in the sky. Thank you, God, for being both light and life.

With You is the fountain of life;
in Your light we see light.

PSALM 36:9 NKJV

God is our standard bearer. His beauty helps us recognize beauty. His truth reveals truth. His light is how we know light. This is opposite from the world. Here, light is easier to pinpoint in darkness. Beauty more obvious against a backdrop of dreariness. A fountain more prized in a parched land.

So how can this be, that in his light—incomparably, incomprehensibly bright—we see light? Because he is light. He is beauty. Without him, refreshment, beauty and light simply wouldn't be.

Beautiful God, you don't just set the standard, you make it possible. You don't just illuminate the path, you make the path and open my eyes to see it. You don't just make things good, you are goodness itself. You are awesome, God. You are everything beautiful, bright, and sustaining. You are life.

What has God's light helped you to see?

Lift You Higher

From the end of the earth I call to you, when my heart is faint.
Lead me to the rock that is higher than I.

PSALM 61:2 NRSV

Have you ever walked through a maze? Even if you can easily navigate one on paper, it's quite a different experience without the bird's eye perspective. In the thick of it all you can see is the hedge or row of corn directly in front of you. Having no other choice, you take it one turn at a time. Inevitably, without that overhead view, you'll make a wrong decision. You may even get lost, repeatedly coming up to the same dead end.

When life feels like that maze, call out to God. Follow his voice to the next turn, and the one after that. Allow his hand to lift you up—higher than your own sight—and show you the way through.

Father God, you are always listening and waiting to guide me. You see whether I am headed the right or wrong way. What a comfort it is to know I can call to you and follow the sound of your voice. I can extend my arms and you will lift me up, showing me more than I can see on my own.

I call to you from the ends of the earth when I am afraid.
Carry me away to a high mountain.

PSALM 61:2 NCV

We can call to the Father for direction and perspective. We can also call to him for rescue. Rather than sink into fear, huddled into a corner of the maze in defeat, we can cry out to God. No matter how far we've travelled, he will hear us. His loving hand can pluck us straight out of our fear and onto the mountaintop of his promises. Our circumstances may not change right away, but our hearts will lighten immediately.

In that high, safe place with him, what could possibly trouble us?

God, you are both guide and rescuer, and you know which I need. When I am just a little lost, your voice gives me direction; your wisdom provides perspective. When I am truly off course, trapped by fear and faced with too many decisions, you lift me up, carrying me to a place where nothing can touch me.

Which could you use more of in your life right now: perspective, direction, or rescue? Call out to him and let him take you higher.

Better than Life

Because Your lovingkindness is better than life,
my lips will praise You.

PSALM 63:3 NASB

"That dress is to die for! Where did you get it?" We have all heard or used such hyperbolic expressions before. While we don't really mean we would dive off a mountain to own the perfect LBD, we use the phrase "to die for" to indicate how great we think something is. Perhaps we use it to describe a delectable dessert or diamond jewelry. It's so delicious or appealing we say we would trade our life for it. In this context, though, these words have little meaning because we would not typically choose death for a brownie or pair of earrings.

Only one thing is truly *to die for*, and that's life with the Lord. Do you believe that even on a perfect day, what God has prepared for you is so much better, you'd gladly give it all up? It's hard to fathom, isn't it? Yet that's what his Word tells us. God's love for us is unimaginably good, and better than even the most wonderful earthly objects and experiences.

Father, your love is hard to fathom. I'm told the best things, moments, and people I've ever known are only an inkling of you. Blessings here are but a taste of the blessings in heaven. Love here is only a kiss of the love there. Beauty here is only a glimpse of what is to come. Life here can be so good, yet you are better than this life! Praise you, God, for your unimaginable goodness.

Your tender mercies mean more to me than life itself.
How I love and praise you, God!

PSALM 63:3 TPT

How intimately the Psalmist must have been connected to God to write these beautiful words. What intimacy to think that a sweet touch from the Lord, a whispered forgiveness, or a tender reprieve was the greatest treasure in his life.

This is the type of intimacy the Lord wants with all of us. How awesome is that?

God, I love you so deeply. to know there are more and more depths of you to explore blows me away. I want to know them all: your kindness, your mercy, and your unfathomable love. Nothing I have matters more than what you want to give me. No connection is more vital than connecting with you. You are better than life because you are life. You are everything to me, God.

What is your most wonderful memory with the Lord? Is there anything you'd trade it for?

Seek Him First

Fill us with your love every morning.
Then we will sing and rejoice all our lives.

PSALM 90:14 NCV

Seek him first. Why are we encouraged both in the Word and by our fellow believers to begin our days with the Lord? If you already begin your mornings with him, you know what a perfect start to the day that is. Settling into his Word and his will first thing creates an awareness of his nearness, a desire to remain close to him, and an overflowing of his love.

We see through his eyes, rendering everything beautiful. We feel with his heart, making everyone lovable. We act with his purpose, giving meaning to our every action. With God's Spirit so near, what else can we do but sing for joy?

Precious God, make my day! Show, move, and lead me in your way. Fill me with compassion, purpose and awe. Allow your overflow to touch everyone I encounter so that together, we'll make their day better too.

*Oh, satisfy us early with Your mercy,
that we may rejoice and be glad all our days!*

PSALM 90:14 NKJV

Good news and bad news. Which do you prefer to hear first?
Most of us choose the bad news, so we can get it over with.
We want to deal with the negative, then move on to happier
matters. The New King James translation of Psalm 90:14
offers a similar perspective.

By pleading early for mercy, we can turn our attention to the
praise, rejoicing and gladness of life with our Lord. By handing
him our burdens first thing, we are unencumbered when it's
time to dance. Seek him first each day, and joy will follow.

*Here they are, God, all the burdens I carry. Take the weight of
worry, guilt, and shame from me so I am free to sing of your great
love. Remove my doubt so I can dance in your glory. Have mercy on
my sins so joy may rule my days.*

What mercy do you need from your Savior, so you can dance
and be glad in his goodness?

Clinging to Dust

My soul clings to the dust;
revive me according to your word.

PSALM 119:25 NRSV

How did this verse sit with you? Your response can tell you about the current condition of your soul. Was your heart pierced with feeling for the writer, and for those you know who are clinging to the dust as well? If your heart responded with compassion is a sign your soul is feeling strong. If this surprises you, take heart, you are doing better than you realized.

If, when you read this, you felt as though you could have written it, sweet friend, then you are laid low. Take care not to let the ground claim you. It will try. Reach up your hand. Grab onto God's and let him revive you. Cling to the promise in his Word: promises of better days, rejoicing, healing, mercy, and grace. Hold on, dear one, and feel your spirit rise.

Savior, what a comfort it is to know that no matter how low I fall, how low I feel, you are there to meet me. I need only cry out and your hand of mercy will begin to lift me. I need only hang on, and your promise of healing will continue my rise. I need only remain in your grasp, and your restoration will be mine.

I lie in the dust;
revive me by your word.

PSALM 119:25 NLT

Perhaps it's been one of those days. Wearily, you wave your white flag and lie down. "I'm done," you declare. "I give up." It may seem like the best place to be, but we're vulnerable lying low. The enemy doesn't respect the white flag. As we curl up in defeat, he layers on sadness. Above the guilt, he piles on shame. But God offers a solution.

"Revive me by your Word." Contained in the pages of Scripture is more hope, encouragement, healing, and promise than you imagine. The next time you find yourself curled up in defeat, rise up from the dust to be revived by the power of the Word.

Oh God, how I love your Word! Whatever I need to hear, you've written it down. Thank you, God, for the living, breathing power of Scripture to revive me. Holy Spirit, remind me when I taste defeat that you offer a better way.

How big a part does the Bible play in your story? Talk it over with God and see if there is more he wants to say to you through his Word.

Choices that Build

The wise woman builds her house,
but the foolish pulls it down with her hands.

PROVERBS 14:1 NKJV

If you were to see a mother bird ripping her nest apart,
how would you feel? Confused? Concerned? A mother dog
refusing her hungry puppies tugs similarly at our hearts.
It's unnatural. Now imagine a woman too busy to make it to
volleyball too harried to pack lunches, or too overwhelmed to
accept an invitation to coffee. It's not as hard to picture, is it?

Twig by twig, we have the option to build our homes—
our relationships, our lives—or to destroy them. Every
"harmless" complaint about a husband, every forgotten
birthday of a friend, every time sleep is more important than
a morning hug goodbye, the nest is weakened. Keeping close
to our Lord, he leads us to the choices that build, sustain and
strengthen our homes. He fortifies us with the love and the
will to keep building.

Dear God, remind me today of what is important. Help me to be a
builder, to reinforce the structures of connectedness, affection, and
respect that make my house strong. Make me wise, Father, and
make me strong.

*The wisest of women builds her house,
but folly with her own hands tears it down.*

PROVERBS 14:1 ESV

"If I knew then what I know now…" Who hasn't thought or said these words before? If only wisdom were innate! Instead, it seems we often get wise by making—or witnessing—foolish mistakes. If only gentle warnings were enough to make us steer clear of choices that weaken our foundation.

Perhaps they can be? Perhaps, if we lean into God's Word, and trust his wise, perfect plan for our lives, our most recent bad decision can be our final bad decision. Of course, we know we will still make occasional mistakes, but how lovely that we grow wiser with each one.

Father, make me wise! Let me bypass learning the hard way by leaning on you and building my house upon your wisdom. Each time I forget and tear down another brick from my house, Let me replace it with one that is stronger.

Does your nest need some attention? Ask God to show you the areas you should focus on rebuilding.

Hear My Prayer

"If my people, who are called by my name, will humble themselves and pray and seek my face and turn from their wicked ways, then I will hear from heaven, and I will forgive their sin and will heal their land."

2 CHRONICLES 7:14 NIV

Cause and effect may be the earliest concept we grasp. A baby cries, and someone comes to soothe her. A toddler sees different results when she asks sweetly or throws a tantrum. We sometimes approach prayer from this simple mindset. If I cry out to God, he'll come running. If I ask nicely, he'll give me what I want. However, that's not how prayer works.

If we want to be heard, we need to come humbly, quietly, and seek first his face. The first step is simply to be in his presence. We must regret that which distances us from him. We need to reject our sins and ask for forgiveness. Then we can await his response.

Father, forgive me for the times I approach you like an infant by wailing my needs without first acknowledging your greatness or asking to see your beautiful face. Forgive the sins I cling to and fail to confess. Hear my prayer, God, offered in love and reverence, and silence my cries.

> "If My people who are called by My name humble themselves and pray and seek My face and turn from their wicked ways, then I will hear from heaven, will forgive their sin and will heal their land."

2 CHRONICLES 7:14 ESV

"My people who are called by My name…" What an extraordinary thing to be called by the name of God. We are children of the King, beloved of the Savior, and family in Christ. As the Church, we are even his bride. When we joined his family, he gave us his name. What confidence this inspires, what hope!

He will always hear our prayers and, surely, as we come humbly before him, there is nothing he won't do for us.

God, I may have thought of myself as your child, or as the bride of Christ, but I've not really considered what it means to be called by your name. Oh, the power I have against darkness, and the favor I have in your presence! What a blessing, God, to share your beautiful name.

Think of your last name. What does it mean to be a _____? Think of God's many names. What does it mean that he gives this blessing to you?

Keeping Watch

He will not let you stumble;
the one who watches over you will not slumber.

PSALM 121:3 NLT

What is the longest you've ever gone without sleep? Most of us have at least one all-nighter in our memory. Chances are, you collapsed into sleep at the first opportunity afterwards. No matter how important our assignment, or how vital our vigil, we all eventually need to stop and sleep.

God is the exception. The one who watches over you and makes sure you won't stumble as you navigate today's rocky terrain, never stops watching. While you work, sleep, struggle, and settle, Lord keeps watch.

Savior God, you never take your eyes off me. How can this be? Each step and moment of rest I take are of concern to you. You won't let me fail. you refuse to lose me. With each wrong turn, you guide me back to the right path. every hour I sleep, you watch over me and replenish my strength. Thank you, God, for your constant presence.

He will not let your foot be moved;
he who keeps you will not slumber.

PSALM 121:3 ESV

If this is true, where was God when my father died, when my daughter became addicted, when my husband cheated? It can be tempting to dismiss a verse like this when it doesn't seem to reflect our experience. My foot has been moved plenty of times.

What, then, are we to make of these lofty promises? It may feel like this verse was written for others since God clearly must've been sleeping on the job where you are concerned. When your life is filled with stumbling, know the Lord sees it all. He's keeping careful guard over your eternal self, and he will not let you go. He sees your suffering, but he's preparing a place for you with him where every second of pain will be forgotten. He's got you.

It's true, Father, that there are days I'm not sure I believe you're keeping watch. I don't understand why things have to happen the way they do. I strain to see the good and feel your protection. Yet your Word tells me you are faithful and deep in my heart. I know deep down this is true. Thank you, God, for staying with me—especially on the days I doubt it.

Have you doubted God's constant care for you or his presence in your troubles? You can talk to him about it, dear one. He longs to remove that doubt and replace it with his comfort.

187

He Made You His

*You are a chosen people, royal priests, a holy nation, a people for
God's own possession. You were chosen to tell about the wonderful
acts of God, who called you out of darkness into his wonderful light.*

1 PETER 2:9 NCV

Did you know God chose you for life in the family of Christ? It's
the most wonderful invitation all of history, and it was extended
to you. He knew just when and how to reach out to you: he
planned it from the moment he dreamed you up. Had he not
ordained it, your heart would have remained closed to him.

Maybe he gave you a longing for more meaning in your life and
then led you into Christian community? Perhaps he allowed
you to hit rock-bottom, to need a radical life change, and then
he lifted you out of the depths? Regardless of how it happened,
he chose you. He called you by name and made you his.

*God, I'm continually amazed that you chose me. You imagined
me, made me, and let my life unfold in just such a way that I
would end up choosing you back. Reaching into the darkness,
you took hold of my heart and lifted me into light, love, and hope.
Today, and forever, I am gratefully yours.*

You are God's chosen treasure—priests who are kings, a spiritual "nation" set apart as God's devoted ones. He called you out of darkness to experience his marvelous light, and now he claims you as his very own. He did this so that you would broadcast his glorious wonders throughout the world.

1 PETER 2:9 TPT

Athletes make great coaches, addicts make wise treatment counselors, and sinners make the best preachers because they have learned from personal experience, not just theory. We learn best from someone who has been where we are. They can better relate to us.

Just as he may have used someone else's story to reach you, God wants your story to reach someone who *is* where you *were*. He lifted you out of the darkness towards him because he wanted to be with you, but also so you could tell others about life in the light. Isn't that beautiful?

God, I love how everything you do has such purpose. I remember how you reached me, and who you used to show me there was a better, more beautiful way to live. to think that I get to be part of someone else's story is wonderful. Creative, loving God, you are wonderful.

How might God want to use your story as an invitation for someone new to join his family?

Worthy of Glory

Honor the LORD for the glory of his name.
Worship the LORD in the splendor of his holiness.

PSALM 29:2 NLT

Imagine walking into you home and noticing a gift on the counter with your name on it. It's not your birthday, or a holiday or an otherwise special time in your life. *What's the occasion*, you wonder? *I was just thinking about you* is written on the card attached. Or maybe you got a postcard in the mail or a kind text from someone who wants to show they care for no other reason than that they do. It feels wonderful, doesn't it, to be appreciated just for being you?

As lovely as it is to receive such surprises, we should enjoy giving them even more. Do you surprise the people you love with gifts, notes, or hugs to let them know you love them simply for being who they are? More importantly, when is the last time you praised God just for being God? He loves to receive spontaneous gifts of honor and praise just as much as we do but he is far worthier of such glory.

God, above all other names, I worship yours. I contemplate your
holiness and perfection, and I realize I can never thank you or
worship you enough. I love you, Father, for who you are,
and I thank you for who you are making me.

Give unto the Lord the glory due to His name;
worship the Lord in the beauty of holiness.

PSALM 29:2 NKJV

What are some of your favorite names of the Lord? There are so many to choose from: King of Kings, Lord of Lords, Prince of Peace, Jehovah, Wonderful Counselor, Comforter, Savior, Father, and Lamb of God. Each name deserves such glory and honor. Can we ever do them justice? What of his beauty, grace, holiness, and majesty?

We could sing forever and never come to the end of the ways the Lord is worthy of our praise.

Perfect, precious God, where do I begin? There is truly no end to your perfection, or to the list of ways you deserve my devotion. You are holy. You are worthy. You are beautiful, mighty, glorious, and generous, Father God.

Fall asleep tonight meditating on the ways the Lord is worthy of your praise.

Open My Understanding

Then he opened their minds to understand the Scriptures.

LUKE 24:45 ESV

Can you remember enjoying a book or film as a child, then revisiting it as an adult? How amazed were you to discover all you'd missed? It's like discovering the old, familiar painting in Grandma's attic is a masterpiece by a renowned artist. Our adult minds understand more of the humor, recognize layers of context, and interpret subtext in a way we couldn't as children.

When it comes to understanding Scripture, we are all as children. Different aspects of Christ's character are revealed as we grow and mature in our faith. God chooses when and how to enlighten us, so like that favorite childhood story or movie, every return to a Bible passage can hold fresh revelation.

Lord God, I pray that you will open my mind to the incredible, living truth of your Word. Every day show me more of who you are and who you would like me to be. Thank you for your Word, Father, and for making it eternally new.

He opened their understanding,
that they might comprehend the Scriptures.

LUKE 24:45 NKJV

What an awesome moment this must have been for the
disciples, especially in light of all that had led up to it. After
grieving Jesus' death and fearing for their own lives, he had
appeared among them, invited them to examine his wounds,
and even sat down to a meal with them. All at once, the veil
of understanding was lifted and everything he had ever said
made sense. They were equipped—to understand all he had
done and all they would now do.

Likewise, Jesus wants to open our understanding that *we*
might comprehend the Scriptures.

Jesus, I understand that you gave the disciples knowledge, so
they would share and spread it. Each time you give me a fresh
revelation of your Word, may your Holy Spirit inspire me to do the
same. Whether a quiet word to a friend or something more public,
as you open me to understanding, embolden me to pass it on.

Do you have a journal where you record the things the Lord
is teaching you? How often do you share the fresh insights he
gives you? Ask the Holy Spirit if this might be something he
is eager for you to do.

Room for Humility

*"He must become greater and greater,
and I must become less and less."*

JOHN 3:30 NLT

Imagine you are famous. Everywhere you go, you are followed. Every time you speak, you are listened to. Every choice you make, you are emulated. You are loved, admired, and respected. Now imagine willingly walking away, leaving the spotlight, and silencing your influence. Doesn't sound easy, does it? If it doesn't sound easy in the context of a daydream, how much harder must it be in reality. We are naturally inclined to want approval and love attention.

Humility is hard. It's not a natural instinct, yet it's a requirement of a life centered on Christ. The words of John 3:30 were spoken by John the Baptist, one of the humblest people in the Bible. He knew, when he met Jesus, it was time for prophecy to be fulfilled. As brightly as his light had shone, and as meaningful as his work had been, it was time to direct the light—and people's attention—toward Jesus.

Father, humble me. Let me take the example of one far greater than I and turn any admiration I receive onto you. When people look at me, may they see more and more of you. When I am heard, let the words be yours. If I am followed, let it be on my way to you.

> *"He must increase, but I must decrease."*
>
> JOHN 3:30 NASB

A full garage can't hold another car. A full glass can't contain any more liquid. If we want to bring in more, we must first make room. If we want God to take over and guide our lives, we must first surrender our own plans.

If we desire his will, we must let go of ours. If we want more fruit in our lives—more joy, more peace, more kindness, and humility—we must first set aside the bitterness, tension, selfishness and pride taking up space in our hearts.

Lord Jesus, I invite you to make room for more of you. I understand this means there will be less of me. I welcome such a change. Your plans are far better, your desires purer, and your fruit so much sweeter. Take all the space you desire, Lord. I want to be filled with your goodness.

Visualize exchanging parts of yourself for parts of Jesus. See anger leave and peace move in. Watch jealousy go and selflessness take its place. Feel your heart lighten.

Prize Beyond Value

To the one who works, his wages are not counted as a gift but as his due. And to the one who does not work but believes in him who justifies the ungodly, his faith is counted as righteousness.

ROMANS 4: 4–5 ESV

Even if you have your dream job and every day is a pinch-me-so-I-know-I'm-not-dreaming day, we'd probably stop working if our employer decided they would no longer pay us. Conversely, if we acted as though our paychecks were an entitlement regardless of job performance or attendance, we'd undoubtedly be fired. Both employee and employer have a responsibility to do their part. It's only fair.

This is how it works in the job market, but not how it works with Jesus. In order to earn our "wages" of eternal salvation, all we have to do is believe him. That's it. No work, no rules, and no sacrifice. He's already done it all. It's far from fair, and yet our just God willingly offers it.

Jesus, I will never stop being amazed by your selflessness. You did all the work, made all the sacrifices, and are also the one who pays the wage. The unfairness of it is too great to comprehend. I can never deserve what you did for me. Thank you, God, for the unearned gift of my salvation.

When people work, they earn wages. It can't be considered a free
gift, because they earned it. But no one earns God's righteousness.
It can only be transferred when we no longer rely on our own
works, but believe in the one who powerfully declares the ungodly
to be righteous[a] in his eyes. It is faith that transfers God's
righteousness into your account!

ROMANS 4:4–5 TPT

Frequently, companies will give away a "dream prize" as a way
of generating excitement and attracting new customers. The
spectacular vacation, or shiny new car, or years' worth of free
product can't be purchased or earned. Hopeful winners must
submit their entry and wait.

God dreamed up the first and best sweepstakes ever. The
prize is beyond value. No amount of money or effort could
purchase it. Hopeful winners must submit their entry and…
win! Everybody wins. The prize too valuable to price is free to
anyone who asks for it.

Father God, you are just so good! The generosity and extravagance
of your grace is overwhelming. I can't earn it, but I can have it
anyway. Thank you, Lord. Your love is amazing.

Have you ever won anything? How did it feel? How does it feel
knowing what you've "won" by accepting Jesus' sacrifice?

Where Are You?

The LORD God called to the man, and said to him,
"Where are you?"

GENESIS 3:9 NRSV

When playing hide and seek with a young child, we usually know exactly where they have "hidden" because they are still in plain sight. "Where could she be?" we playfully wonder aloud. For the child's benefit, we pretend to be looking. Believing we can hide in plain sight is a brief and innocent period of life.

When Adam and Eve first sinned, God treated them much the same. He knew where they were hiding. He also knew *why* they were hiding and what they had done. Still, he called out. "Where are you?" For their benefit, he let them answer and come out of hiding. Only by their confession could they begin to heal.

Father, you know every mistake and sin I try to hide. Still, you patiently wait for me to come out of hiding, discover consequences, and learn there is a better way. Though you know where I am and could easily expose me, you wait for me to come to you. Thank you for your loving patience, God.

Then the LORD God called to Adam and said to him,
"Where are you?"

GENESIS 3:9 NKJV

Where are you? The longer we ponder this question, the more
compelling it becomes. It's like catching a dog in the act of
destroying our flower bed, or a child smearing peanut butter
and jelly all over the living room sofa. Though the answer is
painfully clear, we cry out. "What are you doing?" What we're
really asking is, "Why?" What we're really saying is, "Stop!"

When we hear God asking us where we are, it's often a sign we
are not where he intended us to go. Let us follow the example
of Adam and Eve by answering God when he calls out to us
and confessing what we have done wrong.

God, thank you for never letting me stray too far. You call to me
out of love. You ask me where I am because you want me back with
you. Thank you for asking me to stop and notice where I've gone,
so I can get back to where I belong.

Where are you? Sit with the Holy Spirit and this question for
a while.

Wanted and Chosen

Because of his love, God had already decided to make us his own children through Jesus Christ. That was what he wanted and what pleased him,

EPHESIANS 1:5 NCV

Adopted children have the delightful privilege of going through life knowing they were wanted by their adoptive family. Never do they have to wonder if they are in their family by mistake: their very presence in the home is proof they were chosen. What a comfort and a blessing, to know you are wanted and chosen.

This same blessing is afforded to you as a child of God. He chose and adopted you specifically because it pleased him to do so. He didn't bring you into his family to save the world, or to end all war, or for any other grand purpose. He simply wanted you.

Oh, Father, I'm so grateful you chose me, though I confess sometimes I can't imagine why. I focus on my failures and flaws, and I'm tempted to think of how disappointed you must be. But you're not, are you? You love and accept me as I am. Thank you, God, for giving me such a loving home.

God decided in advance to adopt us into his own family by bringing us to himself through Jesus Christ. This is what he wanted to do, and it gave him great pleasure.

EPHESIANS 1:5 NLT

Perhaps you know a couple who spent months or years dreaming of and praying for a child to adopt. You would have witnessed an incomparable anticipation as they awaited this child's arrival. Afterwards, their joy must have been equally incomparable.

Imagine God's delight as he planned out the adoption of each and every one of his beloved children. Imagine the explosion of joy and sound of angels' voices singing in anticipation of our arrival! How beautiful it must have been, and must still be, as he waits for each of his adored ones to come to him.

God, how I love imagining your joy! The music, laughter, colors and light involved — I can't get the smile off my face as I picture it. To know I am the cause of some of that joy fills me with love and gratitude. Thank you for bringing me to you, Lord. There is nowhere I'd rather be.

As you close your eyes tonight, picture all of heaven rejoicing on the day you were adopted into God's family. Imagine the pleasure you brought your Father.

Safe in His Arms

He will cover you with his feathers,
and under his wings you can hide.
His truth will be your shield and protection.

PSALM 91:4 NCV

Like an eagle protecting its young, God shelters us under his mighty wings from every storm or attack. No pelting rain or arrows can touch us. This picture is both powerful and tender. How safe and secure we are, and yet how peaceful it is to be nestled in against his warmth.

Do you rest in God's protection, or do you struggle like a young bird eager to leave the nest and fly? Are you constantly poking your head out, trying to get a peek at the action? Maybe you've even slid out from underneath those sheltering feathers and now you're flying alone, vulnerable to both enemy and elements. If you are, fly home. Nestle in.

God, you are my shield, my protector. Thank you for providing me such a safe place to wait out the storms and hide from the attacks this world hurls my way. Forgive me for the times I leap from your protection, thinking I don't need shelter. I will always need you, Father. Thank you for always being there when I fly home.

His massive arms are wrapped around you, protecting you.
You can run under his covering of majesty and hide.
His arms of faithfulness are a shield keeping you from harm.

PSALM 91:4 TPT

Beyond the physical picture of God's protection, of his mighty wings and strong arms, we have also the safety of his truth.

If he said it, we can stand on it. If we are called to faithfulness, we can rest assured we are called to where he is. On the side of majesty, of beauty, of anything that is good, we are also on the side of his protection.

Mighty God, what comfort I find in knowing that if I fight for good, I fight alongside you. If the arrows come too close, your faithfulness is my shield. When I stand up for truth, I stand with you. No winds or waters can overwhelm me. I'm safe in your arms, you keep me from harm.

If you're in a battle, look for the truth and goodness in the situation. That's where you'll find the Lord and his open, waiting arms.

Respond in Peace

If it is possible, as far as it depends on you,
live at peace with everyone.

ROMANS 12:18 NIV

Does living in peace with everyone you know sound possible to you? Peace with everyone? Paul clearly didn't know anyone like the people I have to deal with. Others among us find this to be one of the easiest commands in Scripture because harmonious relationships are all they know.

Most of us land somewhere between these two extremes. We find people are generally easy to get along with, except that one co-worker, moody child, or rude cashier. As we run down the list, living at peace with everyone can seem like an impossible dream. Look at the phrase tucked into the middle of the sentence, *as far as it depends on you.* We can't do anything about the way people behave toward us, but we do have a choice as to how we respond. Calling on the Holy Spirit's help, may we always respond in peace.

Holy Spirit, hear my prayer. May I always respond in peace. To every slight, slur, and misunderstanding, may I respond in peace. To every disagreement, and to any and all disrespect, may I respond in peace. Through my peaceful responses, please help others to respond back in kind.

If possible, so far as it depends on you, live peaceably with all.

ROMANS 12:18 ESV

Why do you suppose Paul prefaced his encouragement to peaceful living with those two caveats? Perhaps it's because he knew that peace is the ideal we aim for, even if it can't always be the reality.

The first condition is *if possible.* It may not be. There may be relationships that cannot, no matter what you do, be harmonious. It's okay to accept this. It's even okay to end a toxic relationship, especially if you are unsafe. The second qualification is *so far as it depends on you.* All you can do is all you can do. Once you've done all you can, you may need to wait for the other party to do the same. While you wait, dear friend, may you be at peace.

God, how I thank you for your Word! In it, I learn how to live as you did, how you would have me live. Here, I find encouragement to seek and offer peace, and your blessing to walk away from a person who will never offer it back to me. Give me the courage to do all I can, Jesus, and the wisdom to know when to stop.

Was this for you, dear one, or someone you care for? The Lord doesn't call us to toxic or dangerous relationships; he calls us to love.

Not Ours to Know

Just as you do not know the path of the wind and how bones are
formed in the womb of the pregnant woman, so you do not know
the activity of God who makes all things.

ECCLESIASTES 11:5 NASB

Imagine a toddler who has just wrapped her mind around
the meaning and power of what is surely the most wonderful
little word in all of language. "Why?" She will use this word
to try and understand everything that comes across her path:
bedtime, grandma's wrinkles, the food on her plate, the blue
sky, and babies inside mommies. Why? Why? Why?

With maturity, we learn to stop verbally questioning
everything we come across. However, this innate curiosity
remains for our whole lives because we were made to wonder.
Often our questions can be answered. Yet, when it comes to
God's own mind and the decisions he makes, the answers are
not ours to know.

Father, I long to know you! There are so many whys I'd love you to
answer. Help me wait, Lord. Help me rest in your sovereignty and
learn to embrace those things about which I can only wonder.

Just as you cannot understand the path of the wind or the mystery of a tiny baby growing in its mother's womb, so you cannot understand the activity of God, who does all things.

<small>ECCLESIASTES 11:5 NLT</small>

Is your phone nearby? Hold it in your hand for a moment. Test its weight, turn it around, and look at every angle. How does it do all it does? It's incredible, isn't it? Most of us are quite content with not having the first clue how it works, we are simply glad it does.

May we feel the same about the incomprehensible, marvelous mind of God.

God, I don't need to understand you in order to appreciate you, or to marvel at your creativity, your goodness, and your power. You are awesome, and I am very glad of it.

Even the first telephone ever was simply a marvel. Wires and metals and wood working together to transport a voice from one place to another. Astonishing. What amazing inventions, creations or discoveries are you content to simply marvel at?

Intimate Companion

> "God is spirit, and those who worship him must worship
> in spirit and truth."
>
> JOHN 4:24 ESV

How do you define *spirit*? An athlete triumphing over great hardship is said to have an indomitable spirit. A feisty, strong-willed child is sometimes described as spirited. What's being described in both cases is something beyond the body, something intangible.

Though equally intangible, we are able to interact with the Holy Spirit. He works in our lives by teaching, comforting, and protecting us. His promptings tell us when to move closer and when to pull back. The Spirit is our intimate companion, and wholly deserving of our worship.

Holy Spirit of God, I doubt I realize even a fraction of the ways you influence and guide the course of my life, and yet I can't imagine life without you. How can I express enough gratitude for the one who is always with me? How can I show enough love to the lover of my spirit? Though I know it will never be enough, I give you all the worship I can.

> *"God is spirit, and those who worship him must worship in spirit and truth."*
>
> JOHN 4:24 NRSV

Do you believe you have a soul mate? Or perhaps you consider a dear friend a soul sister? There are those with whom we share a bond that defies all the laws of time and space. It's as if when we first saw them our hearts said, *There you are! I've been waiting for you.* Our souls recognized what our minds had not yet time to grasp: we are connected.

This is the worship—the connection—the Lord wants from us. Beyond Bible studies, stirring sermons, and fervent prayers, he wants to connect with our souls. He wants to be our most intimate companion, closer to us than any earthly friend.

Spirit of God, when I close my eyes and think of you, there you are. It's nothing I can see, hear, or taste, but it's real. We are connected. My heart sees you. My soul knows you. And oh, how all of me loves you.

How can you interact with the Holy Spirit tonight?

Even When I Blow It

"For the eyes of the LORD move to and fro throughout the earth that He may strongly support those whose heart is completely His. You have acted foolishly in this. Indeed, from now on you will surely have wars."

2 CHRONICLES 16:9 NASB

You blew it. These three words can carry the weight of a thousand when they are bearing down on us. No one likes to hear them, but it's unlikely we'll get through life—or even April—without feeling the consequences of a bad decision. How wonderful that we can rely on God's grace when we do!

In this passage, Asa is learning his lack of faithfulness has landed him in a cycle of struggle and battle. While we should surely hope to learn from his mistake, let us also take courage from the first half of the verse. God is constantly watching for hearts dedicated to him. When he finds such a heart, he sends all the resources of heaven to support them. Have you blown it? Give your heart back to God and let him help you.

God, I know I act foolishly more often than either of us would prefer. Thank you for being there, for seeing my heart, and for assuring me that even when I blow it, I am yours. You forgive me, support me, and shower me with grace.

"The LORD searches all the earth for people who have given themselves completely to him. He wants to make them strong. Asa, you did a foolish thing, so from now on you will have wars."

2 CHRONICLES 16:9 NCV

For context, here's a little more of Asa's story: Despite the Lord having been faithful and allowing him to defeat much stronger armies in the past, the king took matters into his own hands and made a foreign alliance instead of trusting God.

Where God sees faith, he sends help. Where he finds us thinking we can do better on our own, he allows us to try. Then, because he is so very good, when we blow it and turn back to him, he mercifully welcomes us home.

Oh, Father. It doesn't matter how many times I try to do it my way. The moment I place myself in your trust, you sweep me up and deliver me from whatever I've gotten myself into. Your mercy and patience are my saving grace.

Have you stubbornly refused God's help in a matter, convinced you can handle it on your own? Pray for the strength to open up to his saving grace.

High Standard

*God's truth stands firm like a foundation stone with this
inscription: "The Lord knows those who are his," and "All who
belong to the Lord must turn away from evil."*

2 TIMOTHY 2:19 NLT

When a rule is firm and unchanging, we say it is written in
stone. Between parents and children, most of these rules are
about keeping everyone safe and healthy: no smoking, no
drinking, or no opposite-sex friends behind closed doors.
Almost uncannily, a parent seems to know when one of these
hard-set rules is being or has been broken. They know their
children so well, they know when something's off.

Our Father knows us even better than earthly parents can
know their children. He also commands us to turn from sin.
Together, these two truths form the foundation of our faith.
We are known, and we are called to a high standard. He loves
us and wants us safe, so when we stray he sends conviction
followed by grace to turn us back to him.

*Wise Father, thank you for knowing me and being my firm
foundation. I could say I wish it was easier to break your rules
and not get caught, but it wouldn't be true. I'm so grateful you love
me enough to want to keep me in your grace!*

God's firm foundation stands, bearing this seal: "The Lord knows those who are his," and, "Let everyone who names the name of the Lord depart from iniquity."

2 TIMOTHY 2:19 ESV

Participation trophies are typically not prized possessions. The awards and accomplishments we cherish are the ones not easily obtained. To belong to God is to be known, and also to be held to a high standard. It might seem daunting to meet his expectations. You might feel like you can't do any better than a participation trophy when it comes to always doing the right thing.

Remember, dear friend, God knows you. He is aware of any weaknesses you may have, yet he still sets forth this high standard. How highly he must think of you to expect so much! How eager and willing he is to help you as you try to turn away from evil!

You see me, God, exactly as I am, and you expect good from me. You command it. I love knowing you have so much faith in me that you believe I can live up to your expectations. It gives me the desire to please you and strength to believe I can.

What principles in your life are written in stone?

After the Storm

> *A great and powerful wind tore the mountains apart and shattered the rocks before the LORD, but the LORD was not in the wind. After the wind there was an earthquake, but the LORD was not in the earthquake. After the earthquake came a fire, but the LORD was not in the fire. And after the fire came a gentle whisper.*
>
> 1 KINGS 19:11-12 NIV

Dramatic weather events, such as hurricanes, tornadoes, and tsunamis, are sometimes referred to as "acts of God." The expression means they were not caused—nor could they be controlled—by human hands. That our human hands can't make or stop a tsunami is an easy concept to grasp. However, the other implications of the phrase "an act of God" can lead us to misunderstand who God is, how he works, and how to find him.

Elijah, however, had a better understanding of what acts of God really are. He had sought shelter in a cave and waited through a great wind, an earthquake, and a devouring fire. Only after this commotion, upon hearing a quiet and gentle whisper, did Elijah sense God's presence and leave the cave to meet him.

Father, I yearn for your presence. Help me to see past the fires that consume my attention, stand strong against the winds that would carry me away, and avoid being buried beneath the rubble of the earthquakes. Help me to be still and listen for your whisper.

> *Behold, the LORD passed by, and a great and strong wind tore the mountains and broke in pieces the rocks before the LORD, but the LORD was not in the wind. And after the wind an earthquake, but the LORD was not in the earthquake. And after the earthquake a fire, but the LORD was not in the fire. And after the fire the sound of a low whisper.*

1 KINGS 19:11-12 ESV

Following a thunderstorm, a beautiful quiet descends. Ever so gently, raindrops drip from rooftops and leaves. Tentatively, birds resume their songs. The winds have stilled. All is calm.

Isn't this exactly where we might expect to encounter the Prince of Peace?

Oh God, forgive me for ever thinking you would bring calamity and commotion! You bring peace. You are peace! If you do accompany a storm, it's as shelter. Thank you for meeting me in the quiet aftermath, and for whispering gently, "All is well."

April is an unpredictable weather month in most places. Try to get outside tomorrow and listen for God's voice, especially if there's a storm to wait out.

What Is Right

The fruit of that righteousness will be peace;
its effect will be quietness and confidence forever.

ISAIAH 32:17 NIV

Righteousness. What a powerful word. Perhaps you have shied away from it in the past. The term can conjure up images of rigidity and unattainable perfection, especially if we have known someone who was overly self-righteous. If we look closer, though, we see what is promised here when we pursue righteousness: peace, quietness, and confidence. It sounds lovely, doesn't it?

A righteous life is one that puts the Lord first by seeking to honor him in what we say and do. When we love what is right, and we are in turn honored with the gift of peace. Our lives are quiet, because there is no discord. We are confident, because we know we have nothing to be ashamed of.

Father, I want to live righteously. Help me ask, before every
decision, "What is right?" Make love of truth and goodness such
a part of me that with time, I won't even need to ask, because I
will know. And knowing, I will act, speak, love, and live with
righteousness.

*The effect of righteousness will be peace
and the result of righteousness, quietness and trust forever.*

ISAIAH 32:17 NRSV

Can it really be this simple? Can choosing "right" really bring
on peace? Can the result of a life lived for truth and fairness
really be quietness and trust?

Surrendering the struggle to get our own way certainly sounds
peaceful. Taking the road of harmony certainly seems quiet.
Why not try and see?

*God, I'm going to take you at your word. I hereby surrender my
version of what's right in favor of what's right in your eyes. Choose
for me when you must and keep me on the path of righteousness,
so I can have peace. Encourage me to stay in your will, so I can live
a life of quiet trust.*

Where could you benefit from a little quietness, confidence,
and trust? Consider the effect of turning this area of your life
over to God.

One True God

Since the beginning of the world men
have not heard nor perceived by the ear,
Nor has the eye seen any God besides You,
who acts for the one who waits for Him.

ISAIAH 64:4 NKJV

Authenticity matters. We crave it. It's important to us that the gemstone, the handbag, or the promise, is real. We want to know if we can trust people and if they are telling the truth. If we have been let down or lied to, we will scrutinize situations in the future to be sure of authenticity.

What a comfort it is to worship the one, true God! We needn't scrutinize. We don't have to ask. All his promises are true. All his gifts are good. His love is authentic, and it is ours.

Almighty God, you are the one and only God. I trust you, I love you, and I believe you. How is it that you care for me, and actively participate in even the tiniest details of my life? It awes me daily. May my worship reflect this awe; may it be authentic.

From ages past no one has heard, no ear has perceived, no eye has seen any God besides you, who works for those who wait for him.

ISAIAH 64:4 NRSV

The Bible contains many mentions of lower-case gods. Our culture is filled with them as well. Since the beginning, people have sought out and made up substitutes. Those of us who know the one true God are puzzled by these false, lesser gods. Why would anyone want a created deity over the Creator?

No made-up god exists purely to love and be loved the way our Lord does. Who but God longs to serve his servants? What more could we possibly want, and where can we imagine ever finding it?

God, you are matchless! You cannot be equaled, nor can your love. You can have anything, demand anything, and cause anything, yet you choose to ask, to invite, and to allow. You choose to bless. Blessed be your name, Lord.

Pray for the Holy Spirit to open the eyes and heart of someone who is infatuated with a "lower-case" god.

Waiting on God

Humble yourselves, therefore, under God's mighty hand,
that he may lift you up in due time.

1 PETER 5:6 NIV

Have you ever met someone who loves waiting? Sure, we may come across—or even be—a person who enjoys counting down to a vacation or special event, but things like traffic, grocery store lines, and four-hour repair windows are pretty universal trials of patience. But what if they didn't have to be?

Imagine instead we humbled ourselves enough to wait our turn and go with the flow. We could learn to actually enjoy the wait. Once we realize our time is no more valuable than anyone else's, and once we embrace our faith in God's timing, waiting becomes a gift. Like dreaming of a months-away vacation, we can look forward to what he has planned for us, knowing it will be good.

God, I don't have this one nailed yet. I am still frustrated by long lines and overflowing carts at the grocery store or a sea of brake lights on the highway. I feel entitled to getting things done as quickly as I want. Forgive me, God, and humble me. Remind me I'm not waiting on other people, but on you, and I can trust you with every minute of my time.

If you bow low in God's awesome presence, he will eventually exalt you as you leave the timing in his hands.

1 PETER 5:6 TPT

What a beautiful picture lowering ourselves before God is. Heads bowed, eyes closed, and fully surrendered, we wait in quiet trust. At just the right time, which he knows to the minute, we'll feel his hand beneath us as we begin to rise. Heads up and eyes open, what we will see is more than we wanted and all that we need.

Waiting on God will always be worth it. Bow before him and know you will be exalted.

Oh, Father, how I love this image. How I long to make it true. Help me lay myself down. Help me wait, filled with hope, to feel you lift me up.

How do you feel about waiting? How might this attitude and image help you resist it less?

A Generous Heart

The generous man will be prosperous,
and he who waters will himself be watered.

PROVERBS 11:25 NASB

A quick reading of this verse may leave us to conclude that when we give, we get. Let's look at it more thoroughly. Is everyone who gives generous? Does every act of giving result in a blessing? Imagine a child reluctantly breaking a cookie in two, sizing up the pieces, and handing over the smaller one. Is the child happy about sharing? Does the recipient of the smaller half of the cookie feel blessed? Acting out of obligation or duty is not the same as wanting to do something nice.

It is not giving and sharing per se that leads to refreshment and prosperity, but generously giving and share. While giving is an act, generosity is a condition. It is willing. It is born of love. It is the generous heart which is refreshed by giving. It is those with generous hearts our Father eagerly helps prosper.

Holy Spirit, I pray you will fill me with generosity. Each time I start to give reluctantly, pierce me with love for the recipient. When I am tempted to share begrudgingly, fling my arms wide open until I offer both halves of the cookie. May I give willingly and share with love.

A generous person will prosper;
whoever refreshes others will be refreshed.

PROVERBS 11:25 NIV

Think back to the best birthday of your life. What made it
so special? Chances are, it wasn't the presents. When we
look back as adults over the presents we got as children we
probably can't remember what we were given as well as we
can remember who gave us gifts. We remember their act
of generosity more than the gift itself. We remember the
joy they expressed when they handed the present to us. We
remember how cherished we felt receiving a gift.

Now recall the most satisfying gift you ever gave, whether a
gift of time, talent, or material goods. How much did your
heart prosper? How refreshed was your soul as you happily
opened your arms?

Thank you, God, for the incredible gift of generosity. It's amazing
how an unselfish act can lead to such a wonderful, personal
reward. How very like you to reward us most when we think of
ourselves the least.

In your experience, is it better to give than to receive?
Begin a dialogue with the Lord about this.

Sure Foundation

He will be the sure foundation for your times,
a rich store of salvation and wisdom and knowledge;
the fear of the LORD is the key to this treasure.

ISAIAH 33:6 NIV

We wouldn't expect a house of cards built on something soft like a pillow to be very tall or stand for very long. A granite countertop provides a much better foundation. Even a jigsaw puzzle wouldn't hold up very well on the softer surface. We need something solid beneath the things we build.

When it comes to our lives, the principle is the same. Building on our faith in the Lord, we can expect safety. If we piece our future together based on respect for him, wisdom and knowledge will be ours.

God, you are my firm foundation. When I stand on your wisdom, I am strong. Relying on your knowledge, I am sure. Respecting you the way you deserve, my house will go up safe, sturdy, and tall.

*In that day he will be your sure foundation,
providing a rich store of salvation, wisdom, and knowledge.
The fear of the LORD will be your treasure.*

ISAIAH 33:6 NLT

When was the last time you were truly afraid? Whether you were in physical danger or feeling another form of insecurity, you don't ever have to feel that way again. Really. Once you know and revere him and understand the sure foundation on which you stand, no power on earth can shake you.

You are safe. You are treasured. You are his.

Father God, your power is unmatched. I give you my reverence, and you save me. The more I know you, the wiser I become. What a treasure it is to fear you!

How might fearing the Lord erase all other fears?

In His Name

> *"I will do whatever you ask in my name,*
> *so that the Father may be glorified in the Son."*
>
> JOHN 14:13 NRSV

"Use my name," Jesus told his disciples. This is not an offer we extend to just anyone. When we tell someone to use our name, we are giving them permission to receive the special treatment usually reserved for us. We are, in a sense, allowing them to take our place and benefit from it.

Jesus still makes this offer today, to all who love him and seek to do his will. It's a letter of unlimited credit. He promises that whenever we ask in his name, we will be answered. It's extraordinary, isn't it? To be given such favor is a sign of the intimacy we share with him. We can come before the Almighty God in Jesus' name. What a glorious honor.

Jesus, I can never be truly worthy of the incredible favor you show me. The ability to come to God with my needs, my requests, and the cries of my heart in your name—as a representative of you—is an honor beyond any other. Thank you, God, for entrusting it to me.

*"If you ask for anything in my name, I will do it for you
so that the Father's glory will be shown through the Son."*

JOHN 14:13 NCV

Jesus promises to do whatever we ask in his name in order
to glorify the Father. When a prayer seems to be going
unanswered, remember God sees well past today. To bring
glory to God, we sometimes need an answer other than the
one we hope for, no matter how sincere our hearts and how
worthy our requests.

Continue to ask for things in his name but be open to God
answering in the way he sees fit.

*Jesus, I trust you. I know a "no" from you is really a "yes" for me.
Help me see past my immediate concerns to the grand, perfect plan
of the Father. Align my heart with yours, so all I would ask in your
name would bring glory to God.*

What can you ask God for, in his name, tonight?

All We Need

God's glory is all around me!
His wrap-around presence is all I need,
for the Lord is my Savior, my hero, and my life-giving strength.

PSALM 62:7 TPT

Safe inside our homes, seated before a table laid with a feast, and flanked by our loved ones, it's easy to think we have everything we need. Wrapped in the warmth of love and provision, all our cares melt away. Then Uncle George makes a political statement that offends our cousin Jane. Aunt Gladys complains the chicken is a bit dry. One of the little ones needs a diaper change. Our peace and contentment slowly evaporate as we daydream about a solo vacation.

If we draw our peace from worldly sources, we will find it eventually runs dry every time. Earthly relationships are to be treasured, but they can't eternally satisfy like our relationship with God can. Only when God is our strength and provider, and it's his warmth and provision that envelops us, do we really do have all we need.

God, surround me with your glory! When my family and friends are gathered in harmony, I have all I need. When they scatter or start bickering, I will still have all I need. Whether the table is full, or the cupboards are empty, you are my sustainer. Savior God, you are all I need.

On God rests my deliverance and my honor;
my mighty rock, my refuge is in God.

PSALM 62:7 NRSV

The Lord wants you to trust him with everything. He wants to
be your rescuer, and the reason for every honorable thing you
do. He wants to be the place you stand tall and brave, and also
the place you seek shelter. He wants you to know you can call on
him, run to him, be inspired by him, and build your life on him.

Do you trust God to be all you need?

God, I want to give you everything. I want to trust you when I need
saving. I want to be inspired by you to do great things. I want to
stand on you when I'm strong, and take shelter in you when I am
afraid. I want you to be my everything.

When do you feel most surrounded by God's presence:
in moments of need or moments of peace?

Better

A day in your courts is better than a thousand elsewhere.
I would rather be a doorkeeper in the house of my God than dwell
in the tents of wickedness.

PSALM 84:10 ESV

What was the absolute best day of your life? Would you trade that day for an extra year of life on earth? How about an extra three or four years? Most of us would not. Our treasured memories are just that—treasure. What value do we assign a day that yields a lifetime of beautiful memories?

Now imagine a day a thousand times better than your best day ever. Imagine a day in the presence of God. You are in the throne room. You hear the angels and know the unknowable, all the while bathed in the glorious light of his beauty. How many ordinary days, or even years, would you sacrifice to have a day like that?

Thank you, God, for a life so lovely. Thank you for days I wouldn't trade for anything on earth. God, when I remember all the beautiful days you've given me, and all the memories I treasure, it is staggering to think they are nothing compared to a day with you. How glorious it will be when that day stretches to eternity.

A single day in your courts is better than a thousand anywhere else! I would rather be a gatekeeper in the house of my God than live the good life in the homes of the wicked.

PSALM 84:10 NLT

Imagine you have two job offers. The first is in the field you have trained for, reached toward, and dreamed of all your life. The salary and benefits are impressive. There's just one problem: you'll be working in an industry that celebrates excess, depravity and greed. The other position is well beneath your qualifications, experience and compensation level, but the company is dedicated to a cause you believe in wholeheartedly. The employees are all passionate about the cause, and they value and respect one another. Love radiates from the office all the way out to the sidewalk.

Where will you go?

God, if only every choice to remain in your light were so obvious. Instead, I find myself faced with lots of tiny decisions and little invitations to compromise. Thank you for reminding me there is nothing worth stepping outside of where you are.

Ask yourself: Am I living a life that reflects my desire for the Lord? What might need to change? Where might I need to go?

Privilege of Suffering

He has graciously granted you the privilege not only of believing in Christ, but of suffering for him as well.

PHILIPPIANS 1:29 NRSV

There are passages in Scripture, like this one, that confound our sense of logic and challenge us to lean on the Holy Spirit for understanding. How can suffering—the state of undergoing pain, distress, or hardship—be a privilege?

Each time we step into a difficult or painful situation in order to glorify Christ, we have the opportunity to experience his comfort. As we endure pain in pursuit of the things that weigh on his heart, he comes into ours, flooding it with endurance, perseverance, and gratitude.

Lord Jesus, what a privilege it is to experience your comfort and benefit from your strength! I will gladly suffer an aching body from standing all day packing meals, pounding nails, or passing down buckets of life-giving water to experience your comforting strength. I'll happily endure ridicule for my convictions in order to feel your Spirit draw close to me. If it brings me more of you, I'll suffer whatever I must.

God gave you the honor not only of believing in Christ but also of suffering for him, both of which bring glory to Christ.

PHILIPPIANS 1:29 NCV

We can bring glory to the Lord with our lives no matter what season we are in. While running a marathon for charity, toiling over a building project to help others, or facing persecution for our faith all bring glory to Christ, not every day will hold such extreme circumstances. Our quiet prayers, our simple trust, and our open faith honor him as well.

We bring Christ glory by suffering for him and by believing in him.

Precious God, I feel connected to you on days when I am drained in body and spirit. Those days give me an inkling of the weight of the cross. Let me also feel united to your cross on ordinary days. Even if my biggest challenge of the day is simply to trust you or speak out about my faith, let it honor you. Thank you for the privilege of letting my life bring you glory.

Do you feel called to "go big" in order to glorify Jesus? What cause has captured your attention? How can you honor him in the ordinary moments as well?

Trust Him

Trust in the Lord with all your heart,
and lean not on your own understanding

PROVERBS 3:5 NKJV

Picture a TV character leaning against a wall or on a table they thought was secure, only to suddenly fall when it gives way. What appeared to be a sturdy fence was actually weak, rotting wood. This scene is typically used to induce laughter as the actor's legs fly and arms flail before they land on the ground. It's the best of slapstick comedy.

What about when this happens in real life and we are the ones falling? Social success, financial gain, and relationships can all send us flailing if we put all our weight—all our trust—on them. Chances are, we won't be laughing when that happens because it hurts. When we rely on only our own constructs and understanding, we get hurt. Instead, God calls us to place all our trust in him. He is the only truly stable surface we can build on. God will keep us upright with our feet firmly on the ground.

Father, you are my sturdy fence. You surround me with protection.
I know you can bear all my weight. Please help me to trust you
with my relationships, work, and decisions. you are the stable
foundation I want to lean on.

Trust in the LORD with all your heart;
do not depend on your own understanding.

PROVERBS 3:5 NLT

Do you remember how much you thought you knew at eighteen? How wise you thought you were? Having mastered high school, maybe held a job, and learned a recipe or two, you felt confident to conquer the adult world. How long did it take to realize how much you didn't know?

No matter how much life we've lived and how much wisdom we've gained, God's is greater. Whatever he's directing you to or keeping you from, you can trust him.

God, thank you for your wise, loving hand over my life. Help me to trust you, remember you know so much more than I ever will, and know your will for me is perfect. No matter what I think, let me remember that you, God, actually know.

Recall some of the times in your life you trusted your own, limited knowledge and then later realized how much better God's plan was.

We Cannot Lose

In all these things we overwhelmingly conquer
through Him who loved us.

ROMANS 8:37 NASB

Sometimes a team or an athlete is so good they don't just win, they dominate. The race is won by a full lap, or the game by dozens of points. If spectating, you almost feel sorry for the loser. If the victor, you're careful not to celebrate too joyfully. Winning is great, but there's no need to rub it in.

However, when your opponent is darkness and defeat, you can feel free to boast about your win. With Jesus on your team you are assured of not just victory, but overwhelming victory—and you needn't feel the least bit sorry about it. Battling fear, loneliness, or despair? Prepare to annihilate them. When confronting any enemy of the joy that is yours in Christ, know the enemy stands no chance against Christ in you. And you, along with all of heaven, can celebrate as heartily as you want.

Lord Jesus, I love knowing that when we are united, I cannot lose. No enemy of my peace or thief of my joy can stand in your presence: they are ground to dust by your powerful defense. Mighty Christ, thank you for being on my team!

Even in the midst of all these things, we triumph over them all, for God has made us to be more than conquerors, and his demonstrated love is our glorious victory over everything.

ROMANS 8:37 TPT

Who doesn't love an underdog? There's something about the unlikely victory of a come-from-behind triumph that reminds us with faith, anything is possible. We may even feel like the underdog sometimes. We may feel hopelessly week or outmatched but don't despair. Take comfort knowing we cannot lose because God has made us conqueror and promised us glorious victory.

Remember, our promise in Christ is not that we won't struggle, but that we won't be defeated. In the midst of it all, because of his great love, the hard-won battle is ours.

God, sometimes I wish you'd end the struggle, but I understand why you don't. By letting me face a powerful opponent, you show me how truly unstoppable you are, and how unstoppable I am with you.

Think of your most satisfying victory. What made it so special? Thank God for the experience.

Like a Child

"Truly, I say to you, whoever does not receive the kingdom of God like a child shall not enter it."

MARK 10:15 ESV

There's usually nothing polite or tentative about the way a small child opens a gift. Filled with anticipation and delight, they tear through the paper, eager to get to what's inside. Now imagine a grown woman at a birthday lunch with girlfriends, ripping through her gifts this way. It would be comical, and maybe even frowned upon. We're expected not only to have more self-control, but also to be less excited in the first place.

When it comes to receiving the kingdom of God, Jesus tells us he wants that childlike abandon. Run toward it like a kid running to the tree on Christmas morning. Tear past the wrappings to get to the good stuff inside. Jump up and down for joy. He wants to see our eager, happy faces as we gleefully exclaim that what he's given us is exactly what we wanted.

God, like a little child I run to you. I can't wait to see what you have chosen just for me, what you have prepared with me in mind. Gratefully and with no reserve, I receive your gift, your blessing, your love.

"Listen to the truth I speak: Whoever does not open their arms to receive God's kingdom like a teachable child will never enter it."

MARK 10:15 TPT

What are some of the things you believed simply because your parents said so? When we are young, we tend to see our caregivers as oracles of truth. We accept what they say as gospel. This is the innocence—the absolute faith—Jesus wants us to receive God's kingdom with.

If the Father says it, it's true. If Jesus promises it, it will be done.

Father God, sweet Abba, I want to open my arms to every promise, command, gift, and plan you speak over me. Help me abandon the caution, doubt, and willfulness that get in the way of the childlike faith you desire. Let your Word be enough to teach my heart, Lord.

How can you pursue a more childlike faith today? What reason or caution can you release?

All He Bore

He was wounded for our transgressions, crushed for our iniquities; upon him was the punishment that made us whole, and by his bruises we are healed.

ISAIAH 53:5 NRSV

Few things make us feel more loved than to know someone has sacrificed or suffered for us. From driving many miles to be by our sides in a crisis, to sharing their time or resources with us, it means something when a friend gives up a piece of their life for ours. We can tell they love us through these small gestures.

How much more, then, must Jesus love us? Remembering all he bore, all he withstood, and all he willingly gave up so that we could receive healing grace, awe is the only worthy response. He did it all for you. And he would do it again.

Precious Jesus, I am in awe of your sacrifice on my behalf. My heart breaks to imagine your pain, and then it bursts with love and gratitude knowing you for it for me. I know I can never deserve your grace, but I willingly, gratefully accept it. Thank you, Lord!

He was pierced for our rebellion, crushed for our sins.
He was beaten so we could be whole.
He was whipped so we could be healed.

ISAIAH 53:5 NLT

The whole class misses recess because someone was talking during the test. Hundreds of workers lose their jobs because a CEO mismanaged the company's finances. It is unfair that the negative actions of one can impact so many who don't deserve it.

Contrastingly, in God's plan, the positive actions of one impact everyone, though we still don't deserve it. We have Jesus, perfect, sinless, and filled with only love, who took the punishment for all the world's sins. It's so unfair, so beautifully, wonderfully unfair.

God, if you were concerned with fairness, heaven would be empty. None of us deserve to be in heaven with you. I'm so grateful for and so awed by your unfair sacrifice. As your beautiful and selfless actions trickle down to so many—myself included—who don't deserve it, all I can do is gratefully receive your healing grace.

How important is fairness to you? How does what Jesus did for you fit with your feelings about what is fair?

Renewed

Do not conform to the pattern of this world, but be transformed by the renewing of your mind. Then you will be able to test and approve what God's will is—his good, pleasing and perfect will.

ROMANS 12:2 NIV

A shower can make you feel like a whole new person, can't it? With bouncy hair and glowing skin, we feel fresh and clean. Then the day happens. By evening, the morning's bounce and glow are forgotten; we are no longer fresh and clean.

Just as we don't expect to shower once and remain clean forever, we shouldn't expect that our acceptance of Jesus as Lord will keep us in a state of sinless perfection. Life happens. Temptation and frustration and sin happen. Christ's renewing love is a stream of cleansing water we must return to again and again. What a gift it is to know that we can always be renewed!

Jesus, you welcome me daily to the cleansing steam of your living water. I stand beneath the flow of your love and goodness, and the day and its grime are washed away. Over and over you change me, God, never tiring of making me clean and new.

Do not be conformed to this world, but be transformed by the renewing of your mind, that you may prove what is that good and acceptable and perfect will of God.

ROMANS 12:2 NKJV

If only we could take one final, permanent shower and stay clean forever. Then again, doesn't the refreshment of the warm water feel wonderful? Even more so, as we shed the influence of the world each day, we are renewed and refreshed by the warmth of God's love and forgiveness. As we resist conforming to the world, he bathes us in truth and goodness.

What a blessing it is to be constantly renewed and transformed to God's good, acceptable, and perfect will!

Father, thank you for the gift of renewal. I appreciate that I can come to you with every sin, doubt, influence, and temptation the world lays on me, and you wash them all away. Refresh and transform me, God, bathing me in truth and revealing your perfect will.

Imagine a warm stream of God's love washing over every part of your day. Feel your mind renew and refresh as everything not of him slips away.

Forgiven

The LORD said to Cain, "No! If anyone kills you, I will punish that person seven times more." Then the LORD put a mark on Cain warning anyone who met him not to kill him.

GENESIS 4:15 NCV

What most people know about Cain is that he murdered his brother, Abel, the one who pleased the Lord. In the passage above God has just sent Cain into exile for this terrible crime, but not before bestowing protection on him. Does this surprise you? Did you know this part of the story?

Despite his unforgivable sin, he was forgiven. Anyone killing Cain would receive a punishment seven times as severe as his. This is the depth of God's love for his children! His capacity to love and forgive us is boundless. This God, this incredible, generous God, is *ours*.

Oh, Lord! Your love amazes me. That you would go so far for Cain, an unrepentant murderer, shows me the depth of your grace. You forgive me, Father, for the wrong I have done and the wrong in my heart. You protect me as you protected Cain: wholeheartedly. May I love you this same way.

The LORD said to him, "Therefore whoever kills Cain, vengeance will be taken on him sevenfold." And the LORD appointed a sign for Cain, so that no one finding him would slay him.

GENESIS 4:15 NASB

Certainly, God's treatment of Cain here is remarkable, and so too is the teaching to all who would harm him. Think of what they learned of God's true character when they read this sign.

Their revenge wouldn't please the Lord; it would cause him to rain down his fury on them. How awed they must have been!

God, you've been trying to tell us who you are since the beginning. You've commanded us to love one another, and you've shown us exactly how deeply. Tonight, I pray that we would comprehend, and be awed.

Is there an unforgivable wrong you need to forgive and leave to God to punish?

Consolation

I am filled with comfort. In all our affliction,
I am overflowing with joy.

2 Corinthians 7:4 esv

Take a moment and imagine yourself in prison. Focus on the isolation, lack of freedom, and your inability to change the situation. Do you feel joyful? It seems an absurd question, right? You may feel lonely, sad, afraid or empty, but feeling joy is unlikely.

With everything you hold dear in this world taken away, it's hard to imagine anything making you happy. The circumstances would be too bleak to find joy by yourself. What a comfort it is, then, to remember we are not alone. Because he'd given himself over entirely to the Lord, Paul was in return given an untouchable peace and inexhaustible joy that could not be taken away, even when everything else had been.

God, what a gift it is to know that no matter what happens to me—
no matter what I lose or ruin—your joy will remain. As long as I
am yours, wherever I go, or I am taken, your comfort will be mine.

I am filled with consolation;
I am overjoyed in all our affliction.

2 Corinthians 7:4 NRSV

How delightful it must be to be filled with consolation and overjoyed in all affliction! This is what our God, in his incomparable generosity, offers us. When we invite the Holy Spirit in, he maximizes our capacity for consolation. As he fills us with joy, our focus is taken away from any suffering or strife.

Our God is so generous, he doesn't stop giving when we have what we need. Instead, he continues to pour out consolation and joy until our hearts overflow and we share it with others.

Holy Spirit, you have the power to shift my focus from any sadness or affliction I face. As you overwhelm me with your love, those negative thoughts and feelings lose their power over me. I invite your joy in. I welcome your consolation. As you give me more than I need, more than I can ever hold, show me where I might bless others with the overflow.

Are troubles taking up space in your thoughts or your heart? Invite the Spirit to wash those troubles away with joy and consolation.

Seek Him Out

Seek more of his strength! Seek more of him!
Let's always be seeking the light of his face.

PSALM 105:4 TPT

If only we could carry the feeling we get from a great church service, Bible study, concert or conference everywhere we go. When we are filled with the Spirit, God's strength is our strength. When we are inspired by praise, we see the world through the Lord's eyes. When open to his amazing power, our wounds can be healed. How pleasant it would be to continuously seek more of him and bask in his light.

Life tends to make continual basking impossible, though. We have bills to pay, tests to study for, and things to clean. We are worn down by stress and struggle. These all distract us from seeking God. Having wandered from that wonderful place, the place we felt him closer than our own skin, we are reminded of how much we crave it—how much we need it. We're reminded to seek, to search, to pursue his presence. When we can't feel his light, we need only turn toward his face. Arms open, he's right where we left him.

God, sometimes I forget it's I who wander away. I find you in the obvious places, in church, in Christian fellowship, in songs that glorify you, and I expect you to follow me into the dark places. You remain in the light, loving me, reminding me, I need only seek your beautiful face.

248

Seek the Lord and His strength;
seek His face evermore!

When separated from our companions in a crowd, we scan
each face, looking for one that is familiar. Once we see the
eyes we know, or the smile we love, we feel at ease. No matter
where we are, their face can us home.

This is what our Lord wants from us. "Seek my face," he tells
us. Look for the eyes that love you more than life. Search out
the smile he's reserved just for you. Come home.

God, I spend most of time seeking things for myself: my purpose,
my possessions, or my comfort. Remind me, God, that nothing
matters more than seeking you. With your strength, I am strong. In
this light of your loving gaze, I am home.

When you seek him, where do you look?

By Your Side

The Lord is faithful; he will strengthen you and guard you from the evil one.

2 THESSALONIANS 3:3 NLT

Faithful means loyal, constant, and steadfast. A faithful friend will never betray you. A faithful pet sticks right by your side. A faithful spouse is one whose eyes will never wander. We are safe, secure, and certain in the midst of faithfulness.

Our Lord is faithful. Let us be strengthened and fortified by this wonderful truth. Whatever the enemy of your soul has planned for you, God remains by your side. Nothing can alter his commitment to you. Be safe, be certain, and be secure in him.

Jesus, I don't deserve such unwavering faithfulness, yet you give it. My own commitment wavers daily as the shiny things of this world catch my eye, or as fear tries to pull me down, away from your side. Today, I thank you for your faithfulness, and I commit to return it. May your Spirit strengthen me to remain faithful to the One who is so wholly committed to me.

The Lord is faithful, and He will strengthen and protect you from the evil one.

2 THESSALONIANS 3:3 NASB

The God remains by our side is gift enough, yet his faithfulness brings other blessings with it.

His constant, lifting presence is our strength. His refusal to ever leave us is our safety. More than just a constant, loving companion, he is also a powerful protector, always instructing evil to leave us be.

God, I spend so much time thinking of you as my most trusted friend, I forget about the fierceness of your loyalty. You would do anything to keep me safe from the evil one. How strong this makes me feel, and how very safe and loved.

How does it feel knowing our beautiful, loving Creator would tear evil limb from limb to keep you safe? Whether empowered or uncomfortable, share your feelings with him.

True Love Abides

As you received Christ Jesus the Lord, so continue to live in him.
COLOSSIANS 2:6 NCV

Few feelings can compare to new love. The anticipation, the discovery, and the excitement are overwhelming. It's hard to think of anything else. Whether a romance, a puppy, or a new friend, as the days go by, excitement is replaced by routine. Discovery gives way to familiarity. If we treasure the love, these feelings, though less intense, will grow deep and remain strong. A good routine takes hold. True love abides.

Falling in love with Jesus can be similar. The overwhelming joy of first finding him in your heart settles into the quiet peace of knowing he's always going to be there. Let us take care to treasure the love, allowing it to grow deep and abide.

Dearest Jesus, I love remembering the way I felt the first time you made yourself known to me, the first time I was certain of your abiding love. Sometimes I long to feel again the intensity of brand new love. And yet, I wouldn't trade the day-to-day joy of knowing you are with me for anything. I thank you for both the thrill of the beginning and the peace of the permanence.

As you received Christ Jesus the Lord, so walk in him,

COLOSSIANS 2:6 ESV

How did you receive Christ? With happiness, relief, or joyful dancing? Whichever way your love began, live it out with equal fervor!

If he gave you peace, walk in peace. If he brought you joy, jump, twirl, and sway in it. Whatever gift he gave your heart, let that gift define your walk with him.

Precious God, remind my heart how it felt to discover you. Inspire my steps with gratitude; move me to the rhythm of your grace. Let your joy be the song I dance to. Let the peace you gave me be the path I walk.

What gifts will define your walk if you determine to live this verse out?

Tell Him

Nothing in all creation is hidden from God's sight. Everything is uncovered and laid bare before the eyes of him to whom we must give account.

HEBREWS 4:13 NIV

Face smeared with chocolate, and t-shirt covered in crumbs, the toddler insists she doesn't know what happened to the rest of the cookies. We can clearly see what she doesn't want us to know. It's almost humorous, the way she thinks that if she denies it, we won't see it.

Perhaps God is similarly amused when we try to keep him from knowing something us. It is quite silly to imagine we can keep secrets from our omniscient Lord. Yet we often act like it's possible to. We think that because we're pretending to have fun, he won't know we are in pain. Because we are denying the problem, he won't see the way it's slowly taking us down. He knows, dear one. He sees. And he adores you. Tell him the truth and see the love with which he responds.

God, I don't know why I try to keep anything from you, why I hide my pain or try to cover up my sin. I know you don't condemn or judge me. I know you find me precious. Please give me the strength to tell you what you already know, so I can have the peace that will follow when I do.

There is no creature hidden from His sight, but all things are naked and open to the eyes of Him to whom we must give account.

HEBREWS 4:13 NKJV

In the mid-1990's, a delightful book called *Naked Babies* was released. It featured, as you might expect, a series of black and white photographs of naked babies in all their roly-poly glory. It was absolutely precious.

We tend to think of our nakedness before God as exposure or weakness, but what if he sees us more like those darling, undressed little ones? No need for shame and nothing to hide, because our Papa thinks we are absolutely precious.

God, thank you that you see everything I do, and you still find me precious. I don't need to live in shame or hide anything from you. Help me to share everything with you, knowing that you already know and you love me unconditionally.

Spend a few minutes searching yourself for anything you are trying to keep hidden and ask God for the faith to lay it bare.

Yet to Do

"I am the vine, you are the branches; he who abides in Me and I in him, he bears much fruit, for apart from Me you can do nothing."

JOHN 15:5 NASB

Were we to go up to a vineyard and cut off a length of vine that held a few ripe grapes and several clusters of promising but still-sour ones, we'd end up with a few good grapes—and a dead branch. It might make an attractive wreath or centerpiece, but it would not be good for much else. Away from its source, the few grapes that had already ripened would be the only fruit that branch ever produced.

Connected to the Lord, we are healthy, nourished vines. Our lives continue to ripen and flourish. Cut off from his life-giving power, we simply wither. Any good deeds we accomplished in the past are from our attachment to him, and any future good relies on this attachment continuing. Let us stay connected, then, and realize our potential. Let's us accomplish all the good we've yet to do.

Jesus, I want to remain in you. I want to produce, ripen, and taste all the fruit I can. Every promising part of me that's as-yet unripe, I want to see come to fruition.

"I am the vine; you are the branches. Whoever abides in me and I in him, he it is that bears much fruit, for apart from me you can do nothing."

If you want to find Jesus at work, follow the fruit. Galatians 5:22-23 tells us what to look for. We're looking for a life that seems to attract and produce love, joy, peace, and patience. We're following the trail of kindness and goodness, of faithfulness, gentleness, and self-control. A life that looks like this is a life abiding in the vine. This is someone who has embraced their need for Jesus, and who relies on him for all their strength.

With God's help and by staying ever-close, may this someone be us.

God, thank you for making sure I know exactly how to find you. Thank you for signs of your work in the lives of my brothers and sisters, and for evidence of your work in me. As I realize more love in my life, may it lead to joy. May that joy lead to peace, and so on, and so on, until your fruit is all I can taste.

Is your branch abiding fully on the vine?

Listen to Your Heart

My heart has heard you say, "Come and talk with me."
And my heart responds, "LORD, I am coming."

PSALM 27:8 NLT

Faced with a crucial decision, a friend will often advise us to listen to our heart. The theory behind this advice is that the deepest part of us already knows what to do. Where we connect with our longing is where the answer awaits.

As a Christ-follower, the Holy Spirit is an active part of your life. Because of this active relationship, your heart will often be directed toward the Lord, to his will, and his way. When your mind has a question, listen to your heart and talk with your God.

God, listening to my heart should always result in hearing from you. I am blessed by your wisdom; you never guide me the wrong way. No matter what I must decide, whether it's major or mundane, may I turn toward you, and hear the words your Spirit speaks to my heart.

My heart said of you, "Go, worship him."
So I come to worship you, LORD.

We all have moments where we just need to honor God.
Sometimes it's a breathtaking sunset, or a sweet moment
with the ones you love the most. It may even be when you're
alone in the dark, uninspired by anything seen or felt, but
drawn to give him praise.

Awe, gratitude, or longing, to worship him is all the heart
wants to do. And when we do worship him? Oh, the sweet,
sweet communion we share with our glorious King!

Father God, my heart longs to sing of your greatness forever.
Because I will never truly be home until I am in heaven,
worshipping you for all eternity, this heart-longing never leaves
me. No song or prayer expresses all you are and all you've done.
Today, and every day, I worship you.

What is your favorite way to worship God? When do you feel
him draw near in response to your praise?

True Home

Our homeland is in heaven, and we are waiting for our Savior,
the Lord Jesus Christ, to come from heaven.

PHILIPPIANS 3:20 NCV

Where is home? Some will always think of the house or town they grew up in, while others have found home is where they chose to settle and raise their own families. Still others may feel most at home with a certain person, regardless of geography. Home feels right. Home feels secure.

Wherever we feel at home on earth, the Lord wants us to remember our true home is with him. All the warmth and love "home" provides us here is just a glimpse of what awaits us in heaven. No person or place can come close to providing the joy and security we will feel when we are united with Jesus.

Lord Jesus, as much as I love my earthly home, and as grateful as
I am for it, I long for the day I am home with you. Eagerly, I wait
for heaven, and for you, my true home.

*We are a colony of heaven on earth as we cling tightly
to our life-giver, the Lord Jesus Christ,*

PHILIPPIANS 3:20 TPT

A trip to Italy won't make us Italian. Regardless of where we
visit, we are citizens of where we are from. A piece of our
hearts remains where it was planted. We eventually grow
homesick, no matter how lovely our surroundings.

We may not remember heaven, but heaven remembers us.
The piece of our hearts that remains there grows homesick
and calls us to our true home.

*Father God, I don't remember heaven, but my heart does. I love
where I am, but I can't wait to be where you are—to come home.*

Where is home the place for you? Who is home the person?
What is it that gives you that feeling of rightness?

Spiritual GPS

I have gone astray like a lost sheep;
seek Your servant, for I do not forget Your commandments.

PSALM 119:176 NASB

It's rare to find ourselves truly lost these days. A GPS points the way almost infallibly when we need directions, and our smartphones keep this technology within easy reach. Yet, occasionally, we find ourselves out of range, or with a map that is out of date. Maybe we made one too many wrong turns and are too muddled up to get back on track. Occasionally, we need more assistance than technology can give. We need someone to show us the way.

This same thing can happen on our faith walk. Despite the guidance from study, prayer and mentors, we may wander off the path and find ourselves lost. When we experience spiritual disorientation, we need God to show us the way. Wonderfully, the Lord's guidance is always infallible. He is never out of range, and his omniscience is never out of date. We can trust his guidance.

God, you are my spiritual GPS. Each time I lose my way, you find me. You hear me when I call, and you light the proper path. I remember your highest command—to love you with all I am—and the way becomes familiar again. As I share your love with others, again I am found.

I have wandered away like a lost sheep;
come and find me, for I have not forgotten your commands.

PSALM 119:176 NLT

God hears the tender, humble pleas of his lost sheep. Whether from distraction or disobedience, when they realize they are lost, he hears their bleating and comes to their rescue. He always hears the cries of those who belong to him. He stays connected to the souls who love their Lord.

Even if getting geographically lost is rare, getting metaphorically lost is still quite common. As we progress along our faith journey, we get distracted, or we stumble, and wander off the path. What a blessing it is to know that the moment we recognize our predicament, we can call, and he will come.

Jesus, you are the Good Shepherd. You see me wander. You know when I have lost my way. Rather than scoop me up and carry me back, you let me learn. You let me remember how much better everything is with you. You wait for me to ask, and then you come.

Together with the Holy Spirit, search your heart. Where have you gotten a little lost? If you are ready, ask your Shepherd to come and find you. If not, pray for the will to call to him soon.

He Is Watching

*The LORD will watch over your coming and going
both now and forevermore.*

PSALM 121:8 NIV

If you've ever taken a little one to a playground, you know to
never let them out of your sight. Around every corner, both
danger and delight await. Every swing, slide, and climbing
structure is hold an invitation to explore and the potential
for pain. The other children could be kind or cruel. You have
to watch and be ready. You don't want to stop them from
exploring and experiencing, but you are there to swoop in if
they are in real danger.

To God, you are very much like a child on a playground. Your
Abba never lets you out of his sight. He wants you to swing
higher, make new friends, and climb to your heart's content.
He's not there to stop you from every potential scrape or
bruise, but he will watch over you and keep you safe.

*Abba, the more I know you, the more I love how you love. Rather
than wrap me up in cotton wool, you let me live! You let me
explore, climb, and engage. Always watching, and always ready,
you are there to make sure I will be okay.*

The LORD will keep your going out and your coming in from this time on and forevermore.

PSALM 121:8 NRSV

You are protected. Again, this doesn't mean nothing bad will happen. This fallen world assures it will. What it means is that the God of the Universe is here, now, with you, to ensure that your soul will be safe.

There are moments this won't feel like enough. Why can't he keep us safe from everything, body and soul? When those moments come, lean in. Lean into the eternal, relentless love of your Lord and know you will be okay.

God, there are days these promises comfort me and days they fill me with fear. Why must I suffer at all? As you watch, why don't you keep me from all harm? Then, gently, you remind me where my true home is, and where my true future lies: with you, safe, forevermore.

Come before God tonight with your honest feelings about the bumps and bruises he allows. Let his eternal, loving Spirit assure you of his protection.

His Poetry

We are His workmanship, created in Christ Jesus for good works, which God prepared beforehand so that we would walk in them.

EPHESIANS 2:10 NASB

Carefully, intentionally, with great foresight and grand plans, God made you. It may not feel like it every day but know this: he knew exactly what he was doing. Everything about you, even the desires of your heart, are there to guide you toward his loving plan for your life.

Remember this the next time you question your worth. When you worry you have nothing to contribute, be assured that you do. There is a specific, beautiful, and one-of-a-kind reason you were born. The unique way you were made, right down to the length of your arms and the passions in your soul, was designed to help you fulfill this divine destiny.

Father, I don't say this enough: thank you for how you made me! Thank you for this body. Though I am hard on it, often focused on the parts I'd like to change, it is a work of art, unique and priceless, like everything you have made. Thank you too, for the dreams I harbor to make a mark for good. They are evidence of your artistry, and a reminder of my own goodness in you.

We have become his poetry, a re-created people that will fulfill
the destiny he has given each of us, for we are joined to Jesus, the
Anointed One. Even before we were born, God planned in advance
our destiny and the good works we would do to fulfill it!

EPHESIANS 2:10 TPT

You are a poem. You are lovely, playful, and lilting language.
You are here to delight and inspire. You are a painting, filled
with color and light and purposed to reflect it outward. You
are a symphony, glorious sound upon glorious sound, all to be
lifted to the one who composed you. You are beautiful. Your
purpose is to be beautiful in exactly the way he intended.

Never forget how unique and priceless you are, dear friend!

God, I long to see myself this way. I don't know why it is so hard.
On the days I feel all wrong— the words, colors, or notes feel off—it
seems impossible this could be true. Inspired by you, though, I keep
writing, painting, or singing. I remember my beauty, and, once
again, I'm ready to share it.

What kind of art do you respond most favorably to? Ask the Lord
to show you how to him, you even more masterfully crafted.

He Knows

When I thought, "My foot slips,"
your steadfast love, O LORD, held me up.

PSALM 94:18 ESV

A practiced assistant knows which instrument the surgeon, mechanic, or chef needs before they even have to ask. An attentive mother spots the first signs of sickness, whether in the body or the heart. She offers the right kind of remedy or comfort instinctively. She knows her child.

As you are his child, the Lord is completely in tune with your needs. Before you even have to ask, he offers just what you need. He sees the slip before it happens, and his arms are waiting to catch you. Before your heart breaks, he prepares to comfort it. He knows his child.

God, I am humbled by your attentiveness to me. The moment I slip, I feel your arm steadying me. If I fail to grab it, you reach down to cushion my fall. As suddenly as sadness and disappointment come upon me, so too does the certainty of your unfailing support and comfort. You are steadfast, God, and I am grateful.

If I say, "My foot slips,"
Your mercy, O Lord, will hold me up.

How very close he must be, to respond the same moment we ask. Whether we call aloud or think our plea, he hears it and comes. No matter if we call to him the second we slip, or after a lifetime of free-falling, he is always anxious and eager to lift us up.

Thank you, Lord, for holding us up with your mercy.

God, what patience you have. You could prevent my slips and falls, but instead, you let me come to you. Knowing I must recognize my need before I can comprehend your mercy, you wait. How closely you remain, though it must be hard to watch at times. Thank you, Father, for sticking so close and for giving so much.

Do you tend to recognize your need for help the moment you slip, or do you need to fall for a while, maybe even hitting the bottom first? Invite the Spirit to speak to you each time you approach a slippery spot.

He Consoles Us

When my anxious thoughts multiply within me,
Your consolations delight my soul.

PSALM 94:19 NASB

How often do we experience anxiety like this? Like mold, one worry builds upon another until a fuzzy, foul surface completely obscures our peace. This is a verse to memorize, dear friend! When stress leads to worry, worry to anxiety, and anxiety threatens to give way to panic, God consoles us. Call to him. Remember him. In the midst of all that swirling chaos, he won't just soothe you, he will delight your soul.

Try this out. Turn to him. The situation may not change, but your perspective will. Watch his loveliness repel the things that try to steal your peace. Remembering his promises will bring you joy and delight right where you are.

God, thank you for showing me how easy it is to obliterate the overgrown anxieties of my thoughts. Your face, your light, and your goodness drown them out the moment I turn my attention to you. Delight replaces doubt, and my worry is overtaken by worship. How wonderful you are!

Whenever my busy thoughts were out of control,
the soothing comfort of your presence calmed me down
and overwhelmed me with delight.

PSALM 94:19 TPT

It would be enough, wouldn't it, if the Father were to stop at comforting us? If all he did was take away our fear and quiet our anxiety, our gratitude would still run deep. But he doesn't stop.

Loving Father that he is, he doesn't leave us simply feeling better. He takes our wringing hands and raises them up. He silences fear by overwhelming us with delight.

Father, how often I feel like a child before you. You hear my cry and replace it with laughter. First you soothe me by drying every tear, and then you make me laugh. First you comfort me, then you invite me to dance.

See how easy it is for your Father to turn your thoughts to wonderful things by trying it now. Surrender every anxiety to him, and see the way he ushers in peace, laughter and joy.

Choose His Way

"Take My yoke upon you and learn from Me, for I am gentle and humble in heart, and you will find rest for your souls. For My yoke is easy and My burden is light."

MATTHEW 11:29-30 NASB

Imagine you're volunteering to work on a farm for a few days, and you get to choose your job. Would you like to break up and move boulders to prepare the field for plowing and planting, or would you prefer to walk behind the plow scattering seeds? Which is more appealing: the back-breaking heavy lifting or the steady purposeful stroll?

Unless we're trying hard to impress someone, or are gluttons for punishment, we're going to choose the seeds, right? This is exactly what it's like to walk with Christ. We can choose his way, and find rest for our souls, or we can go our own way and try to lift those heavy boulders. Which will we choose?

God, here and now, the choice to do life your way is easy. It's only when I get to the field—when I think it has to be hard in order for it to count—that I am tempted to take the harder way. I ask myself, "Am I spiritual enough, working hard enough, and sacrificing enough?" In these moments, remind me of your gentle way, and invite me, again, to choose it.

"Accept my teachings and learn from me, because I am gentle and humble in spirit, and you will find rest for your lives. The burden that I ask you to accept is easy; the load I give you to carry is light."

MATTHEW 11:29-30 NCV

Throughout our lives we seek to learn from those who know more than us. We seek teachers and experts we can trust. We rely on the truth of their knowledge. We are open to their instruction especially when we feel like they have a method that would make things easier for us.

How much better our lives would be if were as open to Jesus' teaching and instruction. Though humble and gentle, he is superior to any earthly expert. If we choose his way, not only will he offer us the best advice and insight, we are also promised a burden that is easy and a load that is light.

God, help me to accept your yoke. help me learn what you teach. You offer protection, grace, and rest. I sometimes eschew these gifts in favor of struggle and burdens. I take on things that are far too heavy. Humble me, God, to accept your peaceful rest.

Are you choosing the hard way over Jesus' way in any areas of your life? What might it feel like to bear his yoke instead?

An Everlasting Rock

Trust in the LORD forever,
for in the LORD God you have an everlasting rock.

ISAIAH 26:4 NRSV

"She's my rock." We know exactly what is meant when we hear this. She is solid, dependable, and constant. No matter where we find ourselves, we know exactly where we'll find our rocks. We also we can trust whatever they tell us, and we can expect safety in their shadow. These people have standards and principles that never change, and a love for us that is just as constant.

Yet, even if the person you depend most on in this world wavers, know that your God never does. He has not, and he will not. He does what he says he will do, and he is who he says he is. Everything he says is true, and he says he is an everlasting rock *for you*. Expect safety, friend. Trust his unwavering love.

Father God, you are the rock. You will not move, nor will you change. I know where to find you, and I know what you tell me is true. In your shadow, I am safe. In your light, I am illuminated. In your love, I am eternally loved.

Trust in the Lord forever,
for the Lord God is an everlasting rock.

Isaiah 26:4 ESV

If you were to place a rock in a box for twenty years, what would you expect to find when you opened the box? The very same rock, right? You wouldn't expect it to grow, turn different colors, or die, because rocks are unchanging. Protected from the elements, they stay as they are.

The people we love the most will all be affected by the changes of this world, and the experiences life brings. God will not. Even if we could place him in a box and forget about him, he would be there, exactly as he always was, the moment we lift the lid. He is the true everlasting rock.

God, to know you would wait, for the rest of my life, for me to come to you, undoes me. In that time, your love for me would not waver. How can you be so constant, so forgiving, and so safe? And how, precious God, can I ever thank you enough for being my rock?

How does it feel to know the permanence of God's love and the constancy of his faithfulness?

Loved for Real

"You shall love the L ORD your God with all your heart and with all your soul and with all your mind and with all your strength.'

MARK 12:30 ESV

If an emergency room doctor worked tirelessly to save your life, would you assume he was in love with you, or that he was doing his job? In another context, if you were dating a man who loved looking at you and showing you off, but didn't enjoy talking to you, would you be satisfied with his love? Would you believe he actually loved you? In real love, more than just effort and attraction are required.

God is no different. He wants to be loved for real. He wants your conversation, not just your admiration. He wants you to know him, not just serve him. He wants to be thought of, not just sung to. He wants it all, just like you do.

God, may my love for you be real. May I serve you in my soul: I don't want to go through the motions, but to be moved with emotion for you. Let my worship be about meeting with you, not about who I might see, or who will see me. Let my prayers be an intimate conversation, God, whispered straight from my heart to yours.

"'You shall love the LORD your God with all your heart, with all your soul, with all your mind, and with all your strength.' This is the first commandment."

MARK 12:30 NKJV

The first rule is usually the most important or essential. It's the one people need to really remember, even if they forget the others. The first rule is the one we want to keep striving to follow.

Rule number one from God? Love God. Love God utterly and completely. Most of us have the first part down: we love him. But is it complete, utter devotion? If we remember nothing else, if we accomplish nothing else, let us die still trying to get this one right.

God, here's my heart. Let all my passion and desire come from you and be for you. Here's my soul. I trust you to keep it for all eternity. Here is my mind. Take captive my thoughts, and lead them toward what matters to you. And God, here is my strength. Use it for your purpose. I love you, Jesus, with all that I am.

The Father wants to be loved utterly, with heart, soul, mind, and strength. Which of these do you find yourself most reluctant to give to him?

Fathom His Glory

> The heavens proclaim the glory of God.
> The skies display his craftsmanship.
> Day after day they continue to speak;
> night after night they make him known.
>
> PSALM 19:1-2 NLT

If you want to be amazed, go outside and look up. Our sky is an endless, ever-changing canvas of awesome. How many shades of blue can there be? How many shapes of cloud? Even on a gray day, how incredible is it that all that vastness is so perfectly hidden? Sunrise and sunset? Breathtaking. Glorious.

When is the last time you stopped to marvel at God's incredible creativity? Take some time, right now, to notice something glorious. Go study a spring bloom. Go read about the miracle that is the human eye. Go look at photos you've taken of beautiful scenery. Try to fathom God's glory. What a craftsman God is!

God, I'm looking up and I am amazed. One day may be gray and dark, but the next is rich in color and light. your sky is the most glorious painting I've ever seen. Sometimes I want to keep it as it is, to freeze time and remain staring at what you've created. Then I remember you are infinitely creative and I look forward to tomorrow, when you do it again.

The heavens declare the glory of God;
the skies proclaim the work of his hands.
Day after day they pour forth speech;
night after night they reveal knowledge.

<small>PSALM 19:1-2 NIV</small>

The night sky has its own mysterious beauty. Swathes of darkest blue and black are punctuated by pricks of light. How far away are the heavens seem. How large, up close, is that tiny, shimmering star? What the day proclaims out loud, the night whispers:

Look at this world! How vast, how lovely. How immeasurable are the stars, like the glory of the God who made it all.

God, you are truly awesome. One look at the night sky shows me how much I don't know. Stars that were there all day long are visible, glimmering symbols of your infinite creativity. As many stars as are visible on the clearest of nights, more are the ways you amaze me.

When you think of God's creation, what are you in awe of tonight?

Whole Again

*Once you were full of darkness, but now you have light from the
Lord. So live as people of light! For this light within you produces
only what is good and right and true.*

EPHESIANS 5:8-9 NLT

When we are sick or injured, a doctor will often take a look
inside to see what's wrong. A dark line on an x-ray indicates a
break in the bone. The dark spots on the MRI show us where
the tumor or clot is. For us to be healthy and whole, these dark
spots need attention and removal before they do more damage.

Similarly, sin creates dark spots on our souls. Jesus is
the life-saving light that wipes them out. He restores our
spiritual health and makes us whole again.

*God, I know I was once filled with dark spots. I felt them, and
I bore the weight of the sickness they created in my spirit. Then
you came with your light, obliterating every trace. May I be ever
grateful for your life-saving light. Because of you, I am healthy
and whole.*

Once your life was full of sin's darkness, but now you have the very light of our Lord shining through you because of your union with him. Your mission is to live as children flooded with his revelation-light! And the supernatural fruits of his light will be seen in you—goodness, righteousness, and truth.

EPHESIANS 5:8-9 TPT

When we pull up a weed, fresh soil gets turned up and new life has a chance to sprout and grow. Similarly, when Jesus removes sin and darkness from our lives, he creates space for his light to shine through. The more darkness he removes, the more brightly we glow.

It is our mission to grow brightly for the Lord, like a lantern. May the goodness, righteousness, and truth he placed in us draw others to his light.

What a beautifully modified picture of my past you paint, Jesus! Every dark spot, every sin, is replaced by light. Make me brave enough to glow, Lord. May my flame burn so bright that anyone mired in darkness may see their way to you and your healing, restorative light.

Does this picture cause you to see your past sins differently? Are there people who could be drawn to your light, were you to let it all shine?

A Protective Wing

Let all who take refuge in you be glad;
let them ever sing for joy.
Spread your protection over them,
that those who love your name may rejoice in you.

PSALM 5:11 NIV

Make a mental list of all the products designed to protect us.
In sports equipment alone, there's a covering for every part
of the body, from helmets, to goggles, to ankle braces. Home
security companies have a lock for every opening, from the
front door to the highest window. From bullet-proof vests to
bodyguards, safety is big business.

God understands how we long to feel safe, and he offers
us refuge more secure than any panic room. He spreads a
protective wing over our very souls, promising everlasting joy
to everyone who trusts and loves him. What bodyguard can
offer that?

Father God, you are safety. From outside threats to the ones I
create all by myself, I find refuge in you. What joy it gives me to
know you are guarding my soul! You cover me from head to toe in
your protection. In you, I have nothing to fear

Let all those rejoice who put their trust in You;
Let them ever shout for joy, because You defend them;
let those also who love Your name be joyful in You.

PSALM 5:11 NKJV

At a sporting event, you don't always have to watch the field to know who is winning. The joyful shouts of the fans, proudly adorned in their team's colors and chanting their team's name, can be telling enough. With every new point scored or shot blocked, their confidence grows, and the cheers get louder.

With Christ on our team, we are assured of victory. With him as our defender, we know we won't be vanquished. Since our victory is over evil, let us shout for joy!

Jesus, because I trust you, I rejoice. Every bit of ground you gain makes me bolder and prouder to be yours. Every attack you stop makes me more confident in our victory. I love your name, Lord. I rejoice in you.

What about Christ's strength gives you the most joy?

Something Different

> *"I am not asking you to take them out of the world but to keep them safe from the Evil One. They don't belong to the world, just as I don't belong to the world."*

JOHN 17:15-16 NCV

We know the out of this world pasta sauce was made right there in our girlfriend's kitchen, and that the singer's otherworldly voice came straight from her lungs. When something is too wonderful to describe, we search for the words to accurately convey its specialness.

As one who belongs to Jesus, you still go to your job, sleep in your bed, and do your best to love well and make a difference, but there is something different about you. You are wonderful in his eyes. A citizen of heaven, you are no longer of this world.

Jesus, I am yours. Though I don't belong here, I still live here and I know this means I need the Father's protection. How wonderful of you, Jesus, to pray that I would have it.

"I do not ask You to take them out of the world, but to keep them from the evil one. They are not of the world, even as I am not of the world."

JOHN 17:15-16 NASB

When we become Christians, God doesn't immediately take us from this world to be with him. If he did, how would anyone else ever learn of his wonderful, redeeming love?

Instead, we remain here, but with a peace and a protection that sets us apart. Through new eyes, we're able to see the devil's schemes for what they are. With a new heart, we're able to love our neighbors with a compassion that draws them near.

Jesus, though I long for the day you call me home to you, I know this is where I belong for now. I have people to love, and a purpose to fulfill. Help me be attentive, God, to all the opportunities you give me to make the most of my time here, and to bring more of my brothers and sisters into your light.

Are there aspects of this world you used to feel a part of that now feel hollow? Rather than avoid them, how might your presence influence others to seek true belonging?

By God

With your help I can attack an army.
With God's help I can jump over a wall.

PSALM 18:29 NCV

Scriptures like this one remind us of God's unlimited power. There is truly nothing he can't do. Things we could never do without him—like attack armies and jump over walls—are possible with his help. This verse is very encouraging, and very easy to misinterpret.

Possible and probable are two different words. It's possible that God will give you super strength and the ability to fly but it's not very probable. Just because God can, doesn't mean he will. And the reason lies right there in the word *will*. The five accomplished, articulate Christian women praying to be chosen as the keynote speaker at an upcoming conference will not all be selected. The two teams ardently praying for a win will not both go home as victors. While the Lord wants us to take confidence in his limitless ability, he also wants us to pray unceasingly to know and do his will.

Father God, I love knowing that within your will, there is truly nothing I can't do. Which walls should I scale, and which should I turn from, Lord? Help me to lean in closely, so I'll hear as you reveal your will.

> *By you I can crush a troop,*
> *and by my God I can leap over a wall.*
>
> PSALM 18:29 NRSV

Having covered the difference between possible and probable, let us now go ahead and embrace the boldness of this verse.

What enemy of your peace needs crushing? By God, you can knock it flat. What wall needs scaling? By your Savior, you can sail right over. Be empowered, friend. By your God, you've got this.

God, I believe you. I believe I can do anything—even scary, impossible things—by you. It is your strength, your might, your courage in me. By you, those enemy troops are going down.

Which aspect of today's verse did you need to lay claim of more, being in his will, or standing in his might?

Unmeasurable Joy

Our light affliction, which is but for a moment, is working for us a far more exceeding and eternal weight of glory.

2 CORINTHIANS 4:17 NKJV

Think of an Olympic diver, sprinter, or swimmer. The short time they spend competing at the Games takes thousands upon thousands of hours to prepare for, and yet it's over in a moment. But think now of what isn't over: the remembered glory of that moment. For the rest of their lives, those athletes can recall the joy they felt achieving their goal—the moment all the pain, sacrifice, and preparation paid off.

This beautiful verse reveals something similar about eternity. What seems hard and is causing us pain now, is just a training session for what's to come. We're getting strong, preparing to hold a glory we can't even comprehend. We'll live with a joy that cannot be measured and, unlike a brief Olympic performance, it will never, ever end.

God, life is heavy sometimes. Please help me remember these are training days to strengthen my soul for the weight of eternal glory. Remind me on the days I want to buckle under the weight that one day, I'll stand in more joy than I can measure.

We view our slight, short-lived troubles in the light of eternity.
We see our difficulties as the substance that produces for us an
eternal, weighty glory far beyond all comparison.

2 CORINTHIANS 4:17 TPT

If we were to paddle up next to an iceberg while kayaking, we'd probably be impressed by its size. If we were to dive below the surface, though, we'd find ourselves overwhelmed by its true mass. Thanks to Titanic, most people know the part of the iceberg that is visible from the surface is only a fraction of the whole, or the tip of the iceberg.

Measuring our daily struggles in light of eternity is akin to seeing the whole iceberg. The tip may look imposing, but as part of our whole story, it's nothing we can't handle.

Father God, up against your perfect, eternal plan, this earthly life is just the tip of the tip of the iceberg. I know the vastness, depth, and goodness of what you have prepared for me. rom that knowledge, I draw courage.

Think of a problem from your past that seemed gigantic at the time, only to be looked back upon as a small bump in the road.

Change the World

Since we have gifts that differ according to the grace given to us, each of us is to exercise them accordingly.

ROMANS 12:6 NASB

Are you creative? It is heartbreaking how many people believe that unless they have a specific skill like painting or writing, they are not creative. This simply isn't true! We are made in the image of an endlessly creative God.

What is something you do well, or something others admire about you? Your creativity may lie in your ability to plan a memorable party, whip up a glorious pasta, or bring a room to laughter. Your gift is the way you positively impact the world around you, and it brings the Father great delight.

God, I confess I don't always see myself as creative—especially when I consider your creation, or I focus on the creative gifts of others. Thank you for the unique way you allow me to shape and change the world. Holy Spirit, help me to discover more of what makes me unique, and to share and celebrate these discoveries with the rest of creation.

In his grace, God has given us different gifts for doing certain things well.

ROMANS 12:6 NLT

Isn't it wonderful how the Lord made each of his children individually? Think of everyone you know. What is their gift? How remarkable it is, how truly awesome, that God made each person according to his place. Every gift he has bestowed is a talent or trait he possesses himself.

The different ways to be amazing are as limitless as the ways he is amazing.

Father God, thank you for unique gifts and the never-ending ways you show us pieces of yourself. Assembling every special quality, every talent, and every passion of everyone I know, a picture of you begins to form—and it is beautiful. How vast you are, God, how unfathomably talented, creative, and good.

What talents do you most admire in others? What talent do others most admire in you?

Every Sweet Moment

People should eat and drink and enjoy the fruits of their labor, for these are gifts from God.

ECCLESIASTES 3:13 NLT

Do you savor your breakfast smoothie, grateful for the gift of year-round berries and the invention of blenders? Do you settle into your desk chair or work space and look around, grateful for a way to earn a living? How often, during a normal day, do you take time to enjoy your day, and to pause and acknowledge that life is a sweet, sweet gift from God?

Every moment is a gift. It's easy to lose sight of this, especially when hurry and worry are at the top of the to-do list. Take a second, right now in your mind, to add "enjoy" above them on the list.

God, thank you for the sweet, simple gifts in my life. I love the smells, tastes, conversations, and experiences you place on my path each day. Thank you, Holy Spirit, for helping me slow down enough to really enjoy them, and to see them for the gifts they are.

It is God's gift that all should eat and drink and take pleasure in all their toil.

ECCLESIASTES 3:13 NRSV

Read the verse again. God wants you to enjoy your life. This means not just the mountaintop moments, but also the ordinary pleasures in your day.

Breakfast with an over-scheduled teenager is a blessing. Enjoy it! Coffee with a girlfriend is a gift. Open it with gladness. Lunch with your love, birthday cake with coworkers, and even quiet dinners with no one but your favorite furry friend are meant to be pleasures, so take pleasure in them.

God, when I think of all the times I rush through my meals, failing to really taste what I am eating or engage with who is with me, I realize all the blessings I've missed, all the gifts I've left unwrapped. Help me to savor these ordinary moments, God, and see them for the blessings that they are.

Do you find it easy, or more of a challenge, to take pleasure in the ordinary moments of life? Invite the Lord to keep you attentive to these sweet blessings.

Lost in Joy

Wearing a linen ephod, David was dancing before the LORD with all his might, while he and all Israel were bringing up the ark of the LORD with shouts and the sound of trumpets.

2 SAMUEL 6:14-15 NIV

The David in this passage is King David, ruler of Israel. He has just seized one of his life's dearest opportunities — to dance with joy before the Lord and the ark. Were he a dancer, or a child, the picture might not seem so surprising, but he's a head of state. Can you picture the President of the United States dancing with all he has, completely abandoned in worship? That would certainly get the media in a frenzy.

We know from the rest of the story that David had his share of open-mouthed onlookers. Even his wife was shocked by his break with decorum. But let's not miss the beauty. David, the king, didn't care what anyone thought. Lost in joy, overwhelmed with love for his King, David danced.

Oh, God, how lovely it would be to know you as intimately as King David did, and to be as abandoned to my love for you that I could worship you without a thought for anyone else. Release me, God, from my attachment to the opinions of others. Let me sing and dance in praise of you with all the abandon you deserve.

David danced with all his might before the Lord. He had on a holy linen vest. David and all the Israelites shouted with joy and blew the trumpets as they brought the Ark of the Lord to the city.

2 Samuel 6:14-15 NCV

For David and the Israelites, this was the absolute best moment ever. The parade, the party, and the spectacle couldn't be too grand. Reunited with the most precious artifact of their faith, they felt reunited with the very presence of God. Joy ruled.

What was the single-best moment of your life? Perhaps you know immediately, or perhaps you need to spend some time remembering all the high points, searching for the one where your joy was most uncontainable. Chances are, you felt the presence of God that day, as well. How did you honor him?

God, when I remember the best moments of my life, I recall joy, perfect peace, and the certain knowledge that you were there. Was my celebration grand enough, Father? Did my gratitude reach you, or was my joy contained? Forgive me, God, if I held back and help me, Spirit, to dance like David the next time you grace me with your presence.

When is the last time you were part of a true celebration, with people openly shouting, dancing, and trumpeting for joy? In light of these readings, did the occasion merit such abandon?

How Rich

You are rich in everything—in faith, in speaking, in knowledge, in truly wanting to help, and in the love you learned from us. In the same way, be strong also in the grace of giving.

2 Corinthians 8:7 NCV

What is the first thing that comes to mind when you hear that someone is rich, and they have everything? Because of the culture we live in, we picture a lavish life of fancy clothes, expensive cars, and multiple homes. Notice Paul mentions nothing material in this letter to the Corinthians.

Were the standards so different then, or was Paul? What was he calling them to understand, and what is this verse speaking to us today? If your standards of wealth matched Paul's, how rich would you be? Instead of dreaming of a bigger home, what if we dreamed of a greater faith? Instead of coveting a newer car, what if we longed for a new revelation of God's goodness?

God, I know you don't condemn me for wanting the shiny things this world offers, but you do call me to want more than just things. You aren't disappointed in me for wishing I was richer, but you do encourage me to seek heaven's riches first. Thank you, God, for showing me continually what wealth really is. By your grace, may I be rich in everything.

*You do well and excel in every respect—in unstoppable faith, in
powerful preaching, in revelation knowledge, in your passionate
devotion, and in sharing the love we have shown to you. So make
sure that you also excel in grace-filled generosity.*

2 CORINTHIANS 8:7 TPT

Looking just at the first phrase of this verse, what do you
imagine? Just as this morning our thought turned to things,
but tonight they probably turned to talents. Intellectual
brilliance, impressive athleticism, and professional success
come to mind. Yet, we see that Paul's standard are attainable
for everyone.

We don't need talent to be faithful, money to gain knowledge,
or skill to share love. We only need Christ.

*Jesus, though you, I can excel in every way that matters. Infuse me
with your unstoppable faith. speak your truth through me. teach
me. Holy Spirit, overwhelm me with passion to serve and to share.
Make me excellent.*

Continue to pray through this list of attributes, inviting the
Lord to increase them in your heart and will.

Only the Beginning

We do not look at the things which are seen, but at the things which are not seen. For the things which are seen are temporary, but the things which are not seen are eternal.

2 Corinthians 4:18 NKJV

We need only recall any high or any low to realize how temporary things here really are. That day you thought you'd never smile again gave way to millions of smiles as your heart mended. The euphoria you felt upon first falling in love turned into a familiar, quieter rhythm, punctuated by occasional moments that felt distinctly not like love.

God really wants us to understand that this world is not our forever home, and this life is only the beginning of an eternity too wonderful to fathom. Our broken hearts will be utterly forgotten, and our deepest loves will be heightened and eclipsed beyond all imagining when we are united with him in heaven.

Father God, on the days I feel the weight of this world is too much to bear, remind me of all that awaits me. Remind me that I won't even recall these moments of pain. And, on the days I am convinced nothing could be better than the joy I'm feeling right then, flood me with the understanding that with you, I will feel all this and more—forever.

We don't look at the troubles we can see now; rather, we fix our gaze on things that cannot be seen. For the things we see now will soon be gone, but the things we cannot see will last forever.

2 CORINTHIANS 4:18 NLT

When is soon? Do you remember asking your parents that, knowing there wasn't a concrete answer? How long will I be waiting? Because the answer can't be known, the Lord invites us to shift our gaze. Past the current situation, past even our hope for the future, we are encouraged to look up.

Whatever has you asking, fix your focus on heaven, and see what hopefulness and light flood your heart.

Thank you, God, for reminding me I can always shift my gaze. Whenever I feel like I can't wait, can't endure, and can't hope, I can look up. Every promise of heaven is in my heart. Fixed upon eternity with you, there is nothing too burdensome for me to bear.

Does this encouragement feel easier said than done to you? Release your worries and let eternity flood your heart.

As We Hope

Rejoice in hope, be patient in tribulation, be constant in prayer.

ROMANS 12:12 ESV

If you really think about it, are we ever *not* waiting? Is there not always a blessing, healing or milestone in the distance? What a wonderful encouragement this is from Paul to make the most of these seasons!

While you hope, rejoice. In expectation of the thing you hope for, celebrate now. While you suffer, find patience. Relax, rest, and lean in to the promise that this too will pass. Pray, remain constant, and be faithful. Believing God's willingness and desire for you to have your heart's desire, bring it continually to him.

It's true, God, I am always waiting. Thank you for reminding me that as I wait, I have reason to hope, patience to persevere, and the privilege of coming to you with all my heart longs for. Because of how you flood my heart with hope, joy, and patience as I pray, waiting is a gift.

Be joyful because you have hope. Be patient when trouble comes,
and pray at all times.

ROMANS 12:12 NCV

God makes everything better. Waiting ushers in hope
when we surrender our concerns to him. Troubles produce
patience, giving us peace and serenity that defy our situation.
Even in the midst of a crisis, our heartfelt prayers can deliver
us beyond our circumstances, to a place of certainty.

As we trust him, as we come before him, and as we hope in
him, he fills us with joy.

Jesus, I need you. Without you, I can barely handle an
unanswered message, let alone endure wondering about and
waiting for an uncertain future. With you, all is certain. I don't
need to know when or how. The hope in my heart is enough. The
patience you provide is sustaining. The way you meet me when
I pray is everything. If this joy is how it feels to hope, I can only
imagine what awaits me when the answers come.

Which of these three encouragements comes the most naturally
to you? With which do you most need the Spirit's help?

He Is with Us

"Do do not fear, for I am with you; do not be dismayed, for I am your God. I will strengthen you and help you; I will uphold you with my righteous right hand."

ISAIAH 41:10 NIV

"Don't be mad, but…" When a conversation begins this way, we automatically brace ourselves for bad news. We know what's about to follow is likely to make us mad. Just as, "Don't laugh…" means what's coming is bound to be funny. What the speaker is trying to tell us is that they hope we'll listen to what they have to say without jumping to an emotional response.

The Bible often tells us to set aside natural instincts like fear and sadness and urges us to instead take courage and consolation from God. How beautiful it is to know he wants to replace our worry and heal our heartbreak. Imagine him coming close, whispering to you: "My darling child, I know this is hard, but it breaks my heart to see you like this. Let me take it from you."

Oh, precious God, how comforting it is to know you want my fear, my sadness, and my pain. Every worry of mine brings you closer, longing to take it away. Help me hear you, God, when anxiety strikes or heartbreak comes. help me let go of my feelings and take on your loving comfort and strength.

> *"Do not fear, for I am with you, do not be afraid, for I am your God; I will strengthen you, I will help you, I will uphold you with my victorious right hand."*
>
> ISAIAH 41:10 NRSV

Few things are harder to endure than being alone and afraid. God knows this. That's why he encourages us again and again to remember we are not alone. We are never alone. When the bad news comes, he is with us. When the waiting gets long, he is with us. When our knees grow weak, he is with us. When we fall to the ground too exhausted to keep fighting, still, he is with us.

He will lift us. He will strengthen us. He will never leave. He is with us.

God, why is it so hard for me to remember I am never alone? I sometimes think no one understands my quiet pain, but you understand. I think no one sees this nagging fear, but you see. I feel utterly alone in my weakness, but you are here. Especially on the days I am certain no one will hold me up, thank you, God, for proving me wrong.

How often do you feel lonely? Invite the Lord to flood your heart, knowing you need never feel lonely again.

Make Me Gracious

"Judge not, and you will not be judged; condemn not, and you will not be condemned; forgive, and you will be forgiven."

LUKE 6:37 ESV

Have you ever made a mistake? Of course, you have — everyone has. Maybe after making a choice you quickly learned it was the wrong one? Or perhaps you spoke without thinking, and, even as the words left your mouth, you wished you hadn't said what you did. Did these bad choices make you a bad person? Of course not. They made you human, in need of compassion, forgiveness and grace.

When someone does us wrong, God gives us the ability to quickly trade places with them in our hearts. How we would want them to respond to us, he invites us to respond to them. Would you want to be forgiven? Forgive. Would you desire the benefit of the doubt? Extend it. As we become known for our compassion, forgiveness, and grace, we become the kind of people who can expect those gifts returned when we need them.

God, only you are perfect, yet I find myself holding others up to your standards. I judge for things I myself am guilty of. I withhold forgiveness, though I know how healing it would be for everyone. Make me gracious, God, that grace would be given back to me.

Jesus said, "Forsake the habit of criticizing and judging others, and then you will not be criticized and judged in return. Don't look at others and pronounce them guilty, and you will not experience guilty accusations yourself. Forgive over and over and you will be forgiven over and over."

LUKE 6:37 TPT

Is there a habit you are proud of overcoming? How did you do it? Conscious, willful attention is vital when we want to change our behavior. We may think we have no control over our thoughts, but we do. Just as we can stop reaching for the phone the second we are bored, or the bag of chips each time we are frustrated, so too can we ditch our critical spirits.

Give up judgement. Embrace forgiveness. Adopt a habit of grace.

God, can it really be this simple? Not that overcoming a time-worn habit is ever easy, but can I decide to be less judgmental, or more forgiving, and have it be so? With your help, I believe I can. Starting tonight, I will to be the gracious, forgiving, and compassionate person you would have me be, Lord. I forsake the habit of criticism and adopt the habit of grace.

How comfortable are you acknowledging and laying down your negative habits before God?

Sharpening

As iron sharpens iron,
so a friend sharpens a friend.

PROVERBS 27:17 NLT

Spend a few minutes thinking about your best friends: those in your life today, and those you remember. What set them apart from your other friends? As you recall memories, moments, and qualities you love, consider something you may not have before: how do you feel about yourself when you are with them? Chances are, you rather like the "you" they bring to light.

Becoming the best version of ourselves is undoubtedly one of the most precious fruits of true friendship. The humor, compassion, adventurousness, generosity, and enthusiasm we so appreciate leave an imprint on us, and our unique qualities do the same on them. Just by being in each other's lives, we make each other better.

Lord God, thank you for my friends. Thank you for the marks they've left on me. Thank you for allowing their qualities to shape me, and mine to shape them. The care you take in choosing who to place in my life, God, is proof of your love. The way I am able to love myself around them is a gift with no price. May I treasure this gift—and these friends—forever.

Iron sharpens iron,
so one man sharpens another.

PROVERBS 27:17 NASB

Who but a friend can recognize a friend? What heart but one that has known pain can speak into our pain? Who besides one who loves can inspire us to love?

We need each other. Every quality we possess is one we have observed. Every mistake we have risen above is one we've been forgiven for—likely by someone who has also made it themselves. We are meant for one another: to season, to shape, and to love.

Father, thank you for the blessing of influence. You design is so perfect, God. We see what we want to be and so become it. Graced by compassion, we become compassionate. Met with love, we become loving. Filled with your Spirit, we shine your light.

What are your very best qualities? Pray for God to show you who influenced these aspects of your character, and who you can share them with now that they are yours.

Heed the Wisdom

*The LORD says, "I will make you wise and show you where to go.
I will guide you and watch over you.*

PSALM 32:8 NCV

Uncertainty arises in situations both crucial and inconsequential. What should I do? As children, we had any number of people to ask: parents, teachers, coaches, counselors, youth leaders, etc. As adults, the list grew shorter. Expected to have more answers, we tentatively reach out to friends, coworkers, spouses, and even the air. We forget, sometimes, that we can ask God—and that he will know the answer. Are we prepared to listen?

The more vital the question, the more vital it is to go to him first. In focused, sincere prayer, we must lay our questions at his feet. He may direct us to a person, a path, or a time of continued prayer. Whichever it is, our job is to trust our hearing and follow his lead. Obey the nudge. Heed the wisdom.

Father God, what should I do? I trust your wisdom. Remind me, patient God, to seek you first and to do what you say. Lead me to people who walk consistently with you and who want what's best, both for the kingdom and for me. Point me to the path you have chosen. Inspire me to pray daily that I remain in your will and learn from your wisdom.

*"I will instruct you and teach you the way you should go;
I will counsel you with my eye upon you."*

PSALM 32:8 NRSV

What's the best advice you never took? How do you know?
Is it because of how things turned out as you went your own
way? It's fascinating how resistant we are to advice, even
advice we asked for. Often, what we're looking for is someone
who will tell us what we want to hear, to affirm the choice our
rebellious heart wants to make.

May we remember, in these moments, that wise, unheeded
counsel. May we turn to our ever-watching God, and ask
expectantly, ready to go wherever he sends us.

*God, I can only imagine how much easier this road would have
been had I listened to every wise person you placed in my path, or
to the sound, loving advice you whispered into my heart. You see
me, always, and you see what's ahead. Will my heart to listen,
God, to your perfect, wise counsel.*

Who do you turn to for advice? Ask the Holy Spirit to help you
search your motives. Is this person chosen for you by God, or
by you, because they affirm your desires?

He Defines You

*Once again you will have compassion on us.
You will trample our sins under your feet
and throw them into the depths of the ocean!*

MICAH 7:19 NLT

I can't believe I did that…again! Why is it certain sins and behaviors just refuse to leave us alone? What is it about certain mistakes that we can't seem to learn from? You'd think the conviction and guilt we feel would be enough to avoid that sin in the future, but it isn't. Close behind guilt, often lurks shame.

Dear friend, if sin is serving up shame in your heart, bolt the door. Where guilt can serve us, shame only hurts us. Recognizing sin is healthy, and an invitation to confess to God and be forgiven. Believing our sin defines us—shame—is toxic. Read the verse again. The Father smashes your sins under his feet and tosses them to the bottom of the ocean. He does this because they don't define you; he defines you. And he says you are precious, priceless, and free.

Father, help me to remember that I am not my sin. Convict me and invite me to confess it so you can take it away, over and over, as often as it takes. I choose you to define me. I choose your perfect, priceless love and forgiveness, because they set me free.

> *He will again have compassion on us;*
> *he will tread our iniquities underfoot.*
> *You will cast all our sins into the depths of the sea.*

Micah 7:19 ESV

We see here what the Lord does with our sins: he tramples them with the hooves of a million horses; he sends them to the bottom of the sea, as far away as it is possible to be. How, then, do they make their way back to us?

Smashed to oblivion, weighted in the depths of the ocean, there is only one explanation. We go after them ourselves. We dive down, retrieve them, and piece their mangled parts back together. Then we sin, again. And he has compassion on us, again.

What a patient, gracious God you are, so strong where I am not, so forgiving when I don't deserve it. No matter how many times I retrieve my favorite sin, again you cast it out. Further and further, you separate me from all that would separate me from you. It's incredible, God, and the most inspiring reason I can think of to leave it where it lies.

Tonight picture God taking all that keeps you from him, smashing it beneath his feet, and hurling it in the sea. Feel the power and permanence of his love for you.

Uncomfortable

Whoever has this world's goods, and sees his brother in need, and shuts up his heart from him, how does the love of God abide in him?

1 JOHN 3:17 NKJV

For little ones, Biblical knowledge consists of a few exciting, inspiring stories. God made the world. Noah built a giant ship and kept the animals alive while it rained. If I ask Jesus into my heart, I will go to heaven. As we grow up—both as people and as Christians—we encounter verses like the one above: verses that, if we're being honest, make us uncomfortable.

Here's some more honesty: Jesus doesn't want us to be comfortable. He wants our hearts broken for those suffering from poverty, hunger, and oppression. He would have us be uncomfortable with having more than we need, so we would instead search eagerly for someone to bless with our excess.

God, you have blessed me with so much—more than I need. Still, I sometimes find myself wanting more. Forgive me. In these moments, remind me of those who have nothing. Make me uncomfortable with my comfort. Give me a longing to get as close to your generous, compassionate heart as I can.

If anyone sees a fellow believer in need and has the means to help
him, yet shows no pity and closes his heart against him,
how is it even possible that God's love lives in him?

1 JOHN 3:17 TPT

It's not any easier to read in another version, is it? What are
we to do with this, this knowledge that no matter how much
we are doing, there is more—so much more—that we could
be doing?

For starters, let us pray.

God, I don't even know where to begin, but you do. Lead me, dear
God, one step at a time, into a more generous life. Let me lose my
taste for luxury; let me long for less and less, that I may help more
and more. Point me toward the next good thing, Father, that you
would have me do. Break my heart wide open, god, that it would
never close to love again.

What step toward a more generous life has hovered in your
mind as you read these devotionals today? What support or
encouragement do you need to take it?

More than Words

They sat down with him on the ground seven days and seven nights, and no one spoke a word to him, for they saw that his grief was very great.

JOB 2:13 NKJV

Women love to make things better, comfortable, and right. We love to beautify and bless. We love to talk it out, to advise, and encourage. Sometimes, though, we can't make things better. Sometimes, there are no words. There is nothing that can be done. When we don't know what to say, it's okay to say that. It's even okay to say nothing at all. A hug, a look, and just our presence can sometimes say more than words ever could.

If you're familiar with the book of Job, you know Job's friends got a lot of things wrong. They speculated, assumed, advised, and accused, and none of it helped or changed a thing. But this part—the loving, silent presence—they got absolutely right. They saw his pain and they remained in it with him. Wordlessly, they told him his grief was theirs.

Father God, thank you for your Word! So often I find the perfect words in it, yet today, I was reminded that when I don't have the perfect words, I can simply be. When the sorrow is too great, my compassion and presence are enough.

Then they sat on the ground with him for seven days and nights. No one said a word to Job, for they saw that his suffering was too great for words.

JOB 2:13 NLT

One of the things that makes the invitation to sit in silence with those who suffer such a challenge is that it hurts to see people hurting. When Christ comes into a heart, he fills it with compassion. The sight of a suffering loved one is almost too much to bear. We'd do anything to take it away.

Before we blurt out clichés like "everything happens for a reason," which offers little comfort to someone in the throes of grief and pain, let us take our own anguish to God. Let us pray, asking him to quiet the pain we feel at witnessing a loved one suffer enough for us to be a comfort to the that loved one.

God, it's true; it hurts to see people hurting! Draw me to you and fill me with your peace, so that my presence brings peace to my hurting loved one.

How do you feel inside when your words can't "fix" something or someone? Ask God to supernaturally strengthen your heart so that you can say everything they need to hear—without uttering a word.

Please Only One

Am I now seeking human approval, or God's approval?
Or am I trying to please people? If I were still pleasing people,
I would not be a servant of Christ.

GALATIANS 1:10 NRSV

How much do approval, popularity, and fitting in matter
to you? A good way to test this is to ask how many different
versions of yourself there are. Would your work friends be
surprised to see the way you act at home? Would your church
friends be shocked to see the way you are when out with the
girls? The more consistent we are from one environment
to the next, the less likely it is we are wrapped up in the
opinions of others.

Paul the Apostle realized someone would always disagree
with him, so he chose to please only one: Christ. The happy
result of this choice is that regardless of what others said or
thought of him, even after they threw him in prison, Paul had
peace. He knew the joy of being the same person—a person
dedicated to pleasing the Lord—everywhere he went.

Dearest Jesus, I want to be one version—the best version—of me.
No matter who I am with or where I am, yours is the approval I
most desire. Help me remember this, God, when I am tempted to
compromise. Grant me the peace of knowing my life is pleasing
first and foremost to you.

Do I now persuade men, or God? Or do I seek to please men?
For if I still pleased men, I would not be a bondservant of Christ.

GALATIANS 1:10 NKJV

We have to choose. If we choose the crowd, we say no to Christ. Saying yes to Christ will eventually result in rejecting the crowd. Jesus and the world want different things from us; where the world wants us to prioritize pleasure, possessions and self, Jesus calls us to sacrifice, giving and compassion.

Let's not pretend this is easy. Instead, let us acknowledge the struggle, and invite the Spirit to lighten the load.

God, as much as I love you, rejecting the world is hard. Refusing to gossip, to over-indulge, or to covet sets me apart in a way that leaves me feeling isolated at times. Come near, sweet Jesus. Send friends who will love these things about me. Send your Spirit to reassure me my life is bringing you glory.

Where do you need help living to please God and not people? Ask him to help you and know that he will. When you fail, know that he has already forgiven you.

In Our Sight

Let your eyes look straight ahead;
fix your gaze directly before you.

PROVERBS 4:25 NIV

Someone with great potential who never realizes it is said to
have taken their eyes off the ball, or lost sight of the prize. To
say someone got off track or lost their way usually means they
made a serious mistake or life-altering poor decision.

Each expression alludes to a journey or path and suggests the
key to success is staying focused. Almost everyone begins life
wanting to be good, and to follow the path of integrity. With
time, our eyes wander, especially towards media and popular
culture, which is a sure way to stumble off the path. Realizing
society's lure but determining to keep our gaze firmly on
Christ is a wonderful way to keep the prize in sight and stay
on the path of wholeness.

God, everywhere I look are temptations to take my eyes off you and
the path I want to travel. The world tells me to focus on pleasing
myself, but I know that's an invitation to lose my way to you. Help
me fix my gaze on you, Jesus. Lead me down the path of integrity.

Look straight ahead,
and fix your eyes on what lies before you.

PROVERBS 4:25 NLT

Have you ever seen a horse wearing blinders? One of
the main reasons for this is so they don't get spooked by
something off to the side. By focusing strictly on what they
see in front of them, they are less vulnerable to distraction
and feelings of insecurity from what is going on around them.

God wants us to stay focused, not only so we won't be lured
off the path, but so we'll remember that as long as we move
forward with him in our sight, we are safe.

It's amazing, God, how everything you ask of me is actually for
me. As I move ever-closer to you, you remind me to keep my eyes
ahead—on you. Glancing off to the side would only disturb and
distract me. What's ahead is all that concerns me. Anything I
don't see, I know you can handle.

How much more peaceful would your life be if you had
"blinders" keeping you from glancing sideways or looking
behind? Invite God to narrow your focus to nothing but the
path he has set before you.

Let Justice Flow

*Let justice roll down like waters and righteousness
like an ever-flowing stream.*

AMOS 5:24 NASB

Somewhere close to where you are this very morning, is a girl with no home. If you have a daughter, she might be the same age. She may even share the same name, favorite color, or birthday. Evil people have taken her freedom, her innocence, and her security.

Stories like this are probably not why we read devotionals, but maybe they should be. We study God's Word to get closer to him, and this girl's story is weighing heavily on his heart. It's crushing him. Take these words from Amos and pray them for her and for every girl in this cruel, broken, ugly situation. Cry out to God, who loves her as fiercely as he loves you, and pray that her hope will be restored.

God, the injustices in this world are too great to number. Forgive me, Father, that I sometimes want to cover my ears and deny the truth. As someone who loves you, I know you expect better from me. Show me what to do to bring justice to the exploited, God. Free their bodies and heal their hearts.

Let justice flow like a river, and let goodness flow like a never-ending stream.

AMOS 5:24 NCV

After weeks without rain, a river still flows. Every day the waters move automatically and unstoppably. The only way to stop it is to build a dam and, even then, the river will simply flow in a new direction.

This is how our Lord wants compassion, rightness, and goodness to be: unstoppable, uncontainable, and constant. For the ones too afraid too sick too hungry or too hopeless to ask for themselves, let us pray it would be so.

Yes, Lord! Let justice flow, and not just like any river, but a mighty, raging, overflowing one. Let compassion spill over the banks so we are all drenched, even here in our comfortable, dry homes. Send goodness past the floodgates and into every heart, urging us to help a heart that is hurting.

Do you pray for social justice, or for victims of human trafficking, extreme poverty, and oppression? If you do not, ask the Lord if he would like you to start. If you do, ask him if it's time for you to do more.

Someone You Choose

A man of too many friends comes to ruin,
but there is a friend who sticks closer than a brother.

PROVERBS 18:24, NASB

Do you have a lot of friends? The answer depends, doesn't it, on how we define friend. Are we referring to those we follow on social media, people we would invite to a large party, those we meet up for coffee with, or the ones we would describe as "like family"? The latter group is necessarily small. True friendship requires an investment of time, trust, and heart.

Who would you rush to in the middle of the night if she needed you? Who would do the same for you? Who has seen you at your absolute worst—and still adores you? These are your true friends, those closer than a brother. If we try to pour this much of ourselves into too many people, none of them gets our best. Therefore, let us save it for those who give us theirs.

God, I adore my friends. Thank you for wiring us for love, and then weaving us together. No matter how I count or classify them, help me value my friendships. May I especially appreciate the rare, beautiful souls you chose to be my friends. The way we love and accept one another gives me a glimpse of the way you feel about me, and I love what I see.

Some friends may ruin you,
but a real friend will be more loyal than a brother.

PROVERBS 18:24 NCV

Whether you have a brother or not, and whether or not that brother is loyal, you know what this proverb means. A brother protects, defends, champions, and encourages, just because you are his sibling.

To find someone who chooses to love you this way, with no family ties or shared history, is a prize beyond value. Equally priceless is the discovery of someone you choose to stand up for, lay down your life for, cheer on, and build up. Friends are treasures.

It is amazing, Father, that you don't just give us the family we're born into, but you also lead us to a family of our choosing. You allow us to meet, and invite us to love, people we'd wade through floodwaters for, and who would swim upstream for us as well. Thank you, God, for the priceless treasure of friendship.

Who are your friends? How do you know, and do they know how much you appreciate them?

Bring Everything

Is anyone among you in trouble? Let them pray.
Is anyone happy? Let them sing songs of praise.

JAMES 5:13 NIV

Are you satisfied with your prayer life? This question doesn't refer to your Bible study, your church attendance, or your fellowship time, just your prayer life. How much time do you spend talking to the Lord, whether through the words of others or your own? Whether you ask for help the moment you recognize you need it or keep a list of things to pray about when you can really focus on it, he loves to hear from you. Whether a quick thank you upon receiving a blessing, or a more thoughtful recitation of all the day's glories at the end of it, he is delighted to receive your gratitude.

As many ways as there are to converse, there are ways to pray. He doesn't care how or when you talk to him nearly as much as that you talk to him. He wants to know your fears, joys, dreams, questions, and needs. He wants to know you.

Lord God, I am continually amazed by your interest in me. Every
need and every praise is music to your ears, simply because I am
the speaker. It's such an honor, God, to be able to come to you for
any reason, and know you'll be delighted I did.

Is anyone among you suffering? Then he must pray.
Is anyone cheerful? He is to sing praises.

JAMES 5:13 NASB

Do you ever feel like you are wasting a prayer or wasting God's time when you come to him with the ins and outs of your life? Be encouraged by this reminder from James.

God wants us to bring everything, from the best to the worst, to him. He wants to lighten heavy hearts, heal hurting bodies, and hear our joyful praises when he does. He wants to forgive us when we fall short, and comfort us when someone lets us down. He wants to hear it all.

Father, forgive me for thinking that what is weighing on my heart is not important enough to trouble you with. If it matters to me, it matters to you. Forgive me for forgetting to praise you for the million ways you make my life better. Search my heart and find it truly grateful for all you are and all you do. I love you, Lord.

Everywhere and Always

If I go up to the heavens, you are there;
if I make my bed in the depths, you are there.
If I rise on the wings of the dawn,
if I settle on the far side of the sea,
even there your hand will guide me,
your right hand will hold me fast.

PSALM 139:8-10 NIV

On the wrong day, this passage can be a little frustrating. It is not possible to get away from God. Wherever we go, there he is: guiding, protecting, loving, and seeing. So that thing we'd prefer he not see? It will be seen. Those words we don't want him to hear? Heard.

On another day, on most days, these same verses offer security and comfort. That fear we're too lost to be found? Never. He's already got us. That nagging wondering: have I gone too far this time? There is no such place. He's already there. All we need to do is turn and fall into his waiting, loving arms.

God, thank you for your steadfast presence. When I try to hide my sin, you see and forgive. When I fear I've taken things too far, and wandered impossibly off the path, you sweep me up and bring me home. What a comfort it is to know you'll never let me go.

If I go up to the heavens, you are there.
If I lie down in the grave, you are there.
If I rise with the sun in the east and
settle in the west beyond the sea,
even there you would guide me.
With your right hand you would hold me.

PSALM 139:8–10 NCV

As amazing as God's omnipresence is, his eternal presence is equally astounding. The Lord is not just everywhere, he is always. Before life begins and after it ends, he is there. As the day and as time itself begins and ends, he is there. Everywhere and all at once, he is there.

Isn't he glorious?

God, I love to try and fathom your unfathomable nature. Words that are hyperbole to humans—everywhere, always, eternal—are just a few of your countless attributes. I can't contain it, Father, the vastness of you, the permanence of you, but I can worship it.

Which is more awesome for you: the everywhere or the always? Talk to him about it.

Loved Not Feared

Better to be patient than powerful;
better to have self-control than to conquer a city.

PROVERBS 16:32 NLT

Remember who Jesus actually was: Emmanuel, God with us. As God, he clearly didn't need to walk everywhere, talking to and healing small groups of people, and speaking into lives. He had the power to move himself—as well as mountains—as he willed. Even on the cross, he could have silenced the jeering crowd and saved himself easily. He could have spared himself the pain and forced everyone to repent of their sins without ever leaving heaven.

Jesus had the all the power of heaven, but he chose patience. He opted for self-control over conquering. Why? Because he wants siblings, not slaves. God wants to love us, not to own us, and love takes time.

Lord Jesus, thank you for taking on flesh and setting the example
of a perfect, patient life. You walked when you could have flown
and made friends when you could have simply demanded your
way. You chose patience over power, love over duty, an death on
a cross over life on a throne, all so we could be with you as your
sisters and brothers.

He who is slow to anger is better than the mighty,
and he who rules his spirit than he who takes a city.

PROVERBS 16:32 NKJV

When the writer of Proverbs said one is better than the other, we can assume he was saying they were better off in life, not inherently more valuable people. The quiet life is a happy life.

The way of peace, patience, and grace will always yield more joy than the way of anger and power. Self-control will always feel better than simply taking. Though both are canines, a golden retriever makes a better pet than a gray wolf.

God, thank you for gentle reminders to keep my temper under control. Nothing I gain in a moment of anger is worth what I could lose. I want to be loved, not feared. I want to receive, not take. I want to be the master of my passions, not mastered by them. Though power feels good for a moment, I choose the enduring peace of a patient life.

What is the best way for you to remain calm in situations where you could become angry?

Choose Optimism

Rejoice always, pray without ceasing, give thanks in all circumstances; for this is the will of God in Christ Jesus for you.

1 THESSALONIANS 5:16-18 ESV

If only all the commandments were this easy: rejoice, pray, and give thanks. This sounds so achievable until you add in the qualifiers. Rejoice always? Pray without ceasing? Give thanks in all circumstances? This actually sounds hard. Is this even possible?

How do we rejoice when our hearts are broken, remember to pray when we're watching TV or laughing with friends, and give thanks for lost jobs, broken appliances, or troubles with family? God knows we can't think of him every moment of every day, but he does want to be our first and favorite thought. For every heartbreak, he wants to be our healer. Before we relax, he wants us to check in. For every disappointment, he wants to be the restorer of our hope.

God, I love how much you care. You want me to take every care to you and when I do, you turn it to joy. You want me to pray about everything and when I do, I find your answers everywhere. You want me to remember to thank you even for the hard things and when I do, you make them easier to bear.

Let joy be your continual feast. Make your life a prayer. And in the midst of everything be always giving thanks, for this is God's perfect plan for you in Christ Jesus.

1 THESSALONIANS 5:16-18 TPT

Choose optimism, the verse tells us. Feast on joy. Live on a prayer. Let gratitude be your constant state of mind.

And why not? Is there not always a ray of light to be discovered? In constant communion with the Lord, mighty joy be always nearby? If a prayer is never formally ended, might life indeed become one lovely, endless conversation with God? And if we are focused on him, might a reason to be thankful be always apparent?

I want to try this, God, right now. I want to see what life is like when I choose optimism. I want to know the peace of a prayer that never ends. I want to keep before me, always, all the reasons I have to give you thanks.

Imagine feasting on joy as you go to sleep tonight. Picture a banquet of choices for a happy life: with what do you fill your plate?

One Who Knows

Faith comes from hearing, and hearing through the word of Christ.

ROMANS 10:17 ESV

A rumor is just a rumor until it's confirmed by someone we trust. Anyone who ever played Telephone knows how words can get twisted and changed as they travel from one mouth to another's ears. If you want to know the truth, ask the one who knows.

This same principle applies to the Lord. We can't text him the way we could a friend, but we can read his sacred text and it will tell us whatever we want to know. Everything God wants us to know is written in Scripture. From who he is, to what Jesus said, to how he loves; it is all there.

God, thank you for telling me in your Word how to live and how to love. You show us who is the wisest and you teach us how we can gain wisdom. Thank you that you have the answers to all my questions. I need only ask you.

Faith comes from what is heard, and what is heard comes through the word of Christ.

ROMANS 10:17 NRSV

It's easy to forget the letters of the New Testament were actual letters to actual people in actual churches. When Paul wrote this to the Romans, he wasn't being figurative. He was explaining to them that they could believe the stories they were hearing.

The good news of a great healer who took on the sin of the world, all so they could be forgiven—was true. What the apostles preached, they heard—straight from Jesus. What Paul wrote inspired faith, as it does to this day.

Jesus, it's incredible to remember these stories I know and love are not just stories. They are truth. We have faith in what we read, because what we read is what you said, what you did, and what it meant. And that means everything to me.

Have you ever felt like you were hearing straight from Jesus? Has a message come through that spoke directly to your heart?

What You Need

The Spirit helps us with our weakness. We do not know how to pray as we should. But the Spirit himself speaks to God for us, even begs God for us with deep feelings that words cannot explain.

ROMANS 8:26 NCV

At a restaurant with a ten page menu, you are spoiled for choice. Choosing just one option out of so many can be a challenge. As the server comes to stand next to you, all that comes out is a sound somewhere between a whimper and a groan. Translation: Help, I don't know what I want!

There are times prayer can feel similarly overwhelming. We know we're hungry, but we can't quite identify the longing. Is it loneliness, emptiness, or simply boredom. Other times, we're in too much pain to speak. We ache, and we need, but the words won't come. Because he lives in our hearts, the Holy Spirit knows exactly what we're trying to say—even when we don't. It's one of the reasons he came to us, to explain what we cannot.

Holy Spirit, what a gift you are! You know me so well, better than I know myself. When all I can utter are cries and disjointed phrases, you turn it into articulate, coherent prayer. You take my need before the Lord and present it in a way I never could. Thank you for your intimate concern.

*The Spirit also helps in our weaknesses. For we do not know what
we should pray for as we ought, but the Spirit Himself makes
intercession for us with groanings which cannot be uttered.*

ROMANS 8:26 NKJV

Spending time with a baby and its mother, you quickly realize
they have a language all their own. The baby cries: "Oh, is she
hungry?" you ask. "No, that's her change my diaper cry," the
mom responds. "I see," you say. Though you don't. Is a cry not
simply a cry? Not to the one who knows you best.

The Spirit knows the difference between hunger, pain, and
frustration. He hears it in your tone and sees it in your heart.
He knows what you need, and he loves to bring that need
before the Father. Like a mother who knows her child, the
Holy Spirit knows you.

*I love this image, God, of your Holy Spirit attending to me as a
mother tends to her baby. How tenderly you love me, and how
eager you are to ease my hunger and end my frustration. How well
you know me, and how cherished that makes me feel.*

If you have any deep, unarticulated needs, spend some
time with the Spirit tonight. You needn't have any concrete
requests; he'll understand your every utterance.

Choose Life

> *"Today I have given you the choice between life and death, between blessings and curses. Now I call on heaven and earth to witness the choice you make. Oh, that you would choose life, so that you and your descendants might live!"*
>
> DEUTERONOMY 30:19 NLT

God is deeply invested in your choices. It's true he isn't on pins and needles to see what you pull out of the closet today but, make no mistake, the Lord will care about something as seemingly insignificant as your t-shirt if it is pulling you away from the life he wants for you.

He has many beautiful plans for you but the choice to see them fulfilled is yours. You can decide to live as a child of the King, or as a slave to your possessions and worldly distraction. Your Father loves you and he wants you, but he will never decide for you. Oh, that you would choose life!

Father, reading these words, the choice seems so simple. I am so certain I will always choose life over death, blessings over curses, but then I don't. Instead of spending time in your Word, I spend time on my phone. Over quality time with my family, I invest in fictional characters, in lives that aren't even real. Oh, that I would choose life, Lord! From the way I dress to the radio dial, help me choose life.

*"Today I ask heaven and earth to be witnesses. I am offering you
life or death, blessings or curses. Now, choose life!
Then you and your children may live."*

DEUTERONOMY 30:19 NCV

If there's not a picture, it didn't happen. Why do certain
situations call for witnesses, whether live or on film? It's so
you can prove you really did conquer your fear and jump off
that quarry cliff or took that oath.

God asks heaven and earth to bear witness to the choice you
make regarding the incredible gift he offers you because he
wants proof—not for him, but for you—of your decision. Heaven
and earth wait, hope, and rejoice when you choose well.

*God, I know how much you love me, how wonderful your plans are
for me. Thank you for calling all of creation to witness my choices.
Their disappointment when I choose poorly calls me back to you,
and their joy when I choose well makes me never want to leave.*

Sit with the weight of all you can choose to embrace or reject.
Ask the Spirit to reveal what it is that holds you back from
choosing well, and for the courage and strength to resist its
lure.

Real Love

*Little children, let us love, not in word or speech,
but in truth and action.*

1 JOHN 3:18 NRSV

It's puzzling, isn't it, when someone's actions don't match
their words. A friend may say you are important to her, but
when she repeatedly cancels your plans you start to wonder.
Am I really? A child claims to respect you, but consistently
breaks the rules. Your heart can't help but question. Do they
really?

Love is about what we do so much more than what we say. You
may not hear the three little words from a teenager, but her
affectionate, respectful manner says it for her. She loves you.
Jesus taught this through his ministry. He didn't tell the sick,
"I'm so sorry you don't feel good!" He healed them. When his
followers were hungry he didn't tell them to go home and eat,
he fed them. With his every action, Jesus loved.

*God, I don't want anyone to have to question my love. Inspire me
to be helpful, encouraging, and generous in all my relationships.
Let my words and my actions declare my love. let me love like you.*

Beloved children, our love can't be an abstract theory we only talk about, but a way of life demonstrated through our loving deeds.

1 JOHN 3:18 TPT

The Passion Translation offers a unique perspective on John's call to love with our lives: love as theory. Imagine it. What if all we ever did was talk about, think about and imagine love?

What a lonely world if we never gave love, received love, or lived love. The living, giving, and receiving are what make it real.

Oh, Jesus, let our love be real. I do think about it, talk about it, and imagine it growing and taking over the world, but don't let my love stop there. As I sleep, fill my dreams with people to whom I can give love. Remind me of all those who show me love and let me notice and be grateful for every loving gesture. You are love, Lord. Filled with you, let me live in love.

Where do you feel the Lord calling you to live out love?

Pleased

Put your heart and soul into every activity you do, as though you are doing it for the Lord himself and not merely for others.

COLOSSIANS 3:23 TPT

Few of us would choose to spend hours scrubbing dish after dish, rinsing glass after glass, and scouring pan after pan. And yet, if the Lord himself asked us to do it, we would throw both rubber-gloved hands into the sink most willingly. A simple shift in perspective can change our whole experience.

Whatever is before us, let us consider that he has asked us himself. We were chosen specifically for this life, this work, and this task that seems so tedious, thankless, or small. You are not volunteering in the toddler room, for example, just because your church needs you; you are doing it because God has asked you to free up an hour of their parents' time, so he might speak into their lives. Caring for noisy little ones, you have pleased your Father.

Father, I want to do all you ask of me. If I change my focus, I can see how my every task can be of service to you. On the days when working for others feels thankless, I do it for your thanks. On the days my job seems soulless, you invite me to pour my own soul into it, and to feel the pleasure of your soul.

Whatever you do, work heartily, as for the Lord and not for men.

COLOSSIANS 3:23 ESV

Imagine weeding a garden. What would inspire you to work with the most enthusiasm: the act of pulling weeds, saving the flowers the weeds are choking out, or knowing it's your final chore before vacation? Does it matter whose garden it is, whether you were hired or compelled?

Whether the task, the reason, or the urgency, whether moved by love or moved by duty, whatever gets you out there digging in the dirt, can it compare to the reward of pleasing the Lord?

Father God, even the work I love the most—what I do just for the pleasure of doing it—takes on more importance when I realize I am doing it for you. And those tasks I dread, the ones I avoid and then halfheartedly complete, are filled with meaning once I remember it is always you I serve.

What are the tasks you dread? How can this shift in perspective infuse them with new meaning, and your work with new life?

Strong Walls

*Those who do not control themselves are like a city
whose walls are broken down.*

PROVERBS 25:28 NCV

While, "Control yourself!" flows freely off our tongues toward
others, it's not easy to say to ourselves—or to do. From
snacking, to making it to the gym, to holding back a sharp
tongue, self-control is easier prescribed than swallowed.
Repeatedly, the Bible encourages us to control ourselves, but
why? Is it really so important we make it to kickboxing class?
Is it really so bad if we speak our minds a little too freely?
Yes, it is.

Like a city with no walls, we are vulnerable when we refuse
self-control. Self-control exists to protect us from things that
would do harm—to us or to others. No one needs to control
herself around a bowl of spinach, but we need that discipline
when we are around chocolate. We needn't hold back words
of encouragement and love, but we need to learn to hold back
criticism and negativity.

*As always, dear God, the things you ask of me you ask for my
good. You love me too much to watch me risk my health and
relationships, so you admonish me to use the self-control I possess
through your Spirit. Help me, Holy Spirit, to stand strong and
fortified against any choice that would bring harm.*

*Like a city that is broken into and without walls is
a man who has no control over his spirit.*

PROVERBS 25:28 NASB

Our mouths don't speak words we haven't thought, nor do our hands carry food to them without our consent. It is not your legs refusing to go outside for a walk, but your will. It is not our bodies, but our spirits we must control.

How wonderful of Jesus to send us his Holy Spirit to help us with this task. The human spirit is selfish and shortsighted, but the Spirit we're given in Christ sees eternity and works tirelessly to see us safely there.

Holy Spirit, you are so good to me! You know the strength of my spirit and the stubbornness of my will, but, because of your love and patience, you come alongside me and help me control them. With your help, my walls are strong, and my life is secure.

Which area of yourself do you feel like you have the least control over? Pray for the Holy Spirit to infuse with the will and the might to reign it in.

We Are Family

*"Are not five sparrows sold for two pennies? Yet not one of them
is forgotten in God's sight. But even the hairs of your head are all
counted. Do not be afraid; you are of more value
than many sparrows."*

LUKE 12:6-7 NRSV

Do you expect to change the world today? Is conquering
Everest, curing cancer or developing a life-changing
piece of technology on you schedule? You may not even
conquer making a healthy lunch, but that won't make your
day meaningless. To everyone whose life you touch with
tenderness or positivity, your day will be worth much.

You are worth much. You are of great value, deeply loved,
and irreplaceable. Your Father has said so. Do you need help
believing it? Run your hands through your hair. Each has a
number. Think of it! How intimately the Lord loves you.

*There are days, God, I question my value. How I thank you for
verses like this which remind me of how specifically and preciously
you regard me. I am filled with meaning and filled with your love
for me. As many as the hairs on my head, so are the ways I am
grateful to you.*

> *"What is the value of your soul to God? Could your worth be defined by an amount of money? God doesn't abandon or forget even the small sparrow he has made. How then could he forget or abandon you? What about the seemingly minor issues of your life? Do they matter to God? Of course they do! So you never need to worry, for you are more valuable to God than anything else in this world."*
>
> LUKE 12:6-7 TPT

Would you sell your mother? How about your sister or daughter? It's preposterous, insulting, and unthinkable, right? They are your family and worth more than any sum offered.

So much more unthinkable is that God would allow anything to take his child's soul from his care. While suffering and pain will come, rest tonight in the assurance that he holds your eternal soul right next to his heart, and he wouldn't let it go for anything.

Father, who am I that you keep me so close, that you love me so much? There is no price high enough, no sin great enough to cause you to give me up. We are family. I am yours.

Do you struggle to believe your pricelessness to your Father? Share this with him and ask him for a glimpse of what he feels for you. Rest among the waves of his love.

A Holy Calling

*The king was very pleased and gave orders for Daniel
to be taken up out of the den. So Daniel was taken up out
of the den and no injury whatever was found on him,
because he had trusted in his God.*

DANIEL 6:23 NASB

With every year of life, trust becomes harder to give. Before
we've even gone to school, we've learned a hard truth: the
world is not entirely safe. The only truly trustworthy thing in
this world is not of this world: God. In our minds, we know
this. We're called to trust him and deep down we know we
can, but there are days when it's hard to live this out.

Rarely has one been more called to trust in God than Daniel.
From the moment he was taken from his home to be a slave
in Babylon, his belief in God's faithfulness was tested, and
never more so than in the lion's den. We know the outcome:
he came out completely unscathed. Daniel's trust was
rewarded, and his story became a reason for our own.

*God, I pray for the faith of Daniel. Whatever you ask of me, let me
do it with the trust of one who knows you will protect me. Let my
faith be rewarded, and if you will it, let my story be a reason for
someone else to entrust her life to you.*

*The king was exceedingly glad and commanded that
Daniel be taken up out of the den. So Daniel was taken up
out of the den, and no kind of harm was found on him,
because he had trusted in his God.*

DANIEL 6:23 NRSV

Focused too closely on Daniel, we can miss the other miracle
in his story. Darius, king of Babylon, saw a mighty display of
God's power—and believed! History moved in a new direction
as Darius decreed worship of Daniel's God…in Babylon!

What might you be willing to trust God through, if you knew
"Babylon" might be changed for the better?

*Father, it's so easy to forget my story is not always about me. As
your child, I must remember everyone is watching. Each time I
trust you, and each time you come through, you prove yourself to
others who doubt. What an honor it is to face fear for you, God,
what a holy calling to trust you. Use me as you will.*

What "lion's den" might God want to use to reach the world
around you? Are you willing to go in?

The Better Thing

Martha was distracted with much serving, and she approached
Him and said, "Lord, do You not care that my sister has left me to
serve alone? Therefore tell her to help me."
And Jesus answered and said to her, "Martha, Martha, you are
worried and troubled about many things. But one thing is needed,
and Mary has chosen that good part, which will not be taken
away from her."

LUKE 10:40-42 NKJV

Balance is something of an ideal to aspire to in our culture.
We're often presented with an image of a scale: two
sides, equally weighted, hanging together. Maintaining a
consistent, perfect balance in our lives is a fantasy. If you're
a mom, the family side of your scale is undoubtedly heavier
than the everything else side. This is as it should be right
now, but it won't be this way forever.

Though a dream, or a super-fit body, or a clean house may
have risen a little out of reach for now, they are still on the
scale. Unless it crashes to the ground, you are in balance—no
matter how uneven the sides. And as long as you remember to
seek his wisdom and walk in his truth, it isn't going to crash.

God, you are so very wise. You know, always, when I am feeling
out of balance. Lovingly, you remind me: balance isn't about being
even, it's about being where I am called. With many priorities, and
even more dreams, you gently reassure me that as I go where I am
needed, you keep the rest aloft.

Martha was busy with all the work to be done. She went in and said, "Lord, don't you care that my sister has left me alone to do all the work? Tell her to help me."
But the Lord answered her, "Martha, Martha, you are worried and upset about many things. Only one thing is important. Mary has chosen the better thing, and it will never be taken away from her."

Mary has chosen the better thing. At least half of the people who read this story need to wrestle with this line. If Martha didn't "do Martha", how would everyone eat? Taken at face value, this is true. Her work was important—vitally so. It feels unfair to say that Mary's choice was better. The comparison trap is deep and dangerous, isn't it?

To Martha, Mary had chosen *not to help* but to Mary, her choice was *to sit at Jesus' feet*. Perhaps what Jesus wanted Martha to hear was not that Mary had chosen better than Martha, but that she'd chosen better for herself.

Oh, Jesus, I need to hear this and remember it. My decisions are my decisions, not meant to be held up against anyone else's. What would you have me do, Lord? Whatever it is, I know it is the better thing.

Search your heart regarding the comparison trap. Have you fallen in? If so, lift your arm to Christ so he can lift you out.

Example of Love

"I have given you an example, that you also should do just as I have done to you."

JOHN 13:15 ESV

In this gorgeous, humbling passage, Jesus has just taken up a towel, knelt on the floor, and washed the feet of his disciples. The most honored person in the room has just willingly, lovingly taken on the worst job in the house. "Do just as I have done to you," he said. If we listen closely, we can hear him saying it still.

Nothing is beneath us when done in the name of love. The lowlier the job, the higher the demonstration of Christ's love. Where would Jesus go to make someone feel his love? Why wouldn't we go as far? What menial task would he perform, that the beneficiaries might sense their worth? As his instruments, why wouldn't we perform these same tasks?

God, I confess to sometimes wishing for a big, important job to do for you. Why would you give me such passion and potential if only to wipe noses in the nursery, or change bedpans in a hospital? And then I think of you, holding the filthy, blistered feet of your disciples in your beautiful hands. Sign me up, God, I'll do whatever you ask.

> *"I have set you an example that you should do*
> *as I have done for you."*

JOHN 13:15 NIV

Imagine how it would feel to have Jesus' hands holding your tired feet. Consider how tenderly and carefully he'd remove the grime of the dusty road, protecting any blisters, and smoothing the callouses.

Are you able to appreciate it, or are you uncomfortable receiving such service from someone so worthy of being served? What is he teaching you about humility and love as he pours the warm water over your feet, gently dries them off, and ties your sandals?

Jesus, you are too beautiful. I almost can't bear it: this tenderness, this love. The way you care for me is the way I want to care: unreservedly, openly, and willingly. Release me, God, from any illusions I have about what or who is worth my time. If they matter to you, they deserve the humblest service I can offer.

Natural as Breath

*Don't act thoughtlessly, but understand
what the Lord wants you to do.*

EPHESIANS 5:17 NLT

Why did I do that? When is the last time you said this, or could have said it? There are times when acting without thinking is a benefit, such as snatching a running toddler out of the path of a moving car, but, more often than not, the things we do thoughtlessly are the ones we question and regret.

Living for a purpose, specifically for God's purpose, is a habit we would be wise to cultivate. Where to begin? In prayer. In studying and meditating on his Word. In the company of wise mentors. The more we pursue his will, the more likely we are to understand it. The better we understand it, the more naturally we will act in it. With time, we may even do so without thinking.

God, I don't want to act thoughtlessly, especially when my actions reflect poorly on you! I want the things I say and do to reflect you accurately. I want positive, purposeful behavior to come as naturally as breathing. Teach me the way of love; inspire me in the way of truth; lead me in the way of grace. I know this is how you want me to live.

Do not be unwise, but understand what the will of the Lord is.

EPHESIANS 5:17 NKJV

To be unwise is to be foolish or without sense. Here, it would also appear to be the opposite of understanding God's will. He hasn't made it difficult. The Bible is filled with examples of how he wants us to live and who he wants us to be. The Holy Spirit speaks directly to our hearts, helping us discern God's leading and approval. Wise friends and mentors willingly share their discernment when we allow them to.

God gives us so many tools to help us understand his will. To ignore all guidance and go our own way would be unwise indeed.

God, I love how thoroughly you dispense your wisdom. I actually have to go out of my way to avoid your plans, and, I confess, sometimes I do. Foolishly, I ignore the wise advice in your Word and try things my way. I understand how much better life is when I choose your will, Lord. Help me be wise enough to walk in it.

How do you discern God's will? How often? How successfully do you feel you walk in it?

Though We Fail

Because of the LORD's great love we are not consumed, for his compassions never fail. They are new every morning; great is your faithfulness.

LAMENTATIONS 3:22-23 NIV

A morning will always come where our first thought upon waking is, *I wish I could take back yesterday.* Perhaps you said something you can't un-say, or you did something you can't un-do. Look outside. While it's not an official do-over, today is a new day and the Lord has fresh compassion for us.

Every single day, including the morning after your most regretted day, God loves us as if we've never sinned, never made a single mistake. The slate is clean, and his grace overflowing. Forgiven the second we mess up, the very next second is an opportunity to start again. Though we fail over and over again, his compassion never does.

Oh God, how I love the promise of a new day. Like new snow, the morning light blankets everything dark and dingy from yesterday. Thank you for reminding me I am not my mistakes; every morning I am loved, forgiven, and new.

*The steadfast love of the LORD never ceases; his mercies never come
to an end; they are new every morning; great is your faithfulness.*

LAMENTATIONS 3:22-23 ESV

Is there something you always seem to be running out of?
Whatever it is, from milk to fresh berries to paper towels, you
run out because you use it all the time. What a blessing it is
to know it works exactly the opposite way in the kingdom of
God!

The more we love, the more his love grows. The more we are
forgiven, the greater his—and our—supply of forgiveness
becomes. The more mercy we are granted, the more mercy
exists. We never run out of God's blessings; every morning,
they are brand new.

*Once again, Father, I find myself nearly unable to fathom your
loveliness. How can you be so good, so generous, and so loving?
Your love is a well that never runs dry, though we draw bucket
after bucket from it daily. Your mercies stretch far beyond sight, far
beyond even light and sound. They are endless. You are endless.
Thank you, God.*

Is there a limit to what you will forgive? If you're human,
there is. Consider how awesome this promise of God's is and
sit with him in your gratitude.

Seek First

*"Seek the Kingdom of God above all else, and live righteously,
and he will give you everything you need."*

MATTHEW 6:33 NLT

Few sights represent contentment more beautifully than a
sleeping baby. Picture one now, swaddled up and lying in his
crib so peacefully, quietly, and comfortably. Then suddenly
he stirs. A full diaper, empty belly, or loud noise can bring an
abrupt end to that picture of contented peace. His needs are
no longer met, so the wailing begins.

The more we grow, the more we need, or think we need. A
baby is only concerned with their needs—food, sleep, and
safety. Yet, as a baby grows into childhood and adulthood, this
concern changes. Over time needs and wants are conflated.
We start longing for things we have no real need for and
our joy is at risk. Our Father wants true contentment for us,
and he promises we can have it. We need only focus on our
one, real need: him. If we seek him first, he'll take care of
everything else.

*God, I must seem like a wailing child to you at times with all my
wanting. Help me set the distractions of empty desires and run
after you with all the longing in my heart. You know what my true
needs are, and I am content to trust you with them all.*

> *"Seek first His kingdom and His righteousness,*
> *and all these things will be added to you."*

MATTHEW 6:33 NASB

Is it possible we are more amenable to adopting the first part of this instruction than the second? Seek first his kingdom. Okay, I'm in. And his righteousness. Wait, what? I can't just run after God and enjoy all his blessings? I have to pursue righteousness?

Are we really so surprised? What we're after is the contentment of the Lord. Did we really think we could find it without also pursuing a life that looks like his? As is always the case, his commands to us are for us. Righteousness, or right living, is living in love, truth, and peace. Doesn't that sound exactly like the kind of place contentment would be found?

Jesus, of course following righteousness will lead to you. Everything you ever did was right, and every word you spoke was chosen to help us do right as well. You told us to love, and you modeled love. You told us to serve and you served, to give and you gave. You told us to be light, and you, God, were light. Help me live righteously, God, that I might find all I need.

How satisfied are you with your life? Ask Jesus to fill you with a desire for him and to live as he lived.

Godly Friends

Though one may be overpowered by another, two can withstand him. And a threefold cord is not quickly broken.

ECCLESIASTES 4:12 NKJV

One of God's most precious gifts is friendship. Consider Jesus, and how intimately connected he was to his friends. Having godly friends to pray with, share ups and downs with, and seek sound advice from is one of the most important aspects of your Christian walk.

If you find yourself isolated, unable to remember the last time you just sat with a friend and poured into one another, you are vulnerable. We're here to hold each other up, and to keep each other strong in the faith. Whatever you need to rearrange in your schedule, find a way to make time for the life-giving gift of godly friends.

God, thank you for reminding me that friendship is not just for fun, it's a necessity. I appreciate the people of God you've placed in my life, and I want to make sure they know this. No matter how busy I get, remind me how much I need these relationships. They bring me light and keep me strong against the dark.

A person standing alone can be attacked and defeated, but two can stand back-to-back and conquer. Three are even better, for a triple-braided cord is not easily broken.

ECCLESIASTES 4:12 NLT

I've got your back. It means we're being watched out for, that nothing is going to sneak up on us from behind. What a lovely picture of friendship, standing back-to-back so no one is vulnerable to a surprise attack. Eyes forward, alert and watching, we keep each other safe.

Its undeniable things will still come at us. We are not promised a trouble-free life. But at least with good friends at our backs, we'll be ready to fight and defend.

Jesus, thank you for friends that have my back. They know me well enough to know when something's coming, and they break out the shields. Even more, I thank you, God, for having my back. Even if I am surprised, you never are. Prepared for whatever I must face, you build my defenses strong and prepare me to fight.

What life-giving friendships do you need to nurture? As soon as you can, make a date to do just that.

The World Will Know

As God's chosen people, holy and dearly loved, clothe yourselves with compassion, kindness, humility, gentleness and patience. And over all these virtues put on love, which binds them all together in perfect unity.

COLOSSIANS 3:12,14 NIV

Are you wearing compassion today? Did you put on kindness and slip into humility? Don't forget to button up gentleness and patience. Nothing you wear, from the most darling sundress to the cutest strappy sandals, will flatter you the way an outfit of these godly attributes does. Complete the look with head-to-toe love, and you'll be positively glowing.

It's a cute image, and a fun little metaphor, but what if we made it more than that? What if, as we dressed, applied makeup, and spritzed on our signature scent, we consciously clothed ourselves in the characteristics that identify us as Christians? How lovely would we be?

God, as sweet as this sounds, I doubt I can do this on my own. Will you be the one to drape me in compassion and cover me with kindness? Adorn me in your gentleness and patience and wrap me in humility. On top of everything, Jesus, decorate me with love. I want to be lovely, Lord.

God has chosen you and made you his holy people. He loves you.
So you should always clothe yourselves with mercy, kindness,
humility, gentleness, and patience. Even more than all this,
clothe yourself in love. Love is what holds you all together
in perfect unity.

COLOSSIANS 3:12,14 NCV

Just as we wouldn't expect a volleyball player to spike in
hockey pads, or a surgeon to operate in beachwear, as God's
holy people, it's important we dress for the job.

How can we show his mercy if we are not clothed in it? We
can't live out kindness, humility and gentleness if we don't
wear them. Patience is impossible to give if we forget to put it
on. And love? We must choose it daily as the crowning touch.
This is how the world will know we are his.

Jesus, I want to be recognizable as yours! I want to be dressed for
the job. Remind me daily what I must wear if I want to do the
work you assign me, if I want to reflect your goodness and glory.

Pray over this list of virtues to put on, asking the Holy
Spirit to reveal which the world most needs to see you wear
tomorrow, and then be sure to dress in it in the morning.

Allowed to Hurt

We rejoice in our sufferings, knowing that suffering produces endurance, and endurance produces character, and character produces hope.

ROMANS 5:3-4 ESV

Ask any mother, and she'll tell you the day she became a mom, she knew she'd gladly take any pain her child had to go through and endure it for them. Very few things compare to the agony of watching a child go through painful trials. The instinct is to fix, to mend, and to make it go away. It's a beautiful and noble instinct, but it's also not always what's best for the child.

As hard as it is for us to watch our children—or anyone we love—go through illness, injury, loss or failure, it's important to the development of their character. For us to become the people we are meant to be, we have to be allowed to hurt.

God, this is a tough one. I can't stand to see the ones I love suffer. I long to stand in their place, to keep them free from all manner of pain. Help me stay strong enough to let them persevere, to develop character, and to experience the beautiful hope born only in times of suffering.

We also boast in our sufferings, knowing that suffering produces endurance, and endurance produces character, and character produces hope.

ROMANS 5:3-4 NRSV

If you've ever prepared for a grueling physical challenge, you understand exactly what Paul was describing. Take running, for example. When we start out, nearly every step is hard. We're winded, we're blistered, we hurt. As we keep training, our lungs develop more capacity; tender blisters are replaced by tough callouses, and aching muscles adapt and even enjoy the effort. We've learned to endure.

Besides its physical benefits, training regularly develops a work ethic, discipline, and commitment. This helps refine and define our character. These qualities make us confident, bolstering our hope. We can do this! With Christ, we can do anything.

If only all suffering were voluntary, God. If only we had a choice, like going on a run. Still, we do have a choice in how to respond. We can lean in to you, knowing how deeply you care. We can take the gifts of suffering, each leading to something more wonderful, and we can grow something beautiful—even in a garden of despair.

Which is harder to endure for you, your own suffering, or that of the ones you love? Either way, grab onto this gift and know that something beautiful will grow.

A Steady Stream

The mouth of the righteous is a fountain of life,
but the mouth of the wicked conceals violence.

PROVERBS 10:11 NIV

How easily can you recall the most hurtful things anyone
ever said to you? For most of us, a list quickly comes to mind.
More often than not, something spoken by an adult whose
approval we craved sits atop the list. Even with the most
loving personal history, chances are you've been dealt some
harsh words. Before any more time passes, recall some of the
most affirming and encouraging things you've been told. A
well-timed compliment or observation can carry weight even
years after its spoken.

Which list came more easily to mind? Invite the Holy Spirit to
speak words of love and healing into any old word-wounds.
Thank the Lord for the beautiful blessing of the words that
brought life to you.

Father God, thank you for this reminder of the amazing power of
words. They carry weight that can serve as armor, or an anvil.
Bring encouragement, affirmation, and love from my mouth, so
my words build confidence and safety. Let my words be a fountain
of life, Lord!

*The teachings of the lovers of God are like living truth
flowing from the fountain of life,
but the words of the wicked hide an ulterior motive.*

PROVERBS 10:11 TPT

Would you rather be advised by a pastor or a drug dealer?
Sometimes, an outrageous illustration serves to point out just
how baffling some of our choices must look to heaven. We
choose the pastor, right? Obviously, we do.

How obvious is that answer, though? Does the media we take
in, from tv shows to music, flow from the fountain of truth?
What we allow into our heads determines how much truth
and life are allowed to flow there.

*God, help me take an honest look at what I listen to, watch, and
read. Am I taking in a steady stream of truth, allowing light and
life to flow freely through my thoughts? Or, am I polluting them
with images I don't need to see, words I don't need to hear, and
ideas I don't even believe? Remind me everything is a teacher, God,
and teach me to choose carefully from whom I want to learn.*

How closely do your entertainment choices reflect your faith?

Without Reservation

*"I give you a new commandment, that you love one another.
Just as I have loved you, you also should love one another."*

JOHN 13:34 NRSV

Before making the ultimate sacrifice and laying down his very
life, Jesus consistently gave of himself for the sake of others,
not just his friends and family, but also total strangers. His
only desire was to do the Father's will, which was to love
without reservation, hesitation, or thought of self. The last
thing Jesus asked his disciples—and, by inheritance, us—to do
was carry on his legacy. He asked us to love. More specifically,
he asked us to love like he did.

Love? We can do that. Love like he loved? We've got a way
to go.

*Jesus, following you is easy, but living like you is hard! I love, but
with reservation. I don't want to be hurt, so I sometimes hold back.
I love, but I definitely still think of myself. I'll give, I'll serve, and
I'll go, but I'd like to do it at a time that works for me. Forgive my
selfishness, Lord. Forgive my hesitation. Strengthen me to love
wholeheartedly and carry on your beautiful legacy.*

"A new commandment I give to you, that you love one another; as I have loved you, that you also love one another."

JOHN 13:34 NKJV

Women are no strangers to sacrifice. Undoubtedly, we've given something up for love. A hometown for a husband, a career for a child, privacy and independence for an aging parent, and a million other little sacrifices along the way. When you love, sacrifice is just part of the narrative. Still, Jesus calls us to more.

The only way to come close to the love he asks of us is to exchange our many desires for his singular one to do the Father's will. And then, the hardest sacrifice of all: to lay down our lives and trade ourselves for his.

God, I suspect this is one of those commandments you expect us to always be pursuing, and never to master. We love ourselves too much, don't we, to really attain the selfless, perfect love you modeled. Still, what a beautiful project: piece by piece, to exchange bits of our imperfect selves for yours. One desire at a time, to make room for our Father's will to rule our hearts.

Drift off tonight dreaming of ways you can love more like Jesus.

Desperate for You

Like newborn babies, long for the pure milk of the word,
so that by it you may grow in respect to salvation.

1 PETER 2:2 NASB

To help us understand how intensely new Christians should seek to know all they can about God, Peter uses the image of a newborn baby. Nothing matters more to a baby than milk; it's a desperate, greedy, primal longing. It's quite a picture, and no doubt one we don't quite recall living up to. We may have felt passionate but not quite primal.

Minus the kicking and the crying, perhaps, can we not relate? When we first tasted God's goodness, did anything matter more? Was anything as sweet? Met with the incredible truth of his perfect love, did we think it possible we'd ever get enough? Just as a baby outgrows the one-track neediness of infancy, so we mature in our faith. Less desperate, we're content to take him in slowly, savoring each morsel of truth.

God, thank you for the memory of what it felt like to be desperate for you. Though I love the peaceful confidence of knowing and trusting you, I do enjoy recalling those early, hungry days. Am I hungry enough, Lord? Do you still sense my need for you? If I've grown too comfortable, please infuse me with a fresh, desperate cry for you.

In the same way that nursing infants cry for milk, you must intensely crave the pure spiritual milk of God's Word. For this "milk" will cause you to grow into maturity, fully nourished and strong for life.

1 PETER 2:2 TPT

How hungry have you recently been for the Word of God? Is Bible reading a cherished part of your every day, just another task on your to-do list, or a hit-or-miss occasion?

How much of it lives inside you, familiar enough to encourage you or someone else when you need it?

Precious Father, I do so love your Word! I love the way that no matter what I am going through, thinking of, or wondering about, there is a passage of Scripture that points me toward encouragement, answers, and understanding. Give me a greater hunger, God, to get your Word inside me, have it build up and nourish me, and become a part of me.

Sit with your Bible tonight, rereading underlined passages and old notes. Thank God for his living, breathing Word, and invite him to increase your hunger for it.

Great Faith

The LORD was with Joseph and showed him steadfast love and gave him favor in the sight of the keeper of the prison. The keeper of the prison paid no attention to anything that was in Joseph's charge, because the LORD was with him. And whatever he did, the LORD made it succeed.

GENESIS 39:21,23 ESV

When looking for models of faith and perseverance, we needn't look farther than Joseph, son of Jacob, from the Old Testament. Stripped, thrown into a well and sold into slavery by his own brothers, then jailed for a crime he didn't commit, Joseph is a timeless example of how God's blessings can supersede our circumstances.

Because of his great faith, Joseph didn't just survive slavery and imprisonment, he thrived—so much so he became the second-highest official in Egypt. Joseph loved God so much, that he felt his presence everywhere he went. This allowed him to experience joy and success in the worst of circumstances and least likely of places.

God, thank you for reminding me that though many things are out of my control, I always have at least one choice: to love, trust and obey you. When I do this, you bless me with your presence. Because joy and favor accompany your presence, I am always free to choose them as well—no matter where I am.

The LORD was with Joseph and showed him steadfast love; he gave him favor in the sight of the chief jailer. The chief jailer paid no heed to anything that was in Joseph's care, because the LORD was with him; and whatever he did, the LORD made it prosper.

GENESIS 39:21,23 NRSV

Have you ever seen the joy of a young Haitian child, dancing for Jesus? Or the peace in the eyes of an African mother, lifting up a song of praise to her Savior?

The happiness that comes from those surrounded by poverty, disease, and devastation is from the Lord of their hearts, the One who lives with them. That kind of joy is a choice.

Jesus, I choose joy. I choose not to look around, but up instead—at the one who saves, sustains, and grants me peace in every circumstance. When things are bleak, I choose you and find hope. When things are great, I choose you and feel grateful.

As the day closes, bring your concerns and your thanks before the Lord. Be bold and ask for the joy that is consistently yours to take hold of—good days or bad.

Still Good

I say to the Lord, "You are my Lord;
I have no good apart from you."

PSALM 16:2 ESV

Is there something you used to enjoy that, when you look back on it now, has lost its appeal? Maybe it's your favorite sugary cereal from childhood, or a destructive habit you've overcome, or that girlhood crush you're so glad you didn't marry. With time comes wisdom and with wisdom, perspective.

Jesus brings perspective too. Once he's the most important part of our lives, everything in our lives gets better. Because of his kindness, we are kind and our relationships get better. Because of his patience we are patient and our worries become fewer. Now imagine him gone. Would anything, no matter how wonderful, still be good?

Jesus, you don't just make everything better; you are the reason anything is good. Because you are love, without you I'd have no love. You are the reason I see beauty; you are the source of all grace. I can't imagine life without you. Thank you, God, that I don't need to! Because I am yours, we will never be apart.

*I said to the LORD God, "You are my Maker,
my Mediator, and my Master.
Any good thing you find in me
has come from you."*

PSALM 16:2 TPT

Jesus isn't just responsible for the good things in our lives; he's also the author of the good things in us. Your tenderness, humor, and talent? That's Jesus in you. Your faith, perseverance, and loyalty? All the Lord.

You are wonderful. He made you so because he wants you to show the world how wonderful *he* is. Just by being you, you can lead others closer to him.

God, I'm not always comfortable listing out the ways I'm special, but when I realize they are ways you are special, I see them in a new light. Magnify the things that make me attractive to others, Jesus, so I can reflect your goodness to them. Allow me to see the ways you shine in them as well, so I will know even more of the ways you are wonderful.

List out the ways the Lord has made you special. Ask the Spirit to reveal every single one, then thank him for using you to shine his light.

Nothing Can Hide

The LORD is my light and my salvation. Whom shall I fear?
The LORD is the stronghold of my life of whom shall I be afraid?

PSALM 27:1 NIV

Were you afraid of the dark as a little girl? This fear is very common amongst children. It's interesting, isn't it? Though the room and its contents remain unchanged, and though nothing bad may have ever happened to them in the dark, they are instinctively resistant to being somewhere they can't see.

You may still fear the dark, at least on occasion. We want every opportunity to avoid danger and we feel safer when we can see where we are going. We want to know what to expect. With Jesus as our light, we do. He never burns out, never goes dim, and nothing can hide in his glow. There is truly nothing to fear.

Jesus, Light of the World, you keep me. You save me. You light every corner, expose every darkness. It is impossible to be afraid in your presence, Lord! Each time I forget this, flood my fears with your marvelous light.

The LORD is my light and the one who saves me.
So why should I fear anyone?
The LORD protects my life. So why should I be afraid?

PSALM 27:1 NCV

Help is on the way. Don't those words instantly make you feel better when you're lost or scared? Even imagined fears are quelled when we hear these words.

Like a child leaping fearlessly from a height because they know their dad will catch them, when you know Jesus is the light you're walking into and his arms the ones that will catch you, it is easy to jump. When you know the Lord himself is your safety net, what height could possibly be too high?

God, even in the darkest place, I remember you are my light and fear leaves me. Even when in dire need of rescue, I remember you are the one who saves me, and I am saved. Atop the cliff, I fear nothing because you protect my life. Why should I be afraid? And so…I jump into the arms I know will catch me.

Imagine yourself leaping—past every fear you have—into your loving Papa's arms. Don't you feel better?

He Understands You

*The LORD looks down from heaven and sees the whole human race.
From his throne he observes all who live on the earth.
He made their hearts, so he understands everything they do.*

PSALM 33:13-15 NLT

Do you remember how you first felt when you heard that God is always watching you and sees everything you do? Whether you were quite young, or it was just a few years ago, it likely made you a little self-conscious. Everything? What about all the things we'd rather not be seen?

Take heart. Yes, he sees all but remember, as the maker of your heart, he also knows exactly how it works. He understands you. Your Father knows the place your less-than-perfect moments come from and, out of love and tenderness, he forgives them. Immediately and completely, he forgives you.

Father God, I confess there are things I do that I'd rather you not see. But I don't need to fret over it. You made my heart, and you understand the reason for every regrettable word, thought, and action. You get me. You see, you forgive, and you set me free. Why would I ever want to hide?

The Lord looks over us from where he rules in heaven.
Gazing into every heart from his lofty dwelling place,
he observes all the peoples of the earth.
The Creator of our hearts considers
and examines everything we do.

PSALM 33:13–15 TPT

"Watch me, Daddy!" Like a dad watches his little girl on a balance beam, what a comfort it is to know Abba watches your life. Every time you leap and land perfectly, you feel his beaming pride. When you lose your balance and fall off, it's his loving encouragement that bolsters your courage to get back up and try again.

He's watching. He sees. And he's very, very proud of you.

God, just like that little gymnast on the beam, I love to know you are watching me. I love making you proud and hearing you cheer as I land a new skill. Just as much, I love knowing you see my wobbles and falls. It changes nothing about how you feel about me, which makes me eager and confident to try again. Thank you, Abba, for seeing me.

Run through your day in your head, imagining your Father seeing it all. What made him proud? When was he encouraging you not to give up?

Unmistakably Clear

"This command I give you today is not too hard for you; it is not beyond what you can do. It is not up in heaven. You do not have to ask, "Who will go up to heaven and get it for us so we can obey it and keep it?" It is not on the other side of the sea. You do not have to ask, "Who will go across the sea and get it? Who will tell it to us so we can keep it?" No, the word is very near you. It is in your mouth and in your heart so you may obey it."

DEUTERONOMY 30:11–14, NLT

A single, paved road through a dense forest is easy to follow. We don't stand on the road and worry about which way to go. The way is clear. It's obvious. Isn't this passage from Deuteronomy wonderful? It's almost amusing, isn't it? A modern translation might say, "It's basic addition people, not rocket science!"

Have you ever wondered how Jesus feels about love? Probably not, because he made himself perfectly, unmistakably clear on that front. When the Lord wants us to understand something, he makes sure we can.

Father God, though I love the way certain passages may take my whole life to understand, I also appreciate how simple you make the big things. When it comes to life, salvation, and eternity, you've made yourself unmistakably clear. Like a road through a forest, you show me exactly where to go.

> "This commandment which I command you today is not too
> mysterious for you, nor is it far off. It is not in heaven, that you
> should say, 'Who will ascend into heaven for us and bring it to us,
> that we may hear it and do it?' Nor is it beyond the sea, that you
> should say, 'Who will go over the sea for us and bring it to us, that
> we may hear it and do it?' But the word is very near you, in your
> mouth and in your heart, that you may do it."
>
> DEUTERONOMY 30:11–14, NKJV

I don't know how I know, I just know. I feel it in my heart.
It's the right thing to do.

One of God's most beautiful gifts to us is our conscience.
Innately, even before we ask Jesus into our hearts, a sense
of right and wrong lives there. Once we have surrendered
our hearts to Christ, his Holy Spirit gives us an even more
powerful understanding of how he would have us speak,
live, and be.

*Lord Jesus, thank you for your Holy Spirit. Living in me is the
knowledge and conviction of how to honor you with my life. I
carry your commitment to love, grace, and service in my heart.
These are the virtues you call me to live out.*

What are the things you "just know"? Thank the Lord for your
conscience and intuition.

Where You Live

LORD, *I love the house where you live,*
he place where your glory dwells.

PSALM 26:8 NIV

You know that house, the one where, every time you're in it you just feel good? It may be picture-perfect, without a pillow out of place or a stray crumb in sight, or it may be the messiest, most mismatched home you know. Decorations and dust bunnies have nothing to do with it - a house feels good when love lives there. When love lives there, so does the Lord.

A home where the Lord's presence is welcome is a home where we feel not just welcome but wanted. We feel at home. There needn't be devotionals on every table or Bible verses stenciled on the walls; his presence dwells in the presence of love—of those who love him.

God, I want my home to be that house. The moment someone walks in my door, whisper "welcome" to their hearts. Make my heart and table equally open, God, so every guest will love my home and recognize it the house where you live.

Lord, I love your home, this place of dazzling glory,
bathed in the splendor and light of your presence!
PSALM 26:8 TPT

Just as our homes don't need to be grand to hold his glory,
neither does the place we go to be in the presence of our
Lord. While it may be a beautiful church, with stained glass
and worn hymnals, it may also be a coffee shop where you
gather with girlfriends, trail you run on, or a lake you sit by.

The glory belongs to him, not the place. The light of his
presence is the source of its splendor.

God, anywhere I find you becomes dazzling to me. Whether my
church, my friend's table, or my own living room, everywhere takes
on a dazzling warmth when you come to meet with me. I love your
home, God, wherever I find it.

Where's your favorite place to meet with God?

Guarding Hearts

"I say to you, Love your enemies and
pray for those who persecute you."

MATTHEW 5:44 NRSV

There's no doubt this is one of Jesus' tougher commands, both to understand and to follow. If you've got this one nailed, then write a book: the rest of us could use your help! An enemy is defined as someone who actively opposes us. How do we love someone who wants to see us fail, and is actively trying to topple us?

This is a perfect time to remember the love Jesus calls us to is a behavior, not necessarily a feeling. He isn't expecting us to doodle their names on the backs of our hands because we feel love for them. What he is expecting is that we show love to them. Return rudeness with kindness, patience, and warmth. He's guarding our hearts, so rather than let the spirit of our enemies get inside us, he wants to keep us filled with his.

Jesus, your command to love my enemies feels impossible some days. the way some people behave, they're almost impossible to even like. What a relief it is to know that I don't need to feel all warm and fuzzy towards them. You want me to show them love through my actions, so I will do so by remaining patient and kind. Thank you, God, for guarding my heart.

"I say to you, love your enemies. Pray for those who hurt you."

MATTHEW 5:44 NCV

How do we pray for the people who want to ruin us? Surely, we don't pray they get what they want. Jesus can't possibly mean we are to wish them success in their efforts to hurt us. Thankfully, that's not what he means.

We pray for their hearts. We pray that through his grace, he changes them into someone who loves him and seeks to do his will. And yes, we pray for their happiness. After all, once he's remade their hearts and filled them with his joy, they'll no longer be our enemies, but our brothers and sisters.

God, I think I can do this. Filled with your compassion, I can pray for the kind of healing and restoration that makes an enemy a brother. Armed with your hope, I can pray for the kind of transformation that unites the whole world in love.

How different could the world become if all God's children dedicated a portion of their prayer time to those who do not wish them well? Might wars end, and many struggles cease, if we truly became one family?

Called to More

"You therefore must be perfect, as your heavenly Father is perfect."
MATTHEW 5:48 ESV

Taken out of context, this verse can be discouraging, perhaps even alienating. Why would Jesus ask us to do something he knows is impossible? Nobody's perfect. Why would he even want us to try? It hardly seems worth it. Haven't we been trying our whole lives to accept our imperfections, to believe we are loved and lovable just as we are?

In a word, yes. The perfection Jesus is referring to is not about flawless skin, high achievements, or a well-manicured lawn. You are called to be perfect as your heavenly father is perfect, and he is perfectly loving, perfectly gracious, perfectly just. And while it is most definitely still a challenge, it is a worthy one. With the help of the Holy Spirit and consistent, hopeful prayer, we can get ever closer to true perfection.

Father God, while perfection by any standard is impossible here on earth, I love this invitation to pursue your perfection. Because my heart and soul are the parts of me that will live forever with you, those are the things you are concerned with.

"Be perfect, therefore, as your heavenly Father is perfect."
MATTHEW 5:48 NIV

In Matthew 5:46-47, Jesus spells out exactly what kind of perfect he means. Someone acting in heavenly perfection doesn't only love those who love them. Even the worst amongst us does that, and we are called to more.

As his followers—his representatives here on earth—we are set apart. We need to stand out. What better way than to be kind to everyone, to show the love of God to everyone?

Lord Jesus, what an honor it is to be set apart for you, and to be called to a higher love. And what a responsibility! Strengthen me, Holy Spirit, on the days I'd settle for blending in. Remind me of the perfect Father I represent and help me honor his name.

If perfectionism is an area of struggle in your life, how does re-defining perfect make you feel?

Came to Save

When Jesus heard this, He said, "It is not those who are healthy who need a physician, but those who are sick."

MATTHEW 9:12 NASB

People who don't know a lot about Jesus' ministry might be surprised to learn how much time he spent with sinners. While technically all his time was spent with sinners, as we live in a fallen world, Jesus actively sought out encounters with people society considered undesirable. Tax collectors, prostitutes, and people with awful diseases feature prominently in his narrative.

Religious leaders were not just confused but appalled by this. Why would a messenger of the Lord waste time on people who clearly cared little for his law? Jesus' answer, beautiful in its simplicity, explains. He came to save. Just as a lifeguard wouldn't spend all day dragging happy swimmers back to shore, neither did Jesus waste his time on people who weren't drowning.

Thank you for saving me, Jesus! I was drowning in my sin, waving my arms, gasping for air, and you came for me. You brought me to the surface, saw me to shore, and set me firmly on the ground again. I owe you my life, Lord.

> *When Jesus heard this, he said, "Healthy people*
> *don't need a doctor—sick people do."*
>
> MATTHEW 9:12 NLT

Can you imagine someone having a heart attack trying to get into an emergency room that was filled with people who had minor complaints like splinters or a mild cough, and ran on a first-come, first-served basis. They'd die waiting for the doctors to get to them.

Like the most well-trained triage doctor, Jesus saw where he was most needed. He knew where he could do the most good—and he did it, no waiting in line required.

Jesus, you as you did during your time on earth, you come straight for the hearts that need you, the ones that are in danger of ceasing to beat without your grace and healing. You come, you love, and you heal. Thank you, Jesus, for going where you can do the most good.

Do you know someone who is "sick and doesn't know it?" Pray, as long as it takes, for them to open their hearts to the healing of the Lord.

Easier than Breath

Jesus looked at them and said to them, "With men this is impossible, but with God all things are possible."

MATTHEW 19:26 NKJV

As with so many of Jesus' teachings, context is important. Here, Jesus was talking about the heart. A wealthy young man had just asked him what he needed to do to assure his place in heaven. After Jesus explained he'd need to give up all his wealth, the young man went away. The price was too high.

Concerned no one could be good enough to get into heaven, the disciples asked Jesus if anyone could do enough. Only God, he told them. Only God can change a heart enough for heaven. And he will, the moment we ask him.

God, I used to feel defeated knowing I could never be good enough for heaven on my own. Then I met Jesus, and I learned that's the way you designed it. Only your heart is pure enough for heaven's glory, so only you can make ours worthy. And you will, no matter what we've done. With you, all things are possible. What wonderful news!

Looking at them Jesus said to them, "With people this is impossible, but with God all things are possible."

MATTHEW 19:26 NASB

It's so important for us to remember when Jesus spoke these inspiring words, he wasn't giving the apostles a pep talk before a big race, test, or trial. Jesus wasn't telling his followers that anything they dreamed they would accomplish.

He spoke them to illustrate how much we need him. What we want—to be good enough for heaven—is harder to achieve than getting a camel through the eye of a needle. But for God, who can make the needle bigger and the camel smaller at will, it's easier than breath.

Jesus, I need you. I prove this every day. Apart from you, I start to think the way the world does. Breathe life over me again, Lord. Send my burdens off on the wind. Save me from this world and prepare my heart for yours.

What aspects of the worldly life do you find the hardest to lay aside to follow Christ? Ask him to help you love them less.

Let Wisdom Pour

"To those who listen to my teaching, more understanding will be given. But for those who are not listening, even what little understanding they have will be taken away from them."

MARK 4:25 NLT

Imagine a runner who trains for a marathon, completes it, then stops running. After a year has gone by, she remembers how much fun she had on race day—how satisfying it felt to cross the finish line feeling strong and accomplished. She shows up to run the marathon the next year but, several miles in, she realizes she won't make it. She's lost her base. To go the distance, you can't just want to run; you need to train.

Following Christ is similar. You need to build—and maintain—your base. If you want to follow Christ, you have to be a Christ-follower. Read your Bible. Pray for understanding. Put what you learn into practice every day.

God, thank you for your Word. Every time I read it, I understand more of who you are. From this solid base, more and more of the world makes sense. I am strong. I can go the distance. Give me a hunger to keep listening, God, because I want to grow as strong and go as far as I can.

"For those who listen with open hearts will receive more revelation. But those who don't listen with open hearts will lose what little they think they have!"

MARK 4:25 TPT

You have two water bottles. One has a lid on, the other does not. Both are half full. Held under the faucet, which bottle will be filled?

To be filled to the top with Jesus' wisdom, we must remain open. Closing our hearts to teaching that feels inconvenient, or makes us uncomfortable, leaves them closed to teaching that would help us grow.

Jesus, I give you permission to take the lid off my heart. Let your wisdom pour, let your knowledge fill me to the brim, and let your love overflow. I want to know you so well that everything you say becomes music to my ears.

Is there a teaching of Jesus' you struggle to embrace? Pray for an open mind, so you can understand the heart behind his words.

Free to Love

*"God did not send His Son into the world to condemn the world,
but that the world through Him might be saved."*

JOHN 3:17 NKJV

Despite well publicized protests and social media campaigns,
Jesus didn't come here to rid the world of sinners. That's
good for us, since if he had, we'd never have been born.
Condemnation was so far from his plan, he even invested a
fair part of his time into stopping the practice. Search the
New Testament's red letters all you want; you won't find
among them a list of all the ways we're disappointing God and
a command to pass it on.

What you will find are repeated commands to love. Choosing
to reject someone because of their sin, or refusing to show
them the love of Christ, is essentially rejecting Christ. Again,
isn't this great news? Released from any obligation to point
fingers and assign blame, we're free to treat them as he did.
We're free to love them.

*Oh Jesus, what a beautiful gift, this invitation to simply love one
another. Freed by you from the weight of my own sin, I have no
pointing fingers. Called to your example, I have only open arms.*

"God did not send his Son into the world to judge the world guilty, but to save the world through him."

JOHN 3:17 NCV

Why do you think it is that so many people, including well-meaning Christians, either forget this beautiful, life-giving verse or get it wrong? What was the point of Jesus' death and resurrection, if not to end the ugly cycle of punishment and blame?

Any time a brother or sister in Christ perpetuates this cycle by telling someone their sin is just too great for them to belong, they're saying Jesus failed. But we know otherwise. Let us share the awesome news that guilt has died and we are saved.

God, how it must grieve you when someone professes your name and doesn't love, when they judge and pronounce guilty, or when they sentence a brother or sister to shame. May I never grieve you, Jesus, but rather welcome people into your love.

Is there a sin you tend to judge harshly, whether in your life or someone else's? Pray for the Holy Spirit to help you drop your gavel and give grace.

Welcome and Safe

*"I am the door. If anyone enters by me, he will be saved
and will go in and out and find pasture."*

JOHN 10:9 ESV

When you have a guest in your home, they come and go
through the door. Were they to slip around back and shimmy
in a window, you'd find their behavior odd, probably even
untrustworthy. If you have a security system, they'd likely
set it off. People who are where they are allowed to be don't
need to find a back way in or sneak out. They don't set off the
alarms and all is well.

When deciding what influences to allow in our lives, it helps
to see Christ as a door. Anything welcome, safe, and helpful
will come through the front door, while anything that needs
an excuse or compromise, or that needs to be hidden, is likely
to set off an alarm. The latter are things we are better off not
letting in.

*God, you keep me safe. Thank you for your presence as the door
all influence must pass through. Anything looking to sneak in
through a window, you sound the alarm for. Anything invited and
safe is in agreement with your will for my life. It—or they—can
come and go freely because they mean me no harm.*

*"I am the gate; whoever enters through me will be saved.
They will come in and go out, and find pasture."*

JOHN 10:9 NIV

Whether we've always followed him, or he is new to our lives,
there will come a time when we wonder if we can follow Jesus
and still have fun. Is choosing Christ akin to surrendering
our freedom? According to Jesus, the opposite is true.

Nothing is forbidden because no things have any power over
us. His Holy Spirit stands at the gate and fills our hearts with
a passion for that which will keep us safe and give us life.
Because of our good gatekeeper, we have free reign to explore
the whole pasture.

*Again, Father, I find myself amazed by the freedom of surrender.
When I give my heart to your Son, relinquishing all control, I am
freed from the power of sin. I can move freely knowing his Spirit
guards the gate. As long as I trust him, I will be saved.*

Do you feel as free as Christ says you are? Spend some time
praying about this with him.

Sweet Lasting Fruit

"You did not choose me but I chose you. And I appointed you to go and bear fruit, fruit that will last, so that the Father will give you whatever you ask him in my name."

JOHN 15:16 NRSV

Think of the people you love most in this world. Did you decide to love them, or did it just swell up into your heart? The feeling aspect of loving is a lot like breathing; it just happens. We can try to stop, but only for a short time. Love, like breath, is keeping us alive.

You may be convinced you chose to love and follow Christ. You may even remember the exact moment you made the decision. The overwhelming swell of emotion, purpose, and joy is something you'll never forget. But consider who gave you the desire? Who infused you with that purpose, that joy? Before you chose him, Jesus chose you.

Oh, Jesus, what an undeserved honor it is to be chosen by you! It's overwhelming, realizing you looked specifically at me and thought, yes, her. I choose her. You even chose the moment, God, when I would choose you back. You appointed the joy; you infused me with purpose. Having chosen to respond, I will never be the same.

*"You did not choose me; I chose you. And I gave you this work:
to go and produce fruit, fruit that will last.
Then the Father will give you anything you ask for in my name."*

JOHN 15:16 NCV

Not only did our Lord choose you, he chose your purpose.
Yes, he adores you and wants to bathe you in his affection, but
he also has work for you to do. Perhaps you already know how
you best serve the Kingdom, or perhaps you are still waiting
for him to stir your heart toward your divine calling.

Rest assured of this one thing tonight, beloved. You do have a
calling. It is divine, and you will succeed. Your chosen life in
Christ will bear sweet, lasting fruit.

*God, there are days I know this and feel utterly immersed in your
purpose for my life, and there are days I wonder if I've missed
the call, or if you've changed your mind about me. Because you
loved me enough to choose me, I know you believe in me, and have
chosen a purpose for me only I can fulfill. You will never change
your mind about me, and I will never change mine about you.*

This verse is a hefty one. Spend some time tonight meditating
on both its messages. He chose you specifically, and he has
meaningful work for you to do in his name. He adores you,
and he knows you are up to the task.

Healed Will Heal

We know that for those who love God all things work together for good, for those who are called according to his purpose.

ROMANS 8:28 ESV

Sickness, evil, disaster, and other tragedies are a very real part of the human existence. We can wish, or even pray, for them to skip our house, but bad things happen to wonderful people every day. Rather than give in to the fear the enemy of our souls would like us to dwell on, we can instead turn to the powerful promise in Romans 8:28.

No matter what happens, no matter how impossibly tragic and sad, for those who are called to love and serve our Lord, something good will be born of it. As we reflect on our own past pain, we see clearly this is true. From that pain, something came forward, something that would not have otherwise been, something *good.*

God, you are good. Because you are always with me, even into the most horrible situation, you bring something good. Just through your presence, hope, healing, and loveliness take root. I've seen it before. I know this is true. And though I'd prefer never to hurt again, I know that when I do hurt you'll be there again to make sure something beautiful grows.

We are convinced that every detail of our lives is continually woven together to fit into God's perfect plan of bringing good into our lives, for we are his lovers who have been called to fulfill his designed purpose.

ROMANS 8:28 TPT

God didn't choose your pain for you. Misunderstood, this verse can suggest he did. What he did choose is to make everything in your life matter, and to move you forward into the beautiful, divine purpose he has set for your life.

If you have to suffer—and you do—the Lord will make sure you have the chance to make it count for something. The comforted will comfort. The healed will heal. The restored will lead the broken to restoration.

God, on the days it hurts, I need to remember that you didn't choose my pain, but you do chose to use it for good. This is beautiful, and so very like you. When I recall the sadness, I also recall the comfort, and I am strengthened to comfort someone else. Remembering my brokenness, I also remember the way you put me back together. Even my most painful memories hold sweetness because of you, giving me a message of hope to pass on to someone who hurts.

Reflect briefly on your past pain and the beauty God was able to birth from it. If you are struggling, cry out to the Holy Spirit to show you where God is working for you even now.

Faithful and Strong

Be on your guard; stand firm in the faith; be courageous; be strong.

1 CORINTHIANS 16:13 NIV

In his final words to the church in Corinth, Paul gives this beautiful admonishment to help them hold onto the freedom they have found in Christ. A few thousand years later, this simple advice remains helpful. Be on your guard. Pay attention to the ways the enemy is trying to disrupt your peace and steal your joy. Stand firm in the faith. Temptation to compromise is a sure sign we are being messed with. Would you do or say it if Jesus was sitting right beside you? Well he is, so decide accordingly.

Be courageous. Over and over, the Lord tells us not to be afraid. Remember, there is no fear in love. If you are feeling afraid, reject fear and hold onto Christ—onto love. Be strong. What must you do to gain strength? Work, train, or try? Do it. Be strong.

Once again, God, I must thank you for making the really important lessons so easy to find and to follow. Help me remember who I am. I have all these things and more in you, Jesus. I will watch, be faithful, be brave, and be strong—in you.

Watch, stand fast in the faith, be brave, be strong.

1 CORINTHIANS 16:13 NKJV

Does the first part of Paul's advice seem easier to follow than the next? While paying attention and standing up for our faith may seem easier than being brave and strong, let's not be fooled into thinking we don't need to focus on them. Distraction and temptation are ever-present in our lives. Were this not true and were commitment and a watchful eye not crucial to our well-being, Paul would not have called them out.

As for strength and bravery? We have both traits, whether we feel them or not. Courage is a choice, and one the Lord empowers us to make. Strength is a condition only proven through testing, so let us rise to the occasion and prove ourselves strong.

God, why is it in the morning your commands and encouragements feel easy to follow and by the evening I know how easy it is to fall short? Distraction, temptation, and fear seem to follow me everywhere, and sometimes I lose focus. Holy Spirit, show me where I am vulnerable. Make me faithful, brave, and strong.

Do you memorize Bible verses? If you do, this would be a great addition to the treasures stored up in your heart. If you don't, why not start tonight?

Be Certain

We are pressed on every side by troubles, but we are not crushed.
We are perplexed, but not driven to despair. We are hunted down,
but never abandoned by God. We get knocked down,
but we are not destroyed.

2 Corinthians 4:8-9 NLT

If your life is really going well, especially if you find yourself amazed and wondering how it's all working out, this is a good indication that you are where God is and where he wants you to be. How did you manage to get everywhere you needed to be today? How does this month's bank balance have just enough, when only days ago you were unsure how you'd pay this month's bills?

If you want to be certain God is active in your life, just consider the astonishing fact that you are still standing, thriving, and rising to another day's challenges when you know, without a doubt, you can't possibly be doing it on your own.

God, the evidence of you in me is everywhere. thank you! I know I succeed because of you, I understand because of you, and I remain whole and strong because of you. Things can come at me, and they do, but they cannot break me, because of you.

We are hard pressed on every side, but not crushed;
perplexed, but not in despair; persecuted, but not abandoned;
struck down, but not destroyed.

2 CORINTHIANS 4:8-9 NIV

What did you overcome today? What pressures failed to crush you? What confusion failed to crush your hope? Were you mistreated or misjudged today? Did you still feel supported and loved by your Savior? Maybe you even got knocked down—hard.

How wonderful of our great God to pick you right back up.

God, even on the good days, as I look back on them later I see the many ways you kept me safe and whole. You are so good, God, so attentive! On the hard days, even on the worst ones, I see the ways you kept me here, believing. You are my hope, Lord. You keep me rising.

Sit with your thoughts until the Holy Spirit calls to mind at least one way the Lord kept you today. Marvel at his attentiveness and thank him for it.

What Would Jesus Do

> *Seek his will in all you do,*
> *and he will show you which path to take.*
>
> PROVERBS 3:6 NLT

WWJD? Though it's become a bumper sticker saying, it's still the most important question we can ask ourselves. It only takes a few seconds, and it can change the whole course of our lives. Would he donate, or decline? Serve, or be served? Gossip, or defend? Whatever Jesus would do, we can be assured it is also what he would have us do.

Other translations of Proverbs 3:6 say he will make your path straight. There are infinite roads to where we are going. If we happen to choose poorly he'll make sure we still get there but walking in his will assures us we are on the best route.

God, better than the best navigation tool, you always guide me to the safest, most direct route. I need only ask myself what you would do, and I know what to do. I know where to go. By seeking your will, I can always find my way.

Become intimate with him in whatever you do,
and he will lead you wherever you go.

PROVERBS 3:6 TPT

Like well-rehearsed dance partners, the more intimately we know someone, the more naturally we can follow their movements. A slight pressure against our palms and we step to the right. The gentlest contact with our waist, and we sway to the left.

Dance with Jesus, dear friend. Let him lead you into the graceful rhythm your life is meant to follow.

Jesus, how I love this picture of dancing with you! Lead me, Lord. How I long to know your heart so well, the slightest touch sends me twirling and spinning into the beautiful future you have for me.

How intimately do you understand the Lord's leading? Give in to the gentle pressure of his hand on your shoulder, and dance with him.

Tense

"I know the plans I have for you," says the LORD. *"They are plans
for good and not for disaster, to give you a future and a hope."*

JEREMIAH 29:11 NLT

Have you ever planned a big surprise for someone? Along
the way to the big reveal, moments of confusion and
misunderstanding often arise. You have to turn down their
suggestion to go to a movie, because you know what is waiting
for them at the restaurant. You have to pretend to forget your
purse, because you know what's waiting for them at home.
You know, but they don't. Things may get tense.

There will be many moments in our lives where we don't
understand what God has planned. We won't understand
why he's permitting what he's permitting and closing doors
you felt certain he'd fling open. Things may get tense. Just
remember, sweet friend, while you don't know, *he does*. And
he's God, so you can trust that hope and goodness will follow.

*God, I wish I could see the big surprise now. In the meantime,
I trust that way this whole, crazy life is eventually going to make
perfect beautiful sense. In the meantime, I'm going to trust you.
Your goodness, and your love, are enough to sustain my hope.*

> *"I know the thoughts that I think toward you," says the* LORD, *"thoughts of peace and not of evil, to give you a future and a hope."*
>
> JEREMIAH 29:11 NKJV

Few things hurt more than being misunderstood, especially when someone doubts our intentions. We know our thoughts, and that there was no evil in them. We know how much we want to see good things happen in the lives of the ones we love. Still, misunderstandings occur—mostly because of what's in their thoughts.

Any time you start to doubt God's thoughts toward you, remember he thinks you're lovely. He thinks you're precious. He thinks of you as his.

Oh Father, is this true? Do thoughts of me bring you delight? Do you dream of ways to delight me? Forgive me for misunderstanding you on the days when things are hard. I know how much it hurts me when my love is misinterpreted, and to cause you pain is something I never want to do. I love you, dear Lord. Thank you for loving me.

We all want to be understood, and to have someone "get" us. The Lord is no different in this regard. Any time you feel confused by him, ask the Holy Spirit for a revelation of his heart toward you.

Completely Loved

The LORD answers, "Can a woman forget the baby she nurses?
Can she feel no kindness for the child to which she gave birth?
Even if she could forget her children, I will not forget you."

ISAIAH 49:15 NCV

Far beyond what an earthly mother feels, your heavenly father adores you. Long past the time an earthly father spends thinking of his child, your Abba thinks of you. Greater than the forgiveness of the most generous of parents is his forgiveness for you. Your Father's love for you is perfect. It is complete.

Oh, what ungrateful children we are, always wanting more, continually asking for proof. And yet he gives it. He proves it every day, every moment. He never takes his eyes off us, never are we out of his arms. He couldn't forget us if he wanted to, because we so deeply are we engraved on his hearts, but he doesn't want to, and he never will. He loves us completely.

Abba, Abba. How I love this name for you. You are Daddy, Papa, the one whose arms are never too full for me. Your love is amazing. Your attentiveness is all I will ever need.

*"Can a woman forget her nursing child,
or show no compassion for the child of her womb?
Even these may forget, yet I will not forget you."*

ISAIAH 49:15 NRSV

As impossible as it is to imagine a mother could forget the baby nursing in her arms, God's Word tells us it's that much more impossible he could ever forget us.

How connected we must be for him to feel our needs so readily, and to attend to us so lovingly. How deeply we are loved! How closely we are held!

Lord this picture of your love for me is almost unbearably beautiful. I'm so grateful and humbled by the depth of your feeling. May your Spirit inspire me to return it back to you with all the love that's in me.

Imagine the incredible intimacy of the moment Isaiah uses to describe God's attentiveness to you. Feel him holding you, sustaining you, and loving you with more tenderness than you've ever known.

Wise in My Steps

Look carefully then how you walk, not as unwise but as wise,
making the best use of the time, because the days are evil.

EPHESIANS 5:15-16 ESV

Have you ever been driving, particularly on a route you travel often, and realized you stopped paying attention some time ago? You've managed to miss your exit or pass your turn, and now you'll need to turn around. Depending on where you are and at what time of day, these mistakes can cost valuable time.

When Paul encouraged the Ephesians to look carefully how they walked, he undoubtedly had something similar in mind. Imagine a long journey by foot, and how disastrous a missed milestone could be. Our journey with Christ is an important one, and every step is valuable. We are wise to pay careful attention to how we walk it.

God, though I value my walk with you, it's amazingly easy for me to lose focus. Though my intention is to follow the path you set, I get distracted by my own thoughts, or something grabs my attention, and before I know it, I've missed the turn. Make me wise in my steps, Father, so every single one will count for good.

Be careful how you walk, not as unwise men but as wise,
making the most of your time, because the days are evil.

EPHESIANS 5:15-16 NASB

As easy as it is to lose our way, how much easier is it to lose track of the time? Armed with good intentions and a plan, we set out. Then the phone rings or the computer pings, and we are pulled in another direction. Minutes or even hours later, we wonder where the time went.

Our hours are finite, both in the day and on this earth. In order to make the most of the time we've even given, we must be wise in how we spend it.

God, as the Eternal One, time means nothing to you and yet you never waste a minute. I can't really comprehend it, as I am so adept at losing track of the hours you've granted me. Forgive me, God, for being unwise with this precious gift. I am grateful for it. grant me the discipline to prove it by how I walk.

How often do you lose track of time? Ask the Lord's help in making the hours matter.

Perfect Timing

A time to tear and a time to mend,
a time to be silent and a time to speak,

ECCLESIASTES 3:7 NIV

Everything in its time. We've heard it, and we've likely said it, but how easily and willingly do we embrace it? Ripped jeans are one thing: it's not difficult to decide when to let a tear grow into a fashion statement, or when modesty calls for mending instead. But what about a snag in a relationship? Are we secure in our understanding of which ones should be unraveled, and which should be stitched back together?

Even when we know what to do, don't we sometimes allow pride, history, or other people's opinions to influence our decision? What a comfort it is to take these questions to our Lord. The answer he gives will always be right. His timing can always be trusted.

Father, I confess I've hung on to friendships well past their time out of what I thought was loyalty, but what you revealed to me was pride. I didn't want to fail. I sense too that I've torn other relationships down over a trifle, when to mend them would have blessed both our lives. Thank you for reminding me to take all my decisions to you. Your judgement, and your timing, are perfect.

A time to tear apart and a time to sew together;
a time to be silent and a time to speak.

ECCLESIASTES 3:7 NASB

How often do you speak, then wish you'd held your tongue? If only we could nail the advice in this verse! Maybe we can. Have you ever, even once, spoken when you shouldn't while praying? No? It's amazing how easy it is to forget to come to the Lord in the moments we need him the most.

From now on, the second you feel anger, defensiveness, or spite rise, pray. Pray for wisdom. If the Lord gives you words to say, speak them. If he prompts you instead to listen, settle back and open your heart to hearing.

God, help me with my tongue. Give me a wisdom and economy with words so that when I speak, it is worth listening to. Make my silence meaningful as well, Father, by helping me to listen. Show me when words would stitch together and when they would tear apart and let this be my guide.

Ask the Lord to begin convicting you each time you speak without thought. Invite his Holy Spirit to teach you to listen, rather than wait to talk, and to teach you to recognize immediately the intention and likely effect of the words you speak.

True Desire

He went on a little farther and fell to the ground. He prayed that, if it were possible, the awful hour awaiting him might pass him by. "Abba, Father," he cried out, "everything is possible for you. Please take this cup of suffering away from me. Yet I want your will to be done, not mine."

MARK 14:35-36 NLT

Wholly devoted to his Father, dedicated to doing his will, Jesus' own needs still cried out for relief. His human side was suffering. If there is another way, I'd really like to take it, Father! Still, he knew that despite his current desire, the Father's way was best. Even if he couldn't feel it in the moment, he knew God's will was his heart's true desire.

Do you ever find yourself praying in this dual manner? I really want this, Father, but only if you want it for me! These are God's favorite prayers. He wants to know our feelings and desires, and nothing pleases him more than our honesty— except for our trust. Telling him what we want and then asking him to withhold it if it's not his will pays him the highest respect.

Father, help me to pray like Jesus: honestly, yet submitted to your will. Remind me that whatever I may think I want or need in the moment, it will only satisfy my heart if it's what you will for me.

Going a little farther, he fell on the ground and prayed that, if it were possible, the hour might pass from him. And he said, "Abba, Father, all things are possible for you. Remove this cup from me. Yet not what I will, but what you will."

MARK 14:35-36 ESV

Jesus may have never been more human than when he prayed, and never so beautifully vulnerable than in this hour of anguish. Jesus knew exactly what was going to happen. He knew the pain of the whips, of the crowd's rejection, and of the nails. He knew.

Had he changed his mind, his Father would have saved him. He knew this too. But because he also knew we'd all be lost without him, he submitted. Not what I will, but what you will. He knew, and still he went.

Oh, Jesus, I can't imagine what your agony in the garden was like. I have a hard time forcing myself to tear off a Band-Aid because I know the pain. You knew the worst pain imaginable, and yet you endured it for me. Let me say this and mean it, God, for the rest of my life: Not what I will, but what you will.

How often do you pray for God's will, knowing it may contradict your own? Pray now for the courage to pray this way every time.

Abundance Follows

The plans of the diligent lead surely to abundance,
but everyone who is hasty comes only to want.

PROVERBS 21:5 NRSV

Take your time. It's good advice, especially when we follow it. Rushing through something just to get over with, or to be the first one to finish, seldom results in work we can be proud of. If we make this a pattern for our lives, we're likely to come up wanting.

If we plan our steps and make prayerful, informed decisions, our lives will bear the fruit of our diligence. Researching airfares instead of buying the first ticket we see can save us hundreds of dollars. Getting to know a neighborhood—its schools, safety and amenities—before buying a home can change our family's entire future. So, let us be diligent, that abundance may follow.

God, how odd you must find our haste. You've given us time, made wisdom available, and yet we sometimes rush in—refusing to plan and forgetting to pray. You let us have our way, though, and we come up in want. How much better it is, Father, when we take the time you gave us, and avail ourselves of wisdom. Help us slow down, God, and find the abundant way.

Good planning and hard work lead to prosperity,
but hasty shortcuts lead to poverty.

PROVERBS 21:5 NLT

If lists, calendars, and flowcharts rule our days, verses like this one are great news. If we love making plans, it's affirming to read that it's pleasing to God and is leading us to prosperity.

However, plan with care. Without prayer and remaining close to God's will, we can run ahead of him—and find ourselves lost.

Father, I love to plan and I'm excited to move forward, but only if you are with me. Tell me, Master Planner, are you pleased with my plan? Is that your voice telling me to go forward, or is it my will? Help me to move slowly and stay attentive to your voice, lest I run ahead of you and lose my way. More than anything, God, I want to plan to please you.

Are you a planner, or a jump-in-headfirst gal? Sit with this verse before the Lord and ask for confirmation that your approach is in line with his will and is leading you to prosperity.

Until We Know

*The Lord is not slow to fulfill his promise as some count slowness,
but is patient toward you, not wishing that any should perish,
but that all should reach repentance.*

2 PETER 3:9 ESV

Following Jesus' death and resurrection, many people
expected the final judgement to come shortly after. Each day,
they lived in anticipation of his glorious return, eager to join
him in heaven. As more time passed, they began wonder why
it was taking so long. Because they were ready, they assumed
God was ready too.

God is ready, but he is also willing to wait—as long as it takes—
until all his children are ready. He loves each and every soul
he has breathed life into and won't be ending the world as we
know it until we all know him.

*God, as eager as I am to be with you in heaven, I'm glad you are
willing to wait. So many wonderful people I know just haven't
realized their need for you, and it would be tragic for them to miss
out. Thank you for loving us all so much that you're waiting for us
all to turn to you.*

The Lord is not slow in doing what he promised—the way some people understand slowness. But God is being patient with you. He does not want anyone to be lost, but he wants all people to change their hearts and lives.

2 PETER 3:9 NCV

What if God decided that today was the day he's coming back? How many souls would be lost, whether out of rebellion or ignorance? If eternity started today, would you spend it without someone who matters to you?

How wonderful it is to know we have a patient, loving God! Because he loves us, he wants to make sure that we who belong to him have time to share his heart—and that those who don't yet know it will realize they too are his.

God, I thank you for your patience so often because I so often need it. Never am I more grateful, though, than when I realize how many others need it even more. My future is secure; I'll be with you in heaven. Others, though, including some people I love, have not yet accepted the incredible gift of your grace. Thank you, God, for waiting until they do.

Is the Lord putting someone who doesn't know him yet on your heart today? Ask him how he wants you to respond.

Eager for More

Let us move beyond the elementary teachings about Christ and be taken forward to maturity, not laying again the foundation of repentance from acts that lead to death and of faith in God.

HEBREWS 6:1 NIV

Can you imagine repeating first grade? While nap time and recess may sound like a welcome respite from our hectic lives, it's doubtful we'd stay content for long. Once we've absorbed an elementary level of knowledge, our minds hunger for more.

How much more then must our spirits hunger? How well is yours being fed? Just as you wouldn't stay in first grade forever, neither would you be content with a pastor who taught the same lesson every week, or a Bible study that never moved beyond Genesis. God is wonderfully complex, and eager to reveal more of himself to you each time you meet with him.

God, I love what I know of you and I'm eager for more. It's exciting to know that no matter how much I learn, there will always be more. There is no end to how high I can build on a foundation of faith and repentance, and I'm grateful that as I build, I'm brought that much closer to you.

Now is the time for us to progress beyond the basic message of Christ and advance into perfection. The foundation has already been laid for us to build upon: turning away from our dead works to embrace faith in God.

HEBREWS 6:1 TPT

God has an unlimited capacity to teach and enlighten us. Even a verse you've read a dozen times can take on a new meaning when you listen closely to his voice.

Think of your faith as a fishing boat. The further you row from shore, the bigger the fish get. Grab the oars and row.

God, I don't want to be satisfied with knowing about you, I want to know you. I'm delighted to have been saved, and now I want to savor your complexity. I'm grateful to have turned my back on sin, but now I'm ready to turn toward a life of great meaning. I'm ready, God, to go far from the shore.

If your knowledge of Christ were a grade in school, what would it be? How about your closeness to him? Whether you feel you're at primary school or PhD level, invite him to take you even further from shore.

We Mean Well

"You hypocrite, first take the log out of your own eye, and then you will see clearly to take the speck out of your brother's eye."

MATTHEW 7:5 NASB

Picturing a log protruding from your eye be a bit comical but it should also be convicting. If you aren't convicted, head to a mirror because there's something stuck in your eye. Instead of recalling all the times we felt victimized by a hypocrite, let's try to remember the times we were a hypocrite.

Jesus taught this same lesson another way. Remember the woman who was dragged from her house by an indignant mob prepared to stone her to death? Once Jesus invited them to examine their own sin, how many still threw a rock?

God, thank you for making sure I never get too comfortable with my own righteousness. If I'm spending more time thinking about other people's faults than my own, show me to a mirror. Keep my hands far from the eyes of my friends, Jesus, until the day my own are clear.

> *"You're being hypercritical and a hypocrite! First acknowledge your own 'blind spots' and deal with them, and then you'll be capable of dealing with the 'blind spot' of your friend."*
>
> MATTHEW 7:5 TPT

When we want to call out our friend on their sin, it's because we mean well, right? Seeing that friend mired in a sin, we want to help her out of it. Jesus knows this, and he gives us a way to do just that.

We can pray for her. Privately, just between us and the Lord, we can ask him to show her a better way. After that, it's time to trust him, and to be prepared for whatever he decides to show us about ourselves

I do mean well, Lord. It hurts me to see someone hurting themselves by a sin they don't recognize. What you help me remember is that I am not unique in this. Even as I pray for my friend, somewhere a friend is probably talking to you about me. Thank you, Jesus, for her well-meaning heart and for the humbling work you are doing in mine.

Be willing to sit with any discomfort this verse brought up today. Whether seeing something new about yourself or being willing to trust your friends' 'blind spots' to Jesus, just sit with it until the Lord brings you peace.

Oh Glorious Day

"He will wipe away every tear from their eyes,
and there will be no more death, sadness, crying, or pain,
because all the old ways are gone."

REVELATION 21:4 NCV

Can you even imagine eternity in heaven? Can you envision a time with no more sadness, tears, or pain? Is a world without death, disease or aging even possible to comprehend? The news is filled with all these things; the world is filled with all these things. There is story after story of brother hurting brother, sister mourning sister, and parents grieving children gone too soon.

Imagine Jesus has come, and tears are gone. Death is defeated, sadness forgotten, and crying and pain are no more. The world as we know it is replaced by the world as we are told will come to be. What a beautiful picture!

I love this part of the story, Lord. I need it. I need to know that all the ugliness I see will be replaced by the beauty of your perfect love. I need to know this hurting world won't hurt forever, and that the new world will be better than I can imagine.

> *"God will wipe away every tear from their eyes; there shall be no more death, nor sorrow, nor crying. There shall be no more pain, for the former things have passed away."*
>
> REVELATION 21:4 NKJV

Oh, glorious day! On the days of crying and of death, look toward this glorious day. On the days of sorrow and pain, imagine this glorious day.

On the days this world is getting old, rejoice in the promise of this new and glorious day.

Great and glorious God, how eagerly I wait for this day. I'm ready, God, to see an end to suffering and the beginning of life with you.

Share your imagining of heaven with God. He loves the way you think, and he wants to know how you hope it will be.

Because We Know

*It is by faith we understand that the whole world
was made by God's command so what we see was made
by something that cannot be seen.*

HEBREWS 11:3 NCV

Could you prove creation in a court of law? Could you prove
the Creator? What physical evidence do you have to back up
your faith, any? And yet, could you deny him? Could you deny
what, by faith, you know to be true?

Faith is a beautiful mystery. While proof exists in the physical
world, faith lives in the heart. We know what we know simply
because we know. The instant the Father called us to him, all
that was speculation became truth.

*God, while I couldn't prove your existence to one whose eyes don't
see you, I have more faith in you than everything I can prove. I've
been changed by your Word, healed by your love, and felt your
presence in my soul. all of that is proof enough for me.*

Faith empowers us to see that the universe was created and beautifully coordinated by the power of God's words! He spoke and the invisible realm gave birth to all that is seen.

HEBREWS 11:3 TPT

Once we get past childhood, we typically need to see in order to believe. Hearing that out of nothing that can be seen came everything we see, skepticism is not a surprising response. But for faith, we'd never move past it.

Look at those first three words: faith empowers us. Without faith, believing God created the universe—believing he exists at all—isn't just a stretch; it's impossible.

Father, thank you for my faith. What a fantastic gift, the ability to embrace a truth beyond seeing. Through faith, skepticism is replaced by knowing. In knowing, I am empowered, which inspires even more faith.

Faith is such a gift! How else could we believe so fantastic of a story? Tonight, simply thank God for the gift of your faith.

What He Gives

"Don't be so concerned about perishable things like food. Spend your energy seeking the eternal life that the Son of Man can give you. For God the Father has given me the seal of his approval."

JOHN 6:27 NLT

It's easy to get caught up in this life, isn't it? After all, it's all we know. We want to live well and, in our desire to do so, we find ourselves chasing not just provision, but approval and even excess. Have goals, the world tells us, ones that can be realized here on earth.

Look up. Look to heaven and remember the real goal, the only one worthy of all your striving. In Jesus, our lives have meaning that goes far beyond paychecks and pleasures. What he gives us, no one can ever take away.

Jesus, you are the goal. Forgive me for taking my eyes of you, the real prize, and chasing after things that cannot last. Tilt my chin toward heaven, God, that I would strive only for that which is eternal.

"Do not work for the food which perishes, but for the food which endures to eternal life, which the Son of Man will give to you, for on Him the Father, God, has set His seal."

JOHN 6:27 NASB

Think about your work, and the reasons you do it. How many of them have eternal significance?

If you are working only for a paycheck, consider asking Jesus to infuse you with a greater purpose. You needn't necessarily change jobs; the enduring reward of working for the Lord is finding meaning right where we are.

God, the moment I rise, turn my thoughts to you. I want to live and work for the reward you offer. I want my eternal life to start right now, as you infuse my life with meaning because I've chosen to live it pursuing you.

How could a change in your perspective, or a new, more kingdom-minded goal, help you find more meaning in your current job?

Worth It

*You need to persevere so that when you have done the will of God,
you will receive what he has promised.*

HEBREWS 10:36 NIV

There are days where you just want to be *done.* Even with
the finish line in sight, even imagining the finisher's medal
around your neck, you just want to sit down and say, *enough!*
Hang in there. Hang on. Hang tough. Whatever you have to
do to persevere, don't give up. You've worked hard to get this
far—too hard to quit before the end.

The Lord wants to see you cross the finish line in your faith
walk as well. He knows it's hard to stay pure in a world that's
corrupted, to stay kind in a world so filled with cruelty. He
knows, because he's been here too. He's run this race and
finished, and now he waits, cheering, for you to join him at
the end.

*God, before my day even starts, I sometimes can't wait for it to
end. Work is hard, and my faith walk is hard some days too. It's
tempting to drop the baton, to compromise, to just sit down. But
then I see you and remember I'm running for your glory. I remember
why I'm here: to do your will. I recall the reward you promise, to be
with you, and that's all the strength I need to persevere.*

You have need of endurance, so that when you have done the will of God you may receive what is promised.

HEBREWS 10:36 ESV

Endurance is the ability to withstand suffering. If we want to accomplish the will of God, we need to be tough. We must willingly suffer pain, and no doubt we will wonder at times if it's worth it.

Would a mother say childbirth is worth it? Would a soldier say the freedom of millions is worth it? As awesome as those rewards are, we are enduring for something far greater still and undeniably worth it.

Oh, Jesus, you are worth it. To feel your pleasure, to spread your love and light, to follow your example and willingly endure all this life throws at me in order to bring glory to the Father is a prize worth any temporary suffering. Thank you, God, for power to persevere.

Could your endurance use a boost? Share your struggle—honestly and completely—with the Holy Spirit, and let him infuse you with willing strength.

Come Home

God has made all things new, and reconciled us to himself, and given us the ministry of reconciling others to God.

2 Corinthians 5:18 TPT

He wanted you back. You may not have even realized you were separated, but God did, and he moved heaven and earth to get you back. How loved you are, how loved we all are! Just think of what he did for us, sacrificing his perfect Son so we could come home, fully reconciled, to our Father.

It is part of our mission to bring others back to him as well. He's not asking us all to become missionaries, or traveling evangelists, or to go door-to-door. He will ask this of some, but for most of us, he is simply asking us to live these brand-new lives in the open. Our light will be a magnet, our joy contagious. Drawn to us, they'll find him—and come home.

Father God, I'm so grateful you wanted me back! Forgive me for keeping the amazing joy of life with you hidden at times, for withholding your light on occasion. I know it is your greatest desire that we all come home, and through your Spirit I will do my part to reconcile my brothers and sisters to you.

All these things are from God, who reconciled us to Himself through Christ and gave us the ministry of reconciliation,

2 CORINTHIANS 5:18 NASB

Just as our Father wants all of us reconciled to him, he longs to see our earthly relationships restored. Grudges and feuds grieve his heart. Even if others never choose to reconcile themselves to us, we can choose reconciliation with them in our own hearts.

Every bit of resentment we hold onto pushes out peace; bitterness chokes out grace. Let us invite them, grace and peace, to bloom and grow so completely, we've no room for anything else.

God, I never want to grieve you. Reconciliation matters so much to you, you gave up everything to have it with me. How, then, can I withhold it from anyone? As much as it depends on me, let me be reconciled to everyone I am at odds with. Let me release the weeds of bitterness, resentment, and anything else that chokes out the life-giving, restorative power of peace and grace.

Meditate on reconciliation tonight, asking the Lord to show you everywhere you can ask for, bestow, and receive it.

Proof

*Jesus asked, "Will you never believe in me
unless you see miraculous signs and wonders?"*

JOHN 4:48 NLT

What do I have to do to prove it to you? It's frustrating, isn't it,
when our word is not enough, when even our repeated good-
faith actions are not enough to constitute proof? Sometimes,
it feels like it would take a miracle for certain people to
believe, trust, or forgive us.

Imagine Jesus' ministry: all the healings, all the restored
hearts, all the mouths who had their fill of wine and bread
and fish. Still, so many required their own miracle before
they placed their faith in him, before they believed he was
who he said he was. His response, to all whose hearts were
open, was to prove it.

*Jesus, your patience and willingness to prove yourself are amazing.
You'd already done enough—more than enough—to erase all doubt
and yet you continued to do more. Right up to your last breath and
even beyond, you proved yourself—and you prove it still.*

Jesus said to him, "Unless you see signs and wonders you will not believe."

JOHN 4:48 NRSV

What constitutes a miracle? Must a bone be mended before our eyes, sight restored, disease erased? Is a transformed life miracle enough?

Consider your own heart. Would you be so kind, so patient, so generous had God not changed it? Would you be kind or patient or generous at all? Considering all the ways you are lovely, and all the fruit you bear, is this not miracle enough?

Jesus, I am a miracle. I know my heart without you, and the way you've made it not just whole but holy is astounding. Even if I never see mangled legs stand and walk, even if I never hear the joyful singing of the once mute, the miracle of my own joyful heart is miracle enough.

What is the most miraculous thing you've ever witnessed? Spend some time with this, asking the Spirit to help you recall as many as you can.

Boldly and Humbly

Let us therefore come boldly to the throne of grace that we may obtain mercy and find grace to help in time of need.

HEBREWS 4:16 NKJV

When someone wants your help, how do you like to be asked? We are most pleased by a straightforward request, the kind that shows the asker trusts our willingness and desire to respond. It's almost hurtful when we're approached timidly, as if expected to say no, or to comply only begrudgingly.

Our Father appreciates boldness too. He loves to be approached confidently, as if we know he will grant our requests. For everything from help with our to-do list to begging his forgiveness, he is pleased when we ask expectantly, and so he willingly responds from his endless supply of grace.

God, I come both boldly and humbly before you. I approach you boldly, because I know you want to help me with everything. I know my trust in you brings you joy. I come humbly, because I recognize my great need for you—for your mercy and your grace. Thank you, Father, for welcoming me. Thank you for the way I know you will respond: willingly and with love.

Let us come boldly to the throne of our gracious God.
There we will receive his mercy, and we will find grace
to help us when we need it most.

HEBREWS 4:16 NLT

Lord, have mercy! The right to speak this phrase is a priceless gift, and yet we've allowed it to be reduced to a cliché, a synonym for "wow." Surely this grieves our Father, and yet he continues to have mercy. That's who he is, this God we serve.

As beloved children, we are invited again and again before the throne of grace. Deserved or not, all his mercy is ours for the asking.

Father, have mercy on me! For every time I've taken your grace for granted, have mercy on me. For every time I've treated your grace as an entitlement instead of an irreplaceable, priceless treasure, have mercy on me. For all the times I need it and fail to even ask or see, have mercy on me.

Did you need this reminder of the precious, priceless privilege it is to come before the throne as a child of the King? For mercy already given, pour out your gratitude.

Power of Kindness

You have granted me life and steadfast love,
and your care has preserved my spirit.

JOB 10:12 NRSV

A person with great tolerance is said to have the patience of
Job. Someone enduring a horrible string of circumstances
may say they feel like Job. Most adults are familiar with
at least the basics of Job's story: he's the one who lost
everything—his wealth, his children, and his health, and yet
stayed faithful to God.

Oh, that we would feel like Job! Look at these beautiful words
again, and consider the speaker. His children have all died.
His home and all his wealth have been wiped away. His body
is in constant agony, and none of his friends are standing by
him. By many standards, he has indeed lost everything. But
look at what he has. The things that sustain him are things
that cannot be taken away.

Father, I confess to thinking of Job and being glad his life was not
mine, but when I read these words—when I think of the incredible
joy you must have placed in his heart in order for him to speak
them—I am almost envious. How beautifully you care for your
children! Even if we lose everything, you give us reason for joy.

You gave me life and showed me kindness,
and in your providence watched over my spirit.

JOB 10:12 NIV

One of the more heartwarming aspects of mass media is our access to feel-good stories. Particularly poignant are videos of rescued dogs. The transformation they undergo in the face of kindness is a thing of beauty. From trembling and mistrustful to frolicking as one freely loved, so is the power of kindness.

As much as we have received from our Lord, may we give it to someone who needs it.

God, thank you for your incredible kindness. I feel it all around me, building my trust and calming my fears. You are good. You are kind. And you make me the same. Reminded of how good it feels to receive kindness, let your Spirit move me to give some away.

If kindness were a picture, what would you see? Is it a specific person, an action, or more abstract: a swirl of color and warmth and light? Whatever the picture, hold it in your gaze and be blessed.

The Perfect Spirit

The Spirit of the LORD will rest on Him, the spirit of wisdom and understanding, the spirit of counsel and strength, the spirit of knowledge and the fear of the LORD.

ISAIAH 11:2 NASB

Never has there been a more precious gift than God's Holy Spirit. First given to Jesus, making him wise, compassionate, strong, and faithful, Jesus now shares him with all who call him Savior. Every time help comes from nowhere, with every nudge or moment of clarity, and

every time our heart is moved toward goodness, he makes his presence known.

However imperfect we may be, his Spirit in us is perfect. These are the gifts he gave to Jesus, which enabled him to lead his beautiful, selfless life. Surely, we can allow them to work more beauty into ours.

Oh, gracious God, how I thank you for your Spirit. Flawed as I am, through him I am made wise. Confused and need of counsel, in him I find the answers I seek. Weak in body and faith, in him I am strong and faithful. What a gift, God, what a precious, priceless gift.

The Spirit of the LORD shall rest upon him, the Spirit of wisdom and understanding, the Spirit of counsel and might, the Spirit of knowledge and the fear of the LORD.

ISAIAH 11:2 ESV

Because these are the things Isaiah prophesied over Jesus long before his birth, let us take a closer look. *Wisdom and understanding.* Son of a Nazarene carpenter, Jesus taught with incredible authority, like that of one educated for years inside the temple. *Counsel and might.* His advice was infallible, and his strength beyond this world. *Knowledge and fear of the Lord.* Jesus knew God. He knew his heart, he discerned his will, and he respected him completely.

These are the gifts the Spirit gave to Christ, and the gifts he gives to us.

Jesus, thank you for the gifts you so generously share! Open my eyes to all your Word can teach me and make me wise. Allow me to use this to offer wise counsel, and to stand in confident strength. I want to know you—as you know the Father and as you know me—that I would give you all the fear, respect, and awe you deserve.

Which of these gifts do you most readily recognize in your life? Of which would you like to experience more? Offer God your request and your thanks.

As He Would

> *Whatever you do in word or deed, do all in the name of the Lord Jesus, giving thanks through Him to God the Father.*
>
> COLOSSIANS 3:17 NASB

How amazing would it be to approach all of life gratefully? Imagine entering every conversation, every room, every situation with thanks. Would our minds go straight to the good, would our eyes pick up instantly on the lovely? If we believed, before we ever tried or prayed, that the outcome would be blessed, our hearts would overflow with thanks.

So, what is stopping us? What evidence do we have to contradict God's goodness? Any example we might produce, when seen through the lens of faith and gratitude, will also prove his goodness.

God, when I look at all you have made—when I consider all you have done—what response can I offer but thanks? A break from the August heat, a blooming hydrangea, and the happiness in my own heart are evidence of the ways you are good. I owe you my thanks, Father, and through your precious Son, I am inspired to give it in all I say and do.

Whatever you do or say, do it as a representative of the Lord Jesus,
giving thanks through him to God the Father.

COLOSSIANS 3:17 NLT

Do you see yourself this way, as a representative of the Lord
Jesus? Not just sometimes, like when a friend asks for godly
counsel, but all the time.

Whatever you do or say, you are representing him to a watching
world. Inspiring, isn't it? Inspiring to move through life
gracefully, compassionately, and gratefully, just as he would.

Oh God, how much differently I speak when I remember I speak
for you. How much more generously, kindly, and purposefully
do I behave when I recall it's on your behalf. Let me be the reason
someone falls in love with you because they see your love in me.

What does this inspire you to do more of? Are you moved to
do anything any less?

Deserved Glory

Jesus said to him, "Why do you call me good?
No one is good but God alone."

MARK 10:18 NRSV

Next to the perfection of God, our casual use of the term is convicting. Next to the most exquisite rose, God's brilliance would wither it. The loveliest face we've ever seen appears ordinary next to the beauty of the Lord. Even Jesus, God's own Son refused to accept the honor that belonged rightfully to his Father.

Just think of it! In all his humility, compassion, mercy, tenderness, and wisdom, Jesus declared himself unworthy next to God. How are we to comprehend such goodness, such perfection? Perhaps we are not. Perhaps we are meant only to celebrate it, and to give him the glory he deserves.

God, there is no one like you. You are the definition of everything good, the embodiment of all that is perfect. Forgive me for thinking anything here can compare. I see they are but an inkling, a glimmer of your awesomeness, and I am awed.

Jesus said to him, "Why do you call Me good?
No one is good but One, that is, God."

MARK 10:18 NKJV

Still human, Jesus wanted to make sure no one worshipped him on earth. His sole mission was to draw everyone he encountered into the Father's love. He didn't want them to love his miracles, but the one who empowered him to perform them.

Now that he is glorified in heaven, though, part of the Holy Trinity of Father, Spirit, and Son, Jesus is worthy and wholly deserving of our worship and praise. For his humility on earth, and his majesty in heaven, let us praise him.

Jesus, you are amazing. Filled with all the knowledge and power of God, you still refused to accept any honor. You gave us a perfect example of how to live a humble, God-glorifying life. Risen and exalted, you are God: glorious, perfect, and entirely worthy of all the praise we could ever offer.

How comfortable are you accepting compliments? Is it natural for you to give the glory back to God? Together with the Spirit, search your heart in this.

Swell of Mercy

If you hide your sins, you will not succeed.
If you confess and reject them, you will receive mercy.

PROVERBS 28:13 NCV

It's not so much that you did it, but that you lied about it. Does this sound familiar? Whether spoken or heard, it's likely we've faced the fact that concealment is worse than the sin it hides. Confession indicates remorse, and a heart that wants to be trusted. Rejecting our bad behaviors inspires the mercy of forgiveness.

Why would we expect anything different from God? Denying our sin doesn't erase it and will not lead to his blessing over our lives. Admitting our flaws before him, however, opens the door to a swell of mercy, an ocean of forgiveness which in turn leads to a beautifully transformed and trustworthy heart.

God, I don't know why I try to hide my sins from you. I know you see them all, including the ones I can't even see myself. I think it's because I can't bear to look at anything ugly in myself, knowing how it distances me from you. Holy Spirit, pull my confession from me; turn me away from my sins and into the mercy of your unconditional love.

Whoever conceals his transgressions will not prosper,
but he who confesses and forsakes them will obtain mercy.

PROVERBS 28:13 ESV

When we want to hide something, we take it somewhere out of the way, often somewhere dark. Kept in the dark, our sins nurture condemnation, shame and excuses.

Rather than keeping sins hidden, where no help can find us, let us be bold enough to shine a light into these dark places so that the glow of mercy and healing can overtake them.

God, I know nothing good grows in the dark. You've told me so many times. Still, I retreat there to nurture shame. But why? Why would I nurture something as ugly as shame? Shine your light too brightly for shame to survive. Come into every dark corner of my heart and expose all I try to conceal. I forsake every darkness, trading it for the light of your mercy.

Does the Father's light want to show you something you don't want to see? Be bold, and let his mercy make you new.

Best of You

*If someone does not know how to manage his own household,
how can he take care of God's church?*

1 TIMOTHY 3:5 NRSV

It can be more than a little disheartening to see evidence of
the disintegration of the family in our society. Viral videos of
abuse and neglect circulate daily, as do angry back and forth
rants about the legal definition. It can quickly start to feel
like society is more concerned with discussing and critiquing
family and other people's families than they are about
nurturing their own.

How about you? How about yours? Does your family life bear
witness to your professed, believed value of family? For most
of us, the Lord will reveal an aspect of our family life that
could use our loving attention. Accept what he shows you,
and do what he puts on your heart to do. He loves you—all of
you—so much; he wants your family to thrive.

*God, we've talked before about how hard it is to confront my
shortcomings, but this is a big deal. Family matters! It's the closest
thing I have on earth to the love you feel for me, and I want to get
this right. Show me how to love my family better and grace me
with the humility to do it.*

If he's unable to properly lead his own household well,
how could he properly lead God's household?

1 TIMOTHY 3:5 TPT

Are you in a season of waiting, sensing God's encouragement to a bigger role in his family—feeling a longing to take it on—but not hearing the unmistakable now just yet?

Without condemnation, look at your family. Are they getting your best? Take your time answering, maybe even weeks or months. Ask the Spirit to be present with you as you interact with the ones he's entrusted to you. Once they're getting the very best of you, you can be sure he'll infuse you with more to give to others.

Father, am I like that athlete who phones it in at practice, performs adequately, but not spectacularly at games, then wonders why you won't promote me? Show me, God, if I'm phoning it in with my family. In any way, are they getting less than my best? I love my people, and I want to be sure this is obvious to all.

How did today's devotions sit with you? What do you sense God telling you to do about it?

Constant Change

Jesus Christ is the same yesterday and today and forever.
HEBREWS 13:8 NASB

It's been said that the only constant in this world is change. Technology devices that blew our minds a decade ago are considered dinosaurs today. Last year's most popular fashion statements are already in the thrift stores. Look at a photo of yourself from just this past winter. You've changed, haven't you? It's true; the only constant in our world—is how constantly things change.

As with so many things in the kingdom of heaven, we find the exact opposite in Jesus. Everything he is, he was. Everything he was, he will always be. He never changes his mind, character, or mood. No matter how much the world changes, no matter how much we change, his love for us never, ever will.

God, thank you for your constancy. In a world where the only thing certain is that nothing is certain, it's reassuring to be completely sure of you. Your kindness, your faithfulness, and your goodness are my constants, and your love is my home.

Jesus, the Anointed One, is always the same—
yesterday, today, and forever.

HEBREWS 13:8 TPT

We just grew apart. We hear it said of friendships, romances, and even parents and children. The more of the world we experience, the more we are affected, the more we change.

No matter how connected we once were to someone, those connections fray with time. All except our connection to Jesus. Because he is everywhere, we cannot go away. Because he is in us, we cannot grow apart.

God, I love knowing there is no way for us to grow apart. All around me, you occupy every space I inhabit. The person I was, the person I am, and the person I am becoming all belong to you. Because you are forever, because you are changeless, so are your connection to, and love for, me.

Do you believe this, that no matter how much you change, his love for you will not? His presence in you will not? If you aren't certain, ask him to help you know it's true.

Sweet Whispers

"Do not keep striving for what you are to eat and what you are to drink, and do not keep worrying."

LUKE 12:29 NRSV

Have you ever met someone who seems to need something to worry about? They even worry about not being worried: *I must be missing something. What have I forgotten?* Some of us need only go to the mirror to have a talk with this person; we wear worry like a favorite necklace.

It's to them—perhaps to us—Jesus was speaking here. *Calm down, dear one.* There is food in the cupboard and water in the well—more than we can eat or drink today, and today is the only day that needs our attention. Strive instead to hear from his Spirit. Where would he have you focus your thoughts, your attention, your striving? What sweet whispers will you miss if worry won't be silenced?

I do worry, Lord. I even worry that I worry too much. I worry you'll grow frustrated with all my worry. Help me stop, Jesus. Help me not. I want to silence worry, so I can hear from you. Tell me again to trust you, to believe you, to silence worry. Whisper to me again and again until I do.

> *"I repeat it: Don't let worry enter your life.*
> *Live above the anxious cares about your personal needs."*

LUKE 12:29 TPT

How many times have you listened to your favorite song? How many times have you told the ones you love that you love them? We repeat what is good, what is important, what we do not want forgotten or questioned.

"Don't worry," Jesus says. Repeatedly. He says it for our good. He says it because we forget, and we question. He says it because it's important. If you forget again and start to worry— and you will—don't worry. He'll tell you again.

Jesus, if there's one thing I know I don't need worry about, it's that you will stop trying to help me with worry. It's important to you that I learn to trust you, to believe in your goodness, to remember and rely on your faithfulness. Thank you that your patient reminders sustain my hope.

What if you let worry die? What if you just stopped feeding it, and handed it over to God?

All You Ask

We know love by this that he laid down his life for us—
and we ought to lay down our lives for one another.

1 JOHN 3:16 NRSV

May we never grow unamazed by this. Jesus gave up his life for us. And may we never grow unimpressed by those who take up this noble charge today. All around the world are brothers and sisters willing to set everything aside to bring this incredible truth to those who haven't heard it.

In many countries, evangelism is a crime. Christians sit in jail because they were caught saying Jesus' name, telling others what he did for them. May we not be unmoved—to pray for their provision, protection, and peace.

Lord Jesus, I am awed by those who hear and answer the call to lay it all down, at the risk of life itself, for your message of hope. From the safety and comfort of my home, I am moved to lay down my own concerns today. Protect them. Provide for their needs, and give them peace that sustains them through every danger and trial.

This is how we know what real love is: Jesus gave his life for us.
So we should give our lives for our brothers and sisters.

1 John 3:16 NCV

Within a few blocks, wherever we may be, is someone who waits for the blessing of our time, resources, and talent. We can't all leave it all behind. We can't all lay it all down. But we can all leave something behind. We can all set something aside.

We can't all give our whole lives, but we can all give a piece of time.

Father God, you inspire some to give up all they have, and others to give all they can spare. Help me to hear your call, God, and to willingly give all you ask. Thank you, God, for calling us all to something—that we may all honor Jesus, whom you called to give everything.

Do you know what the Lord wants you to lay down or give? If you do, how are you responding? If you do not, how can you begin listening?

Golden

"Whatever you wish that others would do to you, do also to them, for this is the Law and the Prophets."

MATTHEW 7:12 ESV

Bible translations with added headings and section titles call this section of Matthew 7 "The Golden Rule." Like a gold medal is the ultimate prize, the golden rule is the ultimate standard of behavior. Some may dismiss it as kindergarten advice, but to do so is to miss out on some ultimate golden wisdom.

Do you want to be treated fairly? Be fair. Is it your desire to be loved? Be loving. Using this logic, it would stand to reason that if you want to be met with rudeness, be rude. To be judged, be judgmental. To be gossiped about, gossip. While not certain, it is likely; you'll get what you give.

God, I'm so grateful for your wise advice. Instead of responding to a nasty tone with nastiness, let me give the sweetness I'd appreciate. To impatience, let me reply with peace. And when I am met with graciousness and hospitality, let me respond in kind, so that love and friendship can prosper.

> *"Whatever you want men to do to you, do also to them,
> for this is the Law and the Prophets."*
>
> MATTHEW 7:12 NKJV

This should be easier, don't you think? Why does something so beautifully simple fly in the face of instinct? Instead of doing what we want done to us, we do what is done to us.

Rudeness brings out rudeness, attacks provoke defensiveness and more attacks. Perhaps if we claim it, determine to live it, and pray for the will to overcome instinct in favor of something that will actually bless our lives, it will be easier.

God, will you help me learn to instinctively behave as someone I'd love to have in my life? Let me treat the disrespectful with respect, and the callous with compassion. Let me be the best friend I—or anyone—could ever want. So that I will know love, God, let me love.

How naturally does the Golden Rule come to you? However well you respond to people, pray that God would make you even more of what you'd love in a friend.

Wired For Connection

The LORD God said, "It is not good for the man to be alone.
I will make a helper who is just right for him."

GENESIS 2:18 NLT

The very first thing God did on behalf of Adam was create
Eve. His first concern was that he not be alone; we are wired
for connection. With God and with one another, we are made
for love. While he does rejoice when we choose someone to
build a family with, this is far from the be-all-end-all our
culture can make it out to be.

Every family relationship matters to God, and every
friendship matters as well. Each day, each person we
encounter is an invitation to connect, to give and receive the
love of the Lord. Whether we are married or single, mothers
or not, he does not want us to be alone.

God, how I thank you for the beautiful gift of connection. As many
types of relationship as there are, there are ways to love; each is an
opportunity to know more of you—how you love. Lead me always
to community even when I resist. Inspire me to pour myself into
every gift of a heart to love.

The LORD God said, "It is not good for the man to be alone.
I will make a helper suitable for him."

GENESIS 2:18 NIV

We all have our days when we think the world would be simpler if we were all the same: *I just don't understand men,* we think. They don't always understand women, either, and undoubtedly have the exact same thoughts.

But let's not question God's infallible wisdom for long. Very intentionally, he created two genders—and not just for reproduction. We are different so that we can help, surprise, and complement one another. On the days you momentarily forget this, recall all the lovely ways you know it to be true.

Thank you, God, for the differences between men and women. Thank you too for the differences between individuals of both gender. Even though I sometimes wish for everyone to just agree with me, and see things as I do, I don't mean it. I love that there are those who are stronger and more patient. I love that I have a chance to be the softer one, the practical one. It's our differences that make us so beautifully suited to help each other along.

Think of a few of your favorite people and celebrate the ways you are different.

He Hears

Certainly God has heard me;
He has attended to the voice of my prayer.

PSALM 66:19 NKJV

God hears everything you say, and it is all of great interest to him, but he is particularly mindful of the words you speak to him. He hears and loves your prayers. Just as we may listen delightedly to the voice of two children playing together, our engagement increases when they speak our names—when they address us directly.

We know he hears us, and we can have faith that he will respond. We don't turn away from someone speaking to us as if we haven't heard, and neither does he. He hears our thanks, our praise, our confessions, and our cries for help. He hears it all—and he responds.

Father, I know you hear me always, and I know you listen when I pray. I praise you and you smile on me; I feel your pleasure. I cry out for help and you comfort me; I feel your warmth surround me. I share my dreams, fears, and confessions with you, and you supply hope, security, and grace.

Certainly God has heard;
He has given heed to the voice of my prayer.

PSALM 66:19 NASB

We know he hears, and we know he responds. How well do we listen? It's easy to forget prayer is a two-way conversation sometimes, isn't it? We just go on and on, barely leaving him an opening to get in a word.

As important as it is to call out to God, let's remember to listen for his voice in reply.

Stillness, God, is a part of prayer I can forget. Done with my list, I say "Amen" and move on. Holy Spirit, stop me. Move me to be still, to be quiet, and to listen. Thank you for your patience. No matter how long I go on, you listen. And no matter how long it takes me to listen to you, you wait.

How good are you at being still before God and listening? Invite him to help you learn to listen as hopefully as you pray.

Rest Assured

You will have confidence, because there is hope;
you will be protected and take your rest in safety.

JOB 11:18 NRSV

Our God is the God of hope. He wipes out everything set against us. In him, in the hope he provides, live safety, rest, confidence, and peace. In the hope of the Lord, we have life. It's baffling, isn't it, that we'd choose to hope in anything else—but we do. And when we do, our confidence suffers. Our safety is uncertain.

He calls us back. Again and again, no matter how often we look elsewhere, he calls us back to true confidence and lasting hope. He restores us to confidence, returns us to safety. He fills us—again—with hope.

God of hope, fear doesn't stand a chance against you. I am safe. I can rest. God of hope, uncertainty has nowhere to hide in your glorious light. I am confident. I have hope. God of hope, you are my protection, my confidence, my safety, and my life. All my hope is in you.

You will be secure, because there is hope;
you will look about you and take your rest in safety.

Have you ever tried to fall asleep when you were afraid?
Perhaps in a tent, or alone in the house, every noise you
heard sounded like danger.

Without the hope of safety, we can't find rest. Rest assured.
Almighty God watches over you. He gives you all the
protection you need. Your soul is safe. Your heart is secure.
Your hope is in him.

Unlimited God, in you I have no need of fear. I can rest because
you are my confidence. Nothing can hurt me. In this world there is
danger but in you my soul is safe. Here on earth is insecurity and
doubt but in you my heart is secure. Hoping in you, I find my rest.

How close does hope feel tonight? Take it all before the Lord,
and feel it surround you. Rest assured.

Lit By Love

"Let your light shine before men in such a way that they may see your good works, and glorify your Father who is in heaven."

MATTHEW 5:16 NASB

Think of a person you know who seems to light up every room they enter. What is it about them that makes their lights shine so brightly? Certainly, they're often wearing a smile. Undoubtedly, they listen with their eyes. Inevitably, when they speak, it is with wisdom and compassion. They are lit by love, and it glows from every part of them.

Their lives are an example of all Jesus calls us to be: compassionate, generous, and kind. And how often with these luminous souls do we just know—even before we know them—they belong to Christ? His light is unmistakable. It's bright, pure, and true. Their glow is a spotlight, originating from his heart.

God, thank you for the lovely, warm light of your love. I'm drawn to it, because it comes from you. Around these people who are so good at reflecting your goodness, I feel your warmth and I am inspired to reflect all the love and kindness I absorb in their glow.

*"In the same way, you should be a light for other people.
Live so that they will see the good things you do
and will praise your Father in heaven."*

MATTHEW 5:16 NCV

This little light of mine, I'm gonna let it shine. Aside from being
an adorable Sunday school song, what does this mean to you?

How wonderful would it be to have someone witness your
light and say, "God is so good!" What an awesome blessing:
to reflect him so truly that it is he, not we, they recognize. To
him be the glory!

*God, make me a mirror. I want to be so filled with your light, I can
no longer be seen. I want to be so transformed by your love, I am no
longer recognizable. When they see me, Jesus, let them praise you.*

Where is Jesus calling you to shine more brightly?

Broken Heart

The righteous cry out, and the LORD hears,
and delivers them out of all their troubles.

PSALM 34:17 NKJV

With God, there is no such condition as helpless. We tend to forget this; we work until we've exhausted all our ideas and gone through every human channel. Desolation knocks on the door, but because of our Father, we don't have to answer. Instead, we can cry out to him—knock on his door—and know he will answer.

He sees our sadness, he hears our cries, and he longs to heal us, to comfort us, to hold us, and deliver us. He always offers a way through, always. No matter how bleak things may look, no matter how surprised we are at where he takes us, we can believe it is where we belong.

God, I need to you help me believe this, to seek you first, and act on what I know: you hear me. You long to heal me. You will deliver me, and wherever I end up, whatever means you use, it will be for my good.

> *The LORD is close to the brokenhearted;*
> *he rescues those whose spirits are crushed.*
>
> PSALM 34:17 NLT

The more we break, the closer our Father comes. We are crushed, yes, but every crack in us makes room for him. He waits to fill our broken places with pure gold. HIs mending makes us whole again, and also more beautiful, more valuable.

A spirit crushed by the world has a chance to be reopened, expanded, and smoothed out. We are better, stronger for having borne the weight.

Father God, I sometimes still feel fragile from the blows this life has dealt me, but I also see how they have reshaped me; I know I am better for it all—because of the loving way you have mended me. Thank you for the careful, tender repairs you've made to this broken heart, this battered soul. I trace the lines of my scars and see the beauty you have brought to my brokenness.

How have you been reshaped lately?

The Whole Thing

Devote yourselves completely to the LORD our God, walking in his statutes and keeping his commandments, as at this day."

1 KINGS 8:61 NRSV

Can you kind of lie? Can you be a little bit married? Sort of pregnant? Nor can you be only somewhat devoted to the Lord. The truth is, we are either following him, or we are not. We can't worship Christ on Sunday and around our Christian friends, and then forget him on Friday night at an after-work happy hour.

This doesn't mean we can't and won't make mistakes. The Lord loves our obedient actions, but what he requires is our dedicated hearts. Just as a half-truth is not the truth, a partially surrendered heart is not what Jesus wants from you. He wants the whole thing.

God, I belong to you. I adore you, and I want to live my life fully committed to you. I realize there are days I try to give you only a piece of me, but that is because I am weak, not because I don't want to give you my whole heart. You laid down your life for me, and I want only to honor your sacrifice by doing the same for you.

Let your heart therefore be wholly true to the LORD our God,
walking in his statutes and keeping his commandments,
as at this day.

1 KINGS 8:61 ESV

Imagine a couple on their wedding day, the earnestness with which they speak their vows, the eagerness with which they anticipate their future together. Even in the most loving and stable of marriages, with time the earnestness and eagerness of young love give way to a calmer, quieter, rhythm. Complacency may even settle in.

As a bride of Christ, he wants you to feel like a newlywed—forever. The same commitment with which you started your walk is the commitment he expects on every step of the journey. That same joy you felt when you first gave him your heart, he wants for you today.

Lord Jesus, I renew my vows. Over and over, I choose you. As on the day you first chose me, called me, and showed me your incomparable love, I choose you. I walk in your statutes. I give you my heart.

The Lord is very aware of how human passion fades. As Spirit, he can continually reignite it, if you continually offer him your heart.

Go All In

Each of us will give an account of ourselves to God.

ROMANS 14:12 NIV

"What have you done?" Often, the asker knows the answer to this question already. Like a child who suddenly sees the magnificent mess she's made, when God asks us to give an account of ourselves, it won't be for him to learn what he already knows; it will be for us to see it through his eyes.

Maintaining an awareness of this reckoning can provide a heightened, helpful level of discernment. Just as we learned to think before we acted as we grew older, so too can we learn to foresee our choices through God's eyes as we grow wiser. *What am I thinking?* affords countless opportunities to avoid "What have you done?"

Father God, today I am grateful for discernment. I welcome the opportunity to consider my actions ahead of taking them, so I can see which are wise and pleasing to you. When we review my life together, I want us both to feel proud.

Each one must answer for himself
and give a personal account of his own life before God.

ROMANS 14:12 TPT

What did you do all day? How often would you be somewhat embarrassed to answer this question honestly? But what of the other days, the ones you are just waiting for someone to ask?

While this verse inspires a healthy level of forethought and caution, let it also inspire enthusiasm. Let it inspire you to live a life you can't wait to review with your God.

God, I want to take this "must answer" and make it a "get to answer!" Inspire and empower me to make the choices and live the kind of life I will be delighted to give an account of. Remind me, on the days I am tempted to live half-heartedly, how much joy we will both feel upon recounting the way I chose instead to go all-in.

If you were to give an accounting tonight of your life thus far, how close do you feel it would come to God's plans for you? What are you inspired by this realization to do?

Never Alone

Even if my father and mother abandon me,
the LORD will hold me close.

PSALM 27:10 NLT

It's a common picture of family that even if the whole world gives up on you, you will always have your parents. The ones who loved you first are supposed to be—and often are—the ones to love you longest, last, best. But even if they don't, your Papa will.

There is absolutely nothing you can do to cause him to drop you from his arms. He may hold you more loosely, especially if you invest a lot of time into resisting him, but make no mistake: he will never, ever set you down.

Oh, what a comfort this is, Abba, to remember your arms hold me always. No distance is too far, no sin is too great. Even if I blow it with the ones who brought me into the world, I can never lose the love of the One who gives me life.

If my father and mother leave me,
the LORD will take me in.

PSALM 27:10

Isn't it amazing to realize we are never alone, can never be alone? The Holy Spirit of God is our constant companion. He helps us, guides us, comforts us, even when the world has turned their backs.

On those days, when they come, let us remember that loneliness is a gift. With no one to sit with, talk to or lean on, we are invited to lean in. No one eases loneliness like the Lord.

Spirit, I ask you today to remind me of this on the days I get lonely. My loneliness is a gift from you, an invitation to lean into you, to your comfort, companionship, and peace. Thank you for loving me far too much to ever leave me alone.

How often are you lonely? Take your time considering this, recalling the moments you feel it even surrounded by people. Can you see, in your heart, these moments may be invitations to connect with the Spirit in your heart?

Not A Luxury

It is in vain that you rise up early and go late to rest,
eating the bread of anxious toil;
for he gives to his beloved sleep.

PSALM 127:2 ESV

When we are working too hard, we are working too hard. If you wake up exhausted, please know this is not God's plan for you. He has given us time for everything he intends for us to accomplish. Certainly, times of financial hardship call for some sacrifice and extra hard work, but running your body into the ground is not what your Father expects of you. It just isn't.

Please read in this verse all the love with which it was written! He adores you. He cares deeply about your physical well-being, and the sleep-hours are when he repairs the damage of the day, when he replenishes the energy spent on living. Rest is a need, not a luxury. Because he provides for all our needs, God will always provide for us to rest.

Father, thank you for rest, for sleep. I know I tend to see it as a gift, and tell myself it's selfish to want too much—or even enough. Help me remember, and to lovingly pass on, that rest is a need, and that you, my Provider, take care of every need.

> *It is useless for you to work so hard*
> *from early morning until late at night,*
> *anxiously working for food to eat;*
> *for God gives rest to his loved ones.*

PSALM 127:2 NLT

If we are denying ourselves the healing, restorative power of sleep, we are denying ourselves power. We are also telling God we don't trust his power, and that we think we have a better plan.

If you don't have time to sleep, you are doing more than what God has given you to do. No matter what is going on in your life, rest assured of this: the Lord will make a way for you to rest. You need only walk in it.

God who never sleeps, I am in awe. Tireless, ready to catch me as I collapse from all my effort, you invite me to rest. You designed me for times of great accomplishment, and times of replenishment. Remind me that I need rest and reassure me it's okay to take it. Refresh and restore me as I break from all my striving and help me remember that even in the wake of my best effort, it is you who truly provides.

Do you believe this? Do you trust him enough to rest? Pray for his help, comfort, and rest.

Run to Win

Do you not know that in a race all the runners run, but only one gets the prize? Run in such a way as to get the prize.

1 CORINTHIANS 9:24 NIV

Just within the 21st century, large organized runs have become hugely popular. Where we used to be awed by a marathoner, we now likely know several. We may even be among them. An older person, on hearing you ran a race last weekend, may ask, "Did you win?" For the vast majority of us, it's an amusing, adorable question. "No, Nana, I didn't win."

Whether a 5K or 50K, we're usually just running to run. How much differently would we run—and train—if we were running to win? The dedication, preparation, and all-out effort we put forth when we want to come in first is the kind of effort Paul was encouraging the Corinthian church to apply to their ministry, and the same dedication Jesus loves to see in his followers today. Love like your life depends on it. Give like you have an endless supply. Run to win.

Lord Jesus, I know my faith life jogs along at a pretty comfortable pace. If worship were a race, I'd be in the middle of the pack. I want to sing louder, dance more freely. If service were a marathon, I'd be with the six-hour group, taking walk breaks and pacing myself for minimal aftereffects. I want to serve with passion, running until I collapse. Light my faith on fire, God. I want to run to win.

Do you not know that in a race the runners all compete, but only one receives the prize? Run in such a way that you may win it.

1 CORINTHIANS 9:24 NRSV

Multiple translations lead to wonderful little discoveries in God's Word: "that you may win it." One word, *may*, opens up a whole new line of thinking.

There's a lovely humility to running as if you may win. It acknowledges the abilities and contributions of others. It bows to the will of God. We do what we can to make it possible, but we submit to the Lord in whether it will be.

God, thank you for this unexpected invitation to humility. Tucked inside a verse about going all out with my effort is this lovely reminder to reign in my pride. I will run as though winning is possible, as if I may. I know there may be someone faster, and God, I know it may be your will that I win on another day. Regardless, and humbly, I will run that I may win today.

Spend your quiet time tonight sharing your heart about winning, about competition, with the Lord.

What Marvels

God created great sea creatures and every living thing that scurries and swarms in the water, and every sort of bird—each producing offspring of the same kind. And God saw that it was good.

GENESIS 1:21 NLT

Do you ever just see a creature and laugh, or marvel, or cringe? The huge array of living things in our world is a mind-boggling display of God's inventiveness. What was he thinking when he made the jellyfish, the hammerhead shark, or the starfish? And what of flamingoes, mallards, and even fat, noisy little blue jays?

Even if your days hold no obvious need for creative inspiration, spending a few minutes in awe of God's imagination is bound to infuse you with perspective.

Father God, how you inspire me! The natural world is overflowing with colorful, crazy examples of your playful, intricate mind. Forgive me for taking the variety and complexity of creation for granted. It's a wonderful world.

God created the great sea creatures and every living creature that moves, with which the waters swarm, according to their kinds, and every winged bird according to its kind. And God saw that it was good.

GENESIS 1:21 ESV

In addition to the delightful variety of God's creatures is the incredible way things all fit together.

Studied carefully, every created thing will be found to serve a purpose. There is meaning in the lion's mane, in the mallard's green head, and in the song of the mockingbird. There is purpose in the life of an ant. What many marvels he has made, and all to his delight.

You saw that it was good, God, and so do I. It is so good, this created, creative, ever-changing world. I know I can't begin to comprehend the ways we all work together, so I will just stand in awe of the One who made it so.

How many species of bird can you think of? Why so many, other than to delight the Maker—and those he made in his image?

Keep Pace

Those who wait for the LORD shall renew their strength,
they shall mount up with wings like eagles,
they shall run and not be weary,
they shall walk and not faint.

ISAIAH 40:31 NRSV

In Isaiah 40:31 we have another Bible verse that is easily misinterpreted. This is not a promise for unlimited strength and endurance. It's a promise that when we keep pace with the Lord, we can be assured of having all the power we need.

What strength we spend, he will renew when we wait for him. The distance we run with him will be a distance we can handle. His pace will not cause us to faint.

Father God, thank you for assuring me that a journey with you is a well-balanced, replenishing one. It is only when I run ahead of you that I start to pant, that my legs start to quiver. Alongside you, I can breathe. My body feels strong and capable. It is only when I refuse to slow down, to stop, that I may lose my strength altogether. When I wait for you, when I stay in your rhythm, my strength is continually renewed.

Those who wait for the LORD will gain new strength;
they will mount up with wings like eagles,
they will run and not get tired,
they will walk and not become weary.

ISAIAH 40:31 NASB

God doesn't need rest. He could go for ever. He stops for us. How loving. How beautifully sensitive to our needs he is. He never needs to slow down. In fact, it's probably a bit of an effort for him to move as slowly as we need to go. And yet he slows—for us.

Just think how much faster God could get things done without us. But he doesn't want to do them alone—he wants to walk with us.

Lord God, when I consider how boundless your strength is, and how endless your abilities are, I realize the pace you set is for me. You call me to wait on you—for me. You rest because I need rest. How patient and loving you are, moving at a speed that's right for me despite all you could do without me. Like a father who sees his exhausted child and asks if he can rest, you sense my weariness, then invite me to pause and wait for you.

Bask in the tender, patient love of your sweet Papa tonight.

Precious Burdens

Give your burdens to the L<small>ORD</small>,
nd he will take care of you.
He will not permit the godly to slip and fall.

P<small>SALM</small> 55:22 <small>NLT</small>

If you've ever tried to walk on a slippery or unstable surface while carrying something, you know how much more difficult the challenge was. Not only did you need to balance your body, but you had to balance the burden, which was likely blocking your sight too.

Your Father wants you steady. He can't bear to see you slip and fall. Whatever it is you carry, from sadness to shame to more obligations than time, let him take them off your hands. Let him free you to use your arms for balance. Learn to walk with an unobstructed view. The Lord has your burdens well in hand, as he also has you.

God, I've been carrying these burdens so long, I'm not even sure I can balance without their weight. Hold me up, Father, as I find my feet beneath me, as I get used to being able to see the ground. Help me trust you to carry me—burdens and all.

Here's what I've learned through it all:
leave all your cares and anxieties at the feet of the Lord,
and measureless grace will strengthen you.

PSALM 55:22 TPT

How comfortable are you leaving everything you carry with
someone else? If what you hold is precious, like a child, or
fragile, like glass, it's hard to let it out of your hands, much
less your sight. If your arms hold only laundry, or garbage, to
let it go is sweet relief.

Trust it all to Jesus. What's precious to you is that much more
precious to him, and what's holding you back and weighing you
down is his pleasure to take off your hands. Let him have it.
Leave it at his feet and pick up measureless grace in its place.

*Jesus, when I think of precious burdens, I realize how tightly I
cling to them. No matter how heavy, I convince myself I alone can
carry this priceless cargo. Can I give them to you? I ask not because
I doubt your willingness, but because I question my strength to let
them fall. Pry open my weary arms, God, and replenish them with
your grace.*

What precious burden are you holding too tightly? Ask the
Spirit for the courage to loosen your grip.

Quick to Listen

My dear brothers and sisters, take note of this: Everyone should be
quick to listen, slow to speak and slow to become angry.

JAMES 1:19 NIV

Wait. *Quick to listen?* Shouldn't we take our time as listeners,
be patient? Consider the quickest speed imaginable:
instant. If listening were our instant, immediate, instinctive
response, would we not be quick to listen?

Slow to speak. This, we understand. And yet we struggle.
Thoughts come forth and our instinct is to release them as
speech. But as we first pause, think, and pray, how often
might our silence be more beneficial than those impulsive
words? Were we not merely waiting to talk, how much more
might we hear?

Oh God, that I could learn to listen as you do! You sometimes
let me go on all day before you respond. And yet I know you
are paying attention; your compassion floods my heart. Be my
example, God, and let quiet compassion flow from mine as I
listen. When I do speak, let it be only after hearing from you what
I should say.

This you know, my beloved brethren. But everyone must be quick to hear, slow to speak and slow to anger;

JAMES 1:19 NASB

Slow to anger. This might be the hardest of the three, considering how anger flares like a match—catches fire like parched leaves.

When we feel insulted and indignation rises up, can we train our hearts, with Christ's help, to pause, snuffing anger's spark? When we're denied respect, can we postpone offense? By thinking more and more of Jesus, can we think less enough of ourselves that anger's flame is never fanned?

Only through your power, Jesus, can I be slow to anger. Only as you replace my thoughts of self with thoughts of you can I face my insulter without anger, my offender without offense. But I do have you, Lord. I do have your power. Soak me with so much love for you, for each of your precious children, that even a single spark of anger has no way to form.

How often are you angry? Whether frequent or rare, consider your triggers, and invite the Lord to help you diffuse their power.

As I Wait

> *Be strong and courageous,*
> *all you who put your hope in the Lord!*
>
> PSALM 31:24 NLT

"I know, but…" Why is there so often a "but?" If only knowing were enough. We know the Lord is entirely trustworthy. We know he is actually incapable of deceit. We know God is love. How, then, is it that we question him? In light of all we know, doubt is unreasonable. We know he can. Whatever it is, we know he can.

But we wonder if he will. We worry this thing we hope for may be out of his will. So we fear: perhaps he won't. This is why the Father tells us so often to be strong and courageous. Hope is stronger than fear. Love is stronger than fear. God is stronger than fear.

God, I know you. I know your power, your goodness, and your love. I know you can do anything. Forgive me, precious Savior, for the times I fear your will. I draw strength from what I know of your goodness. I draw courage from what I know of your love. I have hope because you are my Lord. In confidence I pray, "Whatever is your will."

> *Be strong, and let your heart take courage,*
> *all you who wait for the LORD!*

PSALM 31:24 ESV

Waiting is hard. We look for the shortest line, the quickest-moving lane, the fast-forward button on the remote.

When we come to the Lord for help, it's often to request timely solutions to our problems. If he doesn't answer quickly enough, doubt creeps in. Is he listening? Is he there?

Encourage me, dear God, as I wait for your resolution. Remind me you see the whole picture, and that your plan is for the best outcome, which is seldom the quickest. Fortify my heart with patience, courage, and strength while I wait. I trust your plan, and I rejoice in knowing all will be well.

How easy or difficult is it for you to wait for the Lord?

Good News

If you openly declare that Jesus is Lord and believe in your heart that God raised him from the dead, you will be saved. For it is by believing in your heart that you are made right with God, and it is by openly declaring your faith that you are saved.

ROMANS 10:9-10 NLT

If you're wondering how to boil your faith down for someone, to explain it simply and succinctly, this, right here, is the famous good news. There is no complicated set of rules to adopt, no ceremony, no sacrifice required. Believing in Jesus' resurrection wipes your slate clean with God, and saying it out loud assures you a place in heaven.

It is good news, isn't it? The most important decision we'll ever make, the most important sentence we'll ever speak, and it's simple. There is no script, trick, or catch. There is only faith, and the courage to speak it aloud.

You make it so easy, Father! To believe and to speak of the incomprehensible love you showed for me by sending your Son to suffer on behalf of all my sins—confessed and unconfessed, past and future—is all you ask of me. I am forgiven, and I am welcomed into heaven. What wonderful, awesome news.

If you confess with your mouth Jesus as Lord, and believe in your heart that God raised Him from the dead, you will be saved; for with the heart a person believes, resulting in righteousness, and with the mouth he confesses, resulting in salvation.

Romans 10:9-11 NASB

Confession. Most people don't get warm fuzzies from the word, and understandably. In every other case, for something to be confessed implies wrongness: wrong actions, wrong motives, wrong us. We confess to committing a crime, to cheating on a test, to betraying a confidence. We don't confess to getting a promotion, getting engaged, or joining a new Bible study.

But a confession of faith is different. What we're admitting is our admission into God's family—and there's certainly nothing wrong with that.

God, I confess I don't always love to confess. Sometimes, to speak my wrongness is more than I can bear. What a blessing it is to know that just to confess that Jesus died for me—just to believe in my heart you raised him up—is enough to set me right with you.

Are you able to see confession as a gift, as a source of freedom? If you need help with this, ask the Lord.

Warm and Fuzzy

Remind them to be submissive to rulers and authorities,
to be obedient, to be ready for every good work,
to speak evil of no one, to avoid quarreling, to be gentle,
and to show perfect courtesy toward all people.

TITUS 3:1-2 ESV

How many words in the first line of this verse had you
bristling at least a little bit, maybe even considering skipping
today's reading? Submission and obedience—rulers and
authorities—just like last night's "confession," are not exactly
warm and fuzzy words. In fact, in our modern culture, they've
gotten downright prickly.

Because Christ lives in us, it doesn't really matter what
anyone does to us, says about us, or takes from us. Everything
that matters is inside us—inside him—so there is no reason,
none at all, not to be warm and fuzzy to everyone—regardless
of how they behave toward us.

*Jesus, your example of submissiveness and respect, of gentleness
and courtesy are perfect models for how to do this right. You, who
had every right to take authority over all, never did. Because your
citizenship was in heaven, you let earth have its way. All my hope
is in you, so I'll walk gently, peaceably, obediently in your way.*

*Remind the believers to yield to the authority of rulers
and government leaders, to obey them, to be ready to do good,
to speak no evil about anyone, to live in peace,
and to be gentle and polite to all people.*

TITUS 3:1-2 NCV

It's not a whole lot easier to swallow at the end of the day than at the beginning, is it? Strong, modern women are supposed to stand up for themselves, be subject to no one, right?

It's helpful to remember this letter was written for the benefit of early Christians, trying to set themselves apart by their warmth, gentleness, and love. It's equally helpful to remember that is still our goal a few thousand years later. We're called to stand out, and in this world we live in, sweetness, compliance, and lovingkindness are excellent ways to do so.

*God, I long for a world where these behaviors are not unusual!
If we all treated each other with love and respect, we'd have no
reason to fear submission—those in authority would be working
for the same good as we are. Let love rule. I long for the day.*

Take time with your Father tonight praying about your attitude toward submission, authority, and obedience. Invite him to show you his intention for these prickly words.

What You Need

*My God will use his wonderful riches in Christ Jesus
to give you everything you need.*

PHILIPPIANS 4:19 NCV

What do you need? The more you think about it, the smaller the list becomes, and the easier it is to believe the Lord will always make sure you have it. Because of his great love for you, he will make a way to feed and clothe and keep you safe. But beyond that, so far beyond that, he will supply you from the riches of Christ.

This hints at a life of unspeakable joy. This suggests all the patience we require, and the ability to be kind to everyone we meet. This opens the way to an abundance of selfless love. And what more could we possibly need?

God, I get caught up in what I think I need, in this world's idea of riches. But you offer riches in Christ, treasures beyond measure. Make me rich in love, loaded with generosity. Give me a wealth of wisdom, so I will know your riches are all I really need.

My God will supply every need of yours
according to his riches in glory in Christ Jesus.

PHILIPPIANS 4:19 ESV

Have you ever wondered how it is that God always seems to know what you need? How wonderful it is too, that he never tires of supplying it. Even when material needs appear to go unmet, the tender, intimate way he loves us supplies us with a level of joy and peace we may not otherwise have experienced, and didn't know we needed.

The way the Lord ministers to us in our need often illuminates how much we actually have. His sustaining grace has a way of eclipsing suffering and want, giving us a joyful satisfaction in every circumstance.

Father God, you are such a wonderful provider! Some of the most joyful, contented people I've ever seen are those with little more than your love to sustain them. This inspires my heart to trust and fills it with gratitude for the amazing way you've supplied my life. I know I don't deserve it but that never stops you. Your provision is as endless as your love. Provide me now with a heart as grateful as this knowledge deserves.

Tell God what you really need tonight.

Simple Pleasures

I've learned from my experience
that God protects the childlike and humble ones.
For I was broken and brought low,
but he answered me and came to my rescue!

PSALM 116:6 TPT

In a dangerous situation, would it be your instinct to protect a child or a soldier? It's impossible to imagine pushing past a little one to throw ourselves in front of someone armed and prepared. We go where we are needed.

So it is with the Lord. The more confident we are in our own ability, the less vulnerable before him, the less of his protection he offers. Not because he is offended by us, but because he does not force himself on us. But when we do cry to him, humble and helpless, we can be sure he will come to our rescue.

God, help me! Help me first to get over the illusion that I don't need your aid. No matter how strong I feel, I am weak next to your power. No matter how well I think I understand, I am a fool in the wake of your wisdom. Humble me, God, to reach out for your rescuing arms.

The LORD protects the simple;
when I was brought low, he saved me.

PSALM 116:6 NRSV

As vast, holy, and awesome as our God is, he still makes it simple for us to please him. He loves our honest, unadorned prayers, our expressions of gratitude for moments of ordinary happiness. He loves our contentment with a simple, quiet life.

God knows the more we amass by way of possessions, responsibilities, and distractions, the easier it is to lose sight of the simple pleasure of being his child. And he never wants that to happen.

Father God, thank you for simple pleasures. Thank you for reminding me how much it delights you when I recognize sweetness in the details of my life. May worry never cloud my appreciation of a sunset, or the stench of fear cause me to miss the fragrance of a vase of flowers. May I simply be grateful for all you do for me.

Drift off tonight by making a list of your favorite simple pleasures.

The Well

*He gives strength to those who are tired
and more power to those who are weak.*

ISAIAH 40:29 NCV

He knows you are tired; he has strength and more strength to give you. He knows when you feel weak; his power is yours for the asking. How encouraging! And how true. Test him in this; he wants you to.

On a morning that feels like you haven't rested at all, ask confidently for strength. On a day that is simply too heavy, when your burdens have left you weak, call out boldly for power. Expect it. Be ready for it. Because he will supply it.

God, you are my power supply. This is good because my own reserves run continually low. Forgive me for forgetting to rely on you sometimes, for getting far more exhausted than I need to before calling out to you. I call and you supply; it's amazing. How generous you are and how very strong.

He gives power to the faint,
and strengthens the powerless.

ISAIAH 40:29 NRSV

Have you had a day that just drained you, maybe even this one? It's tempting to wonder if the Lord is paying attention, to wonder why he didn't come in and plug the drain, especially if we asked him to.

One of the reasons our Father allows us to become depleted is so we'll remember he is our source. For power, strength, courage, hope, and more, he is the well.

God, your strength can move mountains, and I've got one I could use your help with. Because I know how intimately you attend to me, I know you are aware of my burden. I know you won't allow it to crush me, but there are days it brings me quite low. I need you. Is that why you allow me to bear it, so I'll remember? Remember I need you, remember I have you, always, remember I am never alone.

Pour your heart out to God regarding where you are feeling faint, where the weight grows heavy.

We've Been Paid

> "Beware of practicing your righteousness before other people in order to be seen by them, for then you will have no reward from your Father who is in heaven."

MATTHEW 6:1 ESV

Awards, recognition, promotion, and accolades feel great—even more so when they are unexpected. It's one kind of thrill to enter a contest and come out on top, and a whole other to receive a surprise thank you, celebration, or shout-out. There you were, just doing you, and boom! You didn't even know anyone was watching.

This is the kind of service that is pleasing to the Lord. We give because we are able, help because we are moved. Our hearts are on the giving, on the helping, not on the attention we will receive for doing it. And Jesus' heart is bursting with love for ours.

Holy Spirit, give me this kind of heart. I want to be so focused on what I can give, how I can help, and who I can serve, I don't even begin to notice who sees. I want my goodness to please you. I don't need accolades and awards, just a heart that loves to help.

> *"Be careful! When you do good things, don't do them in front of people to be seen by them. If you do that, you will have no reward from your Father in heaven."*
>
> MATTHEW 6:1 NCV

If you performed a job for your neighbors, you wouldn't expect to be paid by both the husband and the wife. One job equals one payday, right? This is a helpful way to consider what Jesus is saying about our good deeds.

If we work for the attention and approval of people, we've been paid when they notice us, when they tell us how good we are. Why expect the Lord to pay us again?

God, search my heart. You know my motives better than I. Am I volunteering my time to impress my friends, or to please my Father? Do I donate so I can feel good about myself, or so that I can help assure your children are being fed? I want to work for you, God, and for your glory alone.

It's okay to enjoy being appreciated. The Lord encourages us to recognize one another. Approval is a wonderful reward; just let him search your heart, to make sure it's not your motivation.

There Is Nothing

Do not throw away your confidence, which has a great reward.

HEBREWS 10:35 NASB

We'd never throw money in the trash, or an exquisitely prepared meal down the disposal. Our most treasured heirlooms are not in danger of being tossed into the ocean. We hold on to things of value, which is what makes this admonishment from Hebrews so intriguing. Throw away confidence? Why would we do that?

Usually, if something of value is cast aside, it's by accident. Haste, or distraction, causes us not to notice what is happening. Perhaps we set our confidence down when we pick up worry. Perhaps we throw it off to catch a flying load of shame. However, it could happen, let's do all we can to hold on to our confidence like the treasure it is.

Lord Jesus, you give me the gift of confidence. It is the reason I can come before you with my needs, the reason I can fall asleep at night knowing they will be met. It is what allows me to stand apart from a world that tells me to want the world. Don't let me throw it away. Let me hold onto it as I hold onto you.

Do not throw away this confident trust in the Lord.
Remember the great reward it brings you!

HEBREWS 10:35 NLT

Who do you trust? Is it because they've given you no reason to doubt you, they have filled you with confidence in their integrity, ability, and commitment?

This person you trust, can you imagine willingly giving up the closeness you share? It's unthinkable. Equally unimaginable would be to give up on the Lord. The awesome rewards of a life spent loving and trusting Christ are simply too great to throw away.

Jesus, what could be worth giving you up, throwing away my trust in you, placing my confidence elsewhere? There is nothing, there is no one, who could possibly care for me, understand me, and empower me the way you do. Whatever else I hold onto, let none of it come before you.

For as many seconds as you can bear it, imagine your life without the confident hope you have in the Lord. Thank him that this will never, ever be.

He Remains Faithful

If we are faithless, He remains faithful; He cannot deny Himself.

2 TIMOTHY 2:13 NKJV

No matter what, God remains faithful. Just pause for a moment and consider this extraordinary truth. No. Matter. What. The perfect one, deserving of all our devotion, is completely devoted to us. No matter how many times we forget him, doubt him, grieve him, and defy him, he remains faithful. It's just who he is.

There are glimpses of this here on earth: the mother who welcomes home the addicted child, the wife who forgives the wandering husband, and even the sweet retriever who waits nightly by the window for the sound of your car. They are but glimpses of how God forgives, endures, and waits on you.

Father, I pray this picture of your steadfast commitment to me will inspire me to a greater faithfulness to you. You deserve all my dedication, all my love, and I want to give it. Strengthen my resolve to please and honor you; let my gratitude be felt as faithfulness back to you.

If we are not faithful, he will still be faithful,
because he must be true to who he is.

2 TIMOTHY 2:13 NCV

You cry at happy movies, you laugh when you are uncomfortable, and you sneeze when you are nervous. We are who we are.

You can no more change these things about yourself than you can change the number of freckles on your arm. Nor can God change his faithfulness toward you, his love for you, and his unlimited capacity for grace. He is who he is. And oh, aren't you glad?

Lord God, you can only be what you are, and what you are is perfect, and perfectly faithful. I too can only be what I am and today, that is awed and humbled by you. Make me more like you. I want to be known for my faithfulness and recognized by my love. Thank you for your faithfulness to me. Thank you for being who you are.

What are you known for? What would you like to be known for?

Obeying God

> *Peter and the other apostles replied:*
> *"We must obey God rather than human beings!"*
>
> ACTS 5:29 NIV

The boldness of the apostles in Acts is amazing. Over and
over, they refuse to stop teaching, healing, and proclaiming
in the name of Jesus. Jail, beatings, and even shipwrecks
don't deter them from their God-given mission. It really
didn't matter what people wanted them to do; they needed to
do what God wanted them to do.

Somewhere in the world, right this very moment, a
missionary is doing the same. Despite the illegality of
Christianity, they are holding a Bible study in their living
room. They are speaking of Jesus on the subway. They are
praying in a sidewalk café. Their freedom and even their lives
are at risk, but they can't stop to care about that; they need to
do what God has called them to do.

*Awesome. The call you place on some who love you, and the
obedience with which they respond, is awesome, God. I'm
listening in case you want to ask more of me. Compelled by love to
obey you, may the example of my brothers and sisters inspire me to
be as brave as you call me to be.*

Peter and the apostles answered,
"We must obey God rather than any human authority."

ACTS 5:29 NRSV

Obeying God means walking in light, living in love, and speaking the truth. Why would we resist? And yet we do. The pull of the world is strong, and we want to fit in. We want to be liked. We hate to offend. And yet we must.

To walk in light, we must leave darkness behind. Living in love means turning from hate. Speaking the truth requires a willingness to offend in the name of love.

Holy Spirit, I need your help. Compel me to the light, draw me toward love, plant me in truth. I must obey you. Not because you demand it, but because it's all I want from life.

In the absence of a cross necklace or a Bible in your hand, how long would it take for a person to recognize you as a Christ follower? Pray honestly about this, asking the Holy Spirit to speak to your heart.

You Are New

If anyone is in Christ, there is a new creation:
everything old has passed away; see, everything has become new!

2 CORINTHIANS 5:17 NRSV

The Lord makes all things new. The moment you chose to love him, he began transforming you. He washed you clean. Years of sin, guilt, regret and grime are gone. It's hard to grasp, isn't it? You're a whole new you. So how well are you grasping it? Do you really believe you are forgiven? Can it be true that you are new?

You may need help understanding that the old self, the one who needed defenses, regrets, grudges, and contention is truly gone. You may go looking for her. You may try to dig her up. You don't need her anymore. You never did.

Perfect Father, can this be true? Can this bright, joyful, gracious, peaceful person be me? Help me believe it, and help me accept this gift of transformation. Help me leave the old self where she lies and bask in the beauty of my newness in you.

Anyone who belongs to Christ has become a new person.
The old life is gone; a new life has begun!

2 CORINTHIANS 5:17 NLT

There are periods, whether of hours or days, where the newness we have in Christ can feel like a pair of new jeans: a little stiff, a little scratchy. We may long for the worn, frayed familiarity of our old selves.

God understands. He knows newness takes getting used to. That's why we have his Spirit with us, to listen, encourage, and uplift us as we settle in.

Thank you, God, for your endless patience. You don't judge me for reaching back toward the familiar; you love me, then and now, and you understand that newness, even when it's so much better, takes time to settle into. While I find my way to comfort, let me settle into you.

Regardless of how long ago he made you new, do you find yourself looking for—digging up—your old self? Take your thoughts before him and let him set you free from any old chains.

Search Me

> *Search me, God, and know my heart;*
> *test me and know my anxious thoughts.*
>
> PSALM 139:23 NIV

This may be the boldest prayer in all of Scripture. Think about it. Do you really want to ask God to search out every corner of your heart—to put your mind to a test that will reveal all your hidden anxieties? A predictable knee-jerk reaction would be a resounding, "No!" but what if we did ask, what if he did search?

Once God has exposed it all, there's nothing to hide. We may be afraid of discovering hidden flaws, but why? Once they're flushed out of hiding, we can deal with them. He can deal with them. What freedom awaits the sincere speaker of this prayer.

Okay, Lord. Search me. Show me what I've hidden, forgotten, and buried. Show me what has grown in the places I've neglected. Expose the lurking anxieties too vague to name, that they lose their hold on me completely. Lay bare unspoken jealousies and shame, so together we can confront them—and send them away. Search me, God, and set me free.

God, I invite your searching gaze into my heart.
Examine me through and through;
find out everything that may be hidden within me.
Put me to the test and sift through all my anxious cares.

PSALM 139:23 TPT

God sees even what we imagine, hears what we think but do not say. How deeply he must love us to forgive our every thought.

We may be tempted to hide the worst of it: the jealousy, anger, and fear, but then we would miss out on experiencing the depth of his love as he sends it all away. Let him in. Let him overwhelm it all with grace.

Come closer, Father. Is there anything tucked away in my heart that's keeping me from you? I want to show you everything so you can forgive it all, change it all, replace it all with love.

Are you ready to invite this experience? Sit with the Lord in however you are feeling about him sifting through your heart.

So It Will

> *"I will give them one heart, and put a new spirit within them.*
> *And I will take the heart of stone out of their flesh*
> *and give them a heart of flesh."*
>
> EZEKIEL 11:19 NASB

It's an incredible, beautiful, impossible picture: everyone with one heart. Every person on this earth believing, valuing, loving, and working for the same thing. We'd see an end to hunger, to war, and to oppression. None of those things would exist if the whole world had hearts that beat for God. No one could go hungry, because no one could bear to allow it. With nothing to fight about and no one to battle against, all fighting would have to cease.

All bearing the heart of God, all containing his Spirit, this world would be overwhelmed by beauty. There would be no end to grace. There would be no containing joy.

Father God, please do it. Remove my cold, hard heart and replace it with yours. What sound, the synchronous beating? What beauty, the glowing faces of those who are of your flesh. It sounds like heaven, God, and I'm ready for it to come.

"I will give them singleness of heart and put a new spirit within them. I will take away their stony, stubborn heart and give them a tender, responsive heart."

EZEKIEL 11:19 NLT

I will. This isn't a fantasy. It's a promise. There will be a day where we all see eye to eye, and every eye is on the Savior. There will be a day when the Holy Spirit is the spirit that lives in every human soul.

There will be an end to selfishness, stubbornness, and cruelty. He said it will happen, and so it will.

God, I believe you. I believe you will change our hearts, renew our spirits, and unite us in purpose and in love. Your will be done, God, and may it be soon.

What promise of God's do you most eagerly await to see fulfilled?

Don't Lose Heart

*Let us not grow weary while doing good,
for in due season we shall reap if we do not lose heart.*

GALATIANS 6:9 NKJV

You worked and studied, worked and studied, and when it was time to take the test, you earned a B+. Your roommate partied and slept, partied and slept, and on test day, bought a copy of the answers—and herself an A. There are so many things about the situation to be upset with; it's hard to know where to start.

It's hard not to lose heart. We do the right thing because it's the right thing, but when we see people taking shortcuts and getting rewarded for it, it can get a little wearying. *Why do I bother? I might as well cheat...lie...steal...*Where does it end? We must keep heart, take heart, hold onto our hearts with all our might.

I do grow tired, Lord. As I toil away by the rules, I see others making their own rules—and their load seems lighter. Their road looks easier. Don't let me lose heart, God! I do good because you are good, and I want to do things your way. Give me strength of heart as I walk the higher, harder road.

Don't allow yourselves to be weary or disheartened in planting good seeds, for the season of reaping the wonderful harvest you've planted is coming!

GALATIANS 6:9 TPT

Most fruit trees take at least five years to produce a good harvest of fruit. For the first four years, tending a brand-new orchard is bound to be a little disheartening at times. Will all that effort pay off?

So too in our faith life, long seasons of sowing, tending, and waiting can pick away at our peace. Remember every step is progress, even well before the first bloom. The seeds must be planted, the trunk must grow tall and the branches strong before the apple blooms, so keep planting and take heart.

God, how do you not grow tired waiting for us to bloom, to bear fruit? I exhaust myself with all my sidesteps and transplanting, and I am just one of your many children. I will take heart from your patient strength and your willing waiting, and I'll keep sowing seeds. I'll tend the branches, water the roots, and trust that one day, there will be fruit.

Are you planting, tending, or reaping right now?

Precious Pursuit

Surely goodness and mercy shall follow me all the days of my life;
and I will dwell in the house of the LORD forever.

PSALM 23:6 NKJV

What is it about being followed by a puppy, or toddler, or
pretty much anything adorable that makes us feel so special?
When something precious pursues us, we feel precious.
When something lovable wants to be near us, we feel lovable.

What a refreshing, uplifting image this is in Psalm 23, being
followed by goodness and mercy. If goodness is staying close
to us, we must be good. With mercy so near, we need only
turn around to receive it. We must indeed be special for the
Lord to send such welcome blessings to watch over us.

Father God, to feel your goodness and mercy at my back makes
me feel safe, cherished, and special. Thank you, God, for your
relentless pursuit of me, and for giving me grace on the many days
I try to outrun it. Help me slow down so I am overtaken by your
goodness and bombarded with your mercy and love.

Surely your goodness and love will follow me
all the days of my life,
and I will dwell in the house of the LORD forever.

PSALM 23:6 NIV

Where that girl comes, trouble follows. It's an old expression, but one that has held its meaning over time. When we leave a place, we leave something behind.

As children of God, our legacy can be goodness and love. What a goal, to be the kind of person who makes a deposit of love, and leaves a trail of goodness, everywhere we go. And why shouldn't it be when our home is with the Lord?

Yes, God, I want to leave a wake of goodness behind me, a legacy of truth. Like a delicate signature scent, let my presence leave sweet reminders of you behind. Because you are my home, the atmosphere around me is peaceful, generous, and good. Even after I'm gone, let these remain wherever I have been.

What qualities would people say you bring to a room?
What is left behind when you depart?

Moved to Action

When He saw the multitudes, He was moved with compassion
for them, because they were weary and scattered,
like sheep having no shepherd.

MATTHEW 9:36 NKJV

"I was so moved!" More often than not, we say something like this after a stirring speaker, a powerful video, a devastating event. But how often does the emotion we feel lead to actual movement. How often are we moved to tears but not action?

When Jesus was moved, he took action. Seeing thousands of hungry people milling about, he organized and orchestrated a meal for everyone. Seeing the grief of his dear friends, he raised Lazarus' lifeless body from his tomb. May his example move us, beyond feeling and tears, to follow our hearts into action.

Move me, precious Lord. Show me something that breaks your heart, and move mine to get involved. Let the pity I feel for others turn to pain. May it hurt me to see hurting and remain still. May I be moved to action.

When he saw the vast crowds of people, Jesus' heart was deeply moved with compassion, because they seemed weary and helpless, like wandering sheep without a shepherd.

This miracle meal wasn't served in the heart of Ephesus, where those listening could have meandered back to their homes and eaten a meal prepared by servants. The people of the crowd were weary, helpless, and far from home. Jesus was touched by their faith: they'd travelled far and wandered long to hear him teach and experience his healing.

Jesus was moved by their need: without his help, they were as helpless and lost as sheep without a shepherd. The key to his deep compassion was the presence of real need.

God, there are so many places I could help, but I pray you will lead me where I should. Show me a need that's real. I want to act out of compassion over convenience, and faith over fashion. Let me be moved by need, God, and then move me straight to the heart of it.

Pray about your empathy and compassion tonight, without any self-condemnation or pride. Ask the Lord to show you where he'd like to see you move.

Lovely for You

This is my prayer for you: that your love will grow more and more; that you will have knowledge and understanding with your love; that you will see the difference between good and bad and will choose the good; that you will be pure and without wrong for the coming of Christ;

PHILIPPIANS 1:9-10 NCV

What if, as members of God's holy Church, we made this our prayer for one another? What if each morning, starting with this one, we prayed this over one another?

Instead of competing ideologies and cooler buildings and more entertaining social media feeds, what if we prayed that each and every place the gospel is adopted and shared would see this beautiful blessing?

Father God, I pray that your Church—from living rooms to warehouses to cathedrals to campfires—would grow in love today. I pray that our knowledge will increase, our understanding will multiply along with our love. I pray for the difference between bad and good to be clear, and for us to choose the good every time. I pray you will keep us pure. Keep us from wrong. And on the day of Christ's return, may we all be there, together, to welcome him into our waiting, open, eager, outstretched arms.

I continue to pray for your love to grow and increase beyond measure, bringing you into the rich revelation of spiritual insight in all things. This will enable you to choose the most excellent way of all—becoming pure and without offense until the unveiling of Christ.

PHILIPPIANS 1:9-10 TPT

What a beautiful picture it is, all these things working together: measureless love infusing our spiritual knowledge and insight with warmth and affection. Discernment, so that we may choose excellence, always, and to recognize that true excellence is pure.

If we possess all these things, we cannot possibly offend God. He will be well pleased with us when he returns.

As I prepare to meet you, God, I want to prepare well; I want you to be delighted with what you see. Increase my love and also my knowledge of you, so I may love as you do. Grant me wisdom to always choose the best way, the way of purity, excellence, and grace. Make me lovely for you.

Which part of Paul's lovely prayer to the Philippians do you most want to lay hold of? Do you sense the Spirit prompting you to pray for the Church as a whole?

Mightily Blessed

"Whatever you ask in prayer, you will receive, if you have faith."
MATTHEW 21:22 ESV

Lifted out of context, this verse could be used to support either side of an argument about the power of God. A detractor could drum up any number of examples of prayed-for, believed-for healings that never happened. As believers, as supporters of the truth of God's Word, let us appropriate Matthew 21:22 for the side of faith.

Not a promise for all the faithful for all of time, this is a specific example of the kind of power Jesus was bestowing on his disciples. He had just withered a fig tree with his words, and was explaining that with true faith, the faith he'd been living out in front of them, they could do that and more. They could ask a mountain to fling itself into the sea. That's the power Jesus had, and it's the power Jesus gave. That's a lot of power! Whatever fraction he sees fit to give to us, we are mightily blessed to receive.

God, I don't need to move mountains, or curse trees, so I'm content with the power you've granted my prayers. The power to be heard, to be seen, and to be blessed with the answer I need, is blessing enough for me. Thank you for the powerful gift of prayer.

"All things you ask in prayer, believing, you will receive."
MATTHEW 21:22 NASB

While Jesus wasn't speaking to all believers when he spoke this sentence, that does not mean he intends us to believe our prayers are limited.

A fully surrendered heart won't ask for anything Jesus doesn't want it to have. A life overflowing with faith won't doubt the Lord's ability to respond with willingness. So, ask, pray, and anticipate receiving your heart's desire.

God, I know nothing is beyond you. I know nothing I ask, when submitted to your will, is beyond my right to ask. Nothing I want—when you are my greatest desire—is outside your will. And when I believe, with a heart aware of your greatness, that you are for me, there is nothing you won't do. Thank you for hearing my prayer.

Does God want to grow your faith? Does he want to shape your will? What do you sense him saying to you tonight?

Room for Me

"My Father's house has many rooms; if that were not so, would I have told you that I am going there to prepare a place for you?"

JOHN 14:2 NIV

Imbedded in this lovely picture of heaven—room for everyone who calls God, Father—lies an admonishment to trust the Son. *There's more than enough room for you. I'm coming back for you. If I wasn't, why would I have said that I was readying your room?*

"Don't you trust me?" Jesus seems to say. He had never lied to them, never led them on, never made a promise he didn't keep. He did everything he said he would do, and proved every claim he ever made. And still they doubted. Still they feared. As do we. He knows this. He understands, and once he comes to take us home, we'll see how right we were to trust him—from the comfort of our very own room.

Oh Jesus, forgive me for my days of doubt. You are entirely trustworthy, so I know you're coming back for me. You are entirely good, so I know a special place in heaven waits exclusively for me. I just grow fearful sometimes. Like a child waiting to see the shine of Daddy's headlights in the window, I feel better once we're home together.

> *"There are many rooms in my Father's house; I would not tell you this if it were not true. I am going there to prepare a place for you."*
>
> JOHN 14:2 NCV

Think of moving to a new house as a child. What is the first thing you want to see, before the kitchen, the family room, or even the big back yard? It's your room, the space that's just for you. The place that holds your bed and your books, your drawings and your dreams. What did he bring for you? What color did he paint your walls, and when you look out the window, what will you see?

God in heaven, I love imagining you there, trying to picture you at ease. I try to imagine myself there with you, but I don't think my mind has the vocabulary yet. A room—in your house—made specifically for me? I see it filled with things that show how well you know me, how well you've always known me. Thank you for your abiding love. I can't wait to come home.

As you fall asleep tonight, try to picture your place in heaven.

Brave Enough

Though he fall, he shall not be cast headlong,
for the LORD upholds his hand.

PSALM 37:24 ESV

Do you remember as a little girl, playing a game where your job was to fall and someone stronger was to catch you? They were like human bungee cords, ensuring our bounce back to safety. With a hand on our little overalls, or clasped around our own, no matter how many times we fell, we never dropped.

Your Abba's favorite part of you is still that little child, trying new things, falling off edges, confident that you'll be caught, you'll bounce back. Brave enough to fall, because you've never been dropped.

Thank you for playing with me, Abba. You let me jump, twirl, and fly. You let me fail and fall and flail. You let me explore my limits, and yet you keep me safe. You hold my hand in yours, which makes me brave enough to fall.

When he falls, he will not be hurled headlong,
*because the L*ORD *is the One who holds his hand.*

PSALM 37:24 NASB

As the adult in the trust-fall game, we don't suddenly decide, *I'm tired of this game. I think I'll let her drop this time.* If we're not planning to catch her, we make sure she knows it. And just in case she decides to test us, we stay close, ready to catch her if she just has to take one more fall.

So much closer still—and ever ready—is God. His arms will never get too tired, his patience won't wear out. We may fall—or even dive—off the same cliff a million times, but he'll never let us drop. Even if we give up, he never, ever will.

God, I never get tired of thinking about your patience, of thanking you for it. You're such a good Father. Your love for me, your belief in me, are a bottomless chasm. I can't mess this up. I can't lose your love. I can't fall out of your grasp. It's amazing, God. You're amazing.

Is there a fall you keep repeating, or someone else's fall you need to release to God's loving hand?

Better, Sweeter Days

"You will seek Me and find Me
when you search for Me with all your heart."

JEREMIAH 29:13 NASB

When you first wake up in the morning, Jesus wants to be wanted—more than coffee. As you move through your day, he wants to be thought of—more than your work. In the evening, he longs to be pursued—more than your rest. Wherever our heads are, wherever our hearts are, Jesus wants to be at the top of the list.

And when he is? The coffee tastes and smells even better; the tasks go more smoothly and when they don't, we mind much less; relaxation is peaceful, replenishing, and filled with sweetness. When every part of us wants him, every part of life is better.

God, help me seek you all day long, that I may find you and know better, sweeter days. Not just in my prayer time, or my quiet time, but all the time, let my first thought be of finding you. As I go about my day, let me seek you in every conversation, find you at every table; include you in every decision. All day long let me find you.

"If you look for me wholeheartedly, you will find me."
JEREMIAH 29:13 NLT

Remember playing hide and seek on a day you weren't really feeling it? You didn't find everyone, because your heart wasn't really in the search.

A halfhearted search for God—his will, his voice, his blessings—won't be any more productive. He absolutely wants to be found, but not until you're in the game, not until finding him is all you can think about.

God, I don't ever want to simply go through the motions with you, stepping through doorways but not looking behind them, walking through hallways with my eyes straight ahead. I want to find you, so I'm going all in. I'll search everywhere, even the places I've already been. I'm throwing my whole heart into it, because that's what I want from you.

How much of your heart is dedicated to God? Try to spend some honest time with this and see if you feel led to dedicate a little more.

Author of Peace

*May the Lord of peace himself give you peace
at all times in every way. The Lord be with you all.*

2 THESSALONIANS 3:16 ESV

Two people are speaking about a book you love in the next
few weeks: one event features someone who has read the
book, and the other features the author. Which event would
you most like to attend? As intriguing as this other speaker's
thoughts and insights may be, they will not compare to the
thoughts and insights of the one who wrote the words.

God is the author of peace. He dreamed it up; he worked
out the details and wrote it all down. Though there are
many peaceful moments in life, none of them can provide
you with the sustaining peace of a heart that belongs to the
Lord. It defies circumstance and overrides condition; it is
everlasting, and it is yours for the asking.

*Lord of Peace, how I thank you for this beautiful, mysterious gift.
Though circumstances rage and swirl around me, the moment
I turn to you, I am tranquil. It's incredible really. Sometimes it
seems like the crazier life gets, the calmer I feel; this can only be
your peace in me. This can only be you with me. Stay, that I may
live in your peace.*

*May the Lord himself, the Lord of peace, pour into you
his peace in every circumstance and in every possible way.
The Lord's tangible presence be with you all.*

2 THESSALONIANS 3:16 TPT

Things are tense. You're stressed, you're late, and one more thing will be two too many. And then that song comes on, the one that reminds you just exactly how loved you are, how good God is. *Thank you, Lord! I needed that.*

Paying attention, it's astonishing how often God speaks to our hearts, ushering peace into our chaos. The right verse, song, or message comes and just like that, though the chaos remains, we are at peace.

God, you amaze me. Your presence and attentiveness are a constant source of peace. Your creativity in bringing me to the center is so playful, so inventive. I could be facing any manner of storm, and though you may not calm it, you know precisely how to calm me. Thank you, God, for your impossibly perfect peace.

Right now, turn your attention to the peace the Lord provides. Invite him to regularly, creatively bless you with incomprehensible, circumstance-defying peace.

A Generous Heart

"Give, and it will be given to you. They will pour into your lap a good measure—pressed down, shaken together, and running over. For by your standard of measure it will be measured to you in return."

LUKE 6:38 NASB

I didn't want to go, but I forced myself and it ended up being an amazing night! It's so true, isn't it, and so often? When we deny our personal feelings and take one for the team, we are blessed by the experience in ways we wouldn't have imagined. A wife who reluctantly attends a work function for her husband meets a delightful new friend. A beleaguered mother ignores her fatigue and volunteers in her child's classroom, and receives a thank you gift of homemade bath salts.

God sees when our desire to help, to give, to serve outweighs our desire to rest, to hang onto what we have, and to be served. He so loves a generous heart, and especially when our generosity costs us something. He loves to give back even more than we let go.

Generous God, each time I give generously, you pour your blessings back on me. You replace what I gave and more, and you also grant me joy. You bring new people, new blessings, new gifts into my life each time I'm willing to give a piece of it away. Thank you for your generous heart.

> *"Give, and you will receive. You will be given much. Pressed down, shaken together, and running over, it will spill into your lap. The way you give to others is the way God will give to you."*
>
> LUKE 6:38 NCV

Some days, we just don't want to hear this. *I'm generous enough. I do enough.* It's human, and the Lord understands. He doesn't become angry with us or withhold his love. But we do miss out on some joy, and on the unexpected gifts that accompany our willingness to give.

On the days it's hard to go, go anyway. On the days you feel like there's nothing left to give, give anyway. And in so doing, be blessed.

Father God, even though I have seen your blessings a million times, I still have days where I just want to keep what's mine—my time, my resources. Thank you for reminding me it is you who gives them, and you who always replaces anything I willingly give in your name. And with the renewed supply, you add to it joy, friendship, and other beautiful gifts.

Spend some time recalling the many blessings you have received through giving. Thank the Lord for his incredible generosity toward you, and for giving you a generous heart.

Keep Still

The LORD will fight for you,
and you shall hold your peace.

EXODUS 14:14 NKJV

What do you carry into battle? In a literal sense, you bring a weapon and a shield. Battling an illness, you might come armed with medications and a treatment plan. Facing a tough conversation, you hold onto your convictions and your well-rehearsed point of view. How often, in any battle do you consider bringing peace?

"And you shall hold your peace." What a beautiful picture this is, letting God do the fighting while we fill our arms with peace. Imagine heading into every confrontation behind the Lord. He devises the plan of attack, he determines the outcome, and because you trust him, because you know he is good and that he fights for you, you hold onto peace.

Lord God, with you as my sword and shield, my arms are free. Whatever enemy I face, I trust you to lead the fight. Peace is the sword I carry, disarming fear. Peace is also the shield that covers me, protecting me from doubt. Victory is ours and after victory, even more peace.

The LORD will fight for you,
and you have only to keep still.

EXODUS 14:14, NRSV

Shhh. Just keep still. One of the first lessons you learn about hide and seek is the value of stillness. The "enemy" may be only inches from you, but if you don't move, if you don't make a sound, they may leave without realizing you are even there.

Silence can keep you safe. When we trust the Lord to fight for us, one of the best things we can do is be still and let him fight. Resist the urge to run past him, swinging your sword. Keep still, hold your peace, and watch him win.

Oh Father, I don't always get this one right, do I? I ask for your help, I say I'm going to trust you, and then the moment things don't seem to be happening fast enough, or going my way, I jump up and give away my position. Help me to keep still. I know that you are God, and I trust you with my life.

Are you comfortable with keeping still, holding your peace, and trusting the Lord to fight your battles, or do you tend to run into the fray? Call on the Holy Spirit to increase your trust.

Fear Removed

I sought the LORD, and He heard me,
and delivered me from all my fears.

PSALM 34:4 NKJV

Fear steals our peace, joy, rest, and even health. God knows this, so instead of rescuing us from everything we are afraid of, he saves us from fear itself. It isn't the awaited phone call keeping you awake; it's the dread of what you might hear. The checkbook isn't causing your nervous stomach; your worry over its balance is.

Vanquish the fear, and the situation has no more hold on you. Fear has no more hold on you. Pray for the outcome, yes, but pray first for the courage to hand over your fear. This frees you to pray from a place of strength, hope, and grace.

God, you are so wise and wonderful! Instead of removing the situations I fear, you remove the fear. Were you to simply change circumstances, fear would simply find a new hiding place. Instead, you send it away. You empower me with hope; you remind me of your grace, and deliver me from all my fears.

I prayed to the LORD, and he answered me.
He freed me from all my fears.

PSALM 34:4 NLT

Fear is like a thorny vine, wrapping us up, sinking its barbs. It's fast-growing, and it can tear us apart if we get too entangled. Carefully, the Lord sets us free. Gently, he removes every thorn. Once we are out of its grip, he goes after the root, removing it from the soil.

Weeds are tenacious, and often grow back. We may even go back on our own, thinking ourselves stronger this time, able to defeat it on our own. At the first prick of fear, though, he hears our prayers and he answers. Once again, as often as we call him, he comes and sets us free.

Faithful God, you take away fear and all need of it. The only way it serves me is in reminding me to cry out to you, to trust you, to rely on you. No matter how tangled up I become, you free me. Each time it grows back, you free me again. Thank you God, for being so much stronger than my fear.

What do you fear? Armed with the power of God's Holy Spirit, refuse fear's interference over this part of your life.

I Can Rejoice

Rejoice in the Lord always. I will say it again: Rejoice!
PHILIPPIANS 4:4, NIV

Have you ever just decided to be happy? Maybe you didn't really want to be where you were, or be doing what you were doing, but you knew that if you just embraced it, you could find a way to enjoy it? We can't always control our situations, and emotions sneak up on us sometimes, but attitude is a choice. Choose joy!

What might this look like? Praise music—and a bit of dancing like no one's watching—while you clean. Meditating on the Lord's beauty while you wait. Remembering his blessings on your daily commute. You'll still be cleaning, waiting, commuting, but if you choose it, the joy of the Lord can join you there.

I confess it, Lord. My first thought was that this can't be done. I can't always feel joyful. Then, once again, you helped me see through your wise and joyful eyes. I may not feel amazing, but I can still rejoice. I can raise my voice, move my feet, and recall all the ways you bring joy to life. Before I know it, my feelings just may join the song.

Rejoice in the Lord always; again I will say, rejoice.

PHILIPPIANS 4:4 ESV

What of the happy days, where joy comes as easily as breath? Do you remember to invite the Lord to the celebration?

As you revel, as you glory and glee, do you remember the author of joy? A wonderful situation can take our eyes off the One who made it possible. Caught up in the moment, we can forget its Maker. Rejoice in the Lord; he's waiting to dance with you.

Oh, Father, sometimes the best moments are the ones I forget to thank you for. I'm wrapped up in the happiness of the people I love, the fun and the laughter, and I fail to notice you there, smiling, the one who made it happen. I owe all my best memories to you, along with all my thanks and praise. Each time I rejoice, God, let my first thought be of you.

Your Father wants you to be able to rejoice always; which of today's perspectives felt more "for you?"

Heaven Was Near

> *"Repent of your sins and turn to God,*
> *for the Kingdom of Heaven is near."*
>
> MATTHEW 3:2 NLT

When you come to a dead end, or dangerous edge, what is the first thing you do? Stop, and turn around. The Hebrew word *repent* comes from means literally *to turn*. Sin is a dead end, a dangerous edge indeed. Once we recognize this, we need to turn around. If we just stay there looking at it, we'll be stuck, or worse, we might fall in.

Once we've turned around, we're faced with the next decision: where to now? In the case of sin, the choice is beautifully, obviously clear. We head straight into the waiting arms of grace. The One who shows us our sin is the same one who takes us far away from it—into the Kingdom of love and light.

Jesus, you are so good to me. First you show me my sins, and then you save me from them. The moment I choose to turn from them I find you there, arms open, waiting to carry me away. You keep me safe, you make me whole. Yours are the arms of grace, and I turn and run to them now.

John said, "Change your hearts and lives
because the kingdom of heaven is near."

MATTHEW 3:2 NCV

Do you think John knew, when he announced the kingdom of heaven was near, that the King of Heaven himself was so close, that in a matter of days, he would step into the river and ask John to baptize him?

Surely John must have felt Jesus as he encouraged everyone he saw to choose a new life, get a clean heart, and wash sin away.

God, I love the way you weave us together, the way you've always done so. You gave John a passion for the kingdom long before he learned his own cousin was the King. The hearts he helped open he did so for you, rejecting sin and choosing love. The lives he called to change he called for you, rejecting the old way—open to the new.

What dead end or precipice is the Lord calling you to turn from? Sense his nearness and turn toward it.

You Are Perfect

Let no one say when he is tempted, "I am tempted by God"; for God cannot be tempted by evil, nor does He Himself tempt anyone.

JAMES 1:13 NKJV

There are those people we know—and strive to be more like—who are simply above blame. They seem to be incapable of unkindness, jealousy, or any host of attributes we must work so hard to resist. They seem perfect.

One of the most incredible aspects of God is that he actually is perfect. In him is absolutely no darkness at all. Where we face temptation, sickness, disaster, and any form of sin, we can know with certainty he had nothing to do with it: it simply could not have been him.

God, you are perfect. You are light, love, truth, and the power to turn from temptation. You are everything good. Forgive me for ever thinking you could be behind anything evil that befalls me. These are the works of the devil, and the result of my own bad decisions. Your only part is to illuminate a way out, to offer me a hand. Help me take it, perfect God, and leave temptation far behind.

When people are tempted, they should not say, "God is tempting me." Evil cannot tempt God, and God himself does not tempt anyone.

JAMES 1:13 NCV

Because God cannot have any part in temptation, he is our greatest help when we are tempted.

The moment we feel the urge, get the impulse, or recognize the inclination to step out of his will, we can call on his name. He wants—and has—so much better for us than anything temptation offers; all the resistance we need is just one prayer away.

God who cannot be tempted, help me resist temptation. Empower me to resist as you do, immediately and completely, anything that tries to take me from your will. Thank you for staying close as I face the distractions, lures, and empty rewards temptation offers. Remind me your way is better, your name is stronger, and your will is always for my good.

Is it natural for you to call to God for help as you face temptation, or are you more likely to recognize what has happened after you have given in?

Blessed Either Way

*"Whoever exalts himself will be humbled,
and whoever humbles himself will be exalted."*

MATTHEW 23:12 ESV

A natural tendency is to think of this verse as a warning: if you lift yourself up too high, watch out. You're going to get knocked down. Keep looking. Just beyond the warning, might there be a promise? Humility is a blessing, and if we think too highly of ourselves, we will miss out.

Jesus doesn't want anyone to miss out on any of his wonderful rewards. If we get a little too pleased with ourselves—our accomplishments, our gifts, our growth—he will make sure we have a chance to be humbled. By showing us our smallness and our sinfulness, we are able to better see God's glory, to recognize our need for him, and to call on him for grace.

Thank you, God, for the gift of humility. Even when you discipline us, it's because you want us to receive all you have. When we take ourselves too high you bring us low, where the view of your glory is better. Thinking ourselves worthy of looking you in the eye, we miss the mercy and grace of being at your feet.

*"Whoever makes himself great will be made humble.
Whoever makes himself humble will be made great."*

MATTHEW 23:12 NCV

Like a stagehand who, thinking they are alone, bursts into
flawless, glorious song—only to learn the director was sitting
in the darkened seats, your hidden gifts will be recognized.
Like an anonymous donor whose identity is finally
discovered, your silent contributions will be celebrated.

Just as those who seek recognition will one day receive the
gift of humility, so too will those who keep themselves low
receive the gift of recognition. Remember, he wants us to
have it all; he loves us, and he makes sure we are all blessed
either way.

*Generous, loving God, how you adore us all. Because both
humility and glory are blessings, you make sure we will one day
receive what we did not take for ourselves. This inspires me to quiet
greatness, secret giving, humble service, so that my glory will come
from you.*

How has God used this verse to minister to you today? Is he
inviting you to step into the spotlight, or to work behind it?

Letting Him Drive

> LORD, I know that people's lives are not their own;
> it is not for them to direct their steps.
>
> JEREMIAH 10:23 NIV

When you surrendered your life to Christ, how much thought did you put into the fact that you were surrendering your life? *Jesus, Take the Wheel* is a great song, but most of us have a hard time actually removing our hands and letting him drive. It sounds scary—and it would be, if we didn't have such an awesome, faithful God.

We can trust him! With every step we take in faith, we can believe we are moving toward meaning, truth, and light. His plan is perfect, and unlike anyone else we will ever meet, he cannot, will not, steer us wrong.

God, I trust you. I have faith in the plans you have for me, and despite my grasping fingers, I do want you to drive. Every place you lead me is just where I belong, and each time you draw me onward, I know the way will be rewarding and the destination sweet. You will never steer me wrong; I trust you with my life.

I know, O Lord, that the way of human beings
is not in their control,
that mortals as they walk cannot direct their steps.

JEREMIAH 10:23 NRSV

When we follow the Lord, we don't need to know where we are going. We don't have to worry about leading someone else in the wrong direction. When we have trusted him with our journeys, we are free to simply live.

Even if we wander off the path—and we will wander—his marvelous light will show us the way back. What a relief this is, knowing the one we follow knows exactly where we need to go, and will do everything in his awesome power to get us there.

Father, I feel so free when I follow you. I don't need the map: I just need to keep you in my sight. Speeding up and slowing down in rhythm with you, I trust the journey because I trust my leader. I pray that it will be obvious to anyone following me that you are the one true guide.

How much comfort do you take —or resistance do you feel— knowing it is God who directs your steps?

In His Example

The reward for humility and fear of the LORD
is riches and honor and life.

PROVERBS 22:4 ESV

If someone offered to give you a new car if you would simply wash theirs, how long would it take you to grab your bucket and sponge? A reward so much greater than the sacrifice is hard to resist. And yet we do.

All God asks of us in exchange for an abundant, rewarding life is that we give him the respect he deserves. He wants our humble, sincere acknowledgement that his ways are better. He wants our trust. As we place our faith in him, life grows richer in every way. We acknowledge our smallness, and he makes us greater. We willingly offer him all we have, and he gives us more than we ever wanted.

God, what you offer is so much greater than what you ask. For humility, you offer honor. And yet I cling to pride. For respect you offer riches, abundance, and life, and yet I stubbornly insist on my own way. Help me, God, to remember who you are. You are God, the Almighty. You deserve all my love and respect, and in return, though I don't deserve it at all, you give me all of yours.

*Laying your life down in tender surrender before the Lord
will bring life, prosperity, and honor as your reward.*

PROVERBS 22:4 TPT

Perhaps the reason humility is so hard to achieve is that we so
desire its promised reward of honor. Perhaps the reason it's
so hard to give up control is that we so desire the prosperous,
abundant life we are told is waiting.

Focused on the prize, we lose our footing on the path. Doesn't
this prove our smallness, our utter need for him? We simply
cannot do this without the Lord. The glory and riches we
crave are only found in him, in his example. Humbling, isn't
it? And the humbling sets us on our way.

*Precious Jesus, only in you can I find the perfection, the blessings,
and the glory I strive for. I want, I reach, and I grab. And then
I am reminded of you, who wanted only to see me saved; who
reached only toward those who needed healing; who grabbed only
onto the Father's will. And I am humbled. Thank you, God, for
your incredible humility. One step at a time, may I follow your
example straight to my reward.*

What prize have you been too focused on lately? Can you allow
God to step in and help you reach your goal?

Not Just Fair

Every valley shall be lifted up, and every mountain and hill be made low; the uneven ground shall become level, and the rough places a plain.

ISAIAH 40:4 NRSV

Imagine an arena where everyone—in every seat—had the same, unobstructed, close-up view of the stage or field. Imagine a hotel in which every single room had an identical, gorgeous view of the ocean—of both the rising and the setting sun. Imagine everything not just equal and fair, but extraordinary and wonderful. Imagine!

One day we won't have to imagine it. One day, this will be true. All will be well; all will be easy. No climbing, no stumbling, no struggle. No straining to see. Not just fair, but glorious, one day we will all gaze upon the King.

Father, how I love imagining this. The beauty, the glory, the sound—and I with a front row seat. Everyone, everywhere with a front row seat. You are so much more than fair, God; you are generous, extravagant, and gloriously good.

> *Every valley shall be lifted up, and every mountain and hill*
> *be made low; the uneven ground shall become level,*
> *and the rough places a plain.*

There will be days this promise can't come soon enough—
days it may be hard to cling to. Pain, grief and loss can leave
us feeling lost, circling a mountain ever higher, the summit
remaining out of reach.

Keep climbing. Climb with the hope of one who knows the
path will become smooth, flat, and easy. He has said it is so.

*I believe you, God. The struggle ends. I believe you enough to keep
struggling. I know every step I take in faith will be rewarded with
blessings. I know every stumble, switchback, and trip through the
valley is carrying me nearer to you. Your promise gives me hope,
and your hope fuels my steps. All will be right; all will be well.
As far as any eye can see, every path will end at you.*

Which part of the climb do you relate to right now?

If You Let Him

*It's time to be made new by every revelation
that's been given to you.*

EPHESIANS 4:23 TPT

An injured animal will sometimes reject your help.
Experience or instinct may have taught them to fear you, so
you must approach them gently, with open hands. Though
we have no reason to fear the Lord, he knows life can leave us
skittish, like a bird with a damaged wing or a deer caught in
barbed wire. And so, he comes gently.

He won't insist we accept his help; we must allow it. He can
take every broken, damaged, wounded attitude, every ugly,
sinful thought, and make them new—if we will let him. With
your permission, the Spirit offers wholeness where you are
fragmented, confidence in place of your fear, and gentleness
where the world has made you fierce. If you will let him, the
Spirit will make you new.

*Holy Spirit, help me accept the gift of newness you offer. As you
reveal more and more of your goodness, more and more of your
intentions toward me, let me be made new. Where I fear, give me
faith. Where I doubt, give me confidence. Where I would cower,
give me the strength to rise. God, wherever I would resist you, with
your help, I will let you make me new.*

Let the Spirit renew your thoughts and attitudes.

EPHESIANS 4:23 NLT

Is there anything on this earth more difficult to control than the mind? If we could control our anxious thoughts, if we could prevent selfish desires from taking hold, how much easier it would be to stay in God's will.

As with so many things in God's kingdom, the way to this blessed control is surrender. We must give him the thoughts as they arise, hand over the attitudes the moment they show themselves, and let him turn them into something lovely, good, and new.

God, send your ever-helpful Spirit to renew my mind. I need my unworthy thoughts replaced with revelations of your worthiness, remembrances of your beauty. I need fear sent away by confidence and faith. I am too weak, God, my mind is too small. Holy Spirit, replace it with the mind of Christ, and give me strength.

Spend some time baring your mind before the Lord, inviting the Holy Spirit to renew every thought and attitude that is keeping you from experiencing more of the bountiful, blessed life he wants you to have.

Looking Elsewhere

*If any of you is lacking in wisdom, ask God, who gives to all
generously and ungrudgingly, and it will be given you.*

JAMES 1:5 NRSV

Have you ever missed out on something because you were
afraid to ask for it? Maybe you wanted a promotion, but didn't
want to apply, lest your supervisor think you were dissatisfied
or worse, unqualified. Perhaps it was something as simple
as a cupcake. Right up until the last one was claimed, you
thought you'd like to have one, but failed to reach for it.

God has so many blessings for you, and he wants you to
ask. He's waiting for you to ask. All the wisdom you need,
to help you with every other choice you make, is waiting for
you to claim it. He's got a huge helping for you: generous,
overflowing, and completely satisfying. He won't think you
presumptuous, greedy, or dissatisfied. He'll give you all you
ask for.

*Father, I love the gifts you give! I love how freely, lavishly, and
joyfully you bless me. I don't know why I hesitate to ask you for
anything, given how generously you always give. Perhaps it's
because I lack the wisdom to understand your utter goodness, your
inability to feel anything but love and patience for me. Grant me
wisdom, God, that I might be wise enough to know you have—and
you are—all I'll ever need.*

If any of you needs wisdom, you should ask God for it.
He is generous to everyone and will give you wisdom
without criticizing you.

JAMES 1:5 NCV

Knowing what we do of God and his infinite wisdom, why do we look elsewhere? It's amazing, isn't it, that we think we can find it here? No book, mentor, or life experience will teach us even a fraction of what the Lord will place in our hearts if we ask him to.

God knows the answer to every question in our minds, holds all the knowledge and truth we seek in our hearts, and he wants to share it all with us.

Wise, wonderful God, thank you for your grace; you never hold my lack of wisdom against me. Instead, you let me learn from it, thereby growing in wisdom. Forgive me for looking all around when all I need to do is look up! Give me the wisdom, each time I'm tempted to turn to the world or myself for answers that you have them all, and that you share generously with all who ask you.

Where do you lack wisdom in your life? Ask the Holy Spirit to reveal a need, then ask the Lord to make you wiser in it.

In the Moment

Come now, you who say, "Today or tomorrow we will go to such and such a town and spend a year there, doing business and making money." Yet you do not even know what tomorrow will bring. What is your life? For you are a mist that appears for a little while and then vanishes. Instead you ought to say, "If the Lord wishes, we will live and do this or that."

JAMES 4:13-15 NRSV

"Who'd have thought a year ago…" How often we hear and say things like this. At any given moment, we can speculate and even plan on where we'll be and what we'll be doing in the future, but the truth is we have no idea how the days in between today and the one we envision will play out. The imagined day comes, and we laugh at how far off we were. Here in the actual moment, we can't imagine it any other way.

From layoff to promotion, and from unexpected loss to serendipitous windfall, we simply can't plan for the unplanned. This is good news, not a discouragement from planning. It's a wonderful invitation to live in the moment we're in. Fully, attentively, let us plan to live today.

Oh, God, how often I look back on a long-term plan I had and laugh. It's amazing, all the things you knew full well would happen, and how they led me here. Help me to live in the moment, God, to spend each moment seeking your will.

> Look here, you who say, "Today or tomorrow we are going to a
> certain town and will stay there a year. We will do business there
> and make a profit." How do you know what your life will be like
> tomorrow? Your life is like the morning fog—it's here a little while,
> then it's gone. What you ought to say is, "If the Lord wants us to,
> we will live and do this or that."

JAMES 4:13-15 NLT

God loves our dreams; after all, he often gives them to us. He just wants to make sure we remember that when our ultimate dream is to do his will, things will not always follow the course we expect.

If God gives you a vision today for a future goal, he wants you to pursue it wholeheartedly. He also wants you to be prepared for the detours, pit stops, and whole new roads that will take you to your ultimate destination: the one that for now, only he can know.

God, I trust you with the future you planned for me. My ultimate dream is to serve, to follow, and to please you with my life, and I look forward to the journey we take to fulfill it.

Recall a few times you made a plan and then realized God had a different one. Share openly your gratitude, disappointment, and questions with him. He wants to hear it all.

Whenever We Love

No one has ever seen God. But if we love each other,
God lives in us, and his love is brought to full expression in us.

1 JOHN 4:12 NLT

You've never been to the ocean, but on the shores of a large lake, toes in the sand and waves rolling in, you can at least imagine it. It's a hint, a glimpse. We may never make it to Italy, but an authentic meal in a carefully designed restaurant can drive the imagination somewhere lovely.

The face of God—the unimaginable, glorious beauty of it—can't be seen. But, we are told, if we love, he comes to live inside us. The radiance we take on from that love is his glow. And as such it affords a glimpse, an inkling, of the glory we will one day behold. How beautiful is that?

Oh, God, I want nothing so much as to see your face—to behold the greatest beauty there is. To learn that I get a taste of it by loving well? It's awesome. The glow of affection, the radiance of love, the fire of passion: all are tiny glimpses of you—and they are glorious.

No one has ever seen God; but if we love one another,
God lives in us and his love is made complete in us.

1 JOHN 4:12 NIV

Separated from loved ones, pictures, videos, calls, and letters are a comfort; they help us feel closer. While we're physically separated from God, unable to take in his beauty with our eyes, he still wants us to feel him.

Whenever we love, he sends his Spirit to dwell. In the eyes of those we love, we see the love of God reflected. In the kind words we speak to one another, we hear his beating heart.

God, thank you that, while I wait to see you face-to-face and take in all you are, I can feel you in my heart, and in the heart of those I love. To sense your love in their affectionate gaze, to feel your warmth in a comforting hug, is a gift. It helps me feel closer to you, which is all I really want.

Spend some time imagining God's face tonight; ask him for a tiny glimpse and take note of what comes to mind.

Timeless

This world is fading away, along with everything that people crave. But anyone who does what pleases God will live forever.

1 JOHN 2:17 NLT

Like a seven-day-old bouquet of cut flowers, even the fullest and freshest of blooms fades. Our favorite song from a few months ago lost its charm with too many replays. Even desire diminishes with time: think of something from twenty years ago you thought your heart might break without. You got over it, didn't you?

The only thing timeless is the love God has for us, his children. Because he so adores us, he's planned an eternity for us to be together. In a place where blooms don't fade and passions are never extinguished, the Lord has prepared a home for us. Singing a song that is both older than time and new every moment, we will love and be loved forever.

Precious God, every passion, every craving, and every thing of beauty I've beheld has eventually faded, but your love for me is eternal. I'm overwhelmed by this. I can't imagine the beauty, the intensity that awaits when we are together. For your abiding love, God, I will be truly, eternally grateful.

The world and its desires pass away,
but whoever does the will of God lives forever.

1 JOHN 2:17 NIV

Think of the whole span of your life, eternity as you know it. How can it be that our forever is just the tiniest fraction of time to God? It's hard to grasp; there may even be days you are not sure you want to comprehend it.

Life gets exhausting; forever sounds… long. Until you remember God's goodness. He would never design something that wasn't utterly wonderful, so we can count on forever with him being the perfect amount of time.

God, I don't know why forever intimidates me sometimes. I suspect it is because I am here, on this side of eternity, where nothing lasts, not even desire. Though I cannot fully grasp it, I know in my heart that forever can't come a day too soon, and eternity with you won't be even a day too long.

Who or what have you loved "forever?" How has that love changed with time?

A Single Gift

One thing I ask from the LORD, this only do I seek:
that I may dwell in the house of the LORD all the days of my life,
to gaze on the beauty of the LORD and to seek him in his temple.

PSALM 27:4 NIV

How old were you when you learned that the fewer gifts there
were to unwrap at your birthday, the more valuable each
package was? The first time we are presented with a single
gift, we know to expect something truly special.

King David understood this perhaps better than anyone who
has ever lived; forsaking all other requests, he went for the
ultimate gift. *I just want to live with you, God. I just want to see
your beautiful face, to visit you in your temple.* He knew that,
were he to unwrap this precious package, every second of his
life would be blessed.

Father God, I want so many things—so few of them worth having.
I know what I really want is to be happy, and I seek that around
every corner. Let me learn, as David did, that joy lives with you.
Peace, contentment, and almost unbearable beauty—they all live
with you. Let me seek to live with you, God, to understand the
value of that single, perfect gift.

Here's the one thing I crave from God,
the one thing I seek above all else:
I want the privilege of living with him every moment in his house,
finding the sweet loveliness of his face,
filled with awe, delighting in his glory and grace.
I want to live my life so close to him
that he takes pleasure in my every prayer.

PSALM 27:4 TPT

Have you ever spent so much time focusing on a future goal, you missed out on present blessings?

What's most thrilling about David's plea is that he's asking for this blessing now. He's asking to live in God's house today. Every moment. All his days.

God, I forget sometimes that the kingdom of heaven is not so much a place as a condition of the heart. I want to go there. I want to be with you, to see you, to seek you every moment of my life. Now and forever, let me live where you are.

When do you most feel at home with the Lord?

Pure Joy Awaits

My brothers and sisters, whenever you face trials of any kind,
consider it nothing but joy, because you know that the testing of
your faith produces endurance; and let endurance have its full
effect, so that you may be mature and complete, lacking in nothing.

JAMES 1:2-4 NRSV

"Yes! Another hardship!" This is not something we hear every day, and not the first exclamation from our own lips when trouble comes either. Where is the joy in this? We can't help but wonder. It's coming. The joy is coming.

Just as running a mile strengthens us to run another, every test of faith, every bit of suffering, increases our endurance. We grow stronger, wiser, more faithful, more hopeful as we see that Jesus always meets us—every time—in our suffering. We can rejoice when trouble comes because we know that the Lord comes too.

Jesus, though I may never jump for joy the moment a test arrives,
may I become more and more aware of the blessings you bring in
each moment of a trial. May I sense growth and wisdom as they
change me. May I sense your presence as you infuse me with hope.
In that presence, may I find joy.

Dear brothers and sisters, when troubles of any kind come your way, consider it an opportunity for great joy. For you know that when your faith is tested, your endurance has a chance to grow. So let it grow, for when your endurance is fully developed, you will be perfect and complete, needing nothing.

JAMES 1:2-4 NLT

How can endurance make us perfect? Think again of a runner. With little endurance, the needs of a distance runner are great. Rest breaks, water breaks, and medical attention, for example.

But as a runner develops endurance through training and trials, the mind and body adapt as what was once impossible is now not just possible but perfectly enjoyable.

God, I can imagine it. Being perfected through trials that built my endurance, I can see a day where I run and run and run, needing nothing except to keep running—into your arms— where pure joy awaits.

What is something you have developed endurance for— not just to tolerate it, but to truly enjoy? Ask the Lord to show you how he can make this true in every trial you face.

There He Is

> *"Where two or three are gathered in my name,*
> *there am I among them."*
>
> MATTHEW 18:20 ESV

Jesus promised to be present any time his followers gathered together in his name, and he is. You've felt it, haven't you? There is such beauty in friendships born of faith, such a sacred tenderness to the way the body of Christ look after one another's hearts; it could only be the loving presence of Jesus.

Gathering in pursuit of Christ—to know him, to worship him, or to serve him—is to find him. He brings with him a love that transcends age, economics, and worldly interests and unites us in our love for him. Wherever we are, there he is and wherever he is, there is love.

God, I love to meet with people who love you. I know you love it too, because you never stay away. Right where we gather, there you are. As we sing, you hear; as we serve, you swell with love and pride. You bind our hearts together as we gather seeking yours.

> *"Where two or three gather together as my followers,*
> *I am there among them."*

MATTHEW 18:20 NLT

Does Jesus like coffee? What are his thoughts on pedicures? If we get together "just because," does he still come along, or does he only want to be with us when we're talking about him?

Quality time with friends is a pursuit born of love, so whether we are studying the Bible or the fall leaves, serving the homeless, or getting a girlfriend a scone, as the author of joy, the founder of fun, and the very embodiment of love, we can be assured that wherever his lovers are, so is he.

Jesus, I confess sometimes I wonder if I'm cheating on those days that are "just for fun." Thank you for reminding me you invented fun. You created joy. You are love. As long as my heart is yours, you will be mine. As long as I love your presence, you will be here.

Ask the Holy Spirit to remind you the next time you're on a "just for fun" date, how much Jesus is enjoying seeing you enjoy your life and the people he gave you to spend it with.

May Peace Abide

> *"Peace be within your walls,*
> *and security within your towers."*
>
> PSALM 122:7 NRSV

Peace be within your walls. Doesn't that sound amazing? The moment you awaken to greet each new day, how lovely it would be to be greeted first by peace. Before any questions are asked or demands are made, before any to-do calls out to be done, may you encounter peace, and may it accompany you all day long.

And security within your towers. May you feel safe, confident, and untouchable in your home, your neighborhood, and the city beyond. May a sense of God's sovereign strength abide in the places you call yours.

God, I pray for peace within these walls. I pray that each member of this household would be affected by the security and tranquility that comes from trusting you. You are safe; therefore, we are safe. As you are strong, so are we. As you abide in us, so may your peace abide in our home.

> "May there be peace within her walls
> and safety within her strong towers."
>
> PSALM 122:7 NCV

While this psalm is a prayer for Jerusalem, something about the pronoun "her" just calls out to a woman's heart, "Claim it." Not all walls are made of matter; your highest tower may be the place you have hidden your heart for safe-keeping.

Dear child of God, may there be peace within your walls. May your heart feel safe, your soul find rest. May you find sanctuary in the strong tower of the Lord, and may he give you peace.

Father, you are my strong tower. My heart is safe. I search this world for things that will make me feel secure, building walls and erecting towers to protect my heart, but only with you do I find the peace I seek. You are safety. You are security. You, God, are peace.

What peace can the Lord bring inside your walls tonight, both within your home and within your heart?

He Gets It

*He understands humanity, for as a Man, our magnificent King-
Priest was tempted in every way just as we are, and conquered sin.*

HEBREWS 4:15 TPT

Jesus was tempted. Not just in the desert by Satan, but over
and over, for more than three decades, he faced the same
temptations we do—all of them. He gets it. He knows exactly
what it's like to have to deny the part of yourself that prefers
comfort. He's fought down anger. Jealousy has tried to take
him down, and lust has given it a go as well. He knows.

He knows it isn't easy. He was human too. He was attacked
by shame, poked by doubt, and needled by judgement. He
felt weakness, hunger, and unimaginable pain. He knows the
temptation of taking the easy way out. He knows. He gets it.
He gets you.

*Jesus, what a gift you are. So that I would be free to tell you
anything, you suffered through everything. You know what I face
because you faced it too. You don't judge me for my feelings, for
the temptations that assail me—you have mercy on me, loosening
their hold. Though you never failed, you empathize each time I do
and instead of condemnation you show me grace.*

We do not have a high priest who is unable to empathize with our weaknesses, but we have one who has been tempted in every way, just as we are—yet he did not sin.

HEBREWS 4:15 NIV

When you think of the temptations in your own life—all the tricks the devil uses to try and lure you to his side—just imagine how much harder he must have gone after Jesus.

As vital as your purpose is, as much a threat to the kingdom of darkness you are, how much more a threat was the Son of God? And yet he did not sin. How awesome he is!

Jesus, how awesome you are. I know what I face, and how often I fail to resist. All it takes is a little bit of hunger, exhaustion, or frustration and my defenses are down. But you knew more suffering than I ever will and still you did not sin. How wonderful you are, Lord; what an honor it is to know you. As well as you know what it is to be human, may I strive to learn more what it is to be holy.

Open up to the Lord about your biggest temptations and weaknesses, inviting him into the middle of your battle. Ask the Spirit for more of his strength.

Stitched Together

Rejoice with those who rejoice, weep with those who weep.

ROMANS 12:15 NRSV

Do you remember how amazing it felt the first time you realized you were so happy for someone else, you completely forgot yourself? Perhaps envy eventually knocked on your door, and certainly your own struggles returned, but before that—in the moment—you felt all the same joy as the one who celebrated. What a gift empathy is, to feel the feelings of another. What intimacy it forges, to not just see into but actually share a few beats of someone's heart. It's beautiful.

Of course, empathy also invites us into their pain—and there's beauty there as well. To lose oneself completely in the suffering of another creates a sacred bond. Stitched together with the golden thread of our Lord's compassion, we are forever connected to each other and ever closer to our God.

Jesus, how I thank you for the beautiful gift of empathy. As I feel with others we are connected; you connect us. Bound by shared experience, our hearts are joined by your love and closer to it. To soar when others soar, and to hurt when they hurt is to feel as you do for each soul in your care.

Be happy with those who are happy,
and be sad with those who are sad.

ROMANS 12:15 NCV

In this translation, we get a stronger taste of the work of empathy. You can celebrate without being happy; you can even weep without being sad. The call to share in the highs and lows of other people's lives is a call to lay down our own.

On a rough day, we must set ourselves aside in order to be thrilled for a friend's great news. And on a fabulous day too, we must agree to abandon our own good feelings in order to be with a loved one in their pain.

God, help me think more of others than of myself. Each time I am invited into the joy or sorrow of a friend, let whatever I am feeling simply fade. Where there is happiness, make me happy. In their sadness, make me sad. Make me someone who, for the gift of empathy, willingly forgets myself. In other words, Jesus, make me more like you.

How naturally does empathy flow through you? Ask the Lord to help you make sure you don't miss an opportunity to join another's moment, and therefore their heart.

Read Notice

*If we know that he hears us—whatever we ask—
we know that we have what we asked of him.*

1 JOHN 5:15 NIV

Most smartphones have an option in their text messaging program to provide a read notice. With this option turned on, the sender is able to see if—and when—their message was opened. Depending on your communication style, this can be a wonderful or problematic feature. A message that was clearly read, and yet unanswered, can lead to hurt feelings, confusion, and tension.

Our prayers don't come with a "read notice," but we can still be assured he hears us. When we belong to the Lord and when we ask in his name, our prayers are heard and, according to John, they are answered. Because he is a good God, even when the answer appears to be silence, or not yet, or even no, we can know it is the exactly the answer we needed.

God, I sometimes wish my prayers came with that read notice, and that you typed out an instant reply granting me exactly what I asked. And yet I do know you hear me. No matter how long the answer takes to get to me, I know you are working on it. Even before I ask, you are answering every prayer.

If we know that he hears us in whatever we ask,
we know that we have the requests that we have asked of him.

1 JOHN 5:15 ESV

What of the times this verse seems to be simply not the case? What of the times when, needing a job, we prayed for an interview to result in an offer and were rejected—again? What of the prayers of good people, begging for healing, who remain afflicted? What then?

Even then, God hears and he responds. Though we may fail to understand it presently, our Savior responds.

Jesus, help me remember this. On the days you bypass my words to answer the need in my heart, help me remember. You know that a prayer for a job is a prayer for security, or meaning, and you work on my behalf to provide it—though perhaps elsewhere. You know my pleas for a healing are for an end to suffering, and for that you have worked since time began. Remind me, God, how very well you hear me, and how beautifully you answer.

Are there times you doubt he's listening? Take those doubts to him and let him ease your wondering.

Live on Camera

People with integrity walk safely,
but those who follow crooked paths will be exposed.

Proverbs 10:9 NLT

Have you ever imagined—perhaps even dreamed of—your life as a reality TV program, and then been thrilled just a few seconds later that it's not? For all the moments your family is adorable and your daily struggle endearing, how many more are there where you are grateful not to live on camera? How much would it change us, knowing we were being watched?

Our lives may not be broadcast to all the world, but they are—every moment of them—seen. The Lord is always with us. We have his Holy Spirit residing inside us, and be assured, he doesn't miss a thing. If this thought makes you a little uncomfortable, take comfort: he's always been here. He's always seen you, and he still adores you.

Holy Spirit, make me aware of your presence; I want to behave in a way that honors you at all times. Let my life be one of integrity, so nothing I say can hurt someone—so nothing I do will cause harm. Rather, let my life bring glory: to my Father, my Savior, and his holy Church. Were I to live on camera, exposed to all of heaven and earth, let it be for my integrity, for a walk that honors you.

*The one who walks in integrity will experience
a fearless confidence in life,
but the one who is devious will eventually be exposed.*

PROVERBS 10:9 TPT

Can you think of a time when getting caught was a blessing? Maybe your parents uncovered a plot that saved you from a choice you could never unmake, or a trip to rock bottom gave you a chance to climb your way back to the surface. Or perhaps you made a discovery that set someone else back on the path to light and life.

Because he loves us so much, the Lord won't let us stay hidden. All he calls his children will be exposed—and with the dawn, invited to join him and walk in the light.

Oh, beautiful God, even to be exposed by you is to be loved by you. Because we are yours, we simply cannot stay hidden. Bad decisions come to light and are redeemed. Wrong directions are exposed and turned around. Thank you for your brilliant light and for making sure we cannot remain outside it.

What was the best or worst thing the Lord ever saved you from? Thank him for his relentless love.

Carried Hope

*I know that I have not yet reached that goal,
but there is one thing I always do.
Forgetting the past and straining toward what is ahead,*

PHILIPPIANS 3:13 NCV

Imagine a student carrying a backpack they never emptied. Each school year, as new textbooks and notebooks were added to the old, the weight would become overwhelming. Seams would burst, straps would fail, and spines would buckle under the heavy, entirely unnecessary burden.

Have you emptied your backpack recently? Everything done is done. The cumbersome burdens of guilt, regret, and shame are heavy on your shoulders. Let the boundless grace of God lift them off your backs. Let him lighten your load until all you carry is hope.

Gracious Lord, you never asked me to carry the weight of my sin, the shame of regret, the pain of the past. Help me set it down. Turn my eyes forward, toward the goal, and leave all that is past in the past. The grace you offer is weightless, God. It lightens my steps and infuses me with hope.

I don't depend on my own strength to accomplish this;
however I do have one compelling focus:
I forget all of the past as I fasten my heart to the future instead.

PHILIPPIANS 3:13 TPT

Just forget about it. We love to dispense this advice, and we love to believe we would take it, but the truth is, this is far easier said than done. How do we just forget? With the help of the God of the impossible, we can learn to leave the past where it lies and fasten our hearts to the future instead.

We are not called to do any of this on our own; that is how regrets are born. Instead, we call on our glorious, gracious, loving God—changer of hearts, healer of wounds—and rely on his strength.

Father God, you are the healer, the redeemer, the God of all hope.
I carry so much more than I need to, don't I? I hang onto memories
that hurt and weigh me down, allowing them to hold me back
when all I need to do is turn to you. You change my focus. You
place it on you, on the beautiful future you have planned for me.
Lighter and filled with hope, your waiting arms are all I can see.

Spend some focused time in prayer about which burdens from your past are weighing you down and holding you back. Ask the Lord to help you turn away, toward him, and run into the future.

All Praise

Praise the LORD in song, for He has done excellent things;
let this be known throughout the earth.

ISAIAH 12:5 NASB

Our God is so worthy! All praise, respect, honor, and glory
belong with him. Amazed by talent, let us glorify the One who
formed the hands that did the painting. Let us lift up the Father
of the voice who sang the song. Beholding beauty, let us sing of
the glorious mind who imagined, then spoke it into being.

Every time we are dazzled, let our hearts remember our God,
who designs, creates, and blesses us with it all, and let us not
be shy in giving him the credit. As long as we have breath, let
us spend it honoring the one who gives it.

God, there is so much excellence, so much beauty and goodness.
Let all my wonder be directed at you. Instead of "What a great
voice!" let me exclaim, "What a great God!" Let me never worship
beauty, but only you who makes it. You alone are worthy—the
author of it all.

Sing praises to the LORD, for he has done gloriously;
let this be known in all the earth.

ISAIAH 12:5 NRSV

Whether worship music is something you only encounter
in church, or headphones proclaiming his glory never leave
your ears, or anything in between, know that the Lord loves it
when you sing to him. He loves it when you sing of him.

When you join your voice with others singing in praise, he
hears and he comes. When you worship him alone, and only
he can hear, he hears, and he comes. So sing. Sing that he
may come.

Father God, is my voice truly music to your ears? Offkey or out of
tune, is it true you hear only sweetness? Of course it is. Like any
proud Papa, my voice is the loveliest sound you know. Thank you,
God, for giving me a voice to sing, and so very many reasons to lift
my song to you.

Losing all traces of self-consciousness, sing a song
to your Father.

Remain Upright

The godly may trip seven times, but they will get up again.
But one disaster is enough to overthrow the wicked.

PROVERBS 24:16 NLT

God will not let you fall. To know the absolute truth of this, you need only realize one thing: you're here. You're reading this. You're still standing; perhaps wobbly and with no small amount of effort, but nonetheless, you remain upright.

Take heart. Your Father sees every stumble and it changes absolutely nothing about his love for you. Like a baby taking her first steps, he'll take your hands and lift you back to your feet as many times as it takes. And after you're steady, once you can run, he'll be with you stride for stride, for the times you need a steadying arm.

Father, I am so encouraged by you. It's amazing. No matter how many times I trip, stumble, and even fall flat on my face, you won't give up on me. You lift me up. You keep me going. You refuse to leave me down. Thank you, God, for your endless patience, your unwavering support, and your endless love.

A righteous man falls seven times, and rises again,
but the wicked stumble in time of calamity.

PROVERBS 24:16 NASB

God gives us our fight, our tenacity. When we meet someone who has none, the most loving thing we can do for them is pray, and make sure we tell them about the source of our hope—the source of all hope.

A heart that doesn't know God is far too easily broken. A soul without his strength is too easily crushed. Praying for words that would reach their wounded spirits, let us make sure we never leave someone on the ground without them knowing who picked us up.

God, I know it is not your will that any would stumble and stay down. You wait for all to see you, to come to you, to accept your open, waiting hand. Where I can offer hope, embolden me. Where my many stumbles may give encouragement, give me courage to speak of your bottomless grace.

Reflecting on your own "seven falls," how might the Holy Spirit be able to use your story to lift someone who has fallen? Pray that your eyes would be open and your heart would take courage.

He's Right Here

*The LORD replied, "My Presence will go with you,
and I will give you rest."*

EXODUS 33:14 NIV

It's a classic movie scene: paralyzed with stage fright, lines forgotten, the protagonist scans the crowd, looking for that one face. *Is she here? Did she come?* Once spotted, all is well; the show goes on—beautifully, in fact. What is it about the mere presence of someone we trust that can calm us so thoroughly?

This is certainly true of the Lord; peace accompanies love. In his presence, we find acceptance and grace. He is here. The show goes on. Resting inside his unconditional love, we are blessed with the peace of mind to go where we need to go, speak the lines we know by heart, and bask in the glow of his watchful, approving gaze.

Father, everything is different when I know you are with me, when I know you are watching. I have such peace in your presence, I am free to remember who I am and to rest in your approval. How can I fail, and what can I fear as long as you are here?

"My presence will go with you, and I will give you rest."

EXODUS 33:14 ESV

Alone in a crowded airport, how well could you sleep? Even exhausted, anxiety over your belongings, over missing your flight, and for your personal safety would wake you every few minutes. But with a companion, someone wide awake and looking out for you, you could allow yourself the rest you needed.

God is your watchman, guarding every aspect of your safety. He gives you all the time you need to replenish your body and your spirit. He's right there watching, keeping you safe.

Ever-watchful God, I'm so grateful for the rest you offer. It's okay to close my eyes, because yours are always open. You keep constant watch over my life, so I can rest from all my striving. Because of you, I know no fear of harm while my strength is being restored. My heart slows, my breath evens out, and I am renewed.

In which aspect of your life do you most need to rest in the safety of God's presence and restore your strength? Ask him to help you release it to him.

Despite What We Know

The apostles said to Jesus,
"Lord, you must increase our measure of faith!"

LUKE 17:5 TPT

Have you ever prayed for a greater measure of faith? If
you haven't, it probably never occurred to you. Isn't faith
believing? I believe in God, therefore I have faith, right? Why
would I need more?

Consider a rickety bridge across a great canyon. Using our
eyes, we can see the bridge goes from one end of the canyon
to the other, and that it just delivered a group of people safely
to the other side. We saw, and so we believe. Old wood, old
rope, and a high wind, however, can limit our faith in the
bridge to do the same for us. Despite everything we know
about our loving, powerful, and gracious God, we still face
things that run up to the limits of our faith. How blessed we
are that we can always ask for more.

God, increase my faith. On the days I merely know you can,
before you do, allow me to wholeheartedly believe you will. In
the moments I question your provision, before you provide, first
increase my faith. Each time I hesitate to ask for something I fear
you might not choose to give, before you give it, forgive me and
increase my faith.

The apostles said to the Lord, "Increase our faith."

LUKE 17:5 NLT

Every limitation we have is one designed by the Lord. Even
the apostles, witness to every miracle and firsthand hearers
of so much wisdom, needed more faith. It's one of the many
things that remind us he is God and we are not. He wants
us to ask him for it. He loves to fill us with all the blessings
of heaven, all the things we lack, and each time we pray for
them, we acknowledge his greatness.

The moment we think we have enough—faith or anything
else—is the moment we need him most. Lord, increase
our faith.

Father God, I want to see my limitations this way, as an
opportunity to honor you. When I lack grace, generous God,
increase my grace. When I lack wisdom, all-knowing God, make
me wise. When I am short on hope, loving Father, give me hope.
And when I need more faith, perfect God, increase my faith.

What limitations in yourself can you turn to praise and honor
of the Lord?

This Is Grace

*Sin is no longer your master,
for you no longer live under the requirements of the law.
Instead, you live under the freedom of God's grace.*

ROMANS 6:14 NLT

Most bills have a grace period. During this time, the debt is allowed to exist with no accumulating penalty. As long as it's paid before the grace period runs out, no interest or other consequence is applied.

Life with the Lord is a permanent grace period. For the rest of this life and for all eternity, we are not bound by the law. We are not slaves to sin. They simply have no hold on us. Our debt was transferred, paid in full, and then forgiven. This is grace: we are truly free.

Jesus, I can't believe what you did for me. I owed so much, more than I could ever repay, and you paid it all. The day I gave you my heart, you turned around and released it, so I could continue to come willingly, again and again, as one who is not bound but free.

Sin shall not have dominion over you,
for you are not under law but under grace.

ROMANS 6:14, NKJV

How can we adequately thank Jesus for this incredible gift, knowing our minds can't even grasp the full weight of what he forgave—what he continues to forgive on our behalf?

All we've done and all we will still do are forgiven. No sin can claim us now; we can't be lost, because we are his. We are his. Sin will entice us back, but we won't go. We can't go because we are his.

God, it's too wonderful. I don't deserve your grace. It's so unfair, what you, Perfect one, gave up for me. The price you paid—more than I even know—was so great, and yet you didn't hesitate. I am yours, Lord. Because you redeemed me but also and always because I choose you freely, I am yours.

Contemplate the incredible truth that you absolutely cannot be lost to sin. Allow the incredible depth of his love for you to empower you to resist old temptations like never before.

Fully Known

All my longings lie open before you, LORD;
my sighing is not hidden from you.

PSALM 38:9 NIV

"I've never told that to anyone before." How loved we feel when someone says this to us, how trusted. And when we reveal our most secret selves, what a sacred offering we place into the hands of the hearer. This is me. And I trust you.

More than anything, the Lord wants to be the one you trust with all your longings. He wants to hear every sigh, dry every tear, and celebrate every triumph. While it's true he already knows you, there is a level of intimacy he longs to share with you that happens only when you lay yourself bare before him.

Jesus, I want to tell you everything. I want to share every yearning and trust you with every confession. I trust you with me. The more I open up to you, the more you come near. The more of you there is, the more of you I want, so here I am, God, bare before you, hiding nothing.

> *O Lord, all my longing is known to you;*
> *my sighing is not hidden from you.*
>
> PSALM 38:9 NRSV

To be so known as we are by the Lord is to be understood at our core. Even the things we have no voice for, he wordlessly comprehends. It's like opening a gift we never mentioned wanting: having seen it, and knowing us so well, the giver just knew.

Truly, is there anything we long for more than this: to be so fully known and still so entirely loved?

Father, the care you take to know me lets me know I am utterly loved. The way you answer prayers I don't even speak, or provide what I need instead of what I ask for, is such proof of your affection, it's overwhelming. Knowing all my longings as you do, you realize it is this—being known—I long for most of all. Thank you, God, for loving me so perfectly.

Go silently before the Lord and let him reveal some of the things he knows and loves about you.

Blind Spot

*If we say that we have no sin, we deceive ourselves,
and the truth is not in us.*

1 JOHN 1:8 NKJV

Don't forget to check your blind spot. Anyone who has ever driven a car knows exactly what this means. A car that can be seen when it is both further away and closer is temporarily invisible when inside our blind spot. The car is there; it simply can't be seen.

Each of us has a blind spot when it comes to our own sin. This is not a sign we think we are perfect, or that we are mired in darkness; it is simply a side effect of being human. Our peripheral vision can only take in so much. Just as side mirrors, special sensors, and having a passenger help with our driving blind spots, Scripture, the Holy Spirit, and trusted mentors can help us see our hidden sins.

Lord Jesus, I need help with my blind spot. I know there are sins I am unaware of. Holy Spirit, make me aware. I want to represent you well. I want to be wise and safe. Point me to Scriptures that stir the earth around my buried sins. Embolden my friends to shine light on any darkness they see. Give me 360° vision, Jesus. Help me to see.

*If we claim to be without sin, we deceive ourselves
and the truth is not in us.*

1 JOHN 1:8 NIV

There is another possibility regarding hidden sin: denial.
Much easier to recognize in someone else than in oneself,
occasionally a sin can become shameful—or important—
enough to us we simply refuse to acknowledge it.

Like plugging our ears and shouting, "Lalalalalalalalala,"
to avoid unwanted news, our refusal to hear or confront it
doesn't make it any less real. The next time the Lord brings
the matter to our attention, we must be brave enough to allow
the truth inside.

*Holy Spirit, I'm inviting you tonight, while I'm feeling safe and
open to truth, to expose any areas of denial in me. Surround me
with safety and peace as you show me the sins I can't bear to see,
and the ones I can't seem to let go. Tell me the truth, God, so I can
be set free.*

Are you ready for this? The Lord understands if you are not.
Invite him to show you as much as you can handle and trust
him with whatever you see.

Unconditionally Welcomed

"All that the Father gives Me will come to Me, and the one who comes to Me I will certainly not cast out."

JOHN 6:37 NASB

Recall a time you were unconditionally welcomed. Whether a new school, new job, new neighborhood, or new church, it's quite a feeling when, just because you showed up, you are immediately accepted. You're in.

This is life with Christ. The day you responded to his invitation—exactly as you were, filled with questions and sins—you were in. And beautifully, incredibly, you will never be out. He will never grow tired of you, get mad at you, or simply move on. Unlike friendships that falter and fade, your relationship with the Lord is forever.

Jesus, what a wonderful, welcoming friend you are. You saw me at my worst and you chose me. You took me, flaws and all, and you never asked me to change; you simply loved me. There's such freedom in knowing you will never change your mind about me. I feel safe, accepted, and forever grateful.

"Everyone my Father has given to me, they will come. And all who come to me, I will embrace and will never turn them away."

JOHN 6:37 TPT

How does it feel, knowing you were given to Jesus? Long ago, before your soul and body came together and were born on this earth, God had you in mind and he chose you…for Jesus. He knew you would choose him back, that you would love him back, and that love would change you.

He decided that every broken place in you would be available for his Holy Spirit to mend, to heal, to fill with his goodness. It all began the day you stepped inside his embrace, and it will never, ever end. How does that feel?

God, I feel awe. Honor, unworthiness, and awe. Your unconditional acceptance of me is a gift I can't possibly earn or deserve, which is what makes it such a treasure. What did you see that made you choose me? How did I gain such favor? Inspire me to pass this treasure on. To see the people you have chosen for me, in all their flawed, imperfect glory, and embrace them as wholeheartedly as you embrace me.

How does it feel?

Live Forward

Teach us to number our days that we may gain a heart of wisdom.
PSALM 90:12 NIV

Waiting for a big event, it's not uncommon to count the days leading up. Whether by crossing them off on a calendar, shortening a paper chain, or some other means, we mark the passing of time; we can see it getting shorter. We can feel the end of our wait grow nearer. Often, we spend these days in preparation, wanting to be sure we are ready when the big day arrives.

What if we could see our whole lives this way? What if we could understand this is true? Every day we are alive, we are preparing for the day we meet the Lord face-to-face. We can't count backward from an end we don't know, but we can live forward, counting them off. What wisdom might we gain, making each day count?

Wise Father, teach me to value the days you have given me. I want to make the most of the hours I have here, so that I am fully ready to meet you. Let me see not a chain that is growing shorter, but instead make me wise enough to see the days as a ladder carrying me ever closer to you.

Teach us to count our days that we may gain a wise heart.

PSALM 90:12 NRSV

At the beginning of a vacation, the days and hours stretch wonderfully ahead, filled with possibility. Once the midpoint arrives and passes, a sense of urgency may develop; with more time behind than ahead, it feels vital to make the moments count. By the last night, wistfulness may even set in: How can it be over? There's so much we still haven't done! Or, if the days were savored, the last night brings joy: How wonderful this has been! We made every moment count.

This is the Lord's wish for us. Looking back from heaven on this brief time on earth, that we would feel joy.

God, I don't want to miss the value of these days, thinking with so many still ahead it's okay to waste one here and there. This life is your gift to me, a chance to love and live and grow and give, creating memories I will carry into eternity. Inspire me to live with the gratitude and intention this precious offering deserves. Make me wise enough to be grateful for every blessed day.

How do you number your days? Is there anything the Lord wants to speak to your heart, any way he may be trying to help you be wiser?

Knowing He Will

> The LORD will be your confidence
> and will keep your foot from being caught.
>
> PROVERBS 3:26 NASB

Confidence is defined as self-assurance arising from an appreciation of one's own abilities or qualities. It is a belief in our capacity to make something happen. Perhaps it's an ability we seem to have been born with. It may also be a quality we naturally possess. Whatever it is, we just know some things about ourselves.

Beautifully, this verse reminds us not that the Lord demands credit for our outstanding attributes, but that he is the source of the confidence they give us. It is he who invites us to recognize and appreciate the things we do well. He takes such delight in you. He loves your unique talents and special qualities, and through your confidence, he encourages you to delight in you as well.

Father, thank you for the blessing of confidence. What a waste it would be not to enjoy the ways you made me special. Forgive me for playing down my talents, for under-valuing the qualities I bring to my relationships. They are gifts from you, and gifts are meant to be savored.

> *The LORD will be your confidence,*
> *and will keep your foot from being caught.*
>
> PROVERBS 3:26 NKJV

What of the days our confidence is nowhere to be found? What of the situations where, we are correctly convinced the situation before us is entirely beyond our capacity? We are neither qualified, nor gifted, nor prepared, yet here we are.

On this day, just as on the day you are in your sweet spot, the Lord will be your confidence. Rejoice in the moments you are called to and yet know you can't do it on your own. Be confident in the one who can, and through your faith, know that he will.

God, if you brought me to the moment, I know you will bring me through. I have confidence in you. I don't need to know what to say or do; I just need to trust you, obey you, and watch you work. You are my confidence. On the days I have it to spare and on the days I can't find a drop inside me, I have all I need in you.

In what situation are you naturally the most confident? How about the least? Consider that, in both, the Lord is your confidence.

Signaled by Fear

When I am afraid,
I will put my trust in you.

PSALM 56:3 NLT

When something frightens you, what happens? We gasp; we squeal; we even scream. Our muscles tense, all at once. We may throw what is in our hands; our feet may leave the floor. Part of our hardwiring designed to keep us safe, fear is a signal. This is dangerous; you need to take care. Without fear, think of all the situations we would wander into, defenseless and unaware.

Signaled by fear, we can place ourselves in the Lord's care. Trusting him to deliver us, we are calmed. Following the lead of his Spirit, the way through is illuminated. Secure in his loving plans for us, we are delivered.

God, I never thought I'd say this, but thank you for fear. When I am afraid, I know something isn't right. When something isn't right, I know I need you. I put my trust in you. I give you my fear and I believe you will deliver me. With you, even in danger, I know I am safe.

When I am afraid,
I will trust you.

Psalm 56:3 NCV

"Don't be afraid." Does this ever work? Has ever once someone telling you not to be afraid resulted in you losing your fear? Fear, like all emotions, comes entirely unbidden. To deny it is as helpful as to deny our need for breath. And yet, we need not give ourselves over to it.

We have the Lord, and never more than when we are afraid, he invites us to give him all our trust. We will be afraid, but when we trust our God, we needn't stay that way.

God, I give you my fear. I thank you for showing me the danger, and now I invite you to take these feelings away and replace them with trust in you. Because I have you, this fear no longer serves me. So, take it, precious Jesus, and fill me instead with faith.

Have you thought of your fears as something to be conquered or denied? Can you view them instead as an invitation to greater trust in the Lord?

Continued Growth

Grow in the grace and knowledge of our Lord and Savior Jesus Christ. To Him be the glory, both now and to the day of eternity. Amen.

2 PETER 3:18 NASB

How lovely it is to watch something grow. Whether a tree that grows taller each year, or a crocus peeking each spring from the snowy ground and lasting only weeks, growth, change, and bloom are inspiring to behold.

Just as we are delighted by the opening of a rose in summer, or the appearance of crimson leaves in fall, the Lord is enchanted by our growth. Every step toward grace, every new bit of knowledge of Christ's glory is a step deeper into his heart.

Father God, with your help, may I grow ever more graceful. May I bloom, like the loveliest rose, into something that delights your senses. Increase my knowledge, God, of all the ways your Son is worthy. And as I understand him, God, grow these same, glorious attributes in me.

*Continue to grow and increase in God's grace and intimacy with
our Lord and Savior, Jesus Christ. May he receive all the glory both
now and until the day eternity begins. Amen!*

2 Peter 3:18 TPT

Upon receiving an award, the recipient will often thank all
the people who helped them on the journey to the moment.
We've come to expect this, haven't we? Think how shocking
it would be to hear someone say, "I'm so glad you all realized
how awesome I am. I'd say thank you if there was anyone who
deserved any credit, but I did this all by myself."

Let us be sure, as God makes us more like him by the day, we
never fail to acknowledge his contribution. We are gracious,
we are growing wiser, lovelier, and more amazing all the time,
and may he rightfully receive all the glory.

*God, may I never take credit for your good work. As people see me
bloom, grow, and accomplish things in your name, may I glorify your
name. Make me glorious, God, that I would shine brighter for you.*

What ways can you recognize God has caused you to bloom
and grow? Ask him how you might use those qualities to
glorify him.

Thoughts on You

Whatever is true, whatever is honorable, whatever is just, whatever is pure, whatever is pleasing, whatever is commendable, if there is any excellence and if there is anything worthy of praise, think about these things.

PHILIPPIANS 4:8 ESV

It's amazing, isn't it, the way our thoughts can take us captive? One minute we're present and the next, we're a million miles away. Someone says the word "bill," and we're preoccupied with our finances. The smell of burning leaves fills the air and we're back in college, reliving a choice we wish we'd made differently.

It's rare we are not thinking; even asleep, our brains sift through our minds, processing our days. So, what if we turned the tables? With the Lord's help, could this advice become second nature? What a filter for our thoughts. We will think of things that are true, and worthy of honor. We will ask, is this thought fair and pure? We will sift out what is not pleasant, excellent, and worth our precious time. And finally, we will question: would I offer this thought to the Lord as praise?

God, I don't know why I allow my thoughts to capture me. Holy Spirit, help me capture them instead, and send them through this filter of worthiness. In Jesus' name, may I learn to give my thoughts only to what I would give back to him as praise.

Whatever is true, whatever is noble, whatever is right, whatever is pure, whatever is lovely, whatever is admirable—if anything is excellent or praiseworthy—think about such things.

PHILIPPIANS 4:8 NIV

Can this be done? Without the Lord's help, no. The world assails us with images, memories, and temptations all specifically calculated to take us out of beauty and into darkness.

Even a seemingly harmless distraction, like contemplating where to go to lunch after church, is a trap, especially when the thought comes while worshipping the Lord, or contemplating his Word. We can't control the thoughts that come, but we can decide how long they are allowed to stay.

Jesus, help me with my thought life. Show me, immediately, when a thought aims to take me from considering things that are honoring and pleasing to you. Let me see and in so seeing, let me send those thoughts away—instead of holding onto those that are noble, right, and true. Keep my mind pure, God, and lovely. As often as possible, help me keep my thoughts on you.

How often do you find your mind wandering, or your thoughts taking you hostage? Ask the Spirit to help you retrain your mind and believe that he will.

Where Planned

Each one of you should continue to live the way God has given you to live—the way you were when God called you.

1 CORINTHIANS 7:17 NCV

At this precise point in time, do you believe you are living as God intended? If you feel like you are still waiting for your purpose or calling, consider this: would the God who so loved you he numbered each hair on your head, the Lord who saves your tears in a jar, not place you just where he planned for you to be?

You are living according to his purpose. He gave you this job, this community, these people. Unless you believe you hear him and are blatantly denying his call, you are who and where he wants you to be. The Lord is everywhere, and he is desperately in love with everyone. He called you—at this time and in this place—to be a witness for his healing, transforming grace.

God, when I think of how carefully you designed me, how can I doubt that you placed me with equal intention? Forgive my restlessness. I am grateful for where I am and with whom. I am grateful for the way you infuse meaning into every kind gesture, act of service, and moment of patience. I may not be saving the world today, but I can use my life to point to the One who is.

Each of you should continue to live in whatever situation the Lord has placed you, and remain as you were when God first called you.

1 CORINTHIANS 7:17 NLT

This morning, we briefly touched on disobedience. God called us where we were, and he intended for us to stay, at least for a season.

While some of us will never be asked to step outside of the lives we are living now, some of us will. Wherever he calls us, to go or to stay, may we do so expectantly, obediently, and filled with his light.

God, I pray for contentment where I am, and confidence to go wherever you may send me. With you as my contentment, with heaven as my home, I know it doesn't really matter where I am. Whether here at my own dinner table or anywhere else I feel you calling me, let me live as one who belongs to you.

Are you surrendered to the Lord's call, whether to stay or to go? Have you embraced it?

Someone Is Watching

Follow my example, as I follow the example of Christ.

1 CORINTHIANS 11:1 NIV

Do you have a role model—not just someone you admire, but someone whose example you intentionally try to follow? What if someone were to intentionally follow you. How closely would their lives end up following the example of Christ? What faith it takes to invite someone to model their walk after your own.

As role models go, Jesus is clearly the pinnacle. The closer we try to emulate his qualities, and the more sincerely we attempt to learn from those who have followed his path for years, the more imitable our own lives will be. And why does this matter? Because as Christians we can be assured someone is watching. For the sake of anyone who might follow our example, let's be sure we are following Christ.

Jesus, thank you for being such a perfect role model. Your example gives meaning and value to my life. For myself and for anyone who is looking at me for inspiration, I am determined to follow you always.

I want you to pattern your lives after me,
just as I pattern mine after Christ.

1 CORINTHIANS 11:1 TPT

Oh, to have the bold and confident faith of Paul. Can you imagine sincerely speaking these words? As role models, we're more likely to fall on our knees and pray our intentions, rather than our actions, are emulated. We get it wrong, don't we? Often.

Even this, though, is a chance to model a godly life. When we are wrong, we can admit it. We can apologize, ask forgiveness, and try to do better. Surrendered to Christ—just as he surrendered to the Father—even our failings can work for good.

God, let this be true of me. Not just when I am living right, but even, perhaps especially, when I am wrong, let those who look to me see me looking to you. Let them witness me asking for the grace you freely give, washed clean by the forgiveness you gladly offer. Even when I'm wrong, let me point to what is right.

Who is watching you? What are they learning about the ways of Christ?

Buried in the Depths

There is no condemnation for those who belong to Christ Jesus.

ROMANS 8:1 NLT

If at all possible, read this verse aloud—several times. Even if you must be quiet, make some audible sound as you speak these lifegiving words over yourself. This is an important truth, and to deny yourself its message would be a tragedy.

Guilt, condemnation, and shame have no home with Christ. He cast your sin as far as the east is from the west; he sank your shame to the bottom of the ocean floor. While the Holy Spirit will still convict you of new sins, and those old ones you've retrieved, you are never condemned by them. Leave shame where it lies: buried in the depths. You belong to Jesus, and he says you are free.

God, I wish I could release myself as easily as you forgave me. Help me recognize the difference between conviction and condemnation. Remind me, especially as I sin anew, that guilt and shame are not from you. They have no home with you. But I do. And in you I am new; there is nothing to condemn.

There is now no condemnation for those who are in Christ Jesus.
ROMANS 8:1 NASB

One of the more glorious mysteries of life in Christ is life *in Christ*. Through his Holy Spirit and because of his great love for us, we are one with him. Jesus is in us, and we are in Jesus.

It is here, in Christ, we realize condemnation cannot possibly abide. In him is only goodness, love, and light. Where could guilt and shame hope to hide? As no part of him, they can be no part of us. Praise the Lord.

Oh, Jesus, thank you. The day you filled me with your Spirit, the darkness had to go. Exposed, made powerless, condemnation no longer had a home. And as I live in you, I am engulfed by your love. I am overwhelmed by your goodness. I am one with your grace.

Do you believe this? Place this verse where you can see it, often, and speak it over and over, until you know it to be true.

Everything for Good

You intended to harm me, but God intended it all for good. He brought me to this position so I could save the lives of many people.

GENESIS 50:20 NLT

This isn't pleasant to consider, but we may have to suffer in order to become the person God intended. Because there is suffering and evil in the world, we may have been chosen to experience some of it—and to come through stronger by the grace of our God—so we can be a light for others looking for a way out of that same dark place.

In the midst of suffering, it feels like everything is happening to us, but in reality, God is using the situation to lead us to where we need to be. Through even the most devastating tragedies, the Lord leads, holds, and shapes us into instruments of his beautiful healing. Within his perfect plan, even that which others mean for harm can be used by the Lord for good.

Father God, you make all things beautiful, even the most ugly. What comfort I take knowing any suffering I may endure will one day be redeemed by you. Inside your goodness, grief, betrayal, and shame are turned to rejoicing, forgiveness, and grace. Thank you for using everything for good.

You meant evil against me; but God meant it for good, in order to bring it about as it is this day, to save many people alive.

GENESIS 50:20 NKJV

Even the evil in this world turns to loveliness in God's hands. This is the God who used the darkness of jealousy and hatred in Joseph's brothers to bring prosperity to a nation, to reconcile a broken family, and to spare many lives.

This is the God who can and will and does redeem the ugliest deeds imaginable still to this day. We need not fear evil; it cannot possibly prevail against our God.

Father God, I cannot wait to see the beauty you create from the evil in this world. To know the things that happen here, things unspeakable, tragic and wrong, will one day be wrought for good gives me hope, and with that hope, I can face another day.

Share your honest pain and confusion about the evil and suffering in this world, with the Lord. He hates it too, and he longs to bring peace and hope to your heart.

Watch and Learn

*"Let the little children come to me, and do not hinder them,
for the kingdom of God belongs to such as these."*

MARK 10:14 NIV

Jesus was exceptionally fond of children. While there may not
be a preponderance of Bible stories of him interacting with
children, the ones that exist leave no room for doubt. Jesus
believed children to be incredibly special. Have you ever
wondered what it was that so enamored him?

Kids possess a charming lack of self-consciousness. Rather
than think about what they should be, or what they ought
to do, they just are. They just… do. Perhaps it was this
authenticity that he found so pleasing, or perhaps it was their
helplessness, their utter dependence. Both are qualities he
most desires in us.

*God, I come before you as a child: unrehearsed, not self-conscious,
and wholly dependent on you. If I'm hurting, I'll cry. If I'm joyful,
I'll dance. Either way, I recognize my need for you, Jesus. Openly
and utterly, I love you. You are my comfort as well as my joy.*

> "Let the children come to me; do not hinder them,
> for to such belongs the kingdom of God."

MARK 10:14 ESV

Paying close attention, we can see that not only does Jesus want the disciples to admit the children for the children's sake, but for the disciples' own as well. *Watch and learn,* the Lord says between the lines.

The way children are is the way we need to be in order to live in the kingdom of God. Joyful, generous, affectionate, and free, the little ones possessed more than they realized, and more than the disciples could see.

Jesus, with everything you did you taught, and still today you are teaching me. How beautiful and wise you are, using the example of a simple child, guileless and sincere, to point me toward the keys to heaven. How affectionate, inviting me to crawl into your lap and simply be, and in so being realize there is nothing more I need.

What childlike qualities would most benefit your heart, and bring you deeper into kingdom living?

No Holding Back

Let the redeemed of the Lord tell their story—
those he redeemed from the hand of the foe.

PSALM 107:2 NIV

What's your story? Whether it's so complicated, you barely know where to begin, or so "ordinary" you think it scarcely worth telling, know that your story matters. The precise way God claimed you as his own is of great significance, both to him and to all who need to hear its encouraging truth.

God planned everything about you, friend, including your story. He chose you to reach someone—or, perhaps, more than one someone—through the details of your own redemption. Someone needs to know that God calls those who are where you were, who have done what you did, or who live how you once lived. Someone needs to hear your story because it will tell her she also matters to God.

God, compared to your own story, and to so many others, mine seems small. That you chose me to be a part of the saving work of redemption is so wonderful, I can hardly take it in. Thank you for my life, Father, and for my story. With your help, I'm learning to see it as you do: significant, worthy and beautiful.

Go ahead—let everyone know it!
Tell the world how he broke through and delivered you
from the power of darkness and has gathered us together
from all over the world.
He has set us free to be his very own!

How many people know the story of how we first fell in love
with Christ? How many are aware of the intimacy you share
with him: the nudges, the whispers, and the dreams?

Let nothing hold you back. Imagine your life without him and
realize the importance of sharing the amazing truth of how
you came to live with him.

Jesus, maybe it's because my story is so familiar to me, I've never
thought of it as important enough to share, or as something
"everyone" needs to know. But everyone does need to know you,
Lord, that my experience of discovering your perfect love and
saving truth might help someone else meet you fills me with a new
sense of urgency to make sure they hear all about it.

Have you ever written your faith story? Whether a paragraph
or several volumes, consider writing it down—and preparing
to share it with others.

Illusion of Control

Submit therefore to God. Resist the devil and he will flee from you.

JAMES 4:7 NASB

Submit to God and resist the devil. How is it that such straightforward advice seems so difficult to follow? Might it be because our culture seems to so often suggest the exact opposite? In movies or shows, a character living by this advice is presented as a novelty, or an oddity, and typically succumbs to the pressure to be normal or fit in.

Until we get this right and submit to the one who wants only peace, goodness and joy for us, we are under the authority of the one who wants to destroy us. Like a frightened cockroach, he will run for his life once we expose him to the light of God's truth, but not before. Until we stand with God and tell the devil no, he's going to hang around.

God, I regret each time I've chosen dark over light, or what is easy over what is right. I can't believe I ever thought fitting in mattered more than standing proudly next to you. Help me, Jesus, to resist the enemy's lure. Help me resist him and send him scurrying far from me. I don't want to be "normal," God, until I am in heaven— where normal is to spend all my time worshipping you.

Give yourselves completely to God.
Stand against the devil, and the devil will run from you.

JAMES 4:7 NCV

What stops us from giving ourselves completely to God? We fear not having control, even though deep down we know we don't have it anyway. We are deceived into thinking things will be better if we make all our own decisions and fight all our own battles. We are controlled by impulse, entitlement, and a million other of the enemy's tricks.

The devil does all he can to hold us back, because he knows he cannot stand against the Lord. Once we belong completely to God, the devil has no choice but to set us free and run away.

Spirit of God, please help me. Pry open these fingers, clinging so pitifully to the illusion of control. Unclench these fists, holding so tightly to the idea I'm entitled to my "freedom", which is really just another of the enemy's traps. Stretch open my hands, Holy Spirit, and help me lift them heavenward. I hand over my life to you, God. all I am is yours and because of this, I am finally free.

Where are you weak? Whether the struggle is over screen time or a temptation that could ruin your life, ask the Lord to stand with you as you say "No!"

All for Nothing

*I do not nullify the grace of God; for if justification comes through
the law, then Christ died for nothing.*

GALATIANS 2:21 NRSV

Imagine spending months preparing your house to go on the
market. You've repainted every room, remodeled the kitchen,
repaved the driveway, and now it's time to sell the house. At
the first open house, you get a full price cash offer. The only
catch is that the buyer plans to tear the house down. Suddenly
those months of work seem all for nothing.

Anyone who believes they can get to heaven just by working
hard or being a good person, is also implying Jesus' brutal
death was all for nothing. Without accepting his gift of grace,
we toil needlessly, and worse, we relegate Jesus' ultimate
sacrifice and glorious resurrection to the status of a magic
trick. Instead, let us run to the arms of grace with all our
might and tell our Lord his death was not all for nothing
because his death was for us.

*God, forgive me for trying to earn my place in heaven. I know
full well I can never do enough to deserve it, and I can't bear the
thought of rejecting the glorious miracle of grace. Your death was
not all for nothing, It was for me, and I will thank you every day of
my life for accomplishing what I never could.*

I do not treat the grace of God as meaningless.
For if keeping the law could make us right with God,
then there was no need for Christ to die.

GALATIANS 2:21 NLT

If you've ever worked hard to choose the perfect gift and only to have your efforts met with ingratitude, you know how hurtful it can be. Despite the care you took in its selection, and the joy it gave you to give it, it seemed to mean little or nothing to the recipient.

Considering how hurt we can be over the rejection of a something trivial like a child's toy or printed scarf, Jesus' sorrow must be unimaginable when a person he loves refuses the grace offered by his death and resurrection.

Jesus, though I know I can never thank you too much, I feel I still don't try nearly enough. I could tell you every day how blown away I am by the depth of your love, how utterly awed I am that you considered me worth dying to save, and I'd still owe you a million songs of praise. May that song be ever on my lips, God, that you may know how deep my gratitude is.

How often do you consider what Christ did for you? Search your heart and ask if it is often enough.

Hold It Up

*In all circumstances take up the shield of faith, with which you
can extinguish all the flaming darts of the evil one.*

EPHESIANS 6:16 ESV

Knowing a tragedy could have been prevented somehow adds
even more to the pain of loss. I'm sure sometimes we feel like
we'd rather not know. Seatbelts save lives, but only if we wear
them. Smoke alarms save lives too, but only when they're
connected. Lifejackets keep us afloat, but not when they're
forgotten back on the beach. To stay safe, we must make use
of all the things designed to save us.

As part of the armor of God, the shield of faith allows us to
extinguish flaming arrows—but only if we hold it up. It's our
responsibility to hold onto our faith and carry it wherever we
go. Abandoning it, even briefly, leaves us vulnerable to those
fiery darts.

*God, I'm wearing all your armor today. I'm wrapped in your
truth, your righteousness, and the glorious news of the gospel. In
addition to the armor, I lift and carry the shield of my faith. No
flaming arrows will reach me because I will not set my faith aside.*

Use the shield of faith with which you can stop
all the burning arrows of the Evil One.

EPHESIANS 6:16 NCV

It's a well-worn sports idiom that the best defense is a good offense. It's of no consequence how well their forward shoots, their running back sprints, or their cleanup hitter bats when your offense is maintaining control of the game.

Your faith is a shield, and that makes it a formidable weapon. When arrows of fear head your way, hold it up. When doubt tries to take you down, raise it high. When jealousy, bitterness, and spite all tag team against you? Raise that shield!

God, what an amazing gift faith is! Because I believe you will protect me, fear can't pierce my armor. Because I have faith in your goodness, doubt can never scorch me. It really doesn't matter what flames the enemy throws; my faith is a strong defense against every offense he has.

Right now, try using your faith against something that is coming at you. Can you hear those arrows hitting your shield?

Invitation to More

O God, You are my God;
I shall seek You earnestly;
my soul thirsts for You, my flesh yearns for You,
n a dry and weary land where there is no water.

PSALM 63:1 NASB

Do you yearn? Thinking of the deepest desire of your heart, can you see yourself wandering through the desert to bring it to fruition? Though few modern women long as intensely for God as King David did, we mustn't let his passion shame us into believing we are not spiritual enough. David's longing was born of intimacy; if we knew the Lord as David did, our desire for the Lord would be unmatched as well.

Rather than saddling ourselves with guilt for our lack of burning passion, we can read the Psalms as a peek into what's possible and an invitation to more. Knowing what you know of God, and how beautiful your own experience has been, just imagine the communion King David must have had with the King of kings in order to pen such desperate longing. Imagine, and accept the invitation to more.

God, I want to yearn! As much as I long for and enjoy the paltry things of this earth, I can only imagine what it's like to experience you. You are the end of hunger, thirst, and all longing. You are glory itself. I accept your invitation, Lord. Show me more, until my desire for you is all I can see.

O God of my life, I'm lovesick for you in this weary wilderness.
I thirst with the deepest longings to love you more,
with cravings in my heart that can't be described.
Such yearning grips my soul for you, my God!

PSALM 63:1 TPT

Ah, lovesickness. There's nothing quite like it, is there? There's a reason it's called sickness. The feeling is not entirely pleasant—and yet, we remember it for the rest of our lives. Some never stop trying to rediscover it or hoping to feel it just once more.

What as yet unseen side of Jesus could make us become truly, distractedly desperate for more of him? Knowing what you do of human love, don't you want to find out what an indescribable craving for the Lord feels like?

Jesus, these words are so beautiful and intriguing; what more of you is there to know, that would cause my soul to yearn painfully for more still? Can I handle it, Lord? Just how beautiful are you, and how satisfying is your love? I'm longing to know, Jesus. I'm desperate to be desperate for you.

How comfortable or uncomfortable is this idea of desperate, passionate longing for the Lord for you? Take your honest feelings before him, and let him speak directly to your heart of how he wants you to feel for him.

His

Know that the LORD is God.
It is he who made us, and we are his;
we are his people, the sheep of his pasture.

PSALM 100:3 NIV

Know that the Lord is God. We may respond that we know this already, but do we live like this is our ultimate truth? In the wake of this knowledge, aren't all burdens lighter and all sins easier to resist? He is God. Completely sovereign, completely good. He is God.

It is he who made us, and we are his. Again, we know this is true, but do our lives bear witness? He made us. Of all the things he could have made, all the perfect, marvelous things, he made us. Just this way, just as we are, the perfect one made us. And we are his. He made us for himself, to love, to nurture, and simply bring him delight, he made us his. How awesome is that?

Father, I recognize and embrace you as God. Capable of anything, Lord of everything, I trust you with all that I am. As the one who made me all I am, who am I to question your judgement. Because I delight you, because I belong to you, I recognize and embrace my own delightfulness. Thank you, God, for making me yours.

Know that the LORD, he is God!
It is who made us, and we are his;
we are his people, and the sheep of his pasture.

PSALM 100:3 ESV

Let's reflect on the latter part of this verse this evening. As his people, we are God's friends, invited to communion, partnership, and intimacy with him. As his sheep, we are under his protection. We are his responsibility, and he'll risk everything to keep us safe.

Whether it be comforting, carrying, or communing with us, he is here for what we need, always.

Oh, God, you are God, maker of heaven and earth, and yet you choose me as your friend. You love to hear my thoughts and bring my dreams to life. I am such a small part of your creation, yet I matter so much to you. It's both humbling and honoring, this love you have for me. Thank you, Jesus, for who you are and what I am to you.

Which part of the verse spoke the loudest to your heart today?

Comparable

Keep me from looking at worthless things.
Let me live by your word.

PSALM 119:37 NCV

Is there anyone out there who doesn't need this prayer? It's much easier to see in others than in ourselves; we see young people spending hours on mind-numbing television and snapping and sending endless photos of themselves and think, *What a waste of time!* But what us? How many of our distractions and entertainments are truly worthwhile?

Before you slip into a shame cycle, remember there is no condemnation in Christ. Verses like this one are meant to help us have the most meaningful, God-honoring lives we possibly can. Our Lord has so much to offer us, so much to teach and show us, and so many ways for us to grow in love, beauty, and grace! We need only keep our eyes on him.

Holy Spirit, help me keep my eyes on the Lord! Show me irresistible beauty, uncontainable love, and unearned grace. As I am tempted to settle for lesser things, let me constantly question whether they are worthy of my time. God, you are so precious that none of the worldly things I distract or entertain myself with can compare.

Help me turn my eyes away from illusions
so that I pursue only that which is true;
drench my soul with life as I walk in your paths.

PSALM 119:37 TPT

What a life one could live, pursuing only that which is true! Just think of it, the richness of seeing only true art, experiencing real love, and living in authentic service. It's almost overwhelming.

We've conditioned ourselves to believe we need down time, and current culture offers no shortage of ways to numb the mind. But what if that's an illusion—a lie—orchestrated to keep us from knowing the incredible blessing of a life drenched glorious truth?

God, open my eyes! Take away my taste for lesser things, for numbness and substitution. Immersed in your beauty and truth, let all illusions melt away. Illuminate your path with blinding light, until it's all I can see, then overwhelm me with a desire to pursue only excellence, compassion, and love.

What lesser thing, or illusion, has captured too much of your attention? Ask the Lord to change the way you see it, and to show you something better.

All Come True

Mary responded, "I am the Lord's servant. May everything you have said about me come true." And then the angel left her.

LUKE 1:38 NLT

Given the extraordinary news that she, an unwed teenager, will bear the Son of God, Mary unhesitatingly agrees. I am the Lord's servant. Can you imagine? No questions, no doubts, and no fears, just humble acceptance. Look at what she says next: "May everything you have said about me come true." What beautiful faith, what trust!

What do you suppose the Lord has spoken over you and your life? Given his abiding love for you, it can only be something wonderful. Despite our limited understanding of his ways, we can trust—with the certainty of Mary—that anything the Lord speaks over our lives is the only truth we need to fulfill.

Father God, may everything you have spoken over me come true. Empower and embolden me to explore every desire you have placed in my heart, and to develop and use every talent you have given me for the glory of your kingdom. Help me to believe the things you have said about me, to embrace the hope you see in me, and to see it all come true.

Then Mary said, "Here am I, the servant of the Lord; let it be with me according to your word." Then the angel departed from her.

LUKE 1:38 NRSV

What do you suppose Mary relied on when she heard the whispers? From whom did she gather strength when met with disapproving stares? Bringing this news to Joseph, and her parents, where did she get the courage to trust they would believe the unbelievable truth?

The source of Mary's hope is the source of ours too, and the well of her courage the same one we visit. The Lord gives us strength. He is our hope. Let it be with each of us according to his Word.

God, here I am, your servant. I reject the fear of the unknown, of public opinion, and of change. I embrace whatever you have for planned me, knowing there is nothing better. You are my hope, and the well of my strength. My courage is from my faith in you, and I surrender my life to your perfect plan.

What do you believe the Lord has spoken over your life?

Sentry

*Do not worry about anything, but pray and ask God for everything
you need, always giving thanks. And God's peace, which is so
great we cannot understand it, will keep your hearts and minds in
Christ Jesus.*

PHILIPPIANS 4:6-7 NCV

Can peace really be obtained so simply? Indeed, the process
has very few steps. Instead of worrying, hand your concerns
to God. Tell him what you need. Thank him always, for what
he has done and what you know he will do. Once you do this,
you will have peace.

While this process is simple in the sense that it's
straightforward, that doesn't mean the steps are easy to
follow. Anxiety holds fast, like Velcro. We can become so
accustomed to its presence, we fail to see it as a threat, or
even remember it is there. Handing anxiety over to God can
require some extraordinary effort on our part, but it's always
worth it. Hand it over, friend, and make room for peace.

*God, though I often come to you with my cares, I've held them for
so long, they feel like part of my hands—part of me—and so I forget
to leave them at your feet. Help me pry open these fingers, Jesus,
and release my worries to you. In the space they leave open, flood
me with your peace.*

Do not be anxious about anything, but in every situation, by prayer and petition, with thanksgiving, present your requests to God. And the peace of God, which transcends all understanding, will guard your hearts and your minds in Christ Jesus.

PHILIPPIANS 4:6-7 NIV

Take a moment to absorb this astonishing promise: the peace of God will guard your hearts and your minds in Christ Jesus. The moment we agree to give our concerns to God, he places Christ himself at the gateway of our minds, allowing in only that which will bring peace. Our Lord stands sentry over our hearts, banishing anxiety.

All we need to do is present our requests to God through prayer and petition.

Jesus, I give you all my worries. I don't know why I carry them around; they are not serving me at all. You, on the other hand, promise peace and protection. You guard my mind. You take every concern of my heart, and render it powerless. Because I trust you, I have peace. Because that peace is yours, it cannot be taken from me.

As you read today, what worries came to mind? Open your heart to God, share your concerns with him, and see how he comes in to guard you and bring you peace.

Priceless Faith

These troubles come to prove that your faith is pure. This purity of faith is worth more than gold, which can be proved to be pure by fire but will ruin. But the purity of your faith will bring you praise and glory and honor when Jesus Christ is shown to you.

1 PETER 1:7 NCV

In difficult times, it's tempting to sink into questioning. We want to know *why.* Most of the answers are not ours to know on this side of heaven, but Scripture can provide powerful encouragement while we wait. Gold is so precious it was once a universal standard for measuring wealth, yet, according to this verse, faith that remains strong through adversity is even more valuable. Such faith is priceless.

Regardless of what struggles we face, when we keep hold of our faith, we gain a glorious reward: the praise, honor and glory of Christ the King. Faith that withstands the fire of adversity brings blessings beyond all imagining.

God, I invite you to use my pain, both now and in the future, to test and prove my faith. A struggle that deepens my trust in you is a struggle worth enduring. Sorrow that increases my comprehension of your goodness is sorrow I can face. Each time you prove yourself faithful, may my faith become purer.

These trials will show that your faith is genuine. It is being tested as fire tests and purifies gold—though your faith is far more precious than mere gold. So when your faith remains strong through many trials, it will bring you much praise and glory and honor on the day when Jesus Christ is revealed to the whole world.

1 PETER 1:7 NLT

A lie the enemy of our souls would love us to believe is that the Lord himself causes our suffering in order to test us. This is simply not true. God is only goodness, and can bring forth only that which is pure, true and lovely.

This is how he is able to work even the most devastating of circumstances for good, because once he is involved, there is simply no other possible outcome. The Lord, seeing our pain, allows pure, golden, and glorious faith to be born of it.

I believe you, God. I believe that the evil and sadness in this world are not of you. You are far too lovely. Invite me, God, not to look away from pain but to peer in closer—close enough to see the all beauty you can't help but bring to life. Purify my faith, God, as only you can, by protecting what the enemy means to destroy and making it more precious than gold.

How has the Lord refined your faith through trials?

Guard My Tongue

*Let no evil talk come out of your mouths,
but only what is useful for building up, as there is need,
so that your words may give grace to those who hear.*

EPHESIANS 4:29 NRSV

Wait. I didn't mean that. It's happened to all of us. The moment the words left our lips, we knew. We may have meant it in the moment, but we didn't really mean it. Frustration, confusion, and anger can release words that are not a true reflection of our hearts. May God grant us, and those hurt by our careless words, his grace.

For so many of us, there is no body part harder to control than the tongue, especially when it appears to work faster than the mind. How do we ensure our angry, unkind thoughts never become words? We pray. The moment we feel slighted, hurt, or otherwise tempted to speak on impulse, we call on the Lord, and give him control of our speech.

God, guard my tongue. Stay close, protecting my thoughts from becoming words I can't reclaim. Turn my anger to compassion, and my frustration to peace. As I remember who I am in you, I'll find the grace to either stay silent or speak love.

Let no corrupt word proceed out of your mouth,
but what is good for necessary edification,
that it may impart grace to the hearers.

<small>EPHESIANS 4:29 NKJV</small>

Our words need protection from far more than just anger, don't they? Words of criticism, self-promotion, and impulse also fight to be spoken.

In order to speak only life, we must belong to the giver of life. To utter only love, we must live in love. If we truly and fully give him our hearts, he'll fill them with his goodness, which will spill out in our speech. Our words won't need protection when we overflow with grace.

God, take over my heart, please. Replace my critical eye with appreciation for differences. Extract my need for attention and approval and put in its place a desire to build up others. Seize my impulses and make them captives of your grace. When I speak spontaneously, let it be to impart love, goodness, and peace.

In what circumstance are you most likely to speak without thinking, or to say what doesn't need saying? Invite the Lord to nudge you into grace instead.

A Wonderful Aroma

Perfume and incense bring joy to the heart,
and the pleasantness of a friend
springs from their heartfelt advice.

PROVERBS 27:9 NIV

What is your absolute favorite fragrance? From foods to flowers to expertly blended perfumes, our sense of smell can trigger powerful emotions and memories. Simmering red sauce takes us to Grandma's lap, cut grass brings back a perfect summer afternoon, while sandalwood, jasmine and rose transport us to the memory of a magical night.

As with all our senses, our sense of smell is a gift from the Lord. It can keep us safe, and it can bring us joy—through both memory and the sheer pleasure of a wonderful aroma. As you pay attention to the smells around you, take note of the feelings they arouse. Turn your mind to the Lord, maker of all your senses, and thank him for this unique and precious gift.

God, your creativity and intricacy never cease to amaze me.
How can something as simple as the smell of cinnamon evoke
such feelings of happiness and warmth? Maker of my senses,
author of my joy, thank you for your wonderful gifts.

*The heartfelt counsel of a friend is as sweet
as perfume and incense.*

PROVERBS 27:9 NLT

As delightful as any fragrance is to our noses, so to our hearts
are friends who counts us as treasure. Their compassion
brings warmth and security, while their wisdom invites peace.

To be around people who love us by choice, and willingly tether
their hearts to ours, is a gift as sweet as the senses can enjoy.

*God, how sweet is your gift of friendship! These people who
choose to love me, unbound by history and blood, are treasures.
As precious as any sight I might behold, song I might hear, or
fragrance I may smell, the compassion and warm acceptance of
a friend is priceless and rare. Help me to treat my friends with the
love and gratitude they deserve, God, and to be a treasure in their
lives as well.*

Spend some time tonight contemplating the most important
relationships in your life. Thank the Lord for loving you
through them.

Lit from Within

The Lord bless you and keep you;
the Lord make his face to shine upon you, and be gracious to you;
the Lord lift up his countenance upon you, and give you peace.

NUMBERS 6:24-26 NRSV

God bless you! Far more than a mere cliché after someone sneezes, speaking the blessings of the Lord over a person's life is a statement of pure love. May you have all you need and more, we are saying to them. May you be safe, and fed, and well. A life blessed by the Lord is a life of provision, protection, and peace.

When the Lord makes his face shines upon us, we are lit from within. Others are drawn to our light, and they meet him through our changed hearts. As beneficiaries of his grace, we are forgiven. We are free to live shamelessly and blamelessly, eagerly forgiving others.

Father God, may I never take your blessings lightly, and may I never speak them without meaning every word. You are generous, protective, glorious, and gracious. may I grow in these same virtues. May I be grateful, kind, and forgiving, and when they look at me may it be you, shining through me, that they see.

May the LORD bless you and protect you.
May the LORD smile on you and be gracious to you.
May the LORD show you his favor and give you his peace.

NUMBERS 6:24-26 NLT

May the Lord show you his favor and give you his peace. What would you attempt, if you knew you had his favor? What could you lay aside, remembering you can claim his peace? Because, friend, you do, and you can.

Close your eyes and absorb his light. He is with you. He will help you. Open your hands and raise them to heaven; feel your burdens lifted and exchanged for peace.

God, may you show favor, to me and to those I pray for. May our efforts be fruitful and bring glory to you. I crave your peace, God, for every living soul. Thank you for the blessings you offer, blessings I can claim and also give. Your grace knows no limits, Lord; may mine be likewise.

Which part of this beautiful blessing do you most need to claim? Which would you most love to pass on?

Still Pleading

Concerning this thing I pleaded with the Lord three times that it might depart from me.

2 CORINTHIANS 12:8 NKJV

What does it mean when God says no? If he loves us and we are hurting and pleading for relief, why does he withhold it? Even Paul, who gave up everything he had to spread the love of Christ, was not delivered from suffering. Why? We must remember even pain has a purpose. If God is allowing an affliction to persist, its purpose has not yet come to fruition.

Let's say you're suffering from back pain. Perhaps there is a doctor he intends to draw to him through your faithfulness and warmth. In order that you meet, your healing may have to wait. Whatever his timing, you can believe it is exactly right. Whatever his purpose, you can trust it will be entirely good.

God, I get confused when you say no. Because I know you love me, I fail to understand why you would let me hurt. Tilt my chin up, God, past my suffering, and let me see you at work. Remind me pain has purpose, and that purpose equals meaning. As long as I must suffer, thank you, God, that it can be for something good.

Three times I pleaded with the Lord to relieve me of this.

2 CORINTHIANS 12:8 TPT

It is said that pain is a signal that something needs attention. When a problem persists, the pain may get all our attention. All our effort goes into finding relief. Perhaps, instead of pleading with God to take away the problem, we're being invited to lean in to God, as our source of endurance and strength.

Like a child who forgets a sore knee when invited to play tag, so too can we forget all our suffering when we accept the Lord's invitation to turn our attention toward him.

I recognize this, God, this invitation to shift my focus. When my life gets hard, that's all I can think about. You allow things to get harder and harder until I remember you are my source. You bring healing, and when you do not, you bring peace. You are my comfort, God, in suffering and in relief. With my attention fixed on you, I have all I need.

Is there a problem getting more of your attention than the Lord who can give you whatever comfort you need? Ask God what he would have you do and be prepared to receive his answer.

More than Anything

My child, give me your heart,
and let your eyes observe my ways.

PROVERBS 23:26 NRSV

What's the most valuable thing you have ever loaned out? Your car, perhaps? As you handed over the keys, you were telling this person you trusted them. You believed they would treat the car as their own. You also implied they were more important to you than any thing.

To give our heart to someone requires even more trust. In giving our hearts we are placing faith in their willingness to care for our feelings as their own, to want only good for us, and to value us as a treasure. We are taking a risk. Except, of course, when we give our hearts to the Lord. There is no risk in trusting God. The maker of our hearts will treat them *better than* his own. He considers us more important than not just any "thing", but *anything*, and he counts us as his treasure.

You matter more to me than anything, Lord. I don't always behave as though this is true, but when I imagine life without you, I know that it is. I trust you with my feelings, my future, and my hope. God, I trust you. Take my heart. Have my love, all of it. Absorb it into you and multiply it, making me ever-more loving to those I share my life with.

My son, give me your heart and let your eyes delight in my ways.

PROVERBS 23:26 NIV

How often do you find yourself surrendering to God? Remember when you thought it was "one and done"? And then you took a few things back, one at a time, just in case he wasn't paying attention. I trust you, Lord, but I'm just going to take control of my finances. Oh, and my health. And as long as I'm here…

Soon enough, you had most of your life back in your own hands. It's okay. He understands. He loves you, and he's ready, whenever you are, to take it back.

Oh God, I surrender. Please have my heart—again. I trust you to care for it, to protect it, and to choose what it needs most. Have all of me, God: my work, my relationships, and my health. take back the things I've tried to hide and keep for myself, God, and make me wholly yours.

Allow the Lord to show you all the things you've taken back from him and pray for the strength to believe what you know – that you can trust him with it all.

A Kind Word

Encourage one another and build one another up,
just as you are doing.

1 THESSALONIANS 5:11 ESV

One of the most precious things about Christian friendship is the spiritual gift of encouragement. When we are on the receiving end, these lovely people always have a kind word. They see the good in us, and in everyone, and have an inspired, beautifully-timed way of expressing their belief in and fondness for us. It never feels patronizing or gratuitous; the sincere words of an encourager give life.

As an encourager, you may find good thoughts about others come to you constantly, and to share them is as natural as breathing. When people respond to our encouragement with pleasant surprise and sincere gratitude, it's affirming. Keep sharing your good thoughts, friend, because you never know who needs to hear your words, or who needs to know they are seen. Speaking life into someone is a beautiful gift.

Lord God, thank you for the gift of encouragement. I know how amazing I feel when I'm with someone to whom you've given an extra measure. The things they say—the things they see—give me strength and keep me going. God, I humbly ask for the gift of speaking life and spreading love. I want to be shown the beauty of your children and tell them what I see.

Encourage each other and give each other strength,
just as you are doing now.

1 THESSALONIANS 5:11 NCV

After gathering with other people, are you usually uplifted, feeling strong and loving, or are you out of sorts, feeling somewhat empty? If your social time is building you up, you know the Spirit of God is present, giving words of encouragement to say and to receive. Gossip, complaining and venting never seem to make their way into the conversation when he is around. Praise God for his loving presence.

As for the draining encounters, pray things change. Can you be the one to shift the tide, breathing welcome life into the conversation? Might others respond so well to your encouragement they too, begin to be a blessing?

Father, make me sensitive to your Spirit when I gather with others.
Let me sense, share, and appreciate the people I am with when
your light and love are all around us. In conversations that go
dark, give me wisdom. Make me an encourager, contagious with
your warmth.

Prayerfully assess your relationships. Where are you naturally encouraged and encouraging, and where do you need the help of the Holy Spirit to spread light instead of darkness?

Infallible Truth

All Scripture is inspired by God and is useful to teach us what is
true and to make us realize what is wrong in our lives. It corrects
us when we are wrong and teaches us to do what is right.

2 TIMOTHY 3:16 NLT

How many areas of your life have been informed by the Bible?
Unlike any other book, God's Word has power. It has life. If we
are to believe Paul's words to Timothy, God himself inspired
every word—and he did it for us. He knew how many sources
would compete for our attention, how many versions of
"truth" there would one day be, so he gave us infallible truth.

He knew how hard the world, and our own flesh, would try to
justify every wrong choice we make, every wrong desire we
have, and every wrong done to us, so he wrote down all that
is truly wrong—and all that is right. Scripture is a teacher,
an encourager, a guide, a gift, and a lifeline. It is God's love
letter to us.

God, your Word is amazing! No matter what I wonder, want, or
will, the inspired words of Scripture point to what is right and
true. No matter what the world says is right, the Word will tell
me if it's wrong. When I read I learn, I am encouraged, and I
am blessed. The Bible gives meaning and structure to my life; it
reminds you how deeply you love me and shows me how to best
love you. Oh, how I thank you for your Word.

Every Scripture has been written by the Holy Spirit, the breath of God. It will empower you by its instruction and correction, giving you the strength to take the right direction and lead you deeper into the path of godliness.

2 Timothy 3:16 tpt

Reading these beautiful, encouraging words, how can we *not* want to spend more time with God's Word? And yet every so often our Bible will sit untouched for days, maybe weeks. A verse for every question is just a few keystrokes away, and yet we look elsewhere. All the ways we can please him, and all the ways we grieve him are listed on its pages, and yet we wonder how we should act.

Let's try to be empowered, strengthened, corrected, and lead by the Bible every day.

God, increase my desire for your Word, and open my mind to its many mysteries. Reveal new treasures; answer questions I have yet to ask. Convict me of anything that grieves your heart, and lead me to choose what brings you delight. I want to please you, honor you, and bring you glory, God, so let your Word inspire my life.

Pray tonight for inspiration about how to engage more meaningfully with God though his Word. Even if you've read it daily forever, invite him to show you something new.

One of Many

*Then God saw their works, that they turned from their evil way;
and God relented from the disaster that He had said He would
bring upon them, and He did not do it.
But it displeased Jonah exceedingly, and he became angry.*

JONAH 3:10-4:1 NKJV

Even if we think of ourselves as highly flexible, when plans
are established, most of us prefer to see things unfold as
scheduled. Some of us get downright fussy in the wake of
unexpected change. Such a man was Jonah.

After much resistance, Jonah informed the people of Nineveh
that God planned to destroy them for their wickedness in
forty days' time. However, they repented—and so the Lord
relented. Jonah was furious, but why? Was he jealous,
wanting God's mercy only for Israel? Embarrassed his
prophecy was not fulfilled? Or was he just put out, having
come all that way for nothing—a nothing which, to Nineveh,
was life over death?

*It's easy to recognize Jonah's selfishness, God, but do I respond
better when you disrupt my plans? Have I not felt envy,
embarrassment, and entitlement as well? Do I not behave as if my
comfort were your sole concern? Forgive me, God, for questioning
your perfect wisdom. In honor of Nineveh, let me remember I am
but one of many souls, all of whom you love.*

When God saw what the people did, that they stopped doing evil,
he changed his mind and did not do what he had warned.
He did not punish them.
But this made Jonah very unhappy, and he became angry.

JONAH 3:10–4:1 NCV

Answer honestly: have you ever been a little disappointed to
see someone get off easily? Even though it didn't affect you
directly, was your sense of retribution ever offended by mercy?

Matthew 20 has a story of field workers, all of whom got
the same wage, regardless of how many hours they worked.
Again, it's not fair—but it's good, actually very good news for
us. Were God concerned with being fair, none of us would
be on our way to heaven. We don't deserve it. But mercifully,
God isn't fair.

Oh, God, what concern is it of mine if, on the last day, you
decide to forgive everyone everything? It is your will that none
should perish, God, so let me do my part here on earth to share
that amazing news. You may not be fair, but you are incredibly,
unreasonably good. Thank you, God, for the unfair gift of mercy.

How comfortable or uncomfortable are you with this view of
God? Share your heart with him. He loves to help you work
things through.

Cousin of Hope

If we hope for what we do not see, we wait for it with patience.

ROMANS 8:25 NRSV

Whether a docile family pet who tolerates endless tugs on his tail and rides on his back, or a teacher who never raises her voice and can answer the same question over and over without frustration, true patience is a marvel, isn't it? While a precious few are born with a seemingly endless supply, the rest of us must pray for this rare and precious commodity.

Listed among the fruits of the Spirit, patience is not something God expects us to possess abundantly on our own, but a gift he gives to those who seek it. It is the product of peace, and the cousin of hope. From a heart at rest and a belief in the coming rightness of all things, patience is born.

Father God, please help me grow in patience. You gave me a little already and it was just enough to make me recognize my need for more. Humbly, aware of my limits, I ask your Spirit to grant me peace. Give me hope, God, that all I don't yet see is coming, and make me patient as I wait.

If we hope for what we do not see,
with perseverance we wait eagerly for it.

ROMANS 8:25 NASB

What better model of patience could we ask for than the Lord?

Think of the questions, complaints, and confessions he hears from us, day after day after day. And still, he welcomes us. He waits for us: eagerly, expectantly, and patiently. His kindness never runs out, nor does his supply of second chances.

God, your patience knows no limit. I can question you daily, come to you over and over with the same pet sins to forgive, and you oblige. Lovingly, gently, you listen, respond, and grant your grace. Continue to be patient with me, God, as I work on extending my own. You are my example, so I know I'll get this right.

What aspect of God's patience most amazes you? Which shortcoming of your own patience would you most like his grace for, and help with?

Something Is Different

Blessed is a man who perseveres under trial; for once he has been approved, he will receive the crown of life which the Lord has promised to those who love Him.

JAMES 1:12 NASB

Honestly, I wouldn't change a thing. You've heard this kind of story, haven't you? There are countless stories of people who lost everything but found hope. Their stories are uplifting, and we're touched by their courage. They're inspiring, and we're moved to cherish our people. But mostly, if we're honest, we're relieved it happened to them instead of us.

Really? You wouldn't change a thing? From where we're sitting, this is hard to believe. Wouldn't they rather not have suffered? From where we're sitting, we can't imagine they'd say no. And yet, from where they stand, life is clearly sweet in a way we can't comprehend. God is close in a way we can only imagine. Something is different about them—something that just may be worth everything.

God, this is another tough one for me. I can't imagine wanting to suffer, and yet I find myself in awe of the peace and happiness living in the hearts of those who have endured. It's a crown I don't covet, though I see how perfectly it fits and how beautifully it shines. How wonderful you are, God, to pay back pain with joy.

If your faith remains strong, even while surrounded by life's difficulties, you will continue to experience the untold blessings of God! True happiness comes as you pass the test with faith, and receive the victorious crown of life promised to every lover of God!

JAMES 1:12 TPT

No one wants to be tested. No one says, while life is running along smoothly, "I hope something bad happens soon!" When life feels like one big blessing, we're content with those blessings we have.

Looking back, though, on tests we've gone through and passed, we can see how life is richer—how we are wiser. We can feel, having lived through it, how God drew closer, and that he remains.

God, I don't ask for my trials, but having lived through them, I can honestly thank you for them. Thank you for wisdom and a greater measure of faith. Thank you for holding me more tangibly than I've ever been held, for proving my trust, and for crowning my life with the blessings reserved for those who call you Lord.

What surprises has God given you through trials?

Heart that Knows

The wisdom that comes from God is first of all pure, then peaceful, gentle, and easy to please. This wisdom is always ready to help those who are troubled and to do good for others. It is always fair and honest.

JAMES 3:17 NCV

If you're wondering if that nudging you're feeling is from God, there is an easy way to find out. God's heart is pure, and his motives are pure. If there is anything iffy about the situation, it is not from the Lord. Do you feel peaceful when you think of taking the step, speaking the words, or accepting the challenge? God's way is always peaceful and brings contentment to your soul.

What he's telling you won't necessarily be easy, but there will be an absence of contention—if not in those around you, then within your own heart. Your manner will be gentle, and your needs will be few. Feelings of self-righteousness, under appreciation, and inconvenience are not of God. The service he calls you to will be a blessing, to others and to you.

Wise Father, help me to know when I am hearing from you, and when I am listening to other voices. Your way is perfect, so if opposition, unrest and compromise rise up to meet me, remind me these things are not from you. when my heart is full, let me revel in your company. I know when you are there; I can feel it in my soul.

The wisdom that is from above is first pure, then peaceable,
gentle, willing to yield, full of mercy and good fruits,
without partiality and without hypocrisy.

JAMES 3:17 NKJV

Seeking advice is natural, and a wonderful part of God's
intention for friendship. Even the most well-meaning
of friends is still human, though, so the Lord grants us
discernment for weighing their counsel.

Ask yourself if their suggestions in line with what you know
of God's heart? Is your friend encouraging you to take the
road of purity, peace and gentleness? Godly, prayerful
wisdom will be fruitful, honest, and fair. It will be loving. It
will invite you to choose the way of love.

Father God, thank you for the goodness of your counsel. Thank you
for a heart that can distinguish between when I'm being advised
to do as you would have me do, and when more worldly concerns
are trying to slither into my spirit. Thank you for placing people in
my life who love you above all, and who care deeply for my heart.
Make me wise enough to treasure them—and to heed their advice.

Invite the Holy Spirit to speak into all your relationships,
and to alert you to conversations that take a turn toward the
world. Be reminded of the people he has entrusted to love you
as he does and set an intention to nurture those friendships.

My Things

> "Go your way, eat the fat and drink sweet wine and send portions of them to those for whom nothing is prepared, for this day is holy to our LORD; and do not be grieved, for the joy of the LORD is your strength."
>
> NEHEMIAH 8:10 NRSV

God wants you to enjoy your life. Do you believe this? Food doesn't have to be delicious in order to nourish us, and yet it is. Think of the variety of tastes, textures, and seasonings the Lord has provided. Beauty serves no real purpose, and yet we are surrounded by it. Laughter, excitement, and fun aren't vital to our existence, but they invite us into joy.

It's true we will struggle and suffer. We are always either just past, in the middle of, or approaching a new storm. But because of God's goodness, and because he grants us peace and joy that defy our circumstances, even in the middle of the strongest storm, we can taste happiness, witness beauty, and be overtaken by joyful laughter.

God, you are so good to me! Even on my worst days, you give me your best. on my best days, I know all that joy is from you. May I never fail to notice the flavor of a berry, the beauty of a child, or the hilarity of irony, surprise, and memory. Thank you, Father, for such an enjoyable life.

"Go, eat of the fat, drink of the sweet, and send portions to him who has nothing prepared; for this day is holy to our LORD. Do not be grieved, for the joy of the LORD is your strength."

NEHEMIAH 8:10 NASB

The Lord wants us to enjoy what he has blessed us with and he wants us to share it. For some, this generosity comes naturally. Others of us hold on a little more tightly to our bounty. What if we run low tomorrow? What if this is all we get?

The Father understands this impulse. He knows the world would have us keep what's ours, and let others do the same. But he wants more for us! He's waiting for us to open our storehouses, to share everything we have, and after, he will fill them back up to overflowing.

Generous God, create in me a more generous heart. If I give freely of my possessions, help me loosen my grip on my time. If I'm open with my time, swing wide the doors of my heart. God, my strength comes from your joy, not from the things I think are "mine." Whatever I try to keep, God, inspire me to share it joyfully. I trust you to provide all I need and more.

How can you be more generous with all that you've been blessed with?

Past Myself

> "To him who strikes you on the one cheek, offer the other also.
> And from him who takes away your cloak,
> do not withhold your tunic either."

LUKE 6:29 NKJV

Turn the other cheek. Love your enemy. Kill them with kindness. The Bible is filled with suggestions like these. They roll easily off the tongue but are more challenging to live out. Take a moment and imagine if you did live them out. Imagine being stopped on the street by someone demanding your coat. Feeling nothing but the love of the Lord, you give you coat, then slowly lift your feet, removing your boots for them, as well. Imagine their response!

It's disarming, isn't it, to be met with love when we are unkind? Responding with an act of selflessness will invite the aggressor to examine their own heart, and to be curious about the peace and beauty in ours. More convicting—and more attractive—than anything else we could say or do, is our willingness to accept their need and brokenness without retaliation. This introduces them to the God they desperately need to know.

God, the spirit of selflessness goes against my nature, so fill me with yours! Give me a heart that sees past myself and into the brokenness and need that causes one soul to lash out at another. Grant me humility and compassion, God, over defensiveness and self-righteousness. Help me turn my other cheek, that they might see you in me.

*"To those who despise you, continue to serve them
and minister to them. If someone takes away your coat,
give him as a gift your shirt as well."*

LUKE 6:29 TPT

When the Lord encourages you to show his love and humility
to the world, he is not asking you to stay with an abuser, or to
invite someone to go on hurting you. He is protecting your
heart from becoming poisoned. He is protecting your soul from
believing you deserve less than respect and human decency.

By urging us to act in love, he is reminding us how we are
meant to treat one another. If this is not how you are living,
friend, he is calling you change.

*Father God, I pray tonight for my friends around the world who
are in harm's way. Infuse them with your courage, Lord. Empower
them with strength to not retaliate, or be taken down by the evil
that surrounds them, but to instead find their way to safety,
healing, and hope.*

Pray that the Lord will keep your eyes and your heart open to
this truth.

Covenant of Hope

My covenant I will not break,
nor alter the word that has gone out of My lips.

PSALM 89:34 NKJV

We all have a person in our lives we don't rely on, even when they promise. We're actually a little bit surprised when plans aren't cancelled, a little shocked when they come through for us. We don't necessarily feel unloved by them, or believe they don't care about us, we just know that a yes in this moment doesn't guarantee their yes down the road.

And then there is our Lord! Unlike these friends, his promises can never be broken. He measures beyond even the most dependable, loving, and selfless people we know. Nothing will come up. No emergency, forgetfulness, or whim will ever keep him from fulfilling any commitment he has ever made to you.

God, your faithfulness gives me strength. You never break a promise. you honor every commitment. Your covenant is my hope, God, and I thank you with all my heart.

I will not break my agreement nor change what I have said.

PSALM 89:34 NCV

How reliable are you? When you say you will be somewhere, what does it take to keep you away? Is a promise always a promise, no matter what? It's tempting sometimes to accept a more attractive offer, to take a little down time, or to betray a confidence. But oh, how gratifying it is to go anyway, to keep our word, to remain faithful!

We so delight our Lord when we choose what he would, or we do as he does. He sees and rewards our faithfulness with even more of his own.

God, may your steadfastness inspire me to be honorable.
May I come to see going back on my word as going back on you.
may I be, as you are, utterly reliable. Help me drown out the voices
of selfishness, fatigue ,and compromise. Help me hear only you,
encouraging me to walk the road of integrity and honor.

What temptations try to keep you from keeping your word? Ask the Spirit to help you recognize these subtle attacks and resist them.

God's Goodness

O how abundant is your goodness
that you have laid up for those who fear you,
and accomplished for those who take refuge in you,
in the sight of everyone!

PSALM 31:19 NRSV

If we want to see God's goodness for ourselves, we need only look at our brothers and sisters in Christ. Everything that makes them beautiful is an attribute of his—a way he is good and lovely. And oh, is he lovely! Think of the selflessness of a friend who gives herself away without even being asked. Ponder the strength of a brother standing firm in his commitment to live an upright life. They're beautiful. He is beautiful.

And there is more! It's hard to imagine what more there could be, but the Lord has stored up goodness; he dispenses it as we need it, and as he chooses to enrich us. When we make him our home, and make no secret of it, the whole storehouse of his blessings is opened to us.

Good and gracious God, I can't imagine there is more than what I have seen, and yet you say it is so. Selflessness, humility, wisdom, patience, and righteousness—all the things I see in your children inspire me to pursue your goodness with all that I am. You are my home, Lord. May your goodness overflow in me, that I might share it with the world.

Lord, how wonderful you are!
You have stored up so many good things for us,
like a treasure chest heaped up and spilling over with blessings—
all for those who honor and worship you!
Everybody knows what you can do
for those who turn and hide themselves in you.

PSALM 31:19 TPT

When we hide, the goal is not to be seen. We choose a hiding place that conceals us. Hidden in the Lord, our humanity is concealed, while his glory revealed. Our selfishness is overshadowed by his generosity, and our pride is hidden beneath his selfless, humble grace.

Hidden in the Lord, we are beautiful, blessed, and bright.

Beautiful God, I want to hide myself in you! When someone looks at me, I want your compassionate and loving eyes to look back at them. When I speak, I want your wisdom to come forth. In all my actions, may your strength, selflessness, and graciousness be seen and known. Every good thing in me is you.

Were you to hide yourself in God, what would you expect to be concealed? What of his goodness would you most hope would be revealed?

Fast, Strong, or Brave

His pleasure is not in the strength of the horse,
nor his delight in the legs of the warrior;
the LORD delights in those who fear him,
who put their hope in his unfailing love.

PSALM 147:10-11 NIV

As impressive as it is to see an athlete's grace, to hear a singer's unique tone, or to behold a craftsman's handiwork, how much more moved are we by acts of generosity and compassion? As wonderful as it is to see someone doing what comes naturally to them, it's even better to see them choosing honor, humility, and love.

God gave us our unique talents and attributes, and he wants us to use them, but his heart doesn't sing when we do; it sings when we sing to him. He's not moved by your talent; he's moved by your trust. It is not your way with words that delight him, the but words you use to honor him. He doesn't want your performance, but your devotion.

Father God, forgive me for thinking I need to impress you, or anyone else. I enjoy and appreciate the gifts you gave me—the ways you made me special—but I recognize this is not how I prove my love to you. Just as my earthly parents would be more honored by my respect than by my talent, so too would you be. I submit myself to you, Father, gifts and all, to be used as you will.

His delight is not in the strength of the horse,
nor his pleasure in the speed of a runner;
*but the L*ORD *takes pleasure in those who fear him,*
in those who hope in his steadfast love.

PSALM 147:10-11 NRSV

God is unquestionably more pleased by our love and honor than by any act or performance. However, let us not fail to consider how we might use our unique talents to draw attention to his glory.

If God gave us a voice, may we lift it heavenward. If he gifted us with leadership, may we lead toward his grace. If we are fast, strong, or brave, let us run straight to him. Whatever light he has cast on us, may we reflect it back onto his wonderful face.

God, show me how to glorify you through my strengths. As I am tempted to take credit for my abilities, remind me it is you who gives me all the goodness I possess. Whatever draws the world to me, let me use it to draw the world to you.

How are you special? How does the Lord want to use your gifts to illuminate the way to him?

Our Best Teacher

You will be God's servant, fully mature and perfectly prepared to fulfill any assignment God gives you.

2 TIMOTHY 3:17 TPT

Have you ever been helped by someone who actually made your work harder? Baking a cake with a little one or painting a room with someone who's never wielded a brush can definitely increase our load. While we didn't need their help, the patience, companionship, and, possibly, humor of the situation blessed us—and them—in other ways.

The Lord doesn't need our help. He has millions of other people he can use, and he is powerful enough to do everything he intends on his own. He *wants* our help, because it deepens our relationship with him, and because *we* are blessed when we do what he asks of us. He equips us to serve him, because he knows how beautifully our obedience will serve us.

Father, I know you don't need me, but I pray you will use me. I know it would be so much easier to just do things yourself, and that I sometimes make a mess of it, which is why I am so thrilled when you invite me to join you in your work. I love coming alongside you, learning from you, and seeing what moves your heart. In serving you, I feel great joy in mine.

Using the Scriptures, the person who serves God will be capable, having all that is needed to do every good work.

2 Timothy 3:17 NCV

Our best teacher—for lessons in how to serve God—is his own Word. In the pages of Scripture, we find out what breaks his heart, what quickens it, and what fills it with surprise, pleasure, and delight. We learn how we grieve him, and how we bring him joy. He has taught us patience, shown us compassion, and modeled humility.

The more we know his Word, the more capable we are to spread it, to share it, and to live it.

God, I pray for the ability to remember and assimilate your Word. May the words of Scripture live in me, inspiring me to obedience, love, and service in your name. May I remember what makes you proud, and may I be powerfully drawn to these things. May my words give life and reveal your truth. May my life give love and show your grace.

How has your understanding of Scripture equipped you to answer God's call on your life?

Mightily Blessed

Love one another with mutual affection;
outdo one another in showing honor.

ROMANS 12:10 NRSV

As contests go, how wonderful would it be to participate in this one? Outdo one another in showing honor. What if, every day, our first thought was one of thanksgiving to the Lord and our second, how we can show honor to everyone we meet? What days we would have! Send your people out the door feeling cherished, respected, and heard. Don't allow a single compliment to go unspoken, or a moment of respect to be withheld.

And know the same will be done for you. As we give all our honor, love, and respect away, the Lord inspires those we meet to return it. Our genuine love will beget only more love. As contests go, win or lose, we will be mightily blessed.

Father, I love this challenge! How, no matter how much love is given to me, can I give even more? Rather than the competitiveness so ubiquitous in this world, you encourage us to outdo one another in respect—in honor. How can I show more grace? How can I reflect more of you? I can't wait to try.

Love each other like brothers and sisters.
Give each other more honor than you want for yourselves.

ROMANS 12:10 NCV

How do brothers and sisters love? Imperfectly, but permanently. For the sake of family unity, they forgive much. In light of history, and to set an example for future generations, they love with boundless grace.

We should also love this way. We should love appreciatively, aware of faults, but dwelling instead on what we cherish about each other. We should defend one another and abandon our own lives when their need is greater. We ought to love them not as they love us, or even as we want them to love us, but even more than that.

God, I want to love better than I am loved. I want to love as you do, God. For the sake of your family, make me forgiving, selfless, and strong. Make me forgetful of slights and errors, and ever-mindful of the ways my brothers and sisters in Christ are wonderful. Make me gracious, honorable, and true. Make me love like you.

How does applying the concept of familial love inspire you to treat the Body of Christ?

Gloriously Complete

I am sure of this, that he who began a good work in you will bring it to completion at the day of Jesus Christ.

PHILIPPIANS 1:6 ESV

Imagine taking a hike on a scenic, well-worn trail. Clearly, someone took great care to clear a path that is rigorous, yet serviceable. Waterfalls, vistas and other points of interest mark your progress and then suddenly, the trail simply stops. Branches, boulders, and brambles obstruct the path, making it impossible to take another step with any confidence. You've come as far as you can.

God is doing a similar work in your life by clearing obstacles, marking your progress, and rewarding you with opportunities to look out and see what you've done. But be assured, the trail won't end. Your progress will continue. Every good thing he intends for you to do, you will do. Every good quality he wants you to possess, you will acquire. On the day you meet the Lord, you will be beautifully, gloriously complete.

Jesus, I love imaging standing at the top of a mountain with you, looking out at all there is to see, looking back over all I travelled through to get there. I love knowing this work you are doing in me is only getting started, that right up to the day I meet you, you'll be clearing branches, moving boulders, and making me better.

I pray with great faith for you, because I'm fully convinced that the One who began this glorious work in you will faithfully continue the process of maturing you and will put his finishing touches to it until the unveiling of our Lord Jesus Christ!

PHILIPPIANS 1:6 TPT

Are you a finisher? Depending on your strengths, you may be someone who is more inspired to begin projects, or even just to dream them up. It's okay. Whichever way he made you, it was purposeful. You are who he intends you to be.

The Lord is a finisher, and while he will not alter who you are, but he will continue to nurture your growth, slowly making you more and more like him. On the day you meet face to face, you'll be a glorious sight to behold.

God, author and finisher of faith, you are also the author and finisher of my life. Thank you! I love the story so far; I'm hanging on every word. I know how it ends, with me next to you, but I can't wait to see how I get there, and to know I am all you intended me to be.

Where do you feel God working in your life? Is there somewhere he might also be telling you to settle in and embrace? Some aspect of you he wants you to learn to love?

Forever

*A thousand years in Your sight are like yesterday when it is past,
and like a watch in the night.*

PSALM 90:4 NKJV

When we say we've loved someone forever, we mean for all—
or at least most—of our lives. When God says he's loved us
forever, he means forever, stretching out in every direction
in ways we can't quite comprehend. It's dizzying, isn't it,
contemplating the timelessness of the Lord and his love?
Because he is eternal, what feels eternal to us is just an hour,
just a moment. This makes us no less significant to him.
Think of the hours you wouldn't trade for anything. This is
how dearly he treasures your life and your memories.

This does serve to remind us how small our troubles will
one day seem. We can bear to suffer now, because we know
that once we get to forever, these painful hours will be but
seconds, all but forgotten in the wake of wake of eternal joy.

*Forever, Lord. It's hard to comprehend. All the hours of my life
combine into a single, precious moment for you—one you wouldn't
sacrifice, one you treasure. The relative brevity of this life comforts
me in times of sadness—knowing I'll be with you in eternity,
where pain is too brief to be remembered. I'll love you forever, God,
however long that may be.*

A thousand years in Your sight are like yesterday
when it passes by, or as a watch in the night.

PSALM 90:4 NASB

On the heels of a melody, something you haven't thought
about in years can come back in vivid detail. You remember
what you were wearing, what the sun felt like on your skin,
and the precise condition of your heart. Time and memory
are amazing, aren't they? How do we hold it all?

And what of the Lord? The vastness of his experience, the
limitless capacity of his mind to hold our histories, to cherish
them as he cherishes us; how does he hold it all?

God, your timelessness is breathtaking and overwhelming, and
when I think that one day, I'll experience it as reality, I am all the
more amazed. I envision seeing everything, all at once, and as I see
it, understanding how you orchestrated it all—every moment—to
carry me to that one, where I join you in eternity, and forever begins.

Spend some time contemplating forever, inviting the Spirit to
remind you of things forgotten, sweet memories and peaceful
days. Ask him for a taste of eternity while you sleep tonight.

God Is Winning

"O death, where is your victory? O death, where is your sting?"

1 CORINTHIANS 15:55 ESV

God will always win. Even when we can't see it, even when it seems evil has an overwhelming advantage, God is winning. Love is winning. Perhaps especially on the days it seems this can't possibly be true, look around, open your heart, and ask the Lord to open your eyes. You will see him in the hands of volunteers, the arms of first responders, and you will hear him in the ardent, passionate pleas for justice.

In your own heart, God is winning. You may feel like you're losing, like you're giving into frustration, fatigue and despair, but look around—look within. That glimmer of hope, that voice that reminds you of your worth—that's God, and he is winning.

Father God, I'm grateful for your strength and victory. My strength is challenged on the days I see sorrow and tragedy. On those days I may even question your victory. Forgive me, Lord. Let me see, even on the darkest of days, that your love is everywhere, winning.

"O death, where is your victory? O death, where is your sting?"

1 CORINTHIANS 15:55 NASB

Imagine a day where death is taunted. Imagine a day where evil is humiliated, brought to shame, rendered powerless. We will see it, friend, and we can glimpse it even now.

Each time we refuse to be brought low or lose hope, and each time we insist our God is greater than all sorrow and can take away all pain, we can glimpse that day. Store up these glimpses and remember, the victory is the Lord's.

God of hope, I long for the day evil is vanquished. I see its grip on this world. I see people losing hope, God, and I pray that my hope can be enough for others and for myself. Strengthen me, God, for the day when together, we laugh at evil and watch it slink away.

Share your thoughts with God about the evil in the world. Let him quiet your spirit and encourage your heart. He is winning.

Burdens

Bear one another's burdens, and thereby fulfill the law of Christ.

GALATIANS 6:2 NASB

Will you pray for me? Does this sound like something you would say? If it doesn't, the Lord wants you to know that it should. We aren't meant to carry our troubles on our own. He loves our sincere prayers for help, and he hears us. Yet, how much louder are those cries for help when echoed by the voices of our friends and our families?

There are also times our needs extend beyond prayer. Sometimes we need help. When we need it, the Father encourages us to ask for it. As we are all one with Christ, he longs for us to be one with each other by bearing one another's burdens and sharing in his love.

Father, thank you for giving me people who will pray for me. Thank you also for assuring my heart it's okay to ask for help. You have given me a heart that loves to be needed. thank for the reminder that my requests are a gift to those who feel the same.

Bear one another's burdens, and so fulfill the law of Christ.

GALATIANS 6:2 NKJV

Even more important than inviting others to help with our burdens is opening our hearts to help with theirs.

Let us be the kind of friend who doesn't even need to be asked. Let us pray without ceasing, show up with meals, and offer our homes and listening ears to those in need. Let us be there for one another, whether carrying the load together or lifting it to heaven, just as Christ's law commands.

Jesus, I forget that I am not just pleasing you when I help my sisters and brothers, I am obeying you. You ask so little; your commands are so few. Yet you repeatedly insist that we love. Inspire me, Holy Spirit! Open my eyes to ways to ease the load of my friends, to carry the burdens of my brothers. Show me, and then move me to act. As you command it, Jesus, may it be so with me.

How readily do you offer to help with a friend's needs? How sincerely do you pray for others? Ask the Holy Spirit to convict you if your heart needs to be more open to his commands.

Our Father

> *Whoever spares the rod hates his son,*
> *but he who loves him is diligent to discipline him.*

PROVERBS 13:24 ESV

Did you ever thank your parents for disciplining you? At the end of a grounding, or following a period without privileges, were you ever grateful for their correction? If you are a mom, has your child ever come to you and said, "Thanks for making me study instead of play video games!" These scenarios are far-fetched, but not impossible. With the wisdom of age, we can often look back on discipline and see it through the lens of love.

God is our Father, and he will intervene when he deems necessary. Can you imagine him *not* correcting you, any more than you would not correct a child heading down a road you knew was going to harm them? He disciplines us—and tells us no—as all parents do, out of love.

God, I know you want what's best for me and that, sometimes, that means telling me no. Other times it means you make me wait, or even take something away. Forgive me for resisting you, and for acting like a spoiled child. I'm sorry for the times I got angry for not getting my way. I would never give a child something that could hurt them just because they wanted it, and neither would you. Perfect Father, I trust your love—and I thank you for your discipline.

If you do not punish your children, you don't love them,
but if you love your children, you will correct them.

PROVERBS 13:24 NCV

When we think of God the Father, it can be more fun to think of him as Papa or as Daddy. Jesus' word for him was Abba. We may imagine being folded into his robes, and covered in affection and blessings, all while basking in the glow of his adoration. And it is often this way. But, like any loving father, on the days we need it, he gives correction.

For our own good, to help us stay safe and become who he intends, our Father disciplines us.

Abba, I do enjoy the image of snuggling in close, feeling your approval, and being comforted by your love. But I know some days that is not what I need. There are days I run away from you and straight into danger. You could just let me fall, and suffer the consequences, but you don't. When I ignore your warnings, defy your instructions, and resist your rules, I need discipline. Thank you, God, for loving me enough to correct me.

Think of a time the Lord has disciplined you and how you grew from it, and then thank him for it.

Invitation to Ask

> *"Call to me and I will answer you and tell you great and unsearchable things you do not know."*
>
> JEREMIAH 33:3 NIV

Between the dawn of the internet and the advent of handheld technology, our access to information is unprecedented. When you try to explain to a young person that you used to have to go to a library or consult an encyclopedia for information, they stare in disbelief. They simply can't imagine life without everything they want to know right at their fingertips.

When we belong to the Lord, we have access to even more information than a smartphone. God reveals the unsearchable things we can't even name to ask. Exciting, isn't it?

God, you contain all knowledge. All that was and is and ever shall be. As your child, I have access to this knowledge. I'm invited to listen at your feet, to study your Word, and to witness your movements. How amazed you must be when I am content to gaze at what I can hold in my own hands, when yours hold all the secrets of the universe.

> *"Call to me and I will answer you, and will tell you great and hidden things that you have not known."*
>
> Jeremiah 33:3 esv

Don't you just love a good mystery? Our natural sense of curiosity is piqued by a series of clues with an elusive solution.

All mystery begins and ends with the Creator, our Triune God. He has every answer to every question, and he invites us *to ask*. When we do, he won't send us on a wild hunt or keep us in the dark, he'll answer us!

Father, can this be true? You are the author of all mystery and Creator of all that is, was, and will be. Can I ask you questions, and will you answer them? Tell me something good, Lord! Tell me something thrilling, mysterious, and new!

Contemplate our fathomless God. Ask him to teach you something new about him.

Who Is Worthy

*"No one is holy like the LORD, for there is none besides You,
nor is there any rock like our God."*

1 SAMUEL 2:2 NKJV

Many people—often without realizing—use words that
describe the Lord to describe other, lesser things. Next
to our God, is anything truly indescribable, awesome, or
incredible? More importantly, can anyone or anything but
our God be holy? The answer is no. Nothing else and no
other being is worthy of the term that encapsulates the Lord's
perfection, purity, and completeness.

Before we again utter "holy" anything, let us remember who
alone is holy. Let us reserve our awe for him who is awesome,
our praise for him who is worthy, and our worship for him
who is holy.

*Holy God, there is none like you. There will never be anyone like
you. You alone are perfect. You are whole, and you are completely,
uniquely, and indescribably holy. You are pure in a way that
nothing else can be, and beautiful beyond anything that can be
measured. Holy, holy, holy God, I praise you and your holy name.*

"There is no one holy like the Lord, indeed, there is no one besides You, nor is there any rock like our God."

1 Samuel 2:2 NASB

In the latter part of today's verse, God is described as not just a rock, but a rock unlike any other. What are we to make of this distinction? Most often, the rock is a symbol in the Bible of strength and safety. If our God is matchless then no rock is stronger or safer. No foundation for our life is more stable.

The only rock one can build a life on, stake all hope on, and find complete safety in, is our God.

God, you are the rock, the firm foundation of my life. Beneath my feet is your solid support. You are the shelter I seek. above my head, you protect me from both the enemy and the elements. There is none like you. You are the source of all my strength: immovable, unbreakable, and timeless. you, God, are my rock.

How has the Lord proven himself solid, firm and safe in your life? Thank him for being the rock on which you stand.

Getting Anywhere

Jesus said to him, "I am the way, the truth, and the life.
No one comes to the Father except through Me."

JOHN 14:6 NKJV

Anyone who uses a smartphone or car navigation system to plan their driving routes has probably wondered how they ever got anywhere before this? Real-time updates on construction, accidents and other factors affecting travel-time constantly alert you to the best way to get where you are going.

Those who follow Christ can wonder the same thing: how did we ever get anywhere before the Lord showed us the way? How did we make decisions before he pointed us to the truth? How did we even get through the day, before Jesus infused meaning into our lives? When we were lost, deceived, and empty, he found us, chose us, and lead us safely home.

Oh Jesus, how did I manage before you took up residence in my heart? I was lost, deceived, and empty, and I didn't even know it. I couldn't see the barriers, delays, and dead ends ahead of me. I wrongly believed I knew the best way—that I was living the best life. Thank you, God, for your infallible truth, for being my way, and for this beautiful life.

Jesus said to him, "I am the way, and the truth, and the life;
no one comes to the Father but through Me."

JOHN 14:6 NASB

Jesus is the Lord of opportunity. Because of his sacrifice, we are free to make our way to the Father. Because of his grace, we are free to come continually before him to confess our sins, present our requests, and offer our praise. Because of his love, we are free to love others and to invite them to share in his blessings. The world will try to convince us God is but one of many ways. The enemy will try to confuse us with lies and lead us to death.

Let's be clear; God is the way. He speaks and is the truth. In him, we have eternal life.

God, the life you offer is one of endless, timeless opportunity. Instead of making my way through the world, you invite me to come to the Father. Instead of pursuing false hope, perishable things, and empty praise, you open the door to the hope of resurrection, the miracle of grace. You replace self-serving love with self-sacrificing love, and I find I am more loved in return than I could have imagined.

Mediate on each concept of Jesus as way, truth, and life, individually. Where have you most felt his impact? Where do you need to pray for more of his influence?

Delight in Weakness

For Christ's sake, I delight in weaknesses, in insults, in hardships, in persecutions, in difficulties. For when I am weak, then I am strong.

2 CORINTHIANS 12:10 NIV

As awesome as mountaintop moments are—those periods of utter happiness, total victory, and complete peacefulness—there is something even sweeter about the way the Lord meets us in the valley. Perhaps it is the contrast of his joy invading our sorrow, his grace eclipsing our indignation, and his power overcoming our weakness.

In these moments, because what we sense, feel, and know is so unexpected and so unsuited to the circumstances, it can only be Christ. What gifts these invasions are, taking us out of our brokenness and into his wholeness. We can almost look forward to difficulty, knowing the Lord will be there bringing his perfect, easy peace.

Jesus, when I am at my worst, you always meet me with your best. You're amazing. You meet me in the valley, no matter now low I've gone, and you raise me up. You stay, however long it takes, for me to recognize your presence and rely on your strength. you rescue me from my weakness. Whatever I have succumbed to, whether sadness, anger, or pain, you replace it. You always place me back atop the mountain, where I belong with you.

*I'm not defeated by my weakness, but delighted! For when I feel
my weakness and endure mistreatment—when I'm surrounded
with troubles on every side and face persecution because of my love
for Christ—I am made yet stronger. For my weakness becomes a
portal to God's power.*

2 CORINTHIANS 12:10 TPT

We may never achieve Paul's delight in weakness,
mistreatment, and misfortune, but we can learn to joyfully
anticipate Jesus' healing presence. The eagerness with which
we wait can usher in a precious hope, and this hope makes us
stronger. Knowing it's our need that draws him near, we can
finally learn to see our weakness as a portal to God's power.

In this way, even if we can't say we are delighted by our
weakness, we can be sure we aren't defeated by it.

*Father, I don't see myself celebrating when trouble comes my
way, but I can imagine looking forward to how you meet me, help
me, and heal me. While the pain will not delight me, your loving
presence will. Thank you, God, for redeeming every situation,
blessing every circumstance, and righting every wrong. You are my
strength.*

How might Paul's hopeful take on painful circumstances
bless you in a current or future crisis? Can you learn to look
through this lens?

Everything for God

*The answer is, if you eat or drink, or if you do anything,
do it all for the glory of God.*

1 CORINTHIANS 10:31 NCV

Are you busy? Most of us answer in the affirmative. We pack our schedules with commitments, obligations, necessities, rewards, and—hopefully—rest. Like a master juggler, we toss in one more ball, then one more ball, until one of them drops. Scrambling to retrieve it, we also risk those still aloft. These are ideal opportunities to check in and ask why you are juggling so much.

One reason is simple: pride. We enjoy the applause. We bask in the limelight as people marvel at all we accomplish. When our attention turns to the praise we are seeking, the balls begin to drop. Another reason we juggle, though, is to live a God-honoring life. We want to give, serve, experience community, steward our responsibilities, and care for ourselves—for him. We know it is pleasing to God when we make meaningful use of our time. When our motive is to do everything for God, he helps us juggle.

God, I know I try to do too much. Thank you for letting me see when my focal point has left you, God, by letting the balls drop. I want my life to bring you glory, God, and I can't do that when I am focused on myself. When I fall to my knees to retrieve the balls I have dropped, I remember I live to serve you.

Whether you eat or drink, or whatever you do,
do everything for the glory of God.

1 CORINTHIANS 10:31 NRSV

What is more important: following custom or showing
respect? Most often than not, they go hand in hand but
occasionally, as in this verse, we are asked to make a choice.
Here, Paul is helping the church in Corinth decide when it is
okay to eat and drink certain things. His advice is to do what
brings glory to God.

Is it more loving to toast or to abstain? Which will best honor
the Lord? May this Christmas season be filled with choices
that please our God and draw others into his light.

*Father, I wish all decisions were simple. Please allow your Holy
Spirit to help me discern. If it will compromise my integrity,
and confuse others about your statutes, may I decline. If it will
show us both as welcoming, gracious, and filled with love, may I
wholeheartedly partake. May every gift I buy, event I attend, and
glass I raise this Christmas season shine a spotlight on your love
and grace.*

Do you find yourself conflicted about things surrounding
the Christmas season in a struggle between worldliness and
your faith? Invite the Holy Spirit to speak truth to you, so your
heart will be at peace.

Surrounding Love

> *"I am with you always, even to the end of the age."*
>
> MATTHEW 28:20 NASB

God is here. Right now, he is with you. Can you sense his presence? Even when you don't feel him, he never leaves you. What can compare to the moments when you *do* feel him, when every sense confirms he is here? When his love surrounds you, and his power runs through you, only then are you fully and gloriously alive.

How did we become worthy of such a blessing? We can't deserve it, or earn it, and yet he chooses to remain. Out of love for us, he leaves his presence with us. We can't offend him, hurt him, or dishonor him in such a way that will cause him to depart from us. May this inspire us to live lives that are respectful, honoring and aware.

God, how can I adequately thank you for your nearness? The moments I can feel you are the most powerful of my life, and to know you are there even when I can't feel you fills me with peace. I pray that the gift of your presence will create in me a heart that strives, always, to be worthy of it.

> *"I am with you always, even to the end of the age."*
> MATTHEW 28:20 NKJV

Reflecting on the less-than-exemplary moments of our lives, we can spiral into shame when we remember the was with us even then. Sister, this is not his plan. Those feelings are not of him. He seeks to uplift, not condemn.

God reminds us of his presence, so we can live in his grace. With him so near, forgiveness is but a breath away. He is with us for support, encouragement, and, yes, conviction—but conviction that leads to repentance, not guilt and shame. When we sense him witnessing our sin, we can turn into the waiting arms of grace.

Oh, Jesus, there are things I wish you hadn't seen. There are words I'd love you not to have heard, and moments I'd prefer to rewind and live differently. And yet, knowing you were right there— and that you stayed anyway—fills me with a holy conviction. Surprised, I find myself grateful for your witness as I swim in your grace. This grace fills me with hope, God, for which I gladly surrender my shame.

Tonight, be still before the Lord and invite him to make his presence fully felt in you. Swim in his grace, soar in his power, and rest in his love.

Our Comfort

This is my comfort in my affliction,
that your promise gives me life.

PSALM 119:50 ESV

What is your favorite comfort food? Mashed potatoes and gravy? Chicken soup? Ice cream? What is it about a particular meal that gives you feelings of safety or relief? Is it the food itself, or the memories attached to it?

Better than the ultimate comfort food are the Lord's soft and strong arms. His embrace is warm and secure. He has loved, comforted and carried you through a lifetime of memories. Even the comfort we get from our go-to dishes is really from him. It is he who gave us the senses to appreciate the tastes, textures, and temperatures that bring us pleasure, relief, and peace.

Father God, I feel almost silly for turning to comfort food when your arms are so near. The fleeting relief I get from a bowl of ice cream can't possibly compare to the lasting comfort of knowing you hold my life in your hands and count it precious. Thank you for giving me tiny glimpses of your warmth, security, and permanence. thank you all the more for being the true source of all the comfort I'll ever need.

My comfort in my suffering is this:
your promise preserves my life.

PSALM 119:50 NIV

God provides many sources of comfort. Wise words from
our mothers are words he gives them, delivered with a
tenderness born of his own. It is he who gives our fathers the
gentleness and strength to hold us just how we need to be
held. God himself inspires the compassion and generosity
of a friend who meets us in our need. The words of the Bible,
vast in their capacity to comfort and instruct, are words he
breathed into being.

Beyond the comfort he generously bestows, God also gives us
life-preserving promises. What better example is there than
his offer of eternal life through his saving grace?

God, your comfort is everywhere! I never lack for sources of
consolation. Thank you for the people you send to love me, the
wisdom embedded in your Word, and the constant comfort of
communion with you. Your promises, provision, and peace are
perfect, Father.

What are three places you turn for comfort? Can you see the
Lord's hand in each one?

As We Wait

It is not yet time for the message to come true, but that time is coming soon; the message will come true. It may seem like a long time, but be patient and wait for it, because it will surely come; it will not be delayed.

HABAKKUK 2:3 NCV

God's timing is perfect. We know this, and we believe it, don't we? We embrace this truth wholeheartedly—right up to the point where it conflicts with our own timing. Then we doubt. We question. We wonder. What's he doing? What's taking so long? Eventually, we see the wisdom and we are grateful. A missed opportunity leads to a better one. A missed traffic light avoids an accident.

Although the Lord loves a dramatic moment, he also enjoys subtlety. He invites us, as we are waiting, to slow down and look around. Little shots of humor, bits of beauty, and glimpses of grace are everywhere, keeping us company as we wait.

Precious God, your timing is always better than mine. I know this, though sometimes I forget. Thank you for proving, in ways both big and small, that you, the Father of time, know exactly what you are doing, and when you will do it.

*Still the vision awaits its appointed time; it hastens to the end—
it will not lie. If it seems slow, wait for it; it will surely come;
it will not delay.*

HABAKKUK 2:3 ESV

Does staring at the clock make waiting better? Waiting is a part of life, but we aren't called to stop everything we ought to be doing while we wait. Let us be sure to *live* while we wait for the Lord to fulfill his promises, both to us and the world. Read books, run races, play in waves, make babies, and bake bread.

The minutes will pass sixty seconds at a time whether we are watching on the clock or not. The Lord will make sure everything happens in just the right time, so we may as well leave the timing up to him and focus on living.

I believe you, God, and I trust your timing. Help me remember to live as I wait. Show me the beauty of the minutes themselves, lest I get caught up in counting them as they pass. Distract me, God, with beauty, with love, and with meaning, while I wait.

Is there an area where surrendering to the Lord's wisdom and perfect timing would bring peace to your life?

A Delicate Balance

Set your minds on things that are above,
not on things that are on earth,

COLOSSIANS 3:2 NASB

Isn't creation incredible? Isn't God's handiwork infinitely glorious? Our world is dazzling in its beauty, bursting with opportunity, and dizzying in its variety. It's also a tremendous distraction, one the enemy knows we are very susceptible to. We need the Lord's help guarding our hearts from worldliness to strike that delicate balance between appreciating and respecting the work of his hands without making it an idol.

We can get so caught up in our own possessions and problems, and in the vast wonders God supplied to the earth, we fail to remember the Supplier. Instead of being grateful for our homes, we become proud and possessive. The purpose we get from our worldly tasks can morph into obsession. Treating our bodies with respect can veer us into vanity. Remember, none of these earthly things define us. Only the Lord does that. Let him, and his love, be all that consumes us

God, you made the world so wonderful, it's hard to know when appreciation turns to worship. I love the colors, the people, and the millions of special things you filled this earth with, but I love you, author of it all, even more. While I'm grateful for the things I have, I'm more grateful for you, the Giver. Remind me, God, to set my mind on things above.

Think about the things of heaven, not the things of earth.

COLOSSIANS 3:2 NLT

In moments of pure worship, where we feel God next to us, hear his voice, and glimpse his soul, it's hard to imagine wanting anything else. What material thing compares to getting a fresh revelation from the Word? What amount of public approval can match feeling the Lord's pleasure? What physical pleasure comes close to being enfolded in the arms of the Father?

God is better. Heaven is better. Glory be to God above.

I want all my desire to be for you, Lord. Sour my taste for the things of this world, giving me instead a hunger for more and more of the things of heaven. Make your will what I most passionately seek. Make my heart fully yours, God, so that all I want is you.

How much change would be required for your desires to turn first and foremost to the things of heaven? Don't be grieved by how attached you are to the blessings of the world because God understands! He made them for you, and he's glad you enjoy them—just ask his Spirit to help you enjoy him even more.

Engraved and Inscribed

"See, I have inscribed you on the palms of My hands;
Your walls are continually before Me."

Isaiah 49:16 NKJV

Remember doodling your crush's name every? Your notebooks, your jeans, and your hands would end up covered in clumsy cursive. You were always thinking about them so writing and seeing their name made you feel closer to them. Your young love burned sweetly and brightly.

The Lord is deeply, irrevocably in love with you, friend. Not content to merely doodle, you are etched into his palms; you are part of him. Cut into his flesh, your name—and the thought of you—makes God's heart sing. How does that feel, to be so adored, by one so overwhelmingly worthy of adoration?

God, how can I be so special to you? Your Word says I am inscribed on your palm, permanently part of you. It's overwhelming to know I quicken your heart, that you burn with affection for me. It makes me long for the day we're together, the day you show me the space in your hand that's just for me. It makes my love glow all the brighter, to be so adored by you.

> *"See, I have engraved you on the palms of my hands;*
> *your walls are ever before me."*
>
> ISAIAH 49:16 NIV

God can't stop thinking about you. Take that in. Consider how many minutes and hours go by where you forget him, yet he can't stop thinking about you. Thoughts of your comfort, your safety, your longings, and your eternity consume him. You consume him.

You are engraved on his palms. Your heart is entwined with his heart. He couldn't forget you if he wanted to—and he doesn't. He never, ever will.

God, thank you for your perfect love. It's so complete, so utter and absolute, it grieves me to compare it to my own forgetful affection for you. I'm overwhelmed by you, God. So grateful, so safe, so contentedly beloved. In this moment, you consume me too. I pray it will stretch to hours and to days that you might be loved as you deserve.

Without apology or any trace of unworthiness, just rest in the vastness of the Father's love for you.

Above All Else

"Where your treasure is, there your heart will be also."
LUKE 12:34 NASB

Treasure. It's an intriguing word, conjuring images of sunken chests filled with jewels, or ancient tombs overflowing with gold. As a noun, a treasure is something or someone of great value; as a verb, it means to guard carefully and to cherish. What do you value and protect? According to the Word, our answer will give us insight into the condition of our heart.

Outside of people and things, we may treasure intangibles, such as our reputations, talents and time. If we protect our reputation instead of promoting his, we miss opportunities to shine his light. When we care more for our talents than the one who bestowed them on us, we fail to use them for his glory. If we value our time too dearly, we will lose out on time with him. Our treasure should be with him, so our heart will be also.

Jesus, I want to get this right! I want you to be my treasure; I want you to hold my heart. Don't let me love anything more than I love you, Lord. Each piece of my heart I leave elsewhere is a piece separated from you. Take my time, my talent, and my reputation and use them as you will! Above all else, I treasure the opportunity to glorify you.

"Where your treasure is, there will your heart be also."

LUKE 12:34 ESV

Have you ever stopped to marvel at God's ability to make every one of his children his top priority?

Even when we feel forgotten, the truth of God's dedication is undeniable; he's proven himself faithful time and again. Can you honestly even name your number one priority? It sometimes feels like we're just floating from fire to fire, waving our hoses, doesn't it?

Oh God, help me get my priorities in order. Place your values at the top of my heart, so the flames of distraction won't so easily tear me away. Inspire me to make you my treasure, to set honoring and following you as my number one priority. I long to know that whatever captures my heart is what is most on yours.

Make a list (it needn't be numbered) of your priorities and pray over it with the Lord. Write down anything he speaks to you: any new priorities, misplaced loyalties, or deepened commitments.

Lawmaker and Judge

There is only one true Lawgiver and Judge, the One who has the power to save and destroy—so who do you think you are to judge your neighbor?

JAMES 4:12 TPT

Let's take a moment and read that question again. Any time it's asked, it's a sign we've probably overstepped. There will always be people—in every religion, every country, and every culture—who disapprove of others. Let's do all we can to make sure we are not those people.

We know the Judge. We know he is merciful, gracious, and loving. We know that repentance moves him to forgiveness; remorse to compassion. We know he wants his heavenly home filled to overflowing with the redeemed, so who are we to block the entrance?

Father, forgive me for thinking that I know what is in someone's heart, and what is between you and them. Forgive me for thinking the grace given me is only available to me. Who do I think I am? Remind me, God, that I am yours, and that you decided it would be so. As someone who has benefitted by your awesome mercy, may I never wish it withheld from anyone you call your child.

God is the only Lawmaker and Judge. He is the only One who can save and destroy. So it is not right for you to judge your neighbor.

JAMES 4:12 NCV

We may, at times, feel ourselves sinking in the quicksand of public opinion. Whether we've been misunderstood, or the chastisement from the masses is completely deserved, may we remember how very little it matters what others think of us. Just as we should not judge others, others should not judge us. If they do, they are acting in error, and we should brush their words and opinions aside.

Only God defines who we are and decides where we are going.

Father God, I pray for you to help me withstand and ignore the judgements of others. I pray their words will not sway, change, or hurt me, because only your decision stands. Only your opinion matters. If I need conviction, I trust it to come from you. Only you know my heart, God, and only you can change it. I trust it to your keeping, and submit it to your judgement.

Do you battle more with judging, or being judged? Invite the Spirit to speak to your heart regarding both.

Impossible Things

We are not saying that we can do this work ourselves.
It is God who makes us able to do all that we do.

2 CORINTHIANS 3:5 NCV

From tackling a major project at work, to bringing home a brand-new baby, to making our first roasted turkey, we've all taken on challenges that made us realize we were out of our depth. Despite our lack of experience, after a whole lot of prayer (and, perhaps, a little panic), we dove in anyway, did our best, and trusted God.

The older we get, the more we realize how unqualified for most of the tasks life throws at us. But we also realize that its ok! We receive an unexpected freedom from owning our shortcomings and allowing the Father to supply our strength. No matter what he asks of us, and despite our incompetence, we learn confidence. We may not be experienced, qualified, or capable in our own right, but we know God will equip us to carry out any assignment he gives us.

God, you are full of surprises. Through you, I'm learning to love my own incompetence. Each time I'm faced with a task I know is beyond me, I look forward to seeing how you pull it off. Once you come through, I stand back amazed, still unsure of how you used me to do that. You're incredibly, God, and I love it when you use me to do incredible things.

We don't see ourselves as capable enough to do anything in our own strength, for our true competence flows from God's empowering presence.

2 CORINTHIANS 3:5 TPT

What feat is beyond the Lord's capability? For what task is he unqualified?

When you feel overwhelmed and incapable, remember who empowers you. God's omnipotence more than makes up for your shortcomings. Whenever you lack confidence, find it in the One who believes in you. Rely on his presence to do the seemingly impossible tasks he sets before you.

God, I know you will never give me a task without also giving me the grace to complete it. You may allow struggle and striving, but that's so I remember that you are my competence, power, and hope. Make me bold with confidence, God, and fill me with your strength. Empowered by your holy presence in me, I cannot fail.

What dream or calling would you be able to fulfill if you were to embrace God's strength, competence, and confidence as your own?

Blizzard Warning

A wise warning to someone who will listen is as valuable
as gold earrings or fine gold jewelry.

PROVERBS 25:12 NCV

In most climates, it would be unwise to plan a December road trip without checking the weather report. Even more unwise would be to move forward with your driving plans despite a blizzard warning. Accepting the forecaster's advice to stay put will likely save time, money, and possibly even your life.

Weather reports and wise counselors are just a few of the ways God speaks to us in order to keep us safe and on the path to a good and prosperous life. Whether we listen, though, is entirely up to us. If someone loves us enough to call out a questionable relationship or risky behavior, we would do wise to seriously consider their concerns. The wisdom of a godly friend is truly worth more than gold.

God, thank you so much for the people you have called to speak truth and wisdom to me! These blizzard warnings—both real and figurative—have made an invaluable difference in my life. Forgive me for occasionally being too stubborn to listen. thank you for not giving up on me—and for making sure others didn't, either. I treasure their wisdom and insight, and I cherish your truth.

Like an earring of gold or an ornament of fine gold
is the rebuke of a wise judge to a listening ear.

PROVERBS 25:12 NIV

How bold are you when it comes to dispensing godly advice?

If the Lord has called something to your attention, prayerfully discern if he wants you to pass it along. Pray for courage to speak up, compassion to speak lovingly, and patience and humility in the event your counsel is rejected. All you can do is speak the truth in love, and then pray for the hearer to listen.

Father, make me bold, yet loving and humble when you call me to call someone out. Help me stand on Scripture, and not on my own opinions. Take away my pride, and place all my concern on the object of yours. May the advice you speak through me be valued, appreciated, and precious.

Has the Lord ever called you to point out a sin, risk, or another concern to a fellow believer? Ask him to prepare your heart for the next time he wants to use you to bless someone in this way.

Jesus Pursues You

*Let us pursue the things which make for peace
and the things by which one may edify another.*

ROMANS 14:19 NKJV

We so often say we need peace, but based on what we are pursuing, it would seem chaos and dissatisfaction are what have us captivated. We say want to be satisfied with ourselves and with our lives, yet we furiously pursue achievement, self-improvement, and the ever-elusive more.

Take a moment and contemplate this thought: Jesus pursues you. Actively and passionately, he comes after your heart. He woos you. Knowing how deeply you are loved, it's hard not to think of yourself as enough, isn't it? It's hard not to be at peace. What a refreshing change it is to be aware we are beloved. Let us continually pursue such peace-giving and affirming truths.

God, thank you for pursuing me! Help me turn from the chaos of chasing more, and instead content myself simply with being adored by you. Let me rest in the joy of being your beloved. Woo me into pursuing you, God, and when I achieve my goal, I'll rest forever in your peaceful, affirming embrace.

*Let us aim for harmony in the church
and try to build each other up.*

ROMANS 14:19 NLT

The exquisite beauty and astonishing variety of music leaves no doubt that God loves harmony. Voices and instruments working together in a symphony of sound glorify him and draw him near. By contrast, arguments and dissent among believers push him away.

May we always seek harmony by adding our voices to the song, instead of the debate.

Father, I want to be near you always, and I sense you in times of balance and harmony. Any time I am tempted to add to the cacophony of noise that drives you from you own temple, bring a song of praise to mind; let its melody fill my heart and lungs, washing over me until I remember that harmony is worship. Let all my interactions be as part of the symphony, so you are glorified and brought near.

Which do you think the Lord finds more pleasing: a thousand voices singing as one, or a dozen voices speaking their minds and fighting to be heard? Before the Spirit, open your heart regarding harmony in the Church, and ask if he has anything to say to you.

Just Go

He said, "Come." And when Peter had come down out of the boat,
he walked on the water to go to Jesus.

MATTHEW 14:29 NKJV

Peter walked on the water. Simply because he obeyed Jesus, Peter did something otherwise impossible. The verse doesn't say Jesus turned the water to ice, or that he made a bridge, or that Peter levitated. It says Peter walked on the water.

Why do we limit ourselves, and the Lord? That impossible thing he's calling you to, the one you can't stop thinking about? Go. When you know it is from Lord, then you also you know the Lord is with you. Fix your eyes on him, place your faith in him, and go. Don't get bogged down worrying about timing or other practicalities, just go.

I'm coming, Jesus! Wherever you call me, I'm coming. I won't wait for you to make it convenient; I won't resist until you make it comfortable. Your voice—your presence—is enough for me. Your invitation is all the courage, possibility, and belief I need.

He said, "Come." So Peter got out of the boat,
started walking on the water, and came toward Jesus.

MATTHEW 14:29 NRSV

Do you remember what happens in the verses after this one? Peter takes his eyes off Jesus. He looks at the waves, absorbs the impossibility of what is happening, and he panics. His faith shaken, he begins to sink and cries out, "Save me, Lord!" Peter no longer able to stand on the sea, Jesus gives him his hand.

"Why did you doubt me?" Jesus asks. And in this question, Peter hears the subtext. You were doing it! You were almost there. Why did you allow your fear to keep you from getting to me? Indeed, why do we?

God, with all my attention on you, fear is forgotten. I see love, possibilities, and you. Only when I shift my gaze away from you does doubt creep in. When I start questioning everything, I immediately start sinking. Jesus, take my chin, hold my gaze, and remind me anything is possible. Show me where I am. Show me I'm already doing it. I'm almost there.

Where is Jesus inviting you to join him? Ask the Holy Spirit for the courage to just go.

Task by Task

> "He who is faithful in a very little thing is faithful also in much;
> and he who is unrighteous in a very little thing
> is unrighteous also in much."
>
> LUKE 16:10 NASB

Many of us babysat as young girls. We probably started when we in our early tweens, perhaps keeping the kids entertained in one room while their mother got some work done in another. Next, she'd let us take them on a walk, or leave us with them while she ran a quick errand. Our mutual trust and comfort grew, and, eventually, we were trusted with a whole evening.

Just as no mother would leave her baby for a whole night with an inexperienced sitter, the Lord isn't going to call us into leading our church's children's ministry before we've ever spent an hour in the nursery. We won't be speaking to full arenas before ever lead a small group. If we want to see our God-sized dreams come true one day, we need to be sure to respond faithfully to the little assignments he gives us this day.

God, I admit I sometimes want to skip the little steps; I want to run the whole show before I've even read the script. Thank you, Father, for slowing me down. You build my capacity one day at a time, and my strength and faithfulness task by task. Meet me in the small things, God, that I might be proven worthy of much more.

> *"He who is faithful in what is least is faithful also in much;*
> *and he who is unjust in what is least is unjust also in much."*
>
> LUKE 16:10 NKJV

How is it that coffee spills, drops of red sauce, and dirty paws are attracted to our white dresses, not our black top or dark jeans? When, once in a blue moon, you drop a sharpie, it will land on your white blouse. Great advances in laundry products make us able to remove many stains, but occasionally, a single spot can ruin a whole garment.

This same thing can happen in our relationships when broken promises, unfulfilled commitments, and untruths creep in. With God's help, we can be exactly the kind of people we want to know—faithful, fair, and true.

Father God, you see and hear everything, so I know you are aware when my relationships are stained by dishonesty and unreliability. Thank you, God, for forgiving me when I am the cause, and thank you for infusing me with grace when I am the disappointed one. Empower and inspire me to be entirely trustworthy, God.

Do people rely on you? Come before the Lord and invite him to show you why. Whether he commends your faithfulness or convicts you to live with more integrity, know he speaks to you from a place of pure love.

Every Day Act

Commit your way to the LORD
trust in him, and he will act.

PSALM 37:5 ESV

While a wedding is a one-day event that legally and prayerfully establishes a commitment, being married is a daily decision. We are born once, but growing up happens day by day, touch by touch. Getting hired is a single, happy day; being employed requires participation and presence every day.

Faith is no different. The decision to follow Christ is a blessed, life-altering event. In order to grow in our faith and keep him in our sight, we must actually join him on the path. We are only Christ-followers when we are following Christ. We trust him by placing our trust in him, and this is an everyday act.

Jesus, I am committed to you, therefore I commit my way to you. This day, I hand over my plans, my purpose and my trust. I want to follow you, and I know that means I must move as you do. I want my faith to grow, Lord. I long to know more of you. As a bride who stays faithful to her groom, so I will remain with you.

Give God the right to direct your life,
and as you trust him along the way
you'll find he pulled it off perfectly!

PSALM 37:5 TPT

When we are riding shotgun with the Lord, the view out the rear window is awesome. When we trust him with our lives, we can unfailingly look back and see how beautifully he was working out his plan—even on the days it seemed he'd given up on us.

On every day we trust him, and with every step along the journey we take in pursuit of his purpose, we can be assured he is perfectly, lovingly guiding us in the right direction.

God, I love looking back when you are beside me! Your glow
illuminates all the places that seemed dark as I passed through;
I see them now as you did, as important stops along the way.
Each day I entrust to you is a day I am free: free to watch you
work, to join you there, and leave worry far behind.

If you have a journal, flip back through the pages. Look for the answered prayers, and twists and turns, that brought you to where you are now. Praise our brilliant, loving God.

Thank the Lord

*Let us be thankful, because we have a kingdom
that cannot be shaken. We should worship God in a way
that pleases him with respect and fear.*

HEBREWS 12:28 NCV

Thank the Lord. As preparations for another Christmas
reach their peak, pause. No matter how many moments
you have already taken to stop and remember why we feast,
exchange gifts, and gather, take another one now. We are
commemorating God's decision to be born as an infant and
live the human experience for himself. Already perfect, he
was moved by a desire to have even more empathy for us.

Imagine how his love grew for mothers as he was held in
Mary's arms. Imagine the depth of his compassion for those
who are persecuted after his family fled to Egypt. As he
fasted, think of how his heart broke for the hungry. All-
powerful, almighty, and entirely worthy, he humbled himself
for us. Thank the Lord.

*God, my words are so inadequate, my praise so small. Focused
on the color, light, and warmth of the season, , I can lose sight of
what you gave up there in heaven for me to have all these blessings
on earth. Thank you, Lord! Thank you.*

*Since we are receiving a kingdom that cannot be shaken, let us be
thankful, and so worship God acceptably with reverence and awe.*

HEBREWS 12:28 NIV

Of all the gifts of the season, what can compare to the
kingdom of heaven? Instead of a stocking stuffer, God
is giving us a divine inheritance. In this easily-shaken,
never-satisfied world, we are receiving the priceless gift of a
steadfast, satiating kingdom.

Let us be thankful indeed, and let us worship him with all the
reverence, awe, and love he deserves.

*God, as much as I delight in receiving a thoughtfully chosen gift,
your gifts are so much better! I carry your kingdom in my heart,
Lord. therefore, I am unshakeable. Incomparably, you bless my life
with confidence in your promises, joy in your presence, gratitude
for all that you are, and a hope that cannot be taken from me.*

Pause tonight and ask the Lord to fill your heart with a fresh
reverence for the Christmas season and its eternal relevance.

Double Gift

*This message about Jesus Christ has revealed his plan for you
Gentiles, a plan kept secret from the beginning of time. But now as
the prophets foretold and as the eternal God has commanded, this
message is made known to all Gentiles everywhere, so that they too
might believe and obey him.*

ROMANS 16:25-26 NLT

It seems there's a fun-loving soul in every family who enjoys
hiding a gift within a gift. They'll hide a gift card tucked
inside a pair of socks or some cash where you wouldn't expect
it. If the recipient goes too quickly, failing to examine and
appreciate each gift, they could miss one of great value.

Hidden in Romans 16, amidst a lengthy series of greetings,
is one of the most marvelous revelations in all of Scripture.
We were always part of God's plan! Though the entire Old
Testament is about his abiding love for Israel, his chosen
people, the beautiful truth of the New Testament is this: we
are all chosen, since the beginning of time!

*Father God, I am so amazed by your love, and by the intricacy
of your plan! As deep as your love for Israel, as powerful as your
connection to Moses, as eternal as your covenant with Abraham,
so too is your desire for me. Thank you for choosing me, loving me,
and planning all along to call me yours.*

The message about Christ is the secret that was hidden for long ages
past but is now made known. It has been made clear through the
writings of the prophets. And by the command of the eternal God it
is made known to all nations that they might believe and obey.

ROMANS 16:25-26 NCV

Why do you suppose the Lord kept his plan a secret? Consider another type of gift-giver: the secret giver. At Grandma's, as she hugs you goodbye, she slips a bill inside your hand while holding a finger to her lips to keep the exchange clandestine. How special you feel! How singled out!

Years later, you realize all the grandkids got these secret gifts. If everyone got one, why the secret? She simply wanted you to feel special and chosen, and to know you were uniquely loved.

Oh, God, far beyond even a Grandmother's love, you adore us! want us each to know how much we matter, so even though you planned it all along, you let us discover your salvation, your grace, and your boundless, beautiful love for ourselves. May we honor you this Christmas by loving each of our people—and you, precious Lord—individually, openly, and completely.

Do you know someone whose love-language is gift-giving? Be sure to acknowledge how loved and seen you feel by their gifts this year. Be sure to let your Father how loved and seen you feel too.

Your Names

*"A child has been born to us; God has given a son to us. He will
be responsible for leading the people. His name will be Wonderful
Counselor, Powerful God, Father Who Lives Forever, Prince of Peace."*

ISAIAH 9:6 NCV

Reading the powerful words of the prophet Isaiah, written
so many generations before the night in Bethlehem that we
honor tonight, the magnificence and intricacy God's plan is
on full display. The patience, the passion, and the beautiful,
redeeming purpose of it all are simply breathtaking. Through
the foretelling of Christ's birth, along with so much more of
his amazing life, God reminds us all his promises are true.

However, wherever, and with whomever you gather to
celebrate and honor him, leave room for awe. Invite the
Wonderful Counselor to advise you, the Powerful God to help
and strengthen you, the Father Who Lives Forever to give you a
glimpse of eternity, and the Prince of Peace to still your heart.

*Awesome God, in all your names and in all three persons, you
are holy. I worship the Father who planned the world, the Son
who came to save it, and the Spirit who lives in me and helps me
comprehend it all. Thank you, God, for all you are and all you
have done.*

> *"Unto us a Child is born, unto us a Son is given;*
> *and the government will be upon His shoulder.*
> *And His name will be called Wonderful, Counselor,*
> *Mighty God, Everlasting Father, Prince of Peace."*

ISAIAH 9:6 NKJV

As we consider each of the names of Jesus that were revealed to Isaiah, ask God to reveal more of himself to you.

Wonderful. The Lord performed many miracles and wonders, things the world has never seen. *Counselor.* His wisdom was infallible, leading always to love and reconciliation. *Mighty God.* Able to wither trees and quiet a raging sea, Jesus' voice contained all the power of heaven. *Everlasting Father.* Through his resurrection, Jesus reigns forever with—and as—our God. *Prince of Peace.* Through his Spirit, our hearts can rest, now and forever, on the truth of his love for us.

Jesus, how I love your names! all the names you go by, and all the incredible things you have done and continue to do, are cause for praise. I especially want to honor your sacrifice in leaving heaven, becoming human, and all that followed. As helpless babe and as Mighty God, you have my heart.

Meditate on Isaiah's words. Which name of Christ speaks most to you tonight?

No Ordinary Miracle

"Today in the town of David a Savior has been born to you;
he is the Messiah, the Lord."

LUKE 2:11 NIV

Consider for a moment that the Father sent the Son into the world exactly as we enter it: vulnerable, helpless, and small. Not wanting to miss a moment of what it means to be human, to feel as we feel, the Lord empathetically arrived the hard way. He started out tiny, knowing nothing except the sound of his mother's voice and the warmth of her body.

May our remembrance of Jesus' youth and vulnerability soften our hearts toward little ones, giving us more patience for their questions and more delight in their silliness. May our awareness of the loneliness, rejection, and loss he endured open our hearts to the wounded, inviting them into healing and light. May our understanding of patience with which he awaited his purpose increase our hope as we wait for ours.

God, I'm so touched by the picture of your humanity, and so moved by your helplessness and fragility on those first days of your life. Inspire me, Jesus, to reach out to the helpless and fragile. Thank you for your humanity, Lord; I pray my awareness of it increases mine.

> *"There is born to you this day in the city of David a Savior,*
> *who is Christ the Lord."*

Local news shows will often do a short feature on Christmas babies: those sweet, little ones born on the day we honor our Lord's birth. Born on any other day, no particular fanfare would accompany their entrance. Yet, because we have made Christ's birthday such an important day on the calendar, these babies get some special attention.

Now picture the scene long ago, as shepherds followed a glorious light and the instructions of the angels to the birthplace of the original Christmas baby. Imagine their delight as they gazed upon what would be an ordinary miracle on any other day but knowing in their hearts there was nothing ordinary about this child and sensing the world would never be the same.

Jesus, through the ordinary miracle of birth, you came to save the ordinary and the exceptional alike. Already having left heaven, you who are most exceptional became ordinary too. May I never take your sacrifice for granted, Lord. There was nothing ordinary about it.

Ponder the image of Jesus as a tiny, helpless baby.
Imagine the astounding joy of holding him in your arms.

Shine Your Light

> "You are the light of the world. A city set on a hill cannot be hidden. Nor do people light a lamp and put it under a basket, but on a stand, and it gives light to all in the house. In the same way, let your light shine before others, so that they may see your good works and give glory to your Father who is in heaven."
>
> MATTHEW 5:14-16 ESV

You are a role model. You never know who is looking to you for an example to follow. If you're a mother, then your children are always watching and learning from you. It's a huge responsibility, and, in the case of mothers, one we can't easily escape. Kids see and hear everything. May the Holy Spirit empower us to live graciously.

As a Christ follower, other Christians—and people still making up their minds—hang on your words and behaviors. Your optimism and friendliness are contagious; your generosity is inspiring. Shine your light, friend. Illuminate your world with the beauty and warmth of the Lord.

Jesus, there are days I embrace this role gladly, feeling lit up from within with a desire to glorify you and draw others to the light that first attracted me. There are also days I just want to flip the switch and be invisible. Thank you for reminding me, God, that you do not intend for me to ever hide my light. As a representative of you, and a messenger of love, may I glow ever-brightly.

> *"You are the light of the world. A city built on a hill cannot be hid. No one after lighting a lamp puts it under the bushel basket, but on the lampstand, and it gives light to all in the house. In the same way, let your light shine before others, so that they may see your good works and give glory to your Father in heaven."*
>
> MATTHEW 5:14–16 NRSV

Have you ever been tempted to hide your light beneath a proverbial bushel basket? There are certainly days where it feels preferable to stay quiet, or to go dim, but the world is always watching. Our silence, inaction, and decision not to shine speaks volumes. It tells the world we are weary, doubtful, or apathetic about our faith.

Instead, let's shine. In this Christmas season, be a bold beacon of Christ's love. Humbly make your good works visible, that you may give glory to the Father.

Thank you, God, for lighting me up. May I reflect you well, and illuminate a fuller, brighter way to live. may I be emboldened to graciously light the way to truth. Despite any occasional hesitation I may feel, I am never more alive than when I am a light.

Are there times you feel yourself dimming? Ask the Spirit to make you aware so you disable the switch. Trust him to adjust your glow back to its brightest setting.

Just Today

"Our Father in heaven, hallowed be your name.
Your kingdom come, your will be done, on earth as it is in heaven.
Give us this day our daily bread, and forgive us our debts, as we
also have forgiven our debtors. And lead us not into temptation,
but deliver us from evil."

MATTHEW 6:9-13 ESV

Today's verses contain what is perhaps the most well-known prayer in the world. Jesus gave it to his disciples when they asked him to teach them to pray. The Lord's Prayer has within it a basic formula of sorts for our daily conversations with God.

First, acknowledge and praise God for being God. Next, ask for today's needs to be met, today's sins forgiven, and today's temptations resisted. Bring your time before God as a daily act of surrender. You'll notice this prayer doesn't contain anything about the future. This is not God interested in our hopes and dreams; he is! But the day Jesus wants us to be most focused on, and most surrendered to, is this one.

Father God, yours is the name above all names; may it always
be so. May your kingdom rule here on the earth, and may I be
provided with the sustenance, grace and protection I need to walk
with you today.

"Our Father in heaven, may your name be kept holy. May your Kingdom come soon. May your will be done on earth, as it is in heaven. Give us today the food we need, and forgive us our sins, as we have forgiven those who sin against us. And don't let us yield to temptation, but rescue us from the evil one."

MATTHEW 6:9-13 NLT

Perhaps Jesus focused his disciples on today because he was so acutely aware of life's brevity, and of his own imminent death. No matter if we are young or old, focusing on the day we are in is the best way to make sure you are always doing God's will.

What perfect sense it makes that the day he chose to give his attention to was one before him.

Repeat the Lord's prayer with a new intentionality.

How might this focus on the present day reshape your prayer life? There is so much freedom in letting go of your ten-year plan, and just laying this day before the Lord.

Inside Your Love

"As the Father loved Me, I also have loved you; abide in My love."

JOHN 15:9 NKJV

How did you learn to love? Most of what we know of love is through the love we have received. In being held, we learned the warmth and safety of a hug. In being nurtured, we learned to care. In being heard, we learned the gift of listening. In receiving, we learned to give.

Jesus' love is straight from God. While on earth, how did he give it away? He taught, he healed, he fed, and he forgave. With his friends, he shared his life: listening, laughing, and living simply. He abided in the Father's love, and we are invited to do the same.

Jesus, from inside your love, I am so free to love others! Surrounded by the warmth and safety of your approval, it is easy to give mine. Fed by your Spirit, I am filled with grace and truth. Abiding in your love, loved as the Father loved you, I know exactly how you want me to love.

> *"I love each of you with the same love that the Father loves me.*
> *You must continually let my love nourish your hearts."*

JOHN 15:9 TPT

If you plant a sapling with great care and then ignore about it, never watering it or pruning it again, you can't expect it to grow into a towering oak. Likewise, you don't expect today's breakfast to sustain you until tomorrow. Nourishment requires a continuous cycle.

In order to fully abide in the love of Christ, and to be able to love others as he commands, you must yourself be continually nourished by his love.

God, I know I can't just fill up on Sunday and think your love will carry me through the week. I need songs that remind me of your goodness, Scriptures that draw me into your truth, and fellow believers to love and be loved by every day. To know you as I want to, to grow tall, and to abide in your affection, I must come to the well, sit at the table, and be nourished.

What are your sources of spiritual nourishment? Pray earnestly for even more chances to draw from the well.

The Perfect Way

As for God, His way is perfect;
the word of the LORD is proven;
He is a shield to all who trust in Him.

PSALM 18:30 NKJV

When something is perfect, it's just right. There is neither
too much nor too little, and everything is exactly where and
how it should be. A perfect solution works for everyone.
The perfect temperature leaves us neither hot nor cold.
The perfect words fill our hearts with peace and gratitude.
Perfection is a state and a quality we naturally strive for, but
seldom attain.

From the way to respond to a request, to the way we conduct
our lives, the Lord's way is the only perfect way. With no
hidden agendas, and absolutely nothing but goodness in
him, he gives us direction, protection, counsel, and love—all
perfectly. Proven over thousands of years and in billions of
lives, his way can be trusted. What freedom! No striving, no
questioning, or correcting, just trusting in our perfect God.

God, every need I have is perfectly met in you. It's amazing. All my
striving for perfection is really just a longing for you, the Perfect
One. Perfect decisions, provisions, and solutions are all contained
within your Word. Perfect peace is mine within your love. Thank
you, God, for reminding me I don't need to try to be perfect, just to
follow your perfect way.

What a God you are! Your path for me has been perfect!
All your promises have proven true.
What a secure shelter for all those
who turn to hide themselves in you!
You are the wrap-around God giving grace to me.

PSALM 18:30 TPT

Sometimes, it's nice to sit back and gaze at beauty. To stop your thoughts, stop your striving, and take it in. Let's do that. Let's allow ourselves to be overwhelmed by all the ways the Lord is perfect, and how perfectly we are loved.

Think of all the fulfilled promises and all the safe harbors! Think of all the grace! Every single sin has been forgiven, forgotten, and beautifully redeemed. What a wonderful God!

I have no request, God, except to be allowed to rest in your perfection, and to reflect on your perfect love, forgiveness, peace, provision, and protection. There is simply no end to the ways you amaze me. You have my eternal gratitude for all that you've done in my life.

Continue the prayer, resting in God's perfect peace. How many ways can you think of to worship him?

Ring the Doorbell

> *"Ask, and the gift is yours. Seek, and you'll discover.*
> *Knock, and the door will be opened for you."*
>
> MATTHEW 7:7 TPT

Sometimes, the reason we don't get what we need is because we don't ask for it. Right now, you can probably come up with at least a few names of people who would drop everything if they knew you were in need. And if you needed prayer? They'd be on their knees within a heartbeat.

We can waste so much joy wishing someone just knew what we needed, or that the perfect solution would just appear. If we just stand on a doorstep, hoping someone decides to peek outside, we're not likely to be noticed. We need to ring the doorbell! How will anyone know what you need if you won't tell them? How diligently are you looking for what you seek? Are you knocking, loudly enough to be heard, on the door you want opened?

God, thank you for this lesson. I sometimes feel like no one cares, and then you remind me it's because I haven't told anyone what I'm going through. Thank you for friends and family who would forego their needs to meet mine; I am grateful for their unselfish love. Remind me it's okay to need, God, and okay to admit that need and ask for help, from them, as well as from you. Thank you for your faithfulness, Lord; you always welcome me in.

> *"Ask, and it will be given to you; seek, and you will find;*
> *knock, and it will be opened to you."*

MATTHEW 7:7 NASB

How consistently do you bring your needs, concerns and desires before the Lord? How persistently do you repeat them? The Greek word used for *knock* in this verse implies a repeated rapping, not a single, timid tap. Jesus tells several stories commending persistence, especially with women and their need.

If it's important enough to ask for God's help, prove you trust his faithfulness by continuing to ask until he answers.

God, forgive me for my failure to keep asking for as-yet unanswered requests to be met. It grieves my heart to think my timidity may suggest a lack of faith. Make me bold, Holy Spirit! Strengthen my knuckles and my resolve to keep knocking, seeking, and asking, until I have everything I need.

Is there a prayer you may need to pray more consistently, loudly, or faithfully? Ask, seek, knock, and be heard, friend.

Amen

Blessed be the LORD forever.
Amen and Amen.

PSALM 89:52 NRSV

As you say goodbye to another calendar year, it's a wonderful time to reflect on all the ways the Lord has met you during the past 365 days. How many times have you benefitted from his grace, been delivered by his healing, or been awed by his displays of beauty and glory? What sadness and struggles did you walk through together? What surprises and delights?

How have you grown and changed? What new things has he shown you about himself, within his Word? What more have you learned about purpose? What dreams do you have for the next year? What hopeful anticipation is stirring your heart? Pour it all out to him, in honor and praise.

Father God, I love looking back and seeing your incredible faithfulness. What a year it's been, filled with growth and with grace. All my praise is for you, God, as I recall the thousands of ways you are beautiful. Thank you for teaching me, for leading me, and for loving me. To you be all the glory forever, Amen.

Blessed be the Lord forever!
Amen and Amen.

PSALM 89:52 NASB

Are you familiar with the meaning of the word, *amen?* It's more than just a punctuation mark at the end of a prayer or something that means, "I'm done now." Amen is best translated as "so be it," or "let it be so."

When we say amen, we are saying we believe him, we trust him, and we surrender to his will. What a wonderful way to end a year, and begin another, with a humble, hopeful amen!

Precious God, looking back on this year, I recall prayers answered just as I petitioned, and others answered in a way that was immeasurably better. Thank you for providing what I needed over what I thought I wanted. I can also think of answers I am still waiting for. This fills me with such excitement and hope. I can't wait to see how you respond. I trust your wisdom, God, and I rely on your perfect timing. For every need, want, hope and dream, let it be just as you will. Amen.

When you reflect on your year, notice the ways your relationship with the Lord has deepened. Where has he shown himself most faithful? Where did you most benefit from his grace? May God bless you beyond all measure in the year to come. Amen.